Flag State Responsibility

John N.K. Mansell

Flag State Responsibility

Historical Development
and Contemporary Issues

Springer

Dr. John N.K. Mansell
Visiting Senior Fellow
Australian National Centre for Ocean Resources and Security
University of Wollongong
NSW 2522 Australia
jmansell@uow.edu.au

ISBN: 978-3-540-92932-1   e-ISBN: 978-3-540-92933-8
DOI: 10.1007/978-3-540-92933-8
Springer Dordrecht Heidelberg London New York

Library of Congress Control Number: 2009922263

Cover design: WMXDesign GmbH

Printed on acid-free paper

Springer is part of Springer Science+Business Media (www.springer.com)

Acknowledgements

I acknowledge, and offer heartfelt thanks to, my beloved wife Christina, my teenage daughters Anna, Lena, and Sophia and my grown sons James and Matthew. I apologise to them all for the many evenings and weekends when I have deprived them of my company and disappeared "down below" to the study, and thank them all for their collective confidence in my ability to carry out and complete the task. I hope that, in some small way, my undertaking of the Doctoral thesis, upon which this manuscript is based, will demonstrate to them all that learning is a lifelong process and it is never too late. I could not have successfully undertaken and completed the thesis without the encouragement and support of my supervisor, and good friend, Professor Martin Tsamenyi of the Australian National Centre for Ocean Resources and Security at the University of Wollongong, Australia and I offer him my sincere thanks for introducing a simple sailor to the world of academia.

Disclaimer

The views and opinions expressed in this book are entirely those of the author and not those of Maritime New Zealand.

Contents

List of Tables

Acronyms and Abbreviations

ABS	American Bureau of Shipping
BV	Bureau Veritas
CIC	Concentrated Inspection Campaign
Class	Classification Society
COLREG	International Regulations for the Prevention of Collisions at Sea, 1972
CSD	United Nations Commission on Sustainable Development
DIS	Danish International Ship Register
DNV	Det Norske Veritas
DWT	Deadweight tonnage
EC	European Commission
EU	European Union
FAO	(United Nations) Food and Agriculture Organization
FIR	French International Ship Register
FLASCI	Flag State Conformance Index
FOC	Flag of convenience
FSC	Flag State Control
FSI	Sub-committee on Flag State Implementation (IMO)
GATT	General Agreement on Tariffs and Trade
GIS	German International Ship Register
GISIS	Global Integrated Shipping Information System
GMDSS	Global Marine Distress and Safety System
HSC	Convention on the High Seas, 1958
IACS	International Association of Classification Societies
IALA	International Association of Lighthouse Authorities
ICAO	International Civil Aviation Organization
ICJ	International Court of Justice
IHO	International Hydrographic Organization
IIS	International Italian Ship Register

ILO	International Labour Organization
IMCO	Intergovernmental Maritime Consultative Organization
IMO	International Maritime Organization
ISM	International Safety Management Code
ISPS	International Ship and Port Facility Security Code
ITF	International Transport Workers' Federation
ITOPF	The International Tanker Owners' Pollution Federation Ltd
LOAD LINE	International Convention on Load lines, 1966
LOSC	United Nations Convention on the Law of the Sea, 1982
MARPOL	International Convention for the Prevention of Pollution from Ships, 1973/1978
MEPC	Marine Environment Protection Committee (IMO)
MSC	Maritime Safety Committee (IMO)
MTA	Maritime Transport Act, 1994 (New Zealand)
MSA	Maritime Safety Authority (New Zealand)
MNZ	Maritime New Zealand
MOU	Memorandum of Understanding
NIS	Norwegian International Ship Register
NGO	Non-Governmental Organization
OECD	Organization for Economic Co-operation and Development
OEEC	Organization for European Economic Co-operation
OILPOL	International Convention for the Prevention of Pollution of the Sea by Oil, 1954
OPA 90	Oil Pollution Act, 1994
Paris MOU	Paris Memorandum of Understanding on Port State Control
P&I	Protection and Indemnity Club
PSC	Port State Control
PSCO	Port State Control Officer
Qualship 21	Quality Shipping for the 21st Century Program (USCG)
REB	Registro Especial Brasierio
RO	Recognized Organization
SAF	Self Assessment Form
SOAP	Universal Safety Oversight Programme
SOP	Voluntary Safety Oversight programme
SOLAS	International Convention for the Safety of Life at Sea, 1974
SRA	Ship Registration Act, 1992 (New Zealand)
STCW	International Convention on Standards of Training, Certification and Watchkeeping for Seafarers, 1978/1995
STUFT	Ship taken up from trade
TAAF	Terres Antartiques et Anstrales Francaises
TONNAGE	International Convention on Tonnage Measurement of Ships, 1969

TOKYO MOU	Memorandum of Understanding on Port State Control in the Asia-Pacific Region
UK	United Kingdom
UN	United Nations
ULCC	Ultra Large Crude (Oil) Carrier
UNCLOS I	First United Nations Conference on the Law of the Sea
UNCLOS III	Third United Nations Conference on the Law of the Sea
UNCTAD	United Nations Conference on Trade and Development
USA	United States of America
USCG	United States Coast Guard
VIMSAS	Voluntary IMO Member State Audit Scheme
VLCC	Very Large Crude (Oil) Carrier
WTO	World Trade Organization

Chapter 1
Introduction

In an ideal world flag States, whose flags are worn by the world's shipping, would lay down, and enforce upon their shipowners, standards of design, maintenance and operation which would ensure a very high standard of safety at sea. Coastal States, along whose coasts shipping passes, and Port States, at whose ports or anchorages shipping calls, would have no cause to concern themselves with the maintenance of such standards. The present system of Flag State Control falls well short of this ideal … Regrettably it is beyond argument that not all flag States live up to their responsibilities. (Lord Donaldson: 1994)

1.1 Shipping as a Global Industry

Shipping is the oldest truly global industry and continues to play a vital role in the carriage of cargo and people in support of the world economy. Ninety per cent of world trade is currently carried by almost fifty thousand ships crewed by more than one million seafarers of virtually every nationality. Total world seaborne trade has more than quadrupled over the last 40 years to a total of 6.7 thousand million tons carried annually over a distance of four million miles. It has been estimated that the operation of merchant ships contributes about US$380 billion in freight rates within the world economy; about five per cent of total world trade.[1] The 51,538 ships trading internationally in 2007, totalling 737.3 million gross tons, are registered in more than 150 flag States, with the 20 largest flag States accounting for 82% of this total world tonnage.[2]

---

[1] All statistics as at January 2006 from the International Chamber of Shipping website; http://www.marisec.org/shippingfacts/home/

[2] Lloyd's Register – *Fairplay, Statistical Notes 2007*, p.12. Tonnages (in millions of gross tons) of the twenty largest flag States as at January 2007 are: Panama (165.4); Liberia (75.3); Bahamas (41.3); Hong Kong, China (35.8); Greece (35.6); Marshall Islands (35.1); Singapore (35); Malta (27.5); China (23.6); Cyprus (18.8); Norway (NIS) (14.4); United Kingdom (12.7); Italy (12.7); Germany (12.7); Korea (South) (12.5); Japan (11.7); USA (9); Bermuda (8.8); India (8.4); Denmark (DIS) (8.6).

J.N.K. Mansell, *Flag State Responsibility,*
DOI: 10.1007/978-3-540-92933-8_1, © Springer-Verlag Berlin Heidelberg 2009

All of these flag States have the right to sail ships flying their flag on the high seas (LOSC Article 90); and those ships enjoy the freedom of navigation upon the high seas (LOSC Article 87). With this freedom comes a concomitant duty upon the flag State to effectively exercise its jurisdiction and control in administrative, technical, social (LOSC Article 94 (1)) and environmental protection (LOSC Article 217) matters over ships flying its flag.

1.2 Flag State Responsibility

The absence of any authority over ships sailing the high seas would lead to chaos. One of the essential adjuncts to the principle of freedom of the seas is that a ship must fly the flag of a single State and that it is subject to the jurisdiction of that State. (Brown 1994, p. 287)

This opinion of the International Law Commission in 1956 on a draft article of the High Seas Convention (HSC) was a product of its time; a time of traditional maritime States and responsible long-established shipping companies operating for the most part under the effective maritime administrations of their national flag[3]. The Convention establishing the Inter-Governmental Maritime Consultative Organization (IMCO) had not yet received sufficient ratifications for the Organization to begin its work and there was very little international regulation of ships. The traditional flag States of the time relied largely upon a framework of unilateral national law for the regulation of ships flying their flag.

In 1958 the States Parties to the HSC, desirous of "codifying the rules of international law relating to the high seas", recognised the customary right of a State to fix the conditions for the grant of its nationality to ships, for the registration of ships in its territory, and for the right to fly its flag (HSC, Article 5(1)). Agreement was also reached on the measures necessary to ensure the safety of ships flying the flag of a State over which the flag State must exercise jurisdiction (HSC, Article 10). These flag State responsibilities were reaffirmed, expanded upon and clarified through the Law of the Sea Convention (LOSC) in 1982. IMCO took an active role in development of the LOSC to ensure that the instruments IMCO was developing would be consistent with the LOSC[4].

---

[3]See Chap. 6 for a detailed discussion on the state of the shipping industry in the 1950s and its subsequent development through the second half of the twentieth century.

[4]IMO Interface with the Law of the Sea Convention (2000), p.2: "The interaction between treaty making activities at the Third Conference and those at IMO is reflected not only in continuous consultations to avoid overlapping but also in temporary clauses included in IMO treaties indicating that these treaties should not be interpreted as prejudicing the codification and development of the law of the sea being undertaken by UNCLOS III. Another proviso establishes the basis for the avoidance of jurisdictional conflicts between the law of the sea and IMO rules and standards. It stipulates that nothing in these treaties shall prejudice present or future claims and legal views of any State concerning the law of the sea and the nature and extent of coastal and flag State jurisdiction".
http://www.imo.org/InfoResource/mainframe.asp?topic_id = 406&doc_id=1077

The international regulation of ships agreed upon by the member States of the International Maritime Organization (IMO) and the International Labour Organization (ILO) is brought into effect through the national law of those States and "transforming these universally accepted goals and rules into a binding legal obligation is each State's sovereign privilege" (Alderton and Winchester 2002, pp. 35–43). This privilege brings with it the freedom to act, but also, freedom *simpliciter*, the freedom not to act (IMO 2000). The provisions of the LOSC that allow a State the freedom to fix the conditions for the grant of its nationality to ships reflect this principle in international law (LOSC Article 91(1)). Regulatory inefficient flag States can choose to exercise the freedom not to act. "Where the nation State is the bulwark of international regulation, sovereignty is for sale in the context of ship registration, and the State enjoys privilege" (Alderton and Winchester 2002, p. 8).

A nation State, in exercising its sovereignty, can make the conscious economic decision not to exercise certain aspects of its authority as a flag State in order to attract tonnage that either does not, or cannot, conform to acceptable international standards. The sovereign act of grant of nationality, through registration, can be a negation of sovereign responsibility. The ongoing commercial success of such flag States depends upon the benefits that accrue from the grant of that nationality, such as freedom from a regulatory oversight that would require the ship to conform with international standards, and the lack of any constraints upon the shipowner from grant of that nationality, apart from incorporation of a shelf company in that State and payment of annual registration fees.

1.3   The Extant International Regulatory Regime and Associated Issues

The regulatory regime that has been developed by the member States of the IMO over the past half-century has, of necessity, recognized the primacy in international law of the flag State and has also recognised customary State practice of authorization of private organisations to carry out technical inspections, surveys and certification of ships. Standards have been developed by the IMO for this delegation of statutory duties and responsibilities.

A fundamental issue in effective flag State responsibility is the will and ability of flag States to provide the necessary maritime infrastructure and legal capability to administer and enforce the applicable laws they have enacted. An associated issue is the ineffectiveness of the IMO under its present mandate in carrying out an oversight role of flag State implementation and inability to have an enforcement role in the regulation of ships. When considering the effectiveness and fairness of their juridical existence, flag States and the IMO have clearly demonstrated an individual and collective inability to administer and regulate ships in a consistent and uniform manner. The International Commission on Shipping summarised the status quo in 2001:

> There were constant demands for nations registering ships to be held more accountable in performance of their responsibilities. A major concern was the inability of a significant

number of registers to provide adequate legal and administrative infrastructure to meet their obligations in international law, in particular the United Nations Convention on the Law of the Sea, 1982…A general consensus is that there are sufficient regulations to do the job, the problem is their lack of implementation. Major reasons stated for the failure to implement the necessary measures were the lack of competent personnel and financial resources, and a lack of political will in many cases…There was a widespread view throughout the Commission's inquiry that the IMO's work on flag State performance has been largely ineffective. (International Commission on Shipping 2000)[5]

Regulatory inefficient flag States issue statutory safety and pollution prevention certificates to ships, either directly or through delegated power to a recognized organisation and, although they may not be underpinned by survey and inspection, these certificates must be accepted by other nation States[6] as *prima facie* of compliance with international rules and regulations, on the presumption that all nation States are equal. There is a clear conflict between the global business of shipping and reliance upon Conventions being brought into effect under the national law of regulatory inefficient States.

1.4 Effective Flag State Control

In order to effectively discharge flag State duties and responsibilities, along with those as a port and coastal State, it is necessary for there to be an effective national maritime administration. This administration should be adequately resourced, both financially and with appropriately qualified and experienced personnel, and be embedded into the Government structure. The flag State, as a contracting party to Conventions, must have the political will and legal capacity to bring these Conventions into effect in its internal law. The maritime administration should have the ability and resources to register and administer the ships flying its flag on a worldwide basis, and to effectively monitor organisations to which it has delegated statutory responsibilities. The principal maritime and labour Conventions should be brought into effect through the State's internal law and there should be active participation in appropriate standards setting international organisations such as the IMO, ILO, and port State control regimes. Regular reporting of the flag State's activities should be made to the IMO and ILO as required by various instruments.

As well as ensuring that there is effective control over ships flying their flag in administrative, technical, social and environmental protection matters, flag States are charged by the LOSC with conformity to generally accepted international procedures, practices and enforcement (LOSC Article 94 (5)), investigating

---

[5]Paragraphs 2.24–2.26 and 10.46–10.48 relate specifically to flag States.

[6]For example, as provided for by SOLAS I/17 *Acceptance of certificates*: "Certificates issued under the authority of a Contracting Government shall be accepted by the other Contracting Government for all purposes covered by the present Convention. They shall be regarded by the other Contracting Governments as having the same force as certificates issued by them."

reports by other States who believe that the flag State jurisdiction and control is inadequate (LOSC Article 94 (6)), and investigating serious casualties to ships flying their flag (LOSC Article 94 (7)). Flag States are also required to maintain a register of ships (LOSC Article 94(2)(a)); to ensure that ships are surveyed before registration and at appropriate intervals thereafter (LOSC Article 94(4)(a)); that appropriate charts and navigational instruments are aboard (LOSC Article 94(4) (a)); that the ships on their register are crewed by properly trained and qualified personnel (LOSC Article 94(4)(b) and (c)); that those ships do not pollute the marine environment (LOSC Article 217 (1)); are regularly inspected and certificated (LOSC Article 217(3)), and do not proceed to sea unless they are seaworthy (LOSC Article 217(2)). If ships flying their flag pollute the marine environment the State is required to investigate the incident and, if necessary, institute proceedings (LOSC, Article 217(4)).

These flag State duties and responsibilities are succinctly summarised in the Code for the Implementation of Mandatory IMO Instruments (IMO, Resolution A.973(24))[7] that recalls the requirements of the LOSC as follows:

> … the Government of the State must have:
>
> 1. the ability to promulgate laws which permit effective jurisdiction and control in administrative, technical and social matters over ships flying its flag and, in particular, provide the legal basis for general requirements for registries, the inspection of ships, safety and pollution-prevention laws applying to such ships and the making of associated regulations.
>
> 2. a legal basis for the enforcement of its national laws and regulations including the associated investigative and penal processes; and
>
> 3. the availability of sufficient personnel with maritime expertise to assist in the promulgation of the necessary national laws and to discharge all the responsibilities of the State, including reporting as required by the respective conventions.

1.5   Issues of Flag State Implementation

The central hypothesis of this examination of flag State responsibility is that the extant regulatory regime is adequate in law but its implementation and enforcement does not deliver the intent of the LOSC, in that it allows a regulatory inefficient flag State to register ships without any assurance that they are seaworthy. The regulatory regime further allows a flag State to delegate its responsibility for inspection, survey and certification to private organisations that often do not have the capacity

---

[7]Further detailed guidance on the measures required by flag States to effectively discharge their responsibilities are contained in Part 2 of the Annex to A.973(24). A possible framework for national legislation to give effect to the provisions of relevant IMO instruments is referenced to in "Guidelines for Maritime Legislation", a United Nations' publication, ST/ESCAP/1076.

to carry out these technical and administrative duties on behalf of the flag State. Some flag States delegate all of their duties and responsibilities under the LOSC to private organisations. These issues are compounded by reliance in international law upon flag States to exercise effective jurisdiction and control over ships flying their flag, and the lack of any mandate for the IMO to enforce effective implementation of its mandatory instruments. Enforcement of international maritime instruments is, by default, reliant upon other flag States or port States. These problems are researched and analysed and it is concluded that the regulatory framework in itself is adequate. The fundamental problem is ineffective implementation of IMO instruments by regulatory inefficient flag States, and a lack of effective global oversight and measurement of flag State performance.

1.6   Research, Background and Sources

Research carried out in the course of this study focuses upon the historical development of registration and control of ships and, in particular, upon the major changes that have taken place in the shipping industry, and associated regulatory environment, over the past half-century, from adoption of the HSC and foundation of the IMCO in 1958 to the present day. Serendipitously, this timeframe exactly spans the author's working life in the shipping industry and there has, therefore, been a close personal and professional involvement with many of the issues identified in this study. It has been possible to complement and authenticate much of the research carried out from the personal experience of 35 years of seafaring experience, including 20 years in command of ships, and involvement for 14 years at the highest levels of national, regional, and international regulation of shipping.

For the past 14 years the author has been General Manager, Maritime Operations directly responsible, within the maritime administration of New Zealand, for, amongst other things, flag and port State control along with registration of ships and licensing of seafarers. During this time almost all sessions of the Maritime Safety Committee (MSC) were attended between 1995 and 2000; a period during which many of the issues identified in this study were debated. The 10th, 11th, 13th, 14th and 16th sessions of the Sub-Committee on Flag State implementation (FSI) were also attended during which time serious concerns about flag State implementation of IMO instruments resulted in development of the Voluntary IMO Member State Audit Scheme (VIMSAS). The opportunity was taken at these meetings to carry out research in the IMO library.

Under his direct responsibility for port State control matters in New Zealand the author has attended almost all of the meetings of the Tokyo MOU[8] on port State control since its inception in 1993, as well as serving a term of three meetings as Chairman of the Port State Control Committee. This has provided invaluable

---

[8]Memorandum of Understanding on Port State Control in the Asia-Pacific Region (Tokyo MOU) concluded in Tokyo on 1 December 1993 by 18 maritime authorities in the Asia-Pacific region.

opportunities for an in-depth understanding of port State control and its impact upon the flag State issues identified in this study, and for access to data from the Paris[9] and Tokyo MOUs.

The author is recognised by the IMO as an expert consultant on flag, port and coastal State matters and was approved in 2006 as an IMO Auditor under the Voluntary IMO Member State Audit Scheme; taking part in two audits of other Member States of the IMO to date and organising an audit of New Zealand. These experiences have provided an in-depth knowledge of the IMO audit process and contributed to some of the remedies identified to address issues of ineffective flag State implementation and enforcement of IMO instruments.

1.7   Existing Literature

A literature search revealed a limited and fragmented body of work on flag State responsibility; principally on matters of registration of ships, the "genuine link", flags of convenience, and analysis of the safety records of various categories of flag State. Valuable work on various aspects of flag State control is available from reports by the United Nations Conference on Trade and Development (UNCTAD) and the Maritime Transport Committee of the Organization for Economic Co-operation and Development (OECD). Documents from FSI, along with IMO resolutions, circulars and information sheets provide a history of the development of initiatives to address flag State issues as do papers, reports and statistics from port State control regimes. Industry sources proved invaluable, particularly the detailed statistics that have been produced by Lloyd's Register for many years, although it was sometimes difficult to access these at a distance. Journal articles, industry magazines and online sources, such as Google Scholar, also provided useful material.

1.8   Structure of the Book

The starting point for this analysis of flag State jurisdiction and control is to examine the component parts: the flag, the State, and the principles of flag State jurisdiction. The historical development of the flag as a powerful symbol of nationality, and visible evidence of the nationality of a ship, and the protection conferred upon it of the sovereign is recalled. The parallel development of the nation State is traced prior to, and beyond, the Treaty of Westphalia which was adopted at the same time as Grotius was expounding the revolutionary concept of freedom of the seas. The

---

[9] Paris Memorandum of Understanding on Port State Control (Paris MOU) signed in Paris in 1982 between 14 European maritime administrations and Canada.

entwining of the flag and the State into the concept of the flag State is discussed along with the differences in juridical principles between the nation State and the flag State. Differences in law between nation States and flag States are identified as are the historic difficulties faced by landlocked States in registration of ships in their territory.

The LOSC provides for a State to unconditionally grant its nationality to a ship, to register the ship, and authorise it to fly the flag of that State. This most ancient of customary maritime laws was the genesis of flag State jurisdiction in the fourteenth century. The development of registration from a device to provide the protection of the sovereign, through protection of trade, to its present day status is recalled and examined in Chap. 3. The one failed attempt to codify registration in international law is discussed and the reasons why there is no requirement in any mandatory IMO instruments for registration are identified and analysed. The requirement of the LOSC that a ship sail under one flag only is discussed, and it is established that modern registration devices are not the dual nationality forbidden by the LOSC. Transfer of registration to another flag State is analysed and it is concluded that the IMO has failed to establish clear and binding guidelines to address this sometimes vexed issue. The lack of any requirement in maritime law for a survey before a ship is registered to ensure that it is seaworthy is identified along with the resultant implications for maritime safety as demonstrated by a case study.

With the rapid development of steam propulsion for ships, principally in the United Kingdom, a need arose for the State to exercise more jurisdiction and control over the activities of ships and their interaction upon the high seas; principally in matters of signalling and collision prevention. Britain, as the leading maritime power throughout the nineteenth century, took a worldwide lead in the introduction of national law for the safety regulation of ships. Some of these laws applied to foreign ships in British waters and many were adopted by other maritime nations. The development of this national law, which was mainly reactive to shipping disasters, is examined in Chap. 4 along with its consolidation in the Imperial Merchant Shipping Act 1894; the basis of maritime law for most nations well into the twentieth century. The transition of this widely accepted national law into international law is identified, analysed and discussed. It is concluded that the British model of flag State jurisdiction that was developed throughout the nineteenth century was still appropriate for codification through the HSC in the mid-twentieth century.

Chapter Five traces the gradual development of law for jurisdiction and control of ships from its foundation in customary and national law into international law during the twentieth century through the HSC and the LOSC. An analysis is carried out of the powers of jurisdiction and control that were codified through the HSC and it is concluded that they were appropriate for the nature of the shipping industry at that time. The drivers for change in the shipping industry between the HSC at UNCLOS I and the LOSC at the third United Nations Conference on the Law of the Sea (UNCLOS III) are identified; in particular the tanker disasters that occurred during this period. A comparative analysis is carried out of the requirements of the HSC and the LOSC for flag State jurisdiction and control, to test the hypothesis that the lawmakers at UNCLOS III may have been influenced more by environmental than safety issues in matters of jurisdiction and control of ships. It is concluded that this was not the case; that the extant model of flag State jurisdiction was strengthened through the LOSC, but that it was becoming increasingly irrelevant due to the sea change that had taken place in the nature of the shipping industry over the preceding quarter century.

The year of 1958, which saw adoption of the HSC and entry into force of the IMCO Convention, was also the beginning of a major revolution in shipping that was to have significant implications for the suitability of the model of flag State responsibility codified by the HSC. Chapter Six recalls the very traditional state of shipping in 1958 and benchmarks the size of ships, the industry, and crewing levels at this time; again in 1982, the year of adoption of the LOSC; and the present day. The chapter identifies and analyses the drivers for change to the shipping industry throughout the turbulent half-century from 1958, and the impact these changes had upon the size of ships, their crews, and the world map of flag States. It is concluded that the traditional model of flag State jurisdiction and control that was adopted by the HSC, and reinforced by the LOSC, was seaworthy enough to weather the storms of change that occurred throughout the period of this second revolution in shipping, but that implementation and enforcement of IMO instruments was increasingly proving to be inadequate due to the changes that took place over this period in the nature of flag States.

Issues associated with the vast increase in numbers and types of flag States that developed, particularly during the last quarter of the twentieth century, are identified and analysed in Chap. 7. The history of the pejorative term "flag of convenience" is recalled, and supported by a detailed analysis of the development of Panama as a flag State. The beneficial ownership of ships and linkages to flags of convenience, both in definition of the term and in practice, is identified and analysed to demonstrate that the majority of ships registered under so-called flags of convenience are owned by residents of OECD countries that are themselves flag States. In order to provide a framework for analysis of flag State statistics the characteristics of various flag States are identified and these are categorised into four main groups: National, Quasi-National, International and Pseudo-National. All active flag States are identified and are grouped into these four categories. Singapore is used as a case study of the influence of a government upon the nature and category of a flag State. The different types of Classification Society (Recognized Organizations [RO]) are also identified and, for purposes of analysis, are categorised into Conventional RO and Convenient RO. A case study is presented of how issues with the extant regulatory regime can lead to an unseaworthy ship having the ability to trade worldwide.

Chapter Eight closely examines the regulatory regime for discharge of flag State duties that has evolved in international law over the past half-century and the two principal players in this regime: the IMO and Classification Societies. The concurrent development of membership of the UN, IMO, and ILO in the years after the Second World War is summarised to set the scene for discussion of the international regulatory regime. The establishment of IMCO, predecessor to the IMO, is recalled along with early flag State issues of mandate and governance faced by the organisation. The much longer historical development of Classification Societies is also recalled in order to clearly define and explain their changing role in the survey and certification of ships, and issues associated with the conflicts of interest that arise from their dual private and public roles. The ability, under the extant regulatory framework, for a flag State to recognise organisations to carry out statutory functions is identified in the regulatory framework for flag State jurisdiction and control, along with associated issues of exploitation of this ability by unscrupulous flag States and ROs. Burgeoning concerns late in the twentieth century at the IMO over the effectiveness of flag State implementation and the enforcement of mandatory instruments are identified along with initiatives to address these issues. The most effective current measure against substandard ships of port State control is examined in light of the derogation by many flag States of their duties and responsibilities under the LOSC and IMO instruments. Development of the Voluntary IMO Member State Audit Scheme, and its derivation in the aviation industry, is examined along with methods for making this scheme mandatory in international law.

The LOSC requires flag States to effectively exercise jurisdiction and control in administrative, technical and social matters over ships flying their flag. Attention is turned in Chap. 9 to measures of flag State performance for administrative and social matters. Ratification of IMO instruments and compliance with IMO mandatory reporting requirements are used as measures to carry out a detailed analysis of flag State administrative efficiency. Similar measures are used with regard to ILO instruments to measure social performance of flag States. The vital role of the International Transport Workers' Federation (ITF) in promotion of living and working conditions for seafarers is recalled, along with the ITF's identification of flag States that are deemed to be not fulfilling their social requirements. Detailed analysis of a wide range of available data and statistics, including one academic and one industry measure, and data from port State control statistics, confirms the hypothesis that International and Pseudo-National flag States have lower levels of performance of administrative and social duties than the majority of National flag States.

Examination of measures of performance of flag State duties continues in Chap. 10 with analysis of the performance of the various argued categories of flag State and Recognized Organizations in undertaking the technical duties required by the LOSC and IMO instruments. These technical duties primarily involve matters of inspection and survey to verify that the ship meets construction, equipment, and seaworthiness standards. A considerable amount of port State control inspection and detention data is analysed to determine the performance of flag States and Recognized Organizations; both individually and jointly as appropriate. Contributing factors to substandard ships of age, tonnage, and type of ship are analysed in depth to establish any correlation with detention. Non-serious and serious casualties, total losses, and lives lost are also analysed as measures of flag State performance. It is argued that there is a correlation between the safety records of certain National and Pseudo-National flag States and the age and types of ships registered. It is demonstrated that International flag States have lower than average detention and casualty rates.

The final chapter summarises the issues that have been identified throughout the study and concludes that the extant regulatory framework for jurisdiction and control of ships is adequate, albeit flawed in its implementation and enforcement, and requires strengthening in law. A suggested alternative model of governance for ships that does not rely upon the primacy of the flag State is examined and discounted. The customary law of refusal of access to substandard ships is analysed and proposals are made for codification of this sanction. The powers of a coastal State to refuse access for substandard ships to coastal waters under its jurisdiction are examined. The need for increased capacity within the IMO to monitor flag State performance on a global basis, and the transition of a number of critical IMO resolutions in the flag and port State control regulatory framework from voluntary to mandatory, are identified. Included in this tranche of work should be urgent reconsideration by the member States of the IMO of the voluntary nature of the IMO Member State Audit Scheme and inclusion in IMO mandatory instruments of a universal sanction of refusal of entry by coastal States to substandard ships.

1.9   Summary

The maintenance of good order and governance of ships navigating upon the high seas is of critical importance for the safety of those ships, their crews, and for protection of the marine environment. The existing model of governance of ships in international law depends upon the primacy of the flag State and the exercise by that State of effective jurisdiction and control.

This study undertakes, for the first time, a comprehensive examination and analysis of flag State responsibility from an historical perspective. It was not possible to find any literature that draws together the core issues of weaknesses in application of the regulatory framework; the missing link between registration and survey; nor of the historical development of national law for regulation of shipping and its codification into international law. This study provides maritime administrators, lawmakers, and students of international maritime law with a single comprehensive document for information, guidance, and reference.

It is hoped that this study will generate comment and discussion within the international maritime community, and this will be welcomed. As many of the proposed remedies to strengthen the regulatory regime involve the Member States of the IMO, and the instruments drafted by that organisation, it is proposed to introduce this study to the organisation for the information of Member States and possible guidance with regard to future work to strengthen the regulatory framework for jurisdiction and control of ships.

References

Alderton T, Winchester N, (2002) Globalisation and de-regulation in the maritime industry. Marine Policy Vol 26, Issue 1

Brown ED (1994) The International Law of the Sea. Vol 1. Dartmouth Publishing Company Ltd., United Kingdom

Donaldson, Lord (1994) Safer Ships, Cleaner Seas: Report of Lord Donaldson's Inquiry into the Prevention of Pollution from Merchant Shipping. HMSO Cm2560

IMO (2000) Interface with the Law of the Sea Convention. http://www.imo.org/InfoResource/
    mainframe.asp?topic_id = 406&doc_id = 1077
International Commission on Shipping (2000) Ships, Slaves and Competition. Charlestown,
    Australia 2290. http://www.icons.org.au

Documents

Convention on the High Seas (1958) Geneva, 29 April. In force 30 September 1962. 450 UNTS 11
Convention on the Inter-Governmental Maritime Consultative Organization (1948) Geneva, 6
    March. In force 17 March 1958. 289 UNTS 3.
IMO Resolution A.973 (24), Code for the implementation of mandatory IMO instruments.
    Adopted 1 December 2005
United Nations Convention on the Law of the Sea (1982) Montego Bay, 10 December. In force 16
    November 1994. Cmnd. 8941: 21 ILM 1245

Chapter 2
The Concept of the Flag State

Abstract The starting point for this study of flag State jurisdiction and control is to trace the historic development of its component parts: the flag as a symbol of nationality, development of the nation State, and how these two concepts came together to form the flag State that assumed responsibility for jurisdiction over ships flying its flag. The important role that the flag plays as a potent symbol of pride in nationhood is examined from its very earliest records, through its evolution as a visible sign of the protection of a sovereign for ships, to its codification in modern national law as a symbol of the flag State. The development of the nation State is recalled from prior to Westphalia to the present day, along with concurrent formation of the concept of the freedom of the high seas. The concept and evolution of the flag State are discussed along with the status of the flag State in international law. Essential differences between nation States and flag States are identified along with associated matters of exercise of sovereignty and ability to ratify international instruments. Historical issues associated with the ability of landlocked States to register ships are discussed, along with resolution of these issues post the First World War.

2.1 The Flag as a Symbol of Nationality

> Symbols are sacred things, and one of the chief that every man holds dear is the national flag. Deep down in our nature is the strong emotion that swells the heart and brings the tear and makes us follow the flag and die around it rather than let it fall into the hands of an enemy. This is no new emotion, no growth of a few generations, but an inheritance from ages before history began.(Gordon, 1915)

From the vexilloid of ancient Greece, to the ensign flying today from the stern of a Greek ship, including countless pennants, flags, standards, burgees and banners over the intervening millennia, the flag has played a central role in the identity of people, tribes, armies, cities, states and, particularly, ships. Its symbolism has entered our everyday vocabulary, almost entirely from the long-standing traditions formed aboard those ships. We "nail our colours to the masthead" to symbolise

J.N.K. Mansell, *Flag State Responsibility,*
DOI: 10.1007/978-3-540-92933-8_2, © Springer-Verlag Berlin Heidelberg 2009

determination not to surrender, "sail under false colours" to give a false impression, "reveal our true colours", "come in with flying colours" (success), "strike the flag" to surrender, "show the flag", and "fly the flag at half mast" for mourning. The flag is as ancient as that of known civilisation. John Potter's *Antiquities of Greece*[1] makes reference to the *Akrostolia* in the prow of a ship and the *Aphgasta* in the stern where "ribbons of various colours were hung and served, in place of a flag, to distinguish the ship" (Campbell 1980, p. 9). The same publication refers to the *Parasemon*, the name given to the flag that distinguished ships, and the *Tutela*, a flag that always represented one of the Gods, to safeguard and protect the ship.

The Vikings were the first Europeans to display flags at sea; symbols that translated onto coins in Northumbria in the tenth century. Merchant ships trading on the Baltic and North Seas carried a metal gridcross at the masthead; a symbol of the king's protection (Znamierowski 2004, pp. 12, 13). It was not, however, until the Middle Ages that the flag slowly came to represent the port, country of origin, or nationality[2] of a ship (Znamierowski 2004, p. 88)

> At sea, flags became a necessity from the first time a ship ventured out of its home waters. Wherever men have sailed on the oceans their flags have indicated their nationality and allegiance and the ship without a flag has justly been recognised in international law as a pirate (Znamierowski 2004, p. 88 (citing Smith 1970))

Models and paintings of northern European ships of the twelfth century clearly show flags flying from the prow, stern and mastheads; usually of a heraldic design (Phillips-Birt 1971, pp. 94–116) representing the coat of arms of the port of origin, as in Cinque, Hanseatic and Mediterranean ports,[3] or of the owner or patron. These symbols were often very similar but, as ships of the time did not travel great distances, there was no scope for confusion. The ships of the great explorers of the fifteenth century – Magellan, Diaz, Da Gama and Columbus – were festooned with flags, usually with religious associations, as were those of the Spanish Armada. Paintings of British warships of this time, show the cross of St George flying from the mastheads; an early symbol of nationality. This symbolism and evidence of nationality was inextricably linked with the development of registration of ships, as the name and port of registry, along with the ensign (national flag), were the most visible evidence of nationality. The history of the British ensign is of significance in this context; particularly as the legislation that came to underpin it (Merchant Shipping Act 1894, sections 73 and 74) served as a model for most traditional maritime nations well into the twentieth century.

In 1625 the Royal Navy adopted a red ensign to denote one of their squadrons and there are records that blue and white ensigns were also in use in 1633. The use

---

[1] Published in Edinburgh in 1813.

[2] "The first national flags used by ships seem to have been the English cross of St George and the Danish *dannebrog* in northern Europe; the Genoese cross of St George and the Venetian lion of St Mark in the Mediterranean region".

[3] For example Hamburg, Riga, Lubeck, Straslund, Elbing, Danzig, Bremen, Rostok, Konisberg, Wismar, Genoa, Pisa.

of these three ensigns to denote the van, centre and rear divisions, with their associated admirals,[4] remained in force until 1864. Over a period from 1602 to 1634 the Union Flag[5] was flown aboard British merchant ships until a Proclamation of 5th May 1634 ordained that it be reserved for naval ships. English ships were to fly the St George's cross and Scottish ships that of St Andrew (Perrin 1922, pp. 55, 129). A further Proclamation of 1674 ordained that the red ensign with a St George's cross in the canton (upper left hand corner) should be recognised as the special flag of British merchant ships, but wearing of this flag was not mandatory and it continued to be used by naval ships (Perrin 1922, pp. 68–69, 130). The increasing usage of flags caused "Their Majesties", by Proclamation on 12th July 1694, to fire a broadside at all those ships which were flying colours "…which according to Ancient Usage have been appointed as a distinction for Their Majesties' ships…" (Perrin 1922, p. 97) In 1707 the St Andrew's cross was added in the canton and all merchant ships were ordered to wear the red ensign and, in 1801, upon union with Ireland, the present red ensign came into being when the St Patrick's cross was added to the Union flag (Perrin 1922, pp. 71–72, 132).

The British ensigns of today came about by an Order in Council of 9th July 1864 (Admiralty Orders 1904, pp. 46–7) which decreed that the white ensign was restricted to naval ships, the blue ensign to ships in Government or public service and ships in the naval reserve, and the senior naval flag, the red ensign, to merchant ships (Admiralty Orders 1904, pp. 119, 136). The historic Merchant Shipping Act 1894, declared that, for all merchant ships belonging to a British subject, the proper national colours were the red ensign (Merchant Shipping Act 1894, section 73), a requirement that has been carried forward in subsequent national legislation to the present day. In most States, national law exists to both declare which flags are allowed to be used to represent the nation and its ships, and to protect the national flag from abuse.[6]

The flag has come to be an officially sanctioned and very powerful symbol of the State and is the visible evidence of the nationality conferred by the State upon ships registered under its national law.

2.2   Development of the Nation State

[I]f every ethnic, religious or linguistic group claimed Statehood, there would be no limit to fragmentation, and peace, security and economic well-being for all would become ever more difficult to achieve (McCorquodale 2005, p. 184)[7]

---

[4]"Lord Nelson was a Vice Admiral of the White and therefore carried the white ensign at the peak. Before the Battle of Trafalgar he ordered that all his ships bear the white ensign in the presence of the enemy to prevent confusion which different colours might have caused in action". (Perrin 1922, pp. 116, 117)

[5]St George's and St Andrew's crosses joined together and flown in the maintop.

[6]See for example in New Zealand, the Ship Registration Act 1992 and the Flags, Emblems and Names Protection Act 1981.

[7]"Boutros-Ghali's comment, made when he was Secretary-General of the United Nations, indicates some of the reasons why the creation and recognition of states has been so critical to the international community".

At the same time that the flag was being recognised and legitimised as a very visible symbol of nationality in the early seventeenth century, the concept of the nation State that it would come to represent was emerging from the chaos and carnage of the 30 Years' War[8] (1618–1648). Europe had, until the sixteenth century, been a patchwork of kingdoms, principalities, duchies and other feudal identities governed under the moral authority of Holy Roman Law and the military power of the Roman Emperor. These precepts were challenged by Luther in the sixteenth century who, when refused the papal reforms he desired, sought support from certain Lutheran German princes to "assert their power of the State in executing those reforms" (Wasnik 1995). An agreement was concluded in 1555 between the Holy Roman Emperor and these Lutheran Princes: the Peace of Augsburg. The conflicts, however, simmered on with the Hapsburg world empire collapsing in 1557, and profound religious antagonism building during the reign of Holy Roman Emperor Rudolf III (1576–1612) between Roman Catholic and Protestant Germans.

With the creation in 1608 of the Protestant Evangelical Union and its counterpart, the Catholic League, in 1609, the situation deteriorated steadily to the inevitable conflict that was to decimate the population of Germany and involve most of Europe and Scandinavia. The end of this conflict was marked by 4 years of negotiations during which European powers desperately sought to agree upon a framework that would recognise their right to function as independent and sovereign entities having undisputed political control, with the right to uphold freedom of religion, and to reach agreement between neighbouring States on territorial boundaries. The resultant Treaty of Westphalia and its system of nation States "is still recognised by jurists, 350 years later, as the cornerstone of modern international law" (Thomas 2000, p. 11). Not all European powers immediately abandoned "the edifice of Latin Christendom" (Thomas 2000, p. 30) and assumed the notion of Statehood coming out of Westphalia.

> The transition of the Christian Commonwealth to an international system of secular, independent sovereign States was not achieved overnight. Nationalistic and economic imperialism often prevented the Westphalian settlement from being maintained. ... The balance of power doctrine had to be constantly restated at Utrecht in 1713, Aix-la-Chapelle in 1748, Hubertsburg in 1763 and Vienna in 1815, after the Napoleonic Wars. ... From the Congress of Vienna in 1815 until 1900 European State relations were relatively stable (Thomas 2000, pp. 31, 32).

From 1648 to the present day the international system of law and relations between States enabled by Westphalia has played a vital role in the maintenance of good order between States, not least in their ability to engage in trade, and to ultimately agree upon safety standards for ships engaged in that trade. Burgeoning international trade and shipping in the sixteenth and seventeenth centuries reinforced the need for international law and establishment of the nation State to govern relationships.

---

[8]"Modern international law began to develop at the same time as the modern system of states, in the sixteenth and seventeenth centuries" (Akehurst 1988, p. 12).

The era of Portuguese exploration and trade during the sixteenth century following Vasco Da Gama's successful rounding of the Cape of Good Hope in 1498, and the subsequent establishment of trade with the East Indies, was the catalyst for vast extensions of the trading routes of Portuguese, Spanish, Dutch and English ships beyond European waters.

Following this contact with far distant States came a "need for some sort of international law to govern relations ... but medieval Europe was not very suitable for the development of international law, because it was not divided into States in the modern sense" (Akehurst 1988, p. 12). After Westphalia it was possible for nation States to develop international law and for both European and non-European States to recognise each other's sovereignty and to form legal relationships. Shortly before the 30 Years' War the father of international law, Hugo Grotius, published his seminal *Freedom of the Seas*, (a document that emanated from the trading imperatives and self-interests of his employer, the Dutch East India Company, as evidenced by the subtitle[9]), expanding the regional outlook of most European States to consider the concept of freedom of the high seas as the common heritage of all mankind. This doctrine was somewhat at odds with that of the Treaty of Tordesillas, signed in 1494, when Pope Alexander VI had approved the division of the entire world into Spanish and Portuguese territories, and prohibited all other nations from sending out expeditions anywhere in the world; a persuasive argument for secular rather than spiritual law[10].

During the centuries succeeding Westphalia the nation State concept steadily took hold with England becoming a parliamentary constitutional monarchy during the seventeenth century, America voluntarily subjugating the aspirations of individual states to form a nation State, and the French Revolution putting paid to the *Ancient Regime.* By the mid-nineteenth century when increasing international trade and pressures on vessel safety, arising from the transition of sail to steam, required international agreement, the regime of nation States provided a vehicle for amicable resolution of issues and setting of standards. This process was finally given a formal framework with adoption of the Convention on the Inter-governmental Maritime Consultative Organization (IMCO) at Geneva in 1948.

More than 300 years after Westphalia the customary right of States to negotiate treaties was codified through the Vienna Convention on the Law of Treaties[11] which recognises "the ever-increasing importance of treaties as a source of international law and as a means of developing peaceful co-operation among nations, whatever their constitutional and social systems"; a fitting legacy to Westphalia.

---

[9]"... or, the right which belongs to the Dutch to take part in the East Indian trade"

[10]"In Chap. V of his *Mare Liberum* Grotius re-iterated that donation of the East Indies to the Portugese by Pope Alexander was nothing more than 'empty ostentation – since neither sea nor the right of navigating can be the property of any man'" (Anand 1983, pp. 87, 88).

[11]Vienna Convention on the Law of Treaties. Geneva, 22 May 1969. http://www.un.org/law/ilc/texts/treaties.htm

2.3   The Concept of the Flag State

A State may assume a number of roles in a maritime context dependent upon its location, function, sovereignty, boundaries, and relationship with vessels of another State. Some of these maritime associations are reflected in the LOSC such as coastal, flag, port and landlocked States.[12] One commentator (Molenaar 1998, pp. 30–32) uses the term "maritime State" to distinguish, in terms of its focus and influence, a State which has a large merchant fleet under its flag; which fact gives it more influence in maritime matters than it would have as a nation under other aspects of Statehood.[13] Examples of maritime States could be so-called "open registry" States[14] or nations with large distant water fishing fleets. The primary aspect of Statehood relevant to this discussion is that of the flag State and the inextricable link, dating from the thirteenth century, between ship registration, the flag, and nationality. "The flag, together with the marking of the port of registry, are the most obvious manifestation of a ship's nationality, and strict requirements and procedures govern the use of national colours" (Campbell 1980, p. 28).

It is not necessary here to trace the historical development of ship registration[15], suffice to say that customary English law on ship registration, the model for most maritime administrations, was consolidated in 1823 under An Act for the Registering of British Vessels (Campbell 1980, p. 12) and has since been further incorporated into the primary maritime Acts of Britain and most States. However, the resultant flag State of a ship differs from other models of statehood and it is instructive to explore these differences and associated issues, particularly in the twentieth century. Before doing so it is useful to define "State" and "flag State".

Article 1 of the Montevideo Convention on the Rights and Duties of States, 1933, defines the generally accepted four elements of a State in international law as follows:

> The state as a person of international law should possess the following qualifications: (a) a permanent population; (b) a defined territory; (c) government; and (d) capacity to enter into relations with other states.

However, traditional concepts of Statehood do not always apply to international shipping and international maritime law. There are a number of definitions of "flag State": "the State which has granted to a ship the right to sail under its flag" (Churchill and Lowe 1999, p. 208); "the State whose nationality the ship possesses" (Akehurst 1988, p. 182); "a State whose flag a ship flies and is entitled to fly"

---

[12]Others, such as developing and developed States are pertinent to economic and environmental matters, which are not the focus of this study, but which are of relevance regarding the degree of their influence in international maritime fora, such as the IMO, ILO, and the Food and Agriculture Organization (FAO).

[13]This State could well also have roles as a coastal and port State.

[14]For example, Panama, the largest flag State with more than 20% of world tonnage, exercises minimal port State control and, due to its small coastline, has few coastal State responsibilities.

[15]See Chap. 3 for a detailed examination of the registration of ships.

(Convention on Conditions for the Registration of Ships 1986, Article 2); "the State in whose territory a ship is registered" (LOSC Article 91(1)). The flag State's customary role in relation to jurisdiction and control of ships was first codified in 1958 through the HSC and reiterated with minor change in the LOSC.[16] The concept of the State, and the link between the flag and the State, is at the heart of the work of the IMO (as IMCO became in 1982) and international regulation of shipping that reflects the intent of the LOSC. Individual Member States of the IMO have equal voting power regardless of the size of their fleet and have the right to grant nationality to ships flying their flag upon the high seas and to exercise jurisdiction and control over them as flag States.

The necessary elements of a flag State in international law are for a State to have granted ships its nationality through the registration process (LOSC Article 91) and to effectively exercise its jurisdiction and control over those ships in administrative, technical, and social matters, apart from where treaty provisions deem otherwise (LOSC Article 94). The exercise of prescriptive and enforcement jurisdiction by a flag State is more proscribed than that of a State. Whereas a State is generally recognised as having the ability to assert its criminal jurisdiction, and prescribe and enforce its laws through at least five principles – national, territorial, protective, universal, and passive personality (Blay et al 2005, pp. 157–168) – a flag State's jurisdiction is limited to two of those principles: nationality and territoriality.

A flag State clearly cannot exercise criminal jurisdiction through the "passive personality principle", according to which, "aliens may be punished for acts committed abroad harmful to nationals of the forum" (Brownlie 1988, p. 306), nor the "protective security principle", according to which, "nearly all States assume jurisdiction over aliens for acts done abroad which affect the security of the state" (Blay et al 2005, p. 307). There is an association with the powers of a flag State under the LOSC regarding the "universality principle" (LOSC Articles 99–108). A State must ensure that ships flying its flag do not commit universally deplored crimes such as piracy and slavery. Under Article 110 of the LOSC, a warship of a State has the right to board ships engaged in these activities, but the State (government) has the primary duty and responsibility, not the flag State maritime administration.

2.4   Flag States and Sovereignty

There are essential differences in international law between nation States and flag States although both claim sovereignty over their "subjects". Some flag States clearly do not meet the accepted definition of a State with regard to population, defined territory, government, and the capacity to enter into relations with other

---

[16]See Articles 90, Right of navigation, 91 Nationality of ships, 92 Status of ships, 94 Duties of the flag State. Articles 90, 91 and 92 of the LOSC are identical to Articles 4, 5 and 6 of the HSC. Article 94 of the LOSC considerably expands and clarifies the Duties of the Flag State over and above Article 10 of the HSC.

States (Montevideo Convention 1933). This could be due to the legal character of
a flag State due to its dependent status with another State, and its legal relationship
with that parent State; for example, Dependent Territory Registers.[17] The Red
Ensign Group[18] of British crown colonies and dependent territories clearly falls
within this category. Dependent territories are not nation States and do not have the
ability to enter into treaties with other States. They are not States in international
law and are not eligible for membership of the UN, IMO or ILO,[19] yet they have
assumed the ability to establish registers and become flag States.

Second Registers, established by many traditional maritime nations within
the territory of the parent State, in order to offer tax and crewing advantages to
entice ships to remain upon their register,[20] are inextricably linked with the maritime administration and law of the parent State and are, effectively, a State
within a State[21].

Every State has the ability, under the LOSC (LOSC Article 91), to grant its
nationality to ships which then assume the nationality of the State whose flag they
are entitled to fly. Yet a country that does not have the capacity to enter into relations
with other States, for example Taiwan, is not recognised by the international
community as being a State. However, Taiwan still has the ability to become a flag
State and exercise sovereignty over the ships to which it has granted its nationality.

Paradoxically, many countries that meet all the requirements of the Montevideo
Convention to be considered as States choose to effectively sell their sovereignty as
flag States to private organisations for commercial gain, and take no active part in
the exercise of their jurisdiction and control over ships flying their flag.[22]

Distinctions between the nation State and the flag State in international law are
not, in practice, of any great moment. Flag States have the ability to ratify maritime
instruments even though they are not members of the UN, IMO or ILO[23]. Although

---

[17]An example would be the Kerguelen Islands which is a territory of France (The French Southern
Antarctic Territory) but is a flag State that is administered in France. All of the flag States that
shall be defined in this study as Dependent Territory Registers (Quasi-National flag States; see
Chap. 7) fall into this category.

[18]Anguilla, Bermuda, British Antarctic territory, British Indian Ocean Territory, British Virgin
Islands, Cayman Islands, Falkland Islands, Gibraltar, Guernsey, Isle of Man, Montserrat, Pitcairn
Islands, St Helena and Dependencies, Sovereign base areas of Akrotiri and Dhekelia, and the
Turks and Caicos Islands.

[19]See: List of UN Member States: http://www.un.org/Overview/unmember.html; Alphabetical List
of ILO member countries: http://www.ilo.org/public/english/standards/relm/country.htm; IMO
Member States with year of joining: http://www.imo.org/About/mainframe.asp?topic_id =
315&doc_id = 840.

[20]See discussion in Chap. 7.

[21]Further examples of Second Registers are given in Chap. 7.

[22]This derogation of flag State responsibility is at the heart of the issues of flag State control
analysed in this study.

[23]The Cook Islands, for example, is not a member of the UN, and was not a Member State of the
IMO until August 2008, but has ratified a number of maritime Conventions.

a flag State has almost exclusive jurisdiction over ships flying its flag this sovereignty is very narrowly defined and exercised; is limited to the ship upon the high seas[24]; and is sometimes concurrent with that of a coastal or port State (LOSC Article 19 and 27).

One particular type of the State that was historically disadvantaged with regard to registration of ships were those States that do not have a border upon the coast: landlocked States.

2.5   Landlocked States as Flag States

In the early days of the twentieth century issues arose regarding the ability of landlocked States to have access to the sea and to register ships in their territory. Until that time flag States had largely comprised traditional maritime nations operating under their national law. There were no international standards for the operation and safety of ships and no international organisation in place with a mandate for drafting such law. The legal right to grant nationality under national law was, by definition and custom, exclusively that of coastal States on the presumption of customary flag State practice that a ship must be physically capable of departing from and returning to its flag State in order for that State to effectively exercise its administrative functions over the ship (Churchill and Lowe 1999, p. 434). Landlocked States were therefore not recognised as having the opportunity to register and grant nationality to ships in their territory.

The issue came to a head shortly after the First World War when the triumphant powers were deciding the future of Germany and its allies through the Versailles Peace Treaty. It was made clear in Article 321 of this treaty that Germany must *inter alia* provide "freedom of transit through her territories" for vessels and goods from landlocked States and that "no charge, facility or restriction shall depend directly or indirectly on the ownership or on the nationality of the ship". The right of transit through the waters of adjacent States to the sea was codified through the Convention and Statute on the Regime of Navigable Waterways of International Concern[25] that was opened for signature in Barcelona on 20 April 1921. The door had thus been opened for landlocked States to enjoy the same benefits as coastal States, to have free and unimpeded access to the high seas, and, in particular, to register ships in their territory. A Declaration Recognising the Right to a Flag of States having no Sea-coast was attached to an Additional protocol to the Versailles Treaty as follows:

> The undersigned, duly authorised for the purpose, declare that the States which they represent recognise the flag flown by the vessels of any State having no sea-coast which are registered

---

[24]LOSC, Article 92: "Ships shall sail under the flag of one State only and, save in exceptional cases expressly provided for in international treaties or in this Convention, shall be subject to its exclusive jurisdiction on the high seas…"

[25]http://www.legislation.gov.hk/doc/multi_904v1.pdf.

at some one specified place situated in its territory; such place shall serve as the port of registry of such vessels. [26]

It therefore became possible for the nationals of landlocked States, to register their ships at a "notional" port within their territory and to obtain the same rights and protections available to their ships under international law as applied to ships flying the flags of coastal States[27]. This ability was codified in due course through both the HSC[28] and the LOSC[29].

References

Anand RP (1983) Origin and Development of the Law of the Sea. Martinus Nijhoff Publishers, The Netherlands

Akehurst M (1988) A Modern Introduction to International Law, 6th edn. Unwin Hyman, London

Blay S et al (ed) (2005) Public International Law: An Australian Perspective. Oxford University Press, Melbourne

Brownlie I (1988) Principles of Public International Law. Clarendon Press, Oxford

Campbell RD (1980) The Ship's Register: a History of British Ship Status and Registration Procedures including their adoption in New Zealand. Ministry of Transport – Marine Division, New Zealand

Churchill RR, Lowe AV (1999) The Law of the Sea, 3rd edn. Juris Publishing, New York

Gordon WJ (1915) Flags of the World. Frederick Warne & Co, London and New York

McCorquodale R (2005) The Creation and recognition of States. In: Blay et al (ed) Public International Law: an Australian Perspective, 2nd edn. Oxford University Press, Melbourne

Molenaar EJ (1998) Coastal State Jurisdiction over Vessel-Source Pollution. Doctoral Thesis. University of Utrecht, The Netherlands

Perrin WG (1922) British Flags: Their Early History and Development at Sea: With an Account of the Origin of the Flag as a National Device. Cambridge University Press, Cambridge, United Kingdom

Phillips-Birt D (1971) A History of Seamanship. George Allen and Unwin, London

Grotius H (1916) A Dissertation: The Freedom of the Seas, or the right which belongs to the Dutch to take part in the East Indian trade. Scott JB (ed) Oxford University Press, New York

Smith W (1970) The Flagbook of the United States. William Morrow & Co, New York

---

[26] http://www.legislation.gov.hk/doc/multi_905.pdf

[27] The vexed question of freedom of transit by a landlocked State through an adjoining State to the sea has not been as clearly and satisfactorily dealt with under international law. See Churchill and Lowe, Chap. 18, 'Landlocked and geographically disadvantaged States', for a useful summary of the issues surrounding landlocked States.

[28] HSC, Article 3 (1)(b): To ships flying the flag of that (land-locked) State treatment equal to that accorded to their own ships, or to the ships of any other States, as regards access to seaports and the use of such ports.

[29] LOSC, Part X, Right of Access of Landlocked States to and from the Sea and freedom of Transit, Article 131, *Equal treatment in maritime ports*: Ships flying the flag of land-locked States shall enjoy treatment equal to that accorded to other foreign ships in maritime ports.

Thomas MA (2000) The Changing Nature of Sovereignty and International Law since Westphalia. In: Herr RA (ed) Sovereignty at Sea: From Westphalia to Madrid. Wollongong Papers in Maritime Policy No 11. University of Wollongong, Australia

Wasnik AW (1995) Whither Sovereignty: Executive Research Project S19. The Industrial College of the Armed Forces, National Defense University, Washington D.C.

Znamierowski A (2004) The World Encyclopedia of Flags. Lorenz Books, London

Documents

Admiralty Orders in Council II (1904) Abolishing the Use of Squadron Colours in the Royal Navy

Convention on the High Seas (1958) Geneva, 29 April. Entered into force 30 September 1962. 450 UNTS 11.

Convention on the Inter-Governmental Maritime Consultative Organization (1948) Geneva, 6 March. In force 17 March 1958. 289 UNTS 3.

Convention on the Rights and Duties of States (Inter-American) (1933) Montevideo, 26 December, 49 Stat 3097 Treaty series 881.

Treaty of Peace between the Allied and Associated Powers and Germany (1919) Versailles, 28th June. In force 10 January 1920. http://www.lib.byu.edu/~rdh/wwi/versailles.html

United Nations Convention on Conditions for the Registration of Ships, Geneva, 7 February 1986. Not in force. 7 LOSB 87 (1986)

United Nations Convention of the Law of the Sea (1982) Montego Bay, 10 December. In force 16 November 1994. 21 ILM 1245

Vienna Convention on the Law of Treaties (1969) Geneva, 22 May. http://www.un.org/law/ilc/texts/treaties.htm

Chapter 3
Registration of Ships

Abstract The LOSC provides for a State to fix the conditions for the grant of its nationality to ships, for the registration of ships in that State's territory, and for the right to fly its flag. The State is also required to issue ships to which it has granted the right to fly its flag, documents to that effect (LOSC Article 91). The historical derivation of "tunnage" and ship registration is recalled as is the development of the customary law of registration of ships, through national and international legislation, from a restrictive device to one that allows unrestricted global freedom of choice of flag State. The lack of any prescriptive requirement in maritime regulations for registration of ships, and the failed attempt to codify registration of ships through an international instrument is identified and analysed. Issues associated with widespread non-observance of the requirement under the LOSC for a ship to be surveyed before registration to ensure that it is seaworthy are identified and analysed. Dual nationality, and transfer of registration, are discussed in the context of the requirements of the LOSC and the practicalities of everyday operation of ships.

3.1 "Tunnage" and Registration: Historical Development

In order to gain an understanding of the requirement for, and purpose of, ship registration it is useful to recall its historical foundation. This development will be traced through British national law; the foundation for law on ship registration worldwide, with reference to national law as an example of how traditional maritime nations, or "closed registers", have legislated for registration of ships.

The genesis of ship registration is found in a levy, introduced in 1302 during the reign of Edward I upon each 'tun'[1] or cask of wine imported into England; hence the term 'tunnage'. In return for payment of this tax the merchant vintners of Aquitaine "were granted certain freedoms and privileges in England and the sovereign

---

[1]"The tun was a legal standard measurement of wine at that time and was to measure not less than 252 gallons" (Campbell 1980, p. 2).

renounced his right to the 'prise' of two tuns of wine from every ship, one from before the mast and one from behind it" (Campbell 1980, p. 6). Due to incessant war and piracy at this time wine ships were forced to travel in convoy from Europe to England and, to meet the cost of protecting these convoys, taxes known as "tunnage" were raised. This became established as the norm by which ships were levied (Campbell 1980, pp. 4, 5) Statutory tonnage measurement, which was first enacted (9 Hen. 5 c. 10) in 1421 during the reign of Henry V, required small vessels carrying coal to Newcastle be measured and marked. The measurement of tonnage evolved over time into a measurement of the internal volume of the ship in terms of 100 cubic feet to the ton. This measure of gross tons, along with the associated measurement of Net or Register Tonnage (Campbell 1980, p. 18), became inextricably linked with the register of the ship which records these tonnages for reference by all of those who impose levies and taxes upon ships.

Even before the requirement for certain ships to be measured for tonnage, legislation had been enacted in 1381 (5 Ric. 2 c. 3) to ensure that only British ships carried cargo to and from that country, but due to the small number of British ships the law was not enforced (Campbell 1980, p. 2). It was not until 1650, when England had gained colonies in North America and the West Indies, that legislation was enforced that forbade foreign flagged ships from trading between England and these colonies, and required the master and a major part of the crew to be English (English Historical Documents, Vol IX p. 353 (51A–E)). The Navigation Act 1660 (12 Cha. 2 c. 18) first required ships to be registered and also excluded foreign built ships unless the English owner could prove his nationality and could also declare how much was paid for the ship and from whom it was purchased. Upon compliance with these requirements, a certificate was issued and a register of all such certificates was maintained by Customs at London. These requirements formed the foundation of ship registration worldwide. In the present day the ancient requirement for tonnage measurement is codified through the Tonnage Convention 1969.

Over the next two centuries further Acts – An Act for Prevention of Frauds and Regulating Abuses in the Plantation Trade 1696 (7 & 8 Will. 3 c.22), An Act for the further Increase and Encouragement of Shipping and Navigation 1786 (26 Geo. 3 c.60), the Navigation Laws Act, 1817 (57 Geo III c.95), and Acts of 1823 (4 Geo. 4 c. 41), 1825 (6 Geo. 4 c.110), 1833 (3& 4 Will. 4 c.55), and 1845 (8 & 9 Vict. c.89) – consolidated requirements under ship registration. These requirements encompassed ownership, marking of the ship's name and port of registry, transfer of ownership, proof of location of build, tonnage, record of identity and changes of master, and provision of a unique registration number carved into the main beam of the ship to provide indisputable evidence of identity of the ship in case of shipwreck. All of these requirements underwent a major consolidation in the Mercantile Marine Act 1850 (13 & 14 Vict. c.93), which established for the first time a central government department responsible for all shipping matters including registration.

Further consolidation took place with introduction of the Merchant Shipping Act 1854 (17 & 18 Vict. c.104), "An Act to amend and consolidate the Acts relating to Merchant Shipping", under which the privileges under registration were extended to British ships and their crews trading worldwide. Refinements regarding the administration of tonnage measurement, upon which customs taxes, lighthouse dues, pilotage and port charges were, and still are, calculated were introduced through the Merchant Shipping Act 1872 (35 & 36 Vict. c.73). Permanent marking of the ship's name, port of registry, official number and draft marks as a prerequisite for registration were introduced through the Merchant Shipping Act 1873 (36 & 37 Vict. c.110), and Samuel Plimsoll's legacy of concern over unseaworthy and overloaded ships was recognised under an interim Merchant Shipping Act 1875 (38 & 39 Vict..88), which required every British registered ship to be permanently marked with a load line.

The gradual development of ship registration from a device to restrict trade to a comprehensive set of requirements, including tonnage measurement, culminated with its inclusion, amongst many other requirements, in Part 1 of the Imperial Merchant Shipping Act 1894. This Act was the foundation of all modern maritime law, and registration requirements remained virtually unchanged in British and colonial law until replaced by the Merchant Shipping Act 1988,[2] which brought about two fundamental changes. The Merchant Shipping Act 1894 had provided Britain with the administrative capability to force its maritime law on dependent territories (Merchant Shipping Act 1894, section 1). Whether a colony wished to or otherwise it was obliged to register ships as a British ship. The Merchant Shipping Act 1988 brought about the complete domestication of the 1894 Act by confining its effects to the mainland of the United Kingdom (Merchant Shipping Act 1894, section 1).

The second change was to replace the obligation to register with an entitlement to register if the person applying met certain qualifying criteria.[3] This recognised that British nationals had the right to 'flag-out'; that is, register in other States. The subsequent Shipping (Registration of Shipping) Regulations 1993 also provided for registration of ships that are demise, or bareboat chartered by a British national as a British ship. Shipowners could therefore obtain tax advantages equivalent to foreign registration whilst still being able to fly the British flag. The requirement for a load line, and its link to registration, applies in the national law of most administrations through application of the Load Line Convention to "ships registered in countries the Governments of which are Contracting Governments".

3.2 Registration in International Law

The requirement for registration of ships was first codified under international law through Article 5 of the HSC, which states, in (1) and (2) that:

---

[2]"It should be borne in mind that the 1894 and 1988 Acts have been consolidated with consequential repeals by the Merchant Shipping Act 1995." (Hill 1998, p. 5)

[3]Details of registration entitlement qualifications are contained in the Shipping (Registration of Ships) Regulations 1993 which came into force on 21 March 1994.

> Each State shall fix the conditions for the grant of its nationality to ships, for the registration of ships in its territory, and for the right to fly its flag. Ships have the nationality of the State whose flag they are entitled to fly. There must exist a genuine link between the State and the ship; in particular, the State must effectively exercise its jurisdiction and control in administrative, technical and social matters over ships flying its flag.
>
> Each State shall issue to ships to which it has granted the right to fly its flag documents to that effect.

These requirements remained largely unchanged in the LOSC under Article 91 – Nationality of Ships. The requirement in the HSC for the State to "effectively exercise its jurisdiction and control in administrative, technical and social matters over ships flying its flag" was repeated verbatim in Article 94 of the LOSC with the quantum and nature of those duties of the flag State becoming more prescriptive. Under international law, and the national law of all States who wish to grant their nationality to ships, there is, therefore, a requirement for a ship to obtain the nationality of a State through registration in order to be able to trade internationally and enjoy the protection of the flag State. Registration records particulars of the ship and its machinery, provides for proof and transfer of ownership, allows for the ship to be used as security, and, as has been the case for centuries, records the principal dimensions and tonnage of the ship (Campbell 1980, pp. 24–28).

There is no definition of, or requirement for, registration under any IMO instrument. The application of IMO Conventions such as SOLAS and MARPOL is to "ships entitled to fly the flag of States the Governments of which are Contracting Governments".[4] A presumption exists that a State must have brought applicable international instruments into effect through national law, and that ships can only be required to comply with that law if they are registered in that State. There is, therefore, a link between issuance of statutory IMO certificates to a ship that can only be effective if the ship has obtained the nationality of that Contracting Government to the Convention through the process of registration as required by Article 91(1) of the LOSC.

There has, historically, never been an international standard for ship registration but, due to concerns at the proliferation of open registers or "flags of convenience" in the 1970s, work commenced in the United Nations on a Convention on Conditions for Registration of Ships (Registration Convention), that was opened for signature in 1986. The fact that this instrument has received minimal support and is not yet in force is not surprising when the preamble to the Convention is considered. The preamble states that the foundation for the Registration Convention was General Assembly Resolution 35/56 of 1980, which called "for an increase in the participation by developing countries in world transport of international trade". The preamble also recalls the need under the LOSC and the HSC for a

---

[4]SOLAS 1974, Article II. SOLAS 60, Article II was more explicit in stating: "The ships to which the present Convention applies are ships registered in countries the Governments of which are Contracting Governments, and ships registered in territories to which the present Convention is extended under Article XIII."

"genuine link", for effective jurisdiction and control over ships by flag States, and for greater transparency for those responsible for the operation and management of ships, particularly in combating maritime fraud. The Registration Convention also reveals its United Nations Conference on Trade and Development (UNCTAD) derivation by the inclusion of Articles covering "Measures to protect the interest of labour saving countries" and "Measures to minimize adverse economic effects".

The Registration Convention goes into great detail in elaborating the requirements for a "genuine link"; the essence of which can be gained from the headings of the Articles that refer to participation by nationals in the ownership or manning of the ship, ownerships of ships, manning of ships and the role of flag States in respect of the management of shipowning companies and ships.[5] However, the reality of the widespread existence and acceptance by the maritime community of "flags of convenience" was not recognised in drafting the Registration Convention which has the "genuine link" as a cornerstone. This laudable attempt to put in place international standards for ship registration requires acceptance by not less than 40 States, representing at least 25% of world tonnage as at 1985, to enter into force (Registration Convention Article 19). It is not surprising that, to date, only one of the large open registers,[6] which collectively now represent more than 50% of world tonnage, has ratified the Convention, with the other 13 countries[7] that have done so, representing a tiny percentage of world tonnage.

3.3   Registration and Survey: The Missing Link

Every flag State is charged by Article 94(3)(a) and (4)(a) of the LOSC with the duty to take such measures for ships flying its flag as are necessary to ensure safety at sea with regard, *inter alia*, to the construction, equipment, and seaworthiness of ships. The LOSC (LOSC Article 94(4)(a)) goes further and requires that each ship, before registration, and thereafter at appropriate intervals, is surveyed by a qualified surveyor of ships, and has on board such charts, nautical publications and navigational equipment and instruments as are appropriate for the safe navigation of the ship. Article 94(5) of the LOSC also requires States, in taking these measures, to conform to generally accepted regulations, procedures, and practices, and to take any steps which may be necessary to secure their observance.

---

[5]Registration Convention, 1986: Article 6, Identification and accountability; Article 7, Participation by nationals in the ownership and/or manning of ships; Article 8, Ownership of ships; Article 9, Manning of ships; and Article 10, Role of flag States in respect of the management of shipowning companies and ships.

[6]Liberia.

[7]Albania, Bulgaria, Côte d'Ivoire, Egypt, Georgia, Ghana, Haiti, Hungary, Iraq, Libya, Mexico, Oman and Syria.

The HSC codified the duty of a flag State to take such measures for ships under its flag as are necessary to ensure safety at sea with regard, *inter alia*, to the construction, equipment, and seaworthiness of ships, and required States to conform to generally accepted international standards. The HSC did not require States to carry out a survey before registration, for the probable reason that the great majority of ships at that time were regulated by traditional maritime nations that carried out this function as a normal part of their administration of ships under their flag.[8] However, the requirement for a survey before registration is the only duty of a flag State, as enumerated by Article 94 of the LOSC, which has not been codified through an instrument of the "competent international organization" charged by the LOSC with development of "generally accepted standards" for the safety of ships: the International Maritime Organization (IMO).

A possible reason for the lack of any prescriptive requirement in IMO regulations for registration is the implicit nature of registration. The principle IMO instruments are all predicated upon a ship being administered by a Contracting Government to the Convention. Article II of the SOLAS Convention states, for example, that "The present Convention shall apply to ships entitled to fly the flag of States the Governments of which are Contracting Governments". Article 3 of MARPOL 73/78 states that "The present Convention shall apply to (a) ships entitled to fly the flag of a Party to the Convention; and (b) ships not entitled to fly the flag of a Party but which operate under the authority of a party". Further implicit linkages to registration are contained in the definitions of "Administration" in both Conventions. For example, Part A, Regulation 2 of SOLAS states: "Administration means the Government of the State whose flag the ship is entitled to fly". There is, therefore, no doubt that the intent of these and other principal instruments is that a ship is registered as required by the LOSC.

The SOLAS Convention has explicit and detailed requirements for a survey before a newly built ship is put in service and this would normally be carried out before the ship is initially registered. There is no requirement under SOLAS for a survey by the "gaining" flag State if the ship then changes its flag. The ship would normally have a full suite of valid statutory certificates issued by the "losing" flag State and these must be accepted by other States as evidence of compliance with all appropriate instruments regardless of their provenance. An associated issue is that, in many States, the registration process is completely separate to any compliance and statutory certification issues, and does not require evidence of seaworthiness. There is, therefore, a missing link in the extant regulatory chain that, as an aging ship progressively seeks more and more regulatory inefficient flag states and Classification Societies (Recognized Organizations) in an attempt to remain in

---

[8]As an indication of the link between survey and registration see the British Merchant Shipping Act, 1894, section 54, Restrictions on re-registration of abandoned ships: "Where a ship has ceased to be registered as a British ship by reason of having been wrecked or abandoned, or for any reason other than capture by the enemy or transfer to a person not qualified to own a British ship, the ship shall not be re-registered until she has, at the expense of the applicant for registration, been surveyed by a surveyor of ships and certified by him to be seaworthy."

operation, there is often no requirement by the "gaining" flag State for a survey before re-registration to determine the ship's seaworthiness.

It is not clear under Article 94 of the LOSC exactly what aspects of the ship are required to be surveyed before registration. It could be argued that the survey is for the purposes of tonnage measurement prior to registration but, if this were the intent, there would not be an ongoing requirement for surveys "thereafter at appropriate intervals". The tonnage survey is only required once unless the ship undergoes significant alterations which materially affect her internal volume. It could also be argued that the survey is to ascertain whether the ship has the appropriate navigational equipment. Although the requirement to carry this navigational equipment is verified by survey at appropriate intervals, such a survey has a far wider scope than simply navigational equipment and would appear to be that required by Article 94(3)(a) of the LOSC for, *inter alia*, construction, equipment, and seaworthiness of ships.

It is argued that the intent of the LOSC is that the survey before registration imposed by Article 94(4)(a) is to ensure that all of the measures required by Article 94(3)(a) to ensure safety at sea, and expanded upon under Article 94(4), are carried out before[9] the ship is registered, and at appropriate intervals thereafter.[10] The only survey required before registration is completed is that for tonnage measurement as required by Tonnage Convention.

The nature of any survey before registration, within the scope prescribed in Article 94(3) and (4) of the LOSC, and whether a survey or inspection is necessary, can be determined entirely by the flag State in fixing the conditions for the grant of its nationality. There is therefore a vital link missing in the regulatory chain that can lead to potentially serious consequences if unseaworthy ships are to be registered.

Overshadowing this unsatisfactory situation is the ability of the "gaining" flag State to "fix the conditions for the grant of its nationality" (LOSC Article 91) which could preclude a survey before registration even if it was mandatory under IMO instruments. The lack of any explicit requirement for registration in the SOLAS Convention also makes it difficult to prescribe a requirement for change of flag surveys, even if this was the intent of the Convention.

IMO has put in place guidelines for Administrations to ensure the adequacy of transfer of class-related matters between Recognized Organizations (MSC/MEPC 2005, 5/Circ.2) to deal with the matter of "class-hopping", where a ship has the ability to change Classification Society to avoid having to rectify outstanding deficiencies. Recommended procedures for the transfer of ships between

---

[9]See Organization for Economic Cooperation and Development report, Competitive Advantages Obtained by some Shipowners as a result of Non-Observance of applicable International Rules and Standards, Paris 1996, OCDE/GD(96)4, p. 18: "In noting the shortcomings of certain flag States, reference has to be made to the fact that in spite of enjoying unimpeded rights of access, these flag States annual surveys and pre-registration inspections are not always conducted, and that any deficiencies once detected are not always followed up."

[10]Although there is a link to registration through the definition of owner in the Load Line Convention this requirement is completely separate to that of registration.

States have also been agreed and issued as an IMO Circular (MSC/Circ.1140, MEPC/Circ.424) but these merely reiterate the recommendations of a number of IMO Conventions and instruments that there is a voluntary exchange of information between the two States regarding deficiencies, non-conformities, and any other safety related information.

Many flag States already require "change of flag" surveys and IACS Classification Societies have prescriptive requirements for this process under their rules.[11] There is clearly a compelling need for the intent of the LOSC that a ship be surveyed before registration to be codified through IMO instruments and for clear and binding standards to be put in place regarding survey requirements for change of flag State; standards that could be verified through the current voluntary IMO audit of flag States.

3.4 Dual Nationality

Article 92(1) of the LOSC states that:

> Ships shall sail under the flag of one State only and, save in exceptional cases expressly provided for in international treaties or in this Convention, shall be subject to its exclusive jurisdiction on the high seas.

Public order on the high seas depends upon the exclusive jurisdiction of the flag State (LOSC Article 91) in administrative, technical, and social matters (LOSC Article 94), save in exceptional cases provided for in international treaties or in the LOSC. Article 92(2) of the LOSC further states that:

> A ship which sails under the flags of two or more States, using them according to convenience, may not claim any of the nationalities in question with respect to any other State, and may be assimilated to a ship without nationality.

This wording recalls the opinion of the International Law Commission (Brown 1994, p. 287) which clearly stated that the practice of sailing under two flags and using them as convenient, could lead to abuse and was a "practice which cannot be tolerated" (Brown 1994, p. 291). The intent of the Convention is clearly that ships shall not have dual nationality (LOSC Article 92) with the exceptions of ships flying the flag of the United Nations, its specialised agencies and the International Atomic Energy Agency.[12] Even when operating under these provisions of the LOSC, a ship must be registered in a flag State and the flag State's laws will apply even though the visible evidence of "nationality" is, for example, that of the UN.

Bareboat registration is not the "dual registration" forbidden by the LOSC but is, rather, dual documentation and, as such, is sometimes referred to as dual or

---

[11] See Chap. 7.

[12] LOSC, Article 93: "The preceding articles do not prejudice the question of ships employed on the official service of the United Nations, its specialised agencies or the International Atomic Energy Agency, flying the flag of the organization".

parallel registry. The practice of bareboat registration evolved through the German Law of the Flag Act 1951 (Ademuni-Odeke 1998, p. 55) as a device to enable German shipowners to both charter-in and charter-out[13]; practices designed to overcome the problems faced by that State in financing maritime reconstruction following the Second World War (Ademuni-Odeke 1997, p. 651) Chartering-in enabled a shipowner to flag out and then charter back vessels that had been de-registered from the German flag and operate them under German law. Chartering-out (maintaining the German base registration) was a far more widespread practice to obtain lower crew costs and retain financial advantages such as "subsidies and accelerated depreciation, whilst redeeming operational costs" (Ademuni-Odeke 1997, p. 651) The Registration Convention 1986, recognised the concept of bareboat charter registration and the legislation of many States was amended to provide for the granting of nationality to ships on a temporary basis (Ademuni-Odeke 1997, p. 653)

3.5   Transfer of Registration

In the global shipping industry shipowners have the ability under the LOSC and most national legislation to choose the State of registration and also to change flag State in the case of transfer of ownership or for any other reason (LOSC Article 91 and 92).[14] Concerns increasingly arose in international fora in the 1990s about the ease with which this transfer of flag could take place, and the ability of ship-owners to change flag State as a means of avoiding action on serious deficiencies identified by the existing flag State or a port State.[15] The LOSC calls for ships to be surveyed by a qualified surveyor of ships before registration (LOSC Article 94(4)(a)). Not all flag States carry out such surveys to determine the standard of the ship but rely on documents issued by the existing flag State.[16] This issue was highlighted by the seventh session of the United Nations Commission on Sustainable Development (CSD 7) which invited:

---

[13]While the underlying registration of the vessel is maintained in one country (often for financial reasons such as security for mortgages against the ship) the vessel may be permitted to fly the flag of another country temporarily.

[14]For national legislation see, for example, the New Zealand Ship Registration Act 1992, section 8, Entitlement to register certain New Zealand-owned ships and other ships, and section 31, Change of name or address or nationality of owner or mortgage.

[15]"… the transfer of the flag of a vessel, from one State to another, in the efforts of an owner to avoid compliance with applicable requirements or to evade the implementation and enforcement actions of the flag State or even, in some cases, the pressure from a Port State." IMO Paper FSI 7/9/2 submitted by Cyprus to the seventh session of the Sub-committee on Flag State Implementation, 5 February 1999.

[16]For example there is no provision in New Zealand law for a ship to be surveyed before registration. The United Kingdom, upon whose law New Zealand law is based, does require such a survey; see the Maritime and Coastguard Agency website at http://www.mcga.gov.uk/flag/needtoknow/survey.

IMO as a matter of urgency to develop measures, in binding form where IMO members consider it appropriate, to ensure that ships of all flag States meet international rules and standards so as to give full and complete effect to UNCLOS, especially article 91 (Nationality of ships), as well as provisions of other relevant conventions. In this context, the Commission emphasizes the importance of further development of effective port State control. (IMO FSI 2000, p. 2)

The IMO accepted this invitation and tasked the Sub-Committee on Flag State Implementation with the development of a preliminary draft Assembly resolution covering matters of transfer of flag State, "phantom ships",[17] and dual nationality. The principal IMO Conventions[18] all provide that a certificate issued under their provisions becomes invalid when a transfer of flag State takes place, with the clear resultant requirement for the "gaining" flag State to survey the ship as required by the LOSC and to issue new certificates (LOSC Article 94(4)(a)). Although the requirements of these instruments regarding this change of flag survey are not prescriptive, it was suggested by one Member State that they were to determine whether the ship remains seaworthy, and has not undergone any changes to the major items covered by the treaty in question (IMO FSI 1999, p. 2). The different standards that States had evolved for survey of ships for re-registration were also highlighted, if in fact any survey or inspection was carried out, along with the consequent lack of confidence that the ship would meet international standards under the "gaining" flag State.

Proposals were made by Member States of the IMO to the seventh and ninth sessions of the Sub-Committee on Flag State Implementation that the draft resolution should include the principle that a ship should meet all applicable international instruments before transfer of flag State takes place, and that the transfer process should be transparent and fully auditable, and that any disputes should be referred to the IMO for arbitration and resolution (IMO FSI 2000, p. 1). If the ship did not comply with applicable international standards it was proposed that timelines should be agreed with the "gaining" flag State to ensure that applicable instruments are complied with under that flag's jurisdiction, and those timelines should not exceed 6 months.

Discussion took place at a number of meetings of the Sub-Committee on Flag State Implementation, during which suggestions were made by member States that clear guidelines were necessary to provide explicit requirements for minimum survey requirements for transfer of flag State; guidelines that might evolve into mandatory requirements that could be used to assess performance of flag States. The proposed Assembly resolution was finally drafted as an equivocal non-mandatory advisory

---

[17] IMO, Sub-Committee on Flag State Implementation, 2001, p. 1. "The issue of phantom ships has been raised at IMO's Maritime Safety Committee (MSC) as part of concerns surrounding piracy and armed robbery against ships – in some cases a ship has been hijacked and re-registered. There is therefore a need for flag States to be certain that ships are not being registered on the basis of false or inaccurate information."

[18] Regulation I/14(g)(ii) of SOLAS 74 as amended; Regulation 8(3) of Annex 1 and Regulation 12(3) of Annex II of MARPOL 73/78 as amended; Article 20(5) of LOAD LINE 66 and Article 10(2) of TONNAGE 69.

circular (MSC/Circ.1140, MEPC/Circ.424), that did not address these matters of substance but confined itself to the matter of transparency of information between flag States.[19] The opportunity had clearly been missed by the Organization to address this fundamental issue and to draft regulations that would achieve the intent of the LOSC.

References

Ademuni-Odeke (1997) Evolution and Development of Ship Registration. Il Diritto Marittimo, Italy
Ademuni-Odeke, (1998) Bareboat Charter (Ship) Registration. Martinus Nijhoff Publishers, The Netherlands
Brown ED (1994) The International Law of the Sea, Vol 1. Dartmouth Publishing Company Ltd., Aldershot, United Kingdom
Campbell RD (1980) The Ship's Register: a History of British Ship Status and Registration Procedures including their adoption in New Zealand. Ministry of Transport – Marine Division, New Zealand
English Historical Documents Vol IX p. 353 (51A–E). In: Campbell RD (1980) The Ship's Register: a History of British Ship Status and Registration Procedures including their adoption in New Zealand. Ministry of Transport – Marine Division, New Zealand
Hill C (1998) Maritime Law, 5th edn. Lloyd's Practical Shipping Guides, London

Documents

IMO (1999) Sub-Committee on Flag State Implementation, paper submitted by Cyprus, FSI 7/9/2, 5 February
IMO (2000) Sub-Committee on Flag State Implementation, paper submitted by the United Kingdom, FSI, 9/5/1/, 15 December
IMO (2001) Sub-Committee on Flag State Implementation – 9th session: 19–23 February, http://www.imo.org/Newsroom/mainframe.asp?topic_id = 106&doc_id = 453.
International Convention on Tonnage Measurement of Ships, London, 23 June 1969. In force, 18 July 1982. UKTS 50

---

[19]For a ship engaged on international voyages to enjoy the benefits and privileges that may be bestowed upon it, it must be under the jurisdiction of a flag State, the flag of which it is entitled to fly. To facilitate transfer of ships between flag States and to increase transparency in the relationships between former and new flag States in the interests of maritime safety, the following procedure is recommended:

1. upon the registration of a ship new to their registries, flag States should endeavour to ensure that the ship in question complies with the applicable international rules and regulations and, if necessary, liaise with the previous flag State;
2. upon the request of the new flag State, the flag of which the ship is entitled to fly, the former flag State the flag of which the ship was entitled to fly should promptly provide details of deficiencies, non-conformities with their applicable timescales and any other safety related information.

United Nations Convention of the Law of the Sea (1982) Montego Bay, 10 December. In force 16
   November 1994. 21 ILM 1245
United Nations Convention on Conditions for Registration of Ships (1986) Geneva, 7 February,
   *7 LOSB 87.
IMO (2004) MSC/Circ.1140 MEPC/Circ.424, Transfer of Ships between States. 20 December.
IMO (2005) MSC-MEPC.5/Circ.2. Survey and Certification related matters. 26 September
International Convention on Load Lines, London, 5 April 1966. In force 21 July 1968. #640
   UNTS 133

Chapter 4
Development of National Law for Flag State Responsibility

Abstract It is instructive to recall the development of national maritime law for jurisdiction and control of ships, and the drivers behind the codification of this customary law. As Britain was one of the leading maritime nations throughout the period from the seventeenth to nineteenth centuries the legislation drafted by that State, and its effect upon the law of other maritime nations, is examined. The dramatic transition from sail to steam, and the development of passenger services on the North Atlantic, are identified as the principal drivers for development of national law for jurisdiction and control of ships. The translation of this national law into international law during the twentieth century, and the drivers for this development are also identified, analysed, and discussed.

4.1 Master Under God

Throughout the middle ages, due to the limited abilities of both ships and their navigation, and lack of far-ranging international trade, there was no requirement for jurisdiction or control by States of ships trading in and out of their ports. The earliest attempts to regulate ships focussed upon customs duties, carriage of cargo, and nationality, rather than design, construction, equipment or safe navigational requirements. As early as 1302 a tunnage tax was levied on wine imported to England. In 1381, legislation was introduced which required that goods exported from or imported to England be carried on English ships but, owing to the lack of sufficient British ships, the law was never enforced (Campbell 1980, pp. 5, 6). It was not until 1660, when England sought to control the carriage of cargo to and from her new colonies in North America, that the first Navigation Act was introduced: "An Act for the Encouraging and Increasing of Shipping and Navigation", which stated that imports from and exports to any of His Majesty's possessions must be:

> ... in such ships as do truly and without Fraud belong only to the people of England or Ireland, Dominion of Wales or Town of Berwick upon Tweed, or are of the Built of and belonging to any of the said Lands, Islands, Plantations or territories, as the Proprietors and

right Owners thereof, and whereof the master and Three Fourths of the mariners at least are English.

Further Acts were introduced during the eighteenth century as the British Empire expanded, but all were to do with registration, restraint of trade,[1] and fraud[2] (Campbell 1980, pp. 2, 3) rather than safety of navigation. Ships were still free to be built to whatever empirical standard the shipbuilder felt appropriate, and to be operated and navigated entirely under the direction and totally autonomous control of the "Master under God"[3]. The sailing ship was "a fragment detached from the earth"[4] (Conrad1897, p. 25). It was not until the evolutionary, and revolutionary, changes brought about by the development of steam powered propulsion for ships from the dawn of the nineteenth century, and the progressive change from wood to iron to steel construction, enabling ever larger and more powerful ships to be built, that a need arose for the State to intervene and establish standards for construction, loading, operation and navigation of ships: flag State jurisdiction and control.

4.2   The Sail to Steam Revolution

Joseph Conrad (1897) described the sailing ship *Narcissus* as she drifted slowly, swinging round and round the compass, through the days of baffling light airs:

> Under the patter of short warm showers, grumbling men whirled the heavy yards from side to side; they caught hold of soaked ropes with groans and sighs, while their officers, sulky and dripping with rain water, unceasingly ordered them about in wearied voices. During the short respite they looked in disgust into the smarting palms of their stiff hands, and asked one another bitterly: "Who would be a sailor if he could be a farmer?"

The frustrations of voyaging under sail and total dependence upon the elements for propulsion were soon to be replaced by the practical and down-to-earth realism of the marine engineer, as steam began to replace sail as the principal means of

---

[1]For example the Navigation Act, 1660 was entitled "An Act for the Encouraging and Increasing of Shipping and Navigation" (English Historical Documents, Vol XI, p. 556 (388G)).

[2]To prevent "Frauds which may be used in colouring or buying of foreign Ships", section 10 of the Navigation Act 1660, required that, from 1st April 1661, no foreign-built ship would be allowed to pass to England or enjoy the benefits or privileges of an English vessel until the owner declared to the Customs at the port nearest to his abode that he was not an alien and declared an oath that the vessel was purchased for a valuable consideration, how much was paid for it, and also where, when and from whom it was purchased". Further, the Act for preventing Frauds and regulating Abuses in the Plantation Trade 1696 (59 Geo. 3 C. 5) consolidated miscellaneous statutes passed since the 1660 Act and introduced further provisions regarding registration of ships. This was the final Act combining trade and navigation law.

[3]"Captains exercised absolute authority at sea and so were dubbed 'Master under God' by early insurance writs, agreements with shipowners and passengers, and the Board of Trade". http://www.maritimeheritage.org/captains.htm

[4]"The passage has begun, and the ship, a fragment detached from the earth, went on lonely and swift like a small planet".

propulsion. The lyric words of Conrad from his experience as a Master in sail were slowly replaced by the equally poetical views of the marine engineer:

> 'From coupler-flange to spindle-guide I see Thy Hand O God, – Predestination in the stride o' yon connectin'-rod.' (Phillips-Birt 1971, p. 280)

Until the end of the eighteenth century, trade had been carried out for thousands of years exclusively under the propulsion of oars or sail. However, these age-old methods were to change dramatically with the dawn of a new century. For a number of years in the late eighteenth century, individual inventors, working in isolation in France, Great Britain, and the United States of America, had endeavoured to harness steam power to the propulsion of ships. A short-lived experiment in 1788 resulted in successful trials of a small steamship in Scotland but incurred the wrath of James Watt[5] and threats of legal action due to patent infringement. It was not until 1801, after the expiry of Watt's patent, that a prototype steamship was proven in trials at Grangemouth, Scotland. A second, larger prototype, the *Charlotte Dundas*, operated successfully on the Forth and Clyde canal in 1802 but was laid up in 1803, due in part to concerns about the effects of its wash upon the canal banks (Fox 2004, pp. 22, 23)

Regardless of this setback, the steamship had arrived and Scotland remained the principal home of ship and engine design and building for the entire nineteenth century and beyond. The first commercial ocean-going steamship, the *Comet*, was launched in 1812, but such vessels were in a tiny minority with one steam vessel recorded in Britain in 1814 (English Historical Documents, Vol XI, p. 556 (388G)) and one more in the colonies; growing to 24 and 8, respectively, in 1819 (Campbell 1980, p. 11) As these small vessels operated mainly in local waters, they had little or no impact upon the navigation of the thousands of trading sailing vessels but by 1820 the *Prince Coburg*, a steam packet, had commenced a service to the Isle of Wight; a service extended to Le Havre in 1823 (Unwin 2003, p. 184). By 1822, 48 steamers had been launched from the Clyde (Fox 2004, p. 31) and, in 1823, the recorded numbers of steamships were 101 and 10 in Britain and the colonies, respectively, requiring an amendment to tonnage measurement law to allow for the non-earning space occupied by the steam propulsion machinery (Campbell 1980, pp. 11, 12). Steamships steadily grew in size, power, and speed, with the *United Kingdom* of 1826 being 175 feet long and 500 tons with an engine of 200 horsepower (Fox 2004, p. 34).

4.3   Sailing Packets to Steam Power

By the 1830s, with improved steam engines of greater power and more economical fuel consumption, it became theoretically possible to traverse the 3000 miles from the United Kingdom to the United States in 15 days. The "fast" sailing packets

---

[5]Watt had improved upon existing stationary steam engines in 1765 by creating "a separate condenser so that the cylinder could remain at essentially the same temperature throughout the cycle, saving time and fuel because no steam would be lost to condensation from entering a cold cylinder." (Fox 2004, pp. 19, 20)

operating scheduled services across the stormy, foggy, and ice-bound North Atlantic averaged 24 days eastbound and 38 days westbound at this time. By the end of the 1830s the sailing packets had achieved a remarkable degree of speed, size (Fox 2004, p. 6), safety, and reliability:

> Every month a dozen packets left New York for Europe and a dozen more arrived: an average of one ship every thirty hours, all year long, regardless of wind or weather. The packets suffered occasional collisions and founderings at sea, but only two accidents caused any loss of life over the two decades from 1820 to 1840 (Fox 2004, p. 15).

This outstanding record of safety and reliability was inevitably challenged by steam power which, whilst eventually reducing passage times, would not be able to replicate the remarkable safety record of the sailing packets. In April 1838 the charismatic and archetypical Victorian engineer Isambard Kingdom Brunel was vying for the honour of achieving the first entirely steam-powered crossing of the North Atlantic in his *Great Western*, of 236 feet long and 1,320 tons. The *Great Western*'s main rival was the smaller paddle-wheeler *Sirius*, of 700 tons, which had been chartered by a frustrated American, Junius Smith, when his very large vessel of 1800 tons, *British Queen*, was delayed in construction. In the resultant race the *Great Western* crossed the North Atlantic in 15½ days, three weeks faster than a crack sailing packet, and four days faster than the *Sirius* (Fox 2004, p. 80).

4.4   Drivers for Jurisdiction and Control of Ships

The age of the ocean-going steamship had arrived and its relationship with other steamships and sailing ships, and its impact upon the safety of navigation, was soon to be felt, both in accident statistics and resultant legislation to administer and control many previously totally uncontrolled aspects of shipping. The race to have the largest and fastest passenger liner on the North Atlantic led technical developments of ship and engine design from the time of the *Sirius* and *Great Western*, but brought about technological, safety, and navigational issues which were exacerbated in many cases by the complete lack of any agreed standards or regulation. Legislation throughout this period of rapid growth in ship size, speed, and technology was constantly in a catch-up mode, driven by reaction to disasters rather than proactivity. The significant drivers for national law are examined below to identify their causes and outcomes. The key drivers discussed are: technical and social standards, competition, steam power, collisions, unseaworthiness, overloading, the emigrant trade, and lifesaving appliances.

4.4.1   Technical and Social Standards

The focus on maritime legislation in the United Kingdom for the first half of the nineteenth century was driven by William Huskisson, the president of the Board of

Trade. This focus had been, from 1823, away from development and protection of trade through its misleadingly named Navigation Laws, which had nothing to do with the safety of navigation,[6] to a growing acceptance of free trade[7] and attention to other matters of administration of ships[8]. The Mercantile Marine Act, 1850 (13 & 14 Vict. c.93) created a Marine Department of the Board of Trade responsible for administration and qualifications of seafarers (Campbell 1980, p. 16) and the extent of previous lack of regulation of ships and seafarers can be gleaned from the scope of the Act. The new Government department administered compulsory examination of Masters and Mates of foreign-going ships, the establishment of Shipping Offices to superintend contracts between seafarers and shipowners, and dealt with matters such as desertion, discipline, health, log-books, wages, and seamens' discharges (Campbell 1980, p. 80).

The safety and seaworthiness of ships, and recognition of issues such as the lack of lifesaving appliances, inadequate means of signalling distress, and increasing numbers of collisions arising from the rapid development of steamships, was eventually addressed through the Steam Navigation Act, 1851 (14 & 14 Vict. c.79) ten years after the commencement of scheduled steamship services across the North Atlantic. Under this Act, the Government set standards for lifeboats, distress signals and collision regulations; and provided for the appointment of Surveyors of Ships and the issuance of Certificates of Survey. These two Acts of 1850 and 1851 were included in the Merchant Shipping Act 1854 (17 & 18 Vict. c. 104.) (effective 1 May, 1855), an "Act to amend and consolidate the Acts relating to Merchant Shipping". The 1854 Act also repealed most of the law affecting merchant ships and seamen that had been introduced since the Elizabethan era (http://www.1911encyclopedia. org/Laws_Relating_To_Seaman) and was the culmination of the work commenced by Huskisson in 1823.

The Merchant Shipping Act 1854, was the foundation upon which all subsequent shipping legislation was built and set standards in eleven parts[9] dealing mainly with administrative and social rather than technical matters (Campbell 1980, p. 16–17). Part IV of the Act, Safety and Prevention of Accidents, comprised less than 4% of

---

[6]For example: "An Act for the Encouragement of British Shipping & Navigation, 1833, (3 & 4 Will. 4 C.54) provided that all British-built boats or vessels under 15 tons burden, wholly owned and navigated by British subjects, although not registered as British ships, would be admitted to be British vessels in all navigation on the rivers and coasts of the United Kingdom or British possessions abroad." (Campbell

[7]"Foreign flag vessels were admitted to the British foreign-going trade in 1850 and to the British home trade in 1854." (Campbell 1980, p. 15)

[8]For example, the Act for the Registering of vessels 1823 (4 Geo. 4 C. 41) provided that the property in a ship be divided into 64 shares, held by not more than 32 individuals. This provision was retained in the Merchant Shipping Act 1854.

[9]The General Functions of the Board of Trade; Registration of Ships; Masters and Seamen; Safety and Prevention of Accidents; Pilotage; Lighthouses; The Mercantile Marine Fund; Wrecks, Casualties and Salvage; Liability of Shipowners; Legal Procedures; and Miscellaneous matters.1980, p. 14)

the content and focussed upon the main causes of accidents at that turning point in the development of ships: collisions; build and equipment of steamships; surveys of passenger steamers; and reporting of accidents.

4.4.2 Competition and Consequences

At this time the development of larger ships and more powerful steam engines was proceeding ever more rapidly, fuelled by intense competition in the North Atlantic passenger and mail trade, by generous mail contracts from the British and American governments, and by the desire of very competitive shipowners to be able to offer passengers the largest and fastest ship on the route. These were combinations of imperatives that did not always result in the safest navigation on a route beset year round by storms and fog.

A disaster that occurred the same year that the Merchant Shipping Act was enacted – 1854 – dramatically and tragically emphasised the need for some of the measures introduced by that Act, such as safety and prevention of accidents. The Collins Line passenger and mail steamer *Arctic*, of 2,800 tons and 814 horsepower, was launched in New York in 1847 and, by 1851, this ship and her three sisters[10] were the fastest passenger liners on the North Atlantic route, progressively, in turn, bringing the westbound passage time down to under ten days at average speeds of more than thirteen knots (Fox 2004, p. 124). On 20 September 1854 the *Arctic* left Liverpool for New York with 281 passengers, including 109 women and children, and 153 crew. On 27 September, when in fog on the Grand Banks, the *Arctic*, steaming at full speed, collided with a smaller French steamer, the *Vesta*. Four and a half hours later the *Arctic* sank amidst scenes of mutiny and panic by the great majority of the crew, including the Captain. As was typical of ships of the day the *Arctic*'s lifeboats could only carry 40% of the total complement of 434. Only 23 passengers survived and all of the 109 women and children perished. The unimaginable horror of the situation is highlighted by the raw statistic that 61 of the crew survived including 4 out of the 5 senior officers (Fox 2004, pp. 128–132).

The Collins Line immediately voluntarily equipped its ships with watertight bulkheads and more lifeboats (Fox 2004, p. 132) but this was as much by way of a public relations exercise to restore confidence as it was to improve safety. The masters of the Collins Line[11] ships, as did their competitors, continued to steam at full speed in fog, ice and heavy weather, pushing their vessels to the limit to maintain schedules, as instructed by their companies (Fox 2004, p. 137). At this time the

---

[10]*Baltic, Pacific,* and *Atlantic.*

[11]The Collins Line collapsed suddenly in 1857 after it lost all confidence of the travelling public when the *Pacific,* with a crew of 141 and 45 passengers, disappeared without trace in January 1856. The bow section was found only 60 miles from Liverpool, her port of departure, in 1991 but it was not possible to establish the cause of her loss.

great majority of ships were still constructed of wood and carried a considerable amount of sail to complement their paddle wheel propulsion. The use of iron construction[12] in large ocean-going ships (Fox 2004, pp. 142–144) in the late 1830s, coupled with development of the screw propeller[13] eventually led to their combined application in Brunel's revolutionary *Great Britain*, which completed her first crossing of the North Atlantic in 1845 (Fox 2004, pp. 146, 153). This particular application of screw propulsion was not a success. It was not until the 1850s that the concept was resurrected due to increased understanding of its technology, greater efficiency and hence less fuel, and greater capacity for cargo and passengers. Screw propulsion was used mainly on cargo and emigrant ships, as paddle-wheelers were still perceived to give greater comfort on the stormy North Atlantic. Finally, in 1862, Cunard launched a screw ship for its Atlantic service, the *China*: 326 feet long and 2,500 tons, carrying 160 passengers in first class and 770 emigrants in steerage (Fox 2004, p. 190).

4.4.3   Problems with Steam Power

The increased strength, power,[14] and economy of iron-built and screw-propelled ships opened the door to the ability to design and build ever bigger and faster ships, with associated increased risks to safety of the ships and the lives of those aboard, resulting in a need to introduce and constantly update fledgling safety standards and administrative jurisdiction to mitigate these risks. The rapidly increasing boiler pressures required to propel ever larger ships had attendant risks and serve as a graphic example, not only of the human cost of technology, but of the effectiveness of flag State jurisdiction through interventionist legislation.

Between 1866 and 1882 there was an annual average of 45 boiler explosions aboard steamships, causing 59 deaths per year (Malcolm 1912, p. 51). This high number of explosions and deaths resulted in the Board of Trade drafting, in 1882, the Boiler Explosions Act (45 & 46 Vict. c. 22: "An Act to make better provision for Inquiries with regard to Boiler Explosions") which was amended in 1890 (53 & 54 Vict.

---

[12]The first small iron steamboat, the *Aaron Manby*, was constructed in 1821 and carried the first cross-channel cargo under steam propulsion to Le Havre; a cargo of iron and linseed.

[13]The *Archimedes* of 1838 was the first successful steam-powered vessel with screw propulsion, and was the inspiration for Brunel to change from paddle to screw propulsion for the *Great Britain*.

[14]"Maximum steam pressure in the 1830s was about 5 pounds per square inch" (Fox 2004, p. 73). "The Collins Line ships, *America* and her three sisters, of 1846, had boilers which could withstand 18 pounds per square inch" (p. 115) The *Scotia* of 1862 "used 164 tons of coal a day at 25 pounds to produce 1,000 horsepower" (p. 215). "The development of the compound engine and scotch boiler in the late 1860s required yet higher pressures" (pp. 273–274). "The White Star liners *Britannic* and *Germanic*, of 1874 and 1875, respectively, generated 5,000 indicated horsepower from eight scotch boilers operating at 65 pounds per square inch" (pp. 281–282).

c. 35 "An Act to amend the Boiler Explosions Act 1882") and then incorporated into the Merchant Shipping Act 1894. For the period subsequent to the Act coming into effect until 1908, the number of annual explosions and deaths dropped to an average of 24 and 15, respectively, with the lowest annual figures being 17 explosions and 5 deaths in 1904–05. This is compared with the worst year before the 1882 Act, of 91 deaths from 40 explosions in 1876 (Malcolm 1912, p. 51).

4.4.4 Collision

Another significant driver for the development of legislation controlling the activities of ships upon the high seas was the hazard of collision; either between steamships and dimly-lit sailing and fishing vessels[15] or between steamships themselves. The very real threat of collision was also the catalyst for the most proactive international maritime agreements in the nineteenth century.

As early as 1840, Trinity House had devised a set of basic "give way" rules for both sailing and steam vessels and these were incorporated in the Steam Navigation Act 1846. The Act was amended two years later to include Admiralty regulations requiring steamships to carry red and green coloured sidelights as well as a white masthead light (Cockcroft and Lameijer 1990, p. xiv). It was not until 1858 that coloured sidelights were required for sailing vessels. These measures were consolidated in the Merchant Shipping Act 1854 (17 & 18 Vict. c. 104). The minimal "Lights and Fog Signals, and Meeting and Passing" requirements brought into effect by this Act,[16] were significantly updated, in consultation with the French Government, in 1862,[17] and subsequently, by amendment in 1879, 1884 and 1897.[18]

This cooperation amongst maritime States in the regulation of shipping led to the United States calling the first International Maritime Conference in 1889 in Washington D.C. The aim of this Conference was to consider regulations for preventing collision at sea and to consider the question of formation of a world body to regulate shipping. Although the latter proposal was considered and rejected

---

[15]"fishermen in the English Channel referred to the new-fangled and badly handled screw driven steamers … as 'silent death'." (Unwin 2003, p. 191)

[16]Merchant Shipping Act, 1854, s.295, Regulations as to lights and fog signals; s.296, Rules as to ships meeting each other; s.297, Rule for steamers in narrow channels; s.298 If collision ensues from breach of the above rules, owner not to be entitled to recover.

[17]The Merchant Shipping Act Amendment Act, 1862, (25 & 26 Vict. c. 63) s.25, repealed sections 295–299 of the 1854 Act and brought into effect Regulations for Preventing Collisions at Sea.

[18]By Order in Council, 7 July, 1897 (London Gazette, 1897, p. 379), made pursuant to the Merchant Shipping Act 1894 and arising out of the first International Maritime Conference convened by the United States of America and held in Washington in 1889.

on the grounds that "for the present the establishment of a permanent international maritime commission is not considered expedient" some significant amendments[19] to the collision regulations were agreed upon by those States present ("Focus on IMO" 1998, p. 1). A second International Maritime Conference was convened in Brussels in 1910 where wider agreement was reached on the amendments to the collision regulations agreed in Washington in 1889, and the collision regulations remained fundamentally unchanged until 1954.

However, there were still some masters of North Atlantic passenger steamers who were driven more by commercial pressures and the perceived need to maintain a timetable, than the dictates of prudent seamanship when navigating in reduced visibility. This issue was highlighted by the trenchant criticism of Sir Charles Butt in the case of the *Resolution* in 1889 (6 Asp. M.C. 363) when he stated *inter alia* that "...I will not yield to what I know is the strong disinclination of the masters of these large vessels to stop their engines. They hate and abhor the very idea, but it is, to my mind, their duty to do so, if they cannot otherwise reduce their speed sufficiently."

It is clear that for collision regulations to work satisfactorily in the matter of navigation in fog and the many other meeting, crossing, and overtaking situations vessels can find themselves in, they must be observed by ships of all nationalities. This matter, at a time when there were no international safety standards for ships, was addressed for waters under British jurisdiction by the Merchant Shipping Acts Amendment Act 1862 (25 & 26 Vict. c. 63), which required *inter alia* that:

> Whenever foreign ships are within British jurisdiction, the regulations for preventing collision contained in Table (c) in the schedule to this Act, or such other regulations for preventing collisions as are for the time being in force under this Act, and all provisions of this Act relating to such regulations, or otherwise relating to collisions, shall apply to such foreign ships; and in any cases arising in any British court of justice concerning matters happening within British jurisdiction, foreign ships shall, so far as regards such regulations and provisions, be treated as if they were British ships. (Merchant Shipping Acts Amendment Act 1862, s.57)

Whilst this section of the Act dealt with interaction between British and foreign flagged ships within Britain's narrow territorial waters, the Act went considerably further and made the bold move of extending this territorial requirement to ships of any other State willing to accept this standard outside British jurisdiction as follows:

> Whenever it is made to appear to His Majesty in Council that the Government of any foreign country is willing that the collision regulations, or the provisions of Part V of this Act relating thereto or otherwise relating to collisions, or any of these regulations or provisions

---

[19] "Among the new provisions agreed at the Conference were requirements that a stand-on vessel should keep her speed as well as her course, that a giving-way vessel should avoid crossing ahead of the other, and that steamships should be permitted to carry a second white masthead light. The regulations agreed to at the Washington Conference were brought into force by several countries, including Britain and the United States, in 1897." (Cockcroft 1990, p. xv)

should apply to the ships of that country when beyond the limits of British jurisdiction, His Majesty may, by Order in Council, direct that those regulations and provisions shall, subject to any limitation of time conditions and qualifications contained in the Order, apply to the ships of the said foreign country, whether within British jurisdiction or not, and that such ships shall for the purpose of such regulations and provisions be treated as if they were British ships. (Merchant Shipping Acts Amendment Act 1862, s.58)

An increasingly large number of "foreign countries" accepted this offer[20]; which was repeated in section 424 of the Merchant Shipping Act 1894, and went on to make it sweepingly and abundantly clear in s.61 of that Act that "Whenever an Order in Council has been issued under this Act, applying any provisions of this Act or any regulation made by or in pursuance of this Act to the ships of any foreign country, such ships shall in all cases arising in any British court be deemed to be subject to such provisions or regulation, and shall for the purpose of such provision or regulation be treated as if they were British ships." This proactive stance by Great Britain was a graphic illustration of their dominant and all pervasive influence in the development of maritime law throughout the shipping world of the late nineteenth century, and of the ability to establish customary law through agreement between sovereign States in vital matters of safety at sea.[21]

4.4.5   Unseaworthiness and Overloading

An age-old problem that had led to very early regulation of ships, and which was endemic throughout the nineteenth century, was that of the large loss of life of seamen through shipwreck, and through the overloading of often unseaworthy ships. The Scandinavian port city of Visby had passed a law in the thirteenth century that required all ships to have a load line, with significant penalties for non-compliance, and, in the fifteenth century Venice standardised the design of galleys and required them to be marked with a load line (IMO paper, J/8351).

---

[20] For example: By Order in Council, September 5 1880, the Collision Regulations 1879, with the exception of Article 10, apply to the ships of Cochin, Kattyawar, Kelat, Kutch, Muscat, Travecore and Zanzibar. By Order in Council, 27 November 1880, the rules of 1879 apply to ships of Hawaii. By Order in Council, 9 July 1885, the rules of 1884 apply to ships of Turkey. Article 10 of the rules of 1879 and 1884 apply to ships of the following countries: Austria-Hungary, Belgium, Brazil, Chili, Ecuador, France, Germany, Greece, Italy, Japan, Netherlands, Norway, Portugal, Russia, Spain, Sweden, United States. By Order in Council, 7 July 1897, the Collision Regulations apply to ships of the following countries: Argentine Republic, Austria-Hungary, Belgium, Brazil, Chili, China, Costa Rica, Denmark, Ecuador, Egypt, France, Germany, Greece, Guatemala, Italy, Japan, Mexico, Netherlands, Norway, Peru, Portugal, Russia, Siam, Spain, Sweden, USA.

[21] "Similarly, the 'Commercial Code of Signals for the Use of Nations', published by Great Britain as far back as 1857 and which formed the basis of the work of the Washington Conferences of 1889 and 1927, and of the London Conference of 1948, is now in universal use." (Colombo 1968, p. 60).

These early examples of jurisdiction and control of this vital element of ship design and loading had been lost in the mists of time by the nineteenth century, when public concerns at the large number of shipwrecks, and a perceived link with unseaworthiness and overloading, caused the British Parliament to appoint a committee in 1836 to investigate these issues.[22] No jurisdiction and control of these matters ensued at that time. The Mercantile Marine Act 1850 established, for the first time, a central administration through the Board of Trade, and the Steam Navigation Act 1851 provided for surveys of ships. These Acts were consolidated in the Merchant Shipping Act 1854, but there was still no recognition in law of the dangers posed by overloading.

It was not until Samuel Plimsoll entered Parliament in 1868 that seamen found a champion prepared to take up the cudgels on their collective behalf against the greed of unscrupulous shipowners in operating unseaworthy ships (Campbell 1980, p. 19). His book *Our Seamen*, published in 1873, and given to every Member of Parliament, claimed that nearly 1,000 seamen a year were being drowned in ships around the British coast. Plimsoll was successful in introducing the Merchant Shipping Survey Bill 1871, which proposed to make certain ships subject to surveys and to introduce a requirement for a load line beyond which the ship could not be submerged. In spite of the Bill having to be withdrawn through lack of support, a similar Bill introduced by the Board of Trade was successful and became the Merchant Shipping Act 1871 (34 & 35 Vict. c. 110).

One aspect of the Merchant Shipping Act 1871 that caused Plimsoll great distress was the requirement for seamen to go to sea and complete the voyage once they had signed Articles of Agreement, on the pain of a fine or imprisonment, regardless of the seaworthiness of the ship. The Merchant Shipping Acts Amendment Act 1871, s.7, allowed *inter alia* "…proceedings against any seaman or apprentice belonging to any ship for desertion, or for neglecting or refusing to join or proceed to sea in his ship, or for being absent from or quitting the same ship without leave." *The Times* of March 1873 reported the tragic case of the *Peru* where 15 seamen, who had refused to sail as they believed the ship to be unseaworthy, were imprisoned for three months. The ship subsequently departed Cardiff with a new crew; three of whom were lost when the *Peru* sank in the Bay of Biscay (http://www.spartacus.schoolnet.co.uk/Lshipping.htm).

In spite of the sympathy of many Members of Parliament to the claims of shipowners that they should have the unrestricted right to run their businesses, Plimsoll finally

---

[22] "According to testimony from both sides of the ocean, Americans were building and running the finest sailing ships in the world. A London newspaper in 1834, after comparing the safety records of the New York packets and the British government's mail ships, urged the Admiralty to buy American vessels. In 1836, a committee of the British Parliament inquiring into the problem of shipwrecks presented evidence that American ships were better built than their British counterparts (and thus preferred by shippers and insurance agents), and that American commanders and officers were more educated and competent and American seamen more carefully selected, more efficient and better paid – to the point that the best British sailors were defecting to American ships." (Fox 2004, p. 15)

gained the support of many politicians, including Lord Shaftesbury and the Conservative Prime Minister Disraeli, who gave their support to the Unseaworthy Vessels Bill 1875. The successful adoption of this Bill resulted in the Merchant Shipping Act 1876 (39 & 40 Vict. c. 80), which finally required vessels to be marked with a load line; the "Plimsoll Line". The attitude of some shipowners to this long overdue legislation is reflected in the fact that, as the Act did not specify where the load line should be painted, some derisorily painted it on the funnel. Through the Merchant Shipping Act 1890 (53 & 54 Vict. c. 9) the Board of Trade eventually specified exactly where the Load Line should be marked (Bloy, http:// www.victorianweb.org/history/plimsoll.html). The Merchant Shipping Act 1854 was amended again in 1872 (35 & 36 Vict. c. 73, s.8) to require, *inter alia*, that every passenger steamer be surveyed once at least in every year in the manner mentioned in the fourth part of that Act. Plimsoll's efforts were rewarded through further amendments to the 1854 Act in 1876 (39 & 40 Vict. c. 80, s.4), which made it an offence to take an unseaworthy ship to sea, and made provision for foreign flagged ships to be detained in such cases, or in cases of overloading.

The legacy of Plimsoll is partially reflected in statistics for the mortality of seafarers. In 1881 a total of 3,278 seamen aboard British and colonial ships were lost in wrecks and shipboard accidents and there was a mortality rate, out of a total workforce of 187,000, of one in 57 serving seafarers. The chances of accidental death were estimated to be four times as high as in coalmining; at that time the most hazardous of land occupations. Mortality rates appreciably declined towards the end of the nineteenth and into the early twentieth centuries, with the death rate in the British merchant marine 1:117 in 1896 (1,859 deaths out of a total workforce of 218,000). However, the age-old perils of working aboard sailing ships remained, with a death rate at this time of 1:60, as opposed to 1:180 for the crews of steamships (Atkinson 2001, pp. 50, 51).

4.4.6 Issues in the Emigrant Trade

Another significant driver of legislative change was the rapidly growing[23] emigration trade from Ireland after the Great Famine of 1846. This brought about regulation of ships trading internationally, in an attempt to improve living and sanitary conditions aboard these vessels. Over a six-year period from 1846, about 50 ships foundered on their passage from Europe to North America, and five disasters alone caused well over 1,200 deaths:

> At their worst, the emigrant ships ran aground, or sank in storms, or caught fire, or just vanished. In 1847 the *Exmouth*, a tiny vessel of only 320 tons was blown by a storm onto a rocky Scottish coast, killing 240 emigrants; the *Carrick* after six weeks at sea hit a shoal

---

[23] 68,000 emigrants in 1846; 118,000 in 1847; 151,000 in 1848; 180,000 in 1849 and over 184,000 in 1850. (Fox 2004, p. 171)

and broke up off Newfoundland, with about 180 deaths; the *Canton* ran onto rocks near Durness, Scotland, leaving no survivors among the three hundred on board. On the *Ocean Monarch* in August 1848, only a few hours out from Liverpool, someone lit an illegal fire below deck; the ship burned to the waterline, killing over 400 emigrants bound for Boston. In 1849 the *Maria,* heading from Limerick to Quebec, ran into an icefield in a storm, could not get free, collided hard with an iceberg, and went down with 109 people. (Fox 2004, pp. 170, 171)

Further, aboard the *Virginius* in 1847, 158 emigrants out of a total of 476 died from typhus and another 100 were ill upon arrival. This catalogue of disasters prompted action by both the British Parliament and the U.S. Congress. In 1848 the British Parliament "decreed that such vessels should maintain certain standards of ventilation, cleanliness and order, with no open flames or smoking below decks, and marauding sailors banned from passenger quarters" (Fox 2004, pp. 170, 171). This concentration upon living conditions, the dangers of fire, and the predatory natures of seamen did not address the very real issue of lack of lifesaving devices if the unfortunate ship was to succumb to one of the many perils of the North Atlantic.

4.4.7   Lack of Lifesaving Appliances

The large sailing vessel *Washington,* of 1,600 tons, carried 900 emigrants on a voyage from Liverpool to New York in 1850 (Fox 2004, p. 170), and although she arrived safely after a thoroughly miserable voyage during which a dozen children died of dysentery, it is extremely doubtful whether she would have carried enough lifesaving appliances to save such a large complement of passengers and crew. Photographs of the ever larger passenger ships built during the decade from 1840 to 1850 for the competing Cunard and Collins Lines show very few lifeboats. Brunel's mammoth failure, the *Great Eastern* of 1847, twice the length and five times the weight[24] of any ship built previously, carried only sixteen boats for 4,000 passengers, plus over 400 crew.

This fundamental issue of safety was not to receive official attention until 1854, [25]when ships were required to carry a number of boats directly related to the gross tonnage of the vessel, not to the total complement of crew and passengers the vessel was certified to carry; a calculation that was to prove woefully inadequate in

---

[24] *Ibid*, p. 160: 690 feet long and 22,500 tons.

[25] Merchant Shipping Act 1854, Table S (See section 292): "Number and dimensions of Boats with which Seagoing Ships are to be provided". For example, a sailing ship greater than 800 tons and a steamship of 500–800 tons were required to carry 4 and 4–5 boats, respectively, regardless of the number of passengers and crew carried. The scale extended to steamships greater than 1,500 tons which were required to carry 7 lifeboats. The Passenger Act 1855 (18 & 19 Vict. c. 119) s.27, had a similar requirement based upon tonnage: "…provided that no passenger ship shall be required to carry a greater number of boats than are sufficient in the judgement of the emigration officer at the port of clearance to carry all the persons on board the ship." The Passenger Act Amendment Act 1863 (26 & 27 Vict. c. 51) made no changes to lifeboat requirements.

ships carrying very high numbers of emigrants for their relatively small size. Forty
years later, and in spite of many accidents where ships had inadequate lifesaving appliances, the Merchant Shipping Act 1894 still did not adequately address this vital
issue. Section 428 of the Act,[26] "Duties of owners and masters as to carrying lifesaving appliances", was fatally flawed in its general qualifications. The specific
provision that allowed designers, owners, and masters to place a higher premium
upon uncluttered promenade decks for passengers, than the fitting of an adequate
number of lifeboats, was to have tragic consequences 18 years later in the *Titanic*
disaster; the next major catalyst for jurisdiction and control of ships.

After the large loss of life in this disaster, which was a direct outcome of the permissive
regulations for carriage of life-saving appliances, the British Government called a
conference in London which resulted in the adoption in 1914 of the first Safety of Life
at Sea (SOLAS) Convention (IMO paper J/8351, p. 2). This watershed treaty, which
only applied to passenger ships, was the first time that international standards had been
agreed upon to govern the safety of shipping, in particular ensuring that vessels carried
enough lifeboats and lifejackets for all aboard (IMO paper J/8351, p. 2).

4.5   The Merchant Shipping Act 1894

Finally, in tracing the evolution of steamships and associated national law in nineteenth century Great Britain, the foundation of all modern regulation, jurisdiction,
and control of ships was firmly laid through the Merchant Shipping Act 1894 (57
& 58 Vict. c. 60), passed on 25 August 1894 and effective from 1 January 1895.
This Act was, with 14 parts and 748 sections, the longest Act on the statute books.
This major Act consolidated maritime legislation stretching as far back into the
history of England as the reign of Edward II in the fourteenth century (Campbell
1980, p. 23) and remained the cornerstone of the legislation of many States for
upwards of 100 years.[27] The Merchant Shipping Act 1894 was the model for future
codification of flag State jurisdiction and control, containing *inter alia* provisions
for social, administrative, and technical matters.[28]

---

[26] Merchant Shipping Act 1894, s.428: "It shall be the duty of the owner and master of every
British ship to see that his ship is provided, in accordance with the rules for lifesaving appliances,
with such of those appliances as, having regard to the nature and of the service on which the ship
is employed, and the avoidance of undue encumbrance of the ship's deck, are best adapted for secur-
ing the safety of her crew and passengers."

[27] For example, the New Zealand Shipping and Seamen Act 1952, repealed by the Maritime
Transport Act 1994, contained many references to the Merchant Shipping Act 1894.

[28] Such as: Accommodation; Agreements; Anchors and Cables; Boiler Explosions; Board of
Trade; Casualties and Unseaworthiness; Certificates and Certificated Officers; Collisions;
Dangerous Goods; Detention; Equipment and Machinery; Flag and Nationality; Lead, Log and
Look-out; Life-saving Appliances; Lights and Fog Signals; Load-line; Manning; Medical Stores
and Inspections; Registry and Marking; Seamen (Deceased, Desertion and Discipline, Relief and
Repatriation, Wages); Signals; Surveyors and Officers of the Board of Trade; and Tonnage.

By the close of a century of remarkable and unprecedented development in shipping, the British national legislative framework had almost caught up with technological development and provided a framework of laws which acted as a model for other maritime States and for the eventual development of international law for the jurisdiction and control of shipping during the twentieth century.

References

Atkinson N (2001) Crew Culture. Te Papa Press, Wellington

Bloy, M. Samuel Plimsoll's Merchant Shipping Act (1876). http://www.victorianweb.org/history/plimsoll.html

Campbell RD (1980) The Ship's Register: A History of British Ship Status and Registration Procedures including their adoption in New Zealand. Ministry of Transport – Marine Division, New Zealand

Cockcroft AN, Lameijer JNF (1990), A Guide to the Collision Avoidance Rules, 4th edn. Butterworth-Heinemann Ltd, United Kingdom

Colombo CJ (1968) The International Law of the Sea, 6th edn. Longmans, United Kingdom

Conrad J (1897) The Nigger of Narcissus: a Tale of the Sea. In: The Nigger of Narcissus, Typhoon, Shadow Line. 1950. Dent and Sons Ltd, London

Fox S (2004) The Ocean Railway. HarperCollins, London

Malcolm JH (1912) The Merchant Shipping and Relative Acts. William Hodge and Company, Edinburgh and London

Phillips-Birt D (1971) A History of Seamanship. George Allen and Unwin, London

Unwin P (2003) The Narrow Sea. Headline Book Publishing, London

Documents

IMO (1998) Focus on IMO. IMO 1948–1998: a process of change. International Maritime Organization, London

IMO (2003) IMO: Committed people working for Safe, Secure and Clean Seas. Paper J/8351, World Maritime Day 2003, Background paper

Chapter 5
Development of International Law for Flag State Responsibility

Abstract A slow transition of national maritime law from the nineteenth century through bilateral and multilateral agreements to eventual international agreements took place during the first half of the twentieth century. Coinciding with the beginning of the second shipping revolution in the 1950s, the International Law Commission was drafting articles as a basis for codification of customary law for matters including the nationality of ships and their jurisdiction and control. These articles, which were adopted with little change through the HSC, provided a standard for flag States that was appropriate at that time. Consideration is given to the development of this international law for the nationality of ships, and their jurisdiction and control, and the question is asked whether review of these specific matters by UNCLOS III was overshadowed by environmental issues, to the detriment of consideration of suitability of the extant model for jurisdiction and control of ships. A comparative study is undertaken of the codification of flag State responsibilities through the HSC, and their metamorphosis into the LOSC.

5.1 Development of Flag State Control in International Law

Although a dominant theme of the nineteenth century world of shipping had been the development of national law to cope with ever-increasing technological and safety concerns, there were attempts to obtain international agreement on important maritime matters. Great Britain had used its dominant role in international shipping to impose its standards for collision regulations[1] and communications[2] upon foreign flagged ships visiting its ports; standards which, through their acceptance and adoption by other States attained the status of customary law. This dominant role continued into the early twentieth century, as exemplified by Britain's

---

[1] See Chap. 4.

[2] *Ibid.*

lead in 1906 in the application of national load line regulations to all foreign ships calling at British ports.[3] Over the next 20 years these British 'Board of Trade Rules' were used as a model for the national law of twenty-two[4] of the world's leading maritime nations. This buy-in, along with preparatory work by the International Shipping Conference, resulted in adoption of the International Load Line Convention1930 (Singh 1963, p. 58). Within 9 years, 50 States had either ratified or adhered to this important Convention (Singh 1963, p. 101).

International concern early in the twentieth century over collisions as one of the most important factors affecting safety at sea resulted in a number of South American States joining all of the maritime nations of Europe and the United States of America, at a Conference in Brussels in 1910 to address this and other matters affecting the safety of ships (Singh 1963, p. 57). Two Conventions resulted; one on the Unification of Certain Rules of Law with respect to Collisions between Vessels (the Brussels Rules) and the other on Assistance and Salvage at Sea. The Brussels Rules remained in effect until they were revised and annexed to the SOLAS Convention in 1948, and further revision of these collision regulations took place at the London Conference in 1960 when they were annexed to SOLAS 60[5] (Singh 1963, p. 57).

After the *Titanic* disaster of 1912, which brought to a head longstanding concerns regarding the inadequacy of requirements for lifeboats on passenger ships, the British Government called a conference that resulted in the adoption, on 20 January 1914, of the first Safety of Life at Sea Convention: SOLAS 1914 (Singh 1963, p. 114). This watershed treaty included, for the first time, matters such as subdivision, wireless telegraphy, navigation rules, construction of ships, fire protection, and, in particular, ensuring that sufficient lifesaving appliances were carried for all persons aboard[6]. As an aftermath of the *Titanic* disaster an Ice Patrol was instituted in the North Atlantic (IMO paper J/8351, p. 2). The next SOLAS Convention (SOLAS 29), which was greatly expanded from that of 1914 to include cargo ships and "sought to deal with all contingencies arising from an emergency at sea,"

---

[3]Merchant Shipping Act 1906, s.1, states *inter alia*: "sections 437 to 443 of the 1894 Act (which relate to loadline), except 440 (3) and (4), shall, after the appointed day (1st October, 1909), apply to all foreign ships while they are within any port in the United Kingdom, as they apply to British ships, without prejudice…"

[4]Australia, Belgium, Chile, Denmark, France, Germany, Hong Kong, Iceland, India, Italy, Japan, Netherlands, Netherlands Indies (Indonesia), New Zealand, Norway, Portugal, Spain, Straits Settlements, Sweden, United Kingdom, United States of America, Union of Soviet Socialist Republics. (Singh 1963, p. 98)

[5]The Convention was signed by Great Britain, Canada, Australia, New Zealand, the United States of America, Austria, Belgium, Denmark, France, Germany, Holland, Italy, Norway, Russia, Spain, and Sweden.

[6]IMO paper J/8351, World Maritime Day 2003, Background paper: Committed People Working Together For Safe, Secure And Clean Seas. p. 2: The Convention only applied to ships carrying more than 12 passengers.

(Singh 1963, p. 114), was adopted in 1929 and entered into force in 1933. The 1929 SOLAS Convention was further revised in 1948 (SOLAS 48) and 1960 (SOLAS 60).

Tonnage measurement is an essential aspect of registration of ships and consequential levying of dues against the ship. These dues are levied by port and harbour authorities, and by coastal States for provision of aids to navigation, search and rescue, and distress and safety radio. The development of international law for tonnage measurement is a case study in the transition from national to bilateral, multilateral, and, finally, international regulation. As levies based upon the internal volume of the ship (gross tonnage) are charged against ships worldwide, it is important that there be a uniform method for the calculation of tonnage.

The system of tonnage measurement developed by England, the "Moorsom" system, became generally accepted in the nineteenth century and became known as the international system (Singh 1963, p. 630). The first bilateral approach was an agreement signed between the United States of America and the Empire of Russia in 1884 dealing with measurement of ships in each other ports, followed by a similar agreement between United States and Denmark in 1886 (Singh 1963, p. 630). However, due to the lack of an internationally agreed system for tonnage measurement, different methods were used in different countries resulting in the issuance of inconsistent tonnage certificates for the Suez and Panama Canals (Singh 1963, p. 630).

The matter was brought to a head in 1931 by vastly different tonnage measurements of the German ship *Leviathan*, resulting in a urgent call for uniformity of tonnage measurements. This incident was the catalyst for the Technical Committee of the League of Nations Transit Committee to take up the matter, and a draft of regulations for tonnage measurement was prepared and circulated to interested governments with a revised text being concluded in 1939 (Singh 1963, p. 630). Even whilst this drafting was under way, further multilateral agreements were negotiated such as the Convention Relating to the Tonnage Measurement of Merchant Ships, Warsaw, 1934,[7] under which Great Britain, Ireland, the British Dominions beyond the Seas, India, and Poland agreed upon mutual recognition of tonnage certificates. A further agreement was negotiated between the United States and Panama in 1937 (Singh 1963, p. 631).

The Second World War then intervened and all work on the regulations ceased for the duration of the war but resumed shortly afterwards with the Oslo Convention[8] being adopted in 1947. Under the Oslo Convention "all contracting Governments undertook to observe the international regulations circulated by the League of Nations in 1939 on this subject" (Singh 1963, p. 631). This Convention, which was the effort of a group of experts in Copenhagen in 1956, and of IMCO's Sub-Committee on Tonnage Measurement of Ships, eventually resulted in adoption of the extant Tonnage Convention in[9] 1969.

---

[7]Convention Relating to the Tonnage Measurement of Ships. Warsaw, 16 April 1934

[8]Convention for a Uniform System of Tonnage Measurement of Ships. Oslo, 10 June 1947.

[9]International Convention on Tonnage Measurement of Ships. London, 23 June 1969. In force 18 July 1982. 1982 *UKTS* 50 276.. *UKTS* 1935 No 13 (Cmd 4875).

Other matters affecting coastal States responsibilities for navigational safety that were codified during the first half of the twentieth century included international standards for buoyage,[10] maritime signals,[11] lightships,[12] and lighthouse characteristics and radio-beacons.[13] Burgeoning issues of oil pollution from ships were first addressed internationally through adoption of the OILPOL Convention[14] in 1954.

At the mid-point of the twentieth century, at a time that momentum was gathering for a Convention that would codify many wider aspects of the law of the sea previously too difficult to resolve, there was an existing framework of treaties that addressed matters vital to the safety of ships and the marine environment such as communications, lifesaving, fire-fighting, subdivision, and collision regulations (SOLAS 48), prevention of marine pollution (OILPOL 54), overloading (LOAD LINE 30), and the age old task of tonnage measurement.

A conference, convened by the League of Nations at The Hague in 1930, had failed to reach agreement on codification of a number of matters including nationality, State responsibility, and territorial waters. However, its report and draft articles on matters such as the nature and extent of coastal States' rights over the territorial sea, and of the right of innocent passage were not without influence and served as guidance when the ILC, whose first members were appointed in 1948, embarked upon the preparation of draft articles on the high seas and the territorial sea. These articles formed the basis for the work of the 86 States represented at the First United Nations Conference on the Law of the Sea (UNCLOS I) in Geneva in 1958.

5.2   UNCLOS I and the High Seas Convention

The output of UNCLOS I in 1958, the four Conventions[15] opened for signature in Geneva in April 1958, were "generally declaratory of established principles of international law" (Preamble to HSC 1958) and largely codified existing customary law. The Convention on the High Seas 1958 (HSC) is of particular interest in the

---

[10]Agreement for a Uniform System of Maritime Buoyage and Rules Annexed Thereto. Geneva, 13 May 1936. League of Nations (Communications & Transit), No C261 M154, 1936, VIII, 11.

[11]Agreement Concerning Maritime Signals. Lisbon, 23 October 1930. Official Document of the League of Nations (Communications & Transit), No C634 M253, 1930, VIII, 13.

[12]Agreement Concerning Manned Lightships Not on their Stations. Lisbon, 23 October 1930.

[13]Recommendations on Lighthouse Characteristics and Radio-Beacons. Lisbon, 23 O ctober 1930.

[14]International Convention for the Prevention of Pollution of the Sea by Oil. London, 12 May 1954. In force 26 July 1958. 327 *UNTS* 3.

[15]Convention on the High Seas; Convention on the Territorial Sea and the Contiguous Zone; Convention on Fishing and Conservation of Living resources of the High Seas; Convention on the Continental Shelf. See Brown ED (1994) The International Law of the Sea, Vol II, Dartmouth Publishing Company Ltd, United Kingdom, Docs. 4.2, 9.2, 9.12 and 7.2 for the full texts of the four Geneva Conventions.

context of this analysis of flag State responsibility as, for the first time, the long-standing principle under customary international law of the primacy of the flag State in all matters to do with the nationality and operation of ships was codified. It is useful to summarise the powers of jurisdiction and control that were considered to be appropriate at this time, to recall the underlying intent of the ILC for this treaty, and to comment in light of the development of international law and State practice.[16]

The preamble to the HSC reflects the desire of the States Parties to "codify the rules of international law relating to the high seas" and *inter alia* gives all States the right to sail ships under that State's flag on the high seas (HSC, Preamble and Article 4). Every State is under a duty to fix conditions for the grant of nationality to ships, the registration of ships in its territory, and for the right to fly its flag (HSC, Article 5). Ships are to have the nationality of the State whose flag they are entitled to fly.[17]

The HSC also included a requirement that there must be a genuine link between that State and the ship (HSC, Article 5(1)). The ILC, in its draft articles of 1956 (ILC 1956), stated that this link must exist "for purposes of recognition of the national character of the ship by other States". In its Commentary, the ILC "discussed incorporating more definite limits concerning the link between a State and ships flying its flag, particularly with regard to concerns over 'flag of convenience' or 'open registry' shipping." The ILC concluded that existing State practice governing permission to fly the flag was "too divergent to be governed by [a] few criteria" (ILC 1956). The ILC went on to note that:

> While leaving States a wide latitude in [determining the nature of the genuine link], the Commission wished to make clear that the grant of its flag to a ship cannot be a mere administrative formality, with no accompanying guarantee that the ship possesses a real link with its new State. The jurisdiction of the State over ships, and the control it should exercise … can only be effective where there exists in fact a relationship between the State and the ship other than mere registration or the mere grant of a certificate of registry (ILC 1956).

---

[16]"In retrospect, it can be seen that the post-war history of the law of the sea falls into two distinct periods. The first period, from 1945 to 1960, was partly one of consolidation, clarification and codification and partly one of progressive development in response largely to technological change. Both elements are reflected in the four Geneva Conventions on the Law of the Sea produced by UNCLOS I." (Brown 1994, p. 9)

[17]"(These) first two sentences of Article (5 of the HSC) repeat verbatim the ILC's 1956 draft. With regard to these requirements, in its Commentary the ILC noted that: "Each State lays down the conditions on which ships may fly its flag. Obviously the State enjoys complete liberty in the case of ships owned by it or ships which are the property of a nationalised company. With regard to other ships, the State must accept certain restrictions. As in the case of the grant of nationality to persons, national legislation on the subject must not depart too far from the principles adopted by the majority of States, which may be regarded as forming part of international law. Only on that condition will the freedom granted to States not give rise to abuse and friction with other States. With regard to the national element required for permission to fly the flag, a great many systems are possible, but there must be a minimum national element." (Nordquist 1995, p. 106)

Clearly, in hindsight, the intent of the ILC has not been realised nor reflected in international law as "mere registration or the mere grant of a certificate of registry" has proven to be not only possible but actively promoted by some flag States. The HSC further required the State to effectively exercise its jurisdiction and control in administrative, technical and social matters over ships flying its flag (HSC, Article 5(1)). This requirement was adopted to strengthen the concept of the "genuine link" with regard to the nationality of a ship by indicating the matters in which jurisdiction could be exercised by the coastal State (Nordquist 1995, p. 144).

A State was required by the HSC to issue to ships to which it has granted the right to fly its flag, documents to that effect (HSC, Article 5 (2)). Ships can only fly the flag of one State and shall, save in exceptional circumstances expressly provided for in international treaties or in these articles, be subject to its exclusive jurisdiction on the high seas (HSC, Article 6 (1)). A State is expressly required[18] to take such measures for ships under its flag as are necessary to ensure safety at sea with regard *inter alia* to; the use of signals, the maintenance of communications and the prevention of collisions; also, manning of ships and labour conditions for crews taking into account the applicable international labour instruments; and the construction, equipment and seaworthiness of ships (Nordquist 1995, p. 147)

The all-inclusive term 'seaworthiness' is of particular importance and can be defined as "in a fit condition to undergo a voyage, and to encounter stormy weather" (OED, p. 820). However, seaworthiness is generally accepted as having a wider meaning than just the ship itself and is considered to include her design, construction, manning, equipment and, increasingly, functional safety management both aboard and ashore.[19]

In taking measures for ships under its flag as are necessary to ensure safety at sea, each State is required by the HSC to conform to generally accepted international standards and to take any steps which may be necessary to ensure their observance.[20] Further requirements of Article 11 of the HSC clarify jurisdiction in the event of "a collision or any other incident of navigation," (HSC, Article 11 (1)) and the power of the issuing State of a certificate of competence to withdraw that certificate "even if the holder is not a national of the State which issued them" (HSC, Article 11 (2)). Only the flag State has the power to arrest or detain the ship "even as a measure of investigation", after a collision or any other incident of navigation on the high sea (HSC, Article 11 (3)).

---

[18]HSC, Article 10. The use of the words *inter alia* means that there are other unspecified matters the State must take into account to ensure safety at sea.

[19]"The term has been defined as meaning "that reasonably safe and proper condition in which a vessel's hull and equipment, her cargo and storage thereof, machinery and complement of crew, are deemed adequate to undertake a specific sea voyage or to be employed in a particular trade". McEwen, WA and Lewis AH, (1953, 1985) Encyclopedia of Nautical Knowledge. Cornell Maritime Press, Cornell MD, p. 487. See also J. Bes, I (n.d. 1977) Chartering and Shipping Terms. Baker and Howard; W S Heinman, London, New York, p. 466

[20]HSC, Article 10(1) and (2), Generally accepted standards are considered to those set by the "relevant international organizations", the IMO and ILO.

The only other Article of the HSC of direct relevance to a State's responsibility for administrative, technical or social matters over ships flying its flag, is that which requires every State to draw up regulations to prevent pollution of the seas by the discharge of oil from ships "… taking account of existing treaty provisions on the subject" (HSC, Article 24, referring to OILPOL 54).

The HSC entered into force, after receiving 62 ratifications, on 30 September 1962, and has been described by one commentator as "a timely and valuable consolidation and codification of the traditional law on such matters as the freedom of the high seas, nationality of ships, safety at sea, piracy and hot pursuit" (Brown 1994, p. 9). Although the HSC, for the first time, codified the primacy of flag State jurisdiction, the ILC's view that HSC should include a requirement for a "minimum national element" (Nordquist 1995, p. 195) did not prevail, as the use of FOCs requiring no national element had become State practice and had attained the status of customary international law.[21]

5.3   UNCLOS I to UNCLOS III: Drivers for Change

The adoption of the HSC in 1958 had little immediate impact upon law coming out of the newly established Intergovernmental Maritime Consultative Organization (IMCO). From 1958, when IMCO commenced its work, priority was given to updating of SOLAS 48 through adoption of a new version of the International Convention for the Safety of Life at Sea Convention (SOLAS) in 1960,[22] and later, (the legacy of Plimsoll), adoption of the Load Line Convention in 1966 (LOAD LINE). The main focus of IMCO's work from the second half of the 1960s into the 1970s was the rapid adoption of a tranche of Conventions[23] dealing with prevention, and the results of, pollution from ships following the world's first major pollution incident, the *Torrey Canyon* oil spill in 1967.[24] All of these pollution prevention,

---

[21]"To date there are no international standards for the registration of ships apart from those contained in the 1986 United Nations Convention on Conditions for Registration of Ships, Geneva, 7 February 1986 which has never achieved enough support to enter into force." *LOSC* 87 (1986). The Secretary General of IMCO pointed out to the Chairman of the Drafting Committee on the Law of the Sea Convention at UNCLOS III that 'there were no current international regulations on the subject of national registers of shipping.'"

[22]SOLAS 1960 had the Collisions Regulations appended to it.

[23]International Convention relating to Intervention on the High Seas in Cases of Oil Pollution Casualties. Brussels, 29 November 1969, 1975 *UKTS* 7; International Convention on Civil Liability for Oil Pollution Damage (CLC Convention). Brussels, 29 November 1969, 1975 *UKTS* 106; International Convention on the Establishment of an International Fund for Compensation for Oil Pollution Damage (Fund Convention). Brussels, 18 December 1971, 1978 *UKTS* 95; International Convention for the Prevention of Pollution from Ships. London, 2 November 1973, as amended by the protocol, London 01 June 1978 (MARPOL 73/78) 1340 *UNTS* 61.

[24]In March 1967 the first major pollution incident from one of the new generation of supertankers occurred in the English Channel when the *Torrey Canyon* grounded on the Sevenstones between Lands End and the Scilly Isles, spilling 119,000 tons of crude oil.

liability, and compensation treaties explicitly recognised the almost exclusive primacy of the flag State in matters of jurisdiction and control over ships on the high seas, as codified by the HSC, through a standard reference to "contracting governments".[25]

The focus of the MARPOL Convention was on prevention of oil spills from operational activities such as tank cleaning and bilge discharges. However IMCO also recognised the relationship between the problem of major oil spills from shipping casualties through collisions and groundings, and commenced a wide ranging work programme to address preventive measures such as sea-lanes, shore guidance, speed restrictions, navigational equipment, officer and crew training, use of automatic pilots, construction and design of tankers, and identification and charting of hazards.[26]

Meanwhile, tanker disasters continued unabated through the 1970s, the worst decade on record for pollution of the world's oceans, with 252 major oil spills occurring during this period. The worst year on record was 1979 when 640,000 tons of oil was spilt, almost half of which was from one casualty[27]; a calamitous by-product of the huge growth in the size of tankers.[28] During the deliberations at UNCLOS III between 1973 and 1982, a total of 2,643,000 tonnes of oil was spilt, although the annual total dropped dramatically to 48,000 tonnes in 1981 and 12,000 in 1982 (ITOPF 2003). Throughout this traumatic decade IMCO continued its work parallel to that of UNCLOS III whose delegates paid great attention to the principles of the MARPOL Convention in prevention of pollution from ships through the substantial Part XII (Protection and Preservation of the Marine Environment) of the resultant LOSC.

5.4 UNCLOS III and Flag State Responsibility

The drivers for what was to become the LOSC were primarily environmental and territorial, as evinced by initial establishment by the United Nations of an Ad Hoc Committee to study the Peaceful Uses of the Seabed and the Ocean Floor beyond

---

[25]See for example SOLAS, Article I, General obligations under the Convention: (a) The Contracting Governments undertake to give effect to the provisions of the present Convention and the annex thereto, which shall constitute an integral part of the present Convention. Every reference to the present Convention constitutes at the same time a reference to the annex. (b) The Contracting Governments undertake to promulgate all laws, decrees, orders and regulations and to take all steps which may be necessary to give the present Convention full and complete effect, so as to ensure that, from the point of view of safety of life, a ship is fit for the service for which it is intended. SOLAS, Article II, *Application*: The present Convention shall apply to ships entitled to fly the flag of States the Governments of which are Contracting Governments.

[26]For a summary of Conventions that were amended or developed as a direct result of the *Torrey Canyon* disaster see Brown ED, (1994) The International law of the Sea. Vol I, Dartmouth Publishing Company Ltd., United Kingdom. p. 382.

[27]The International Tanker Owners Pollution Federation Ltd., (ITOPF), Oil Tanker Spill Statistics: 2003. p. 3: "The figures for a particular year may therefore be severely distorted by a single large incident. This is clearly illustrated by 1979 (*Atlantic Empress* – 287,000 tonnes), 1983 (*Castillo de Bellver* – 252,000) and 1991 (*ABT Summer* – 260,000 tonnes)."

[28]ITOPF, Oil Tanker Spill Statistics 2003. From 1970–1979 inclusive a total of 3,142,000 tonnes of oil was spilt; predominantly from collisions and groundings.

the Limits of National Jurisdiction. This Committee developed over the next few years into the Third United Nations Conference on Law of the Sea (UNCLOS III) which commenced in late 1973 and carried out its work through a unique process of consensus, until agreement was finally reached on the comprehensive LOSC in 1982.

The HSC codified the right of a State to sail ships under its flag on the high seas (HSC, Article 4) and provided for that State to register ships (HSC, Article 5). Every State was also required to take such measures for ships under its flag as are necessary to ensure safety at sea and, in taking these measures, to conform to generally accepted international standards and to take any steps which may be necessary to ensure their observance (HSC, Article 10). The attention given by UNCLOS III to these flag State duties shall be analysed and the question of whether scrutiny of a flag State's fundamental and critical responsibility for jurisdiction and control of its ships, at a time of rapidly declining standards, was overshadowed by territorial and environmental issues shall be examined. In order to test this hypothesis it is useful to examine the development of flag State responsibility in international law through the HSC and LOSC, through a comparative study of this aspect of these two treaties.[29]

5.4.1   Nationality of Ships

Article 5[30] of the HSC and the corresponding article 91[31] of the LOSC, deal with the grant of nationality by a State to a ship, and the vexed question of a "genuine link" between that ship and its flag State:

> This link is the principal factor for maintaining discipline in all aspects of maritime naviga-
> tion, for the attribution of the responsibility of a State in cases of violations of applicable
> rules by ships of its nationality, and for the exercise of flag State jurisdiction and control
> generally (Nordquist 1995, p. 104).

---

[29]Altered wording from the HSC and new wording in the LOSC above that in the HSC is in bold in the footnote references.

[30]HSC Art.5 (1) (2) (Corresponding to Article 29 of the ILC's draft Articles) (1) Every State shall fix the conditions for the grant of its nationality to ships, for the registration of ships in its territory, and for the right to fly its flag. Ships shall have the nationality of the State whose flag they are entitled to fly. There must exist a genuine link between the State and the ship; **in particular, the State must effectively exercise its jurisdiction and control in administrative, technical and social matters over ships flying its flag. (2) Each** State shall issue to ships to which it has granted the right to fly its flag documents to that effect.

[31]LOSC Articles 91(1) (2) Nationality of Ships. (1) Every State shall fix the conditions for the grant of its nationality to ships, for the registration of ships in its territory, and for the right to fly its flag. Ships shall have the nationality of the State whose flag they are entitled to fly. There must exist a genuine link between the State and the ship. (2) **Every** State shall issue to ships to which it has granted the right to fly its flag documents to that effect.

The wording beginning '…in particular' in article 5.1 of the HSC had not been included in the ILC's 1956 draft but was proposed by France and Italy to provide examples of the matters which the State should take account of through its genuine link with ships flying its flag. This wording, which emphasised that the "State must effectively exercise its jurisdiction and control in administrative, technical and social matters over ships flying its flag" (Nordquist 1995, p. 104), was dropped at the third session of UNCLOS III in 1975.[32] The requirement for these flag State responsibilities was moved to what was to be adopted as article 94 of the LOSC. Apart from an unsuccessful attempt by the Drafting Committee in 1980 to replace "entitled to fly" with "authorised to fly" (Nordquist 1995, p. 106),[33] the wording of article 91.1 then remained as finally adopted.[34]

5.4.2   Status of Ships

There was very little change in the wording of article 92[35] of the LOSC from that of article 6[36] of the HSC, which was in itself identical to that drafted by the ILC in 1956. There was also no substantive debate during the course of UNCLOS III on this important article, which deals with the relationship between a ship and its flag State. The only issue identified was where this article should be placed in the framework of the draft Convention. Throughout the long gestation of the LOSC, Peru made consistent but unsuccessful efforts to place articles 91–96 and 98 in a proposed separate Part of the Convention on general provisions concerning ships. Peru also proposed, unsuccessfully, at the seventh session in 1978, deletion of the words

---

[32]See footnote 1, "Based on proposals by Italy and France. See A/CONF.13/C.2/L.28 (1958), UNCLOS I, IV Off. Rec. 123 (Italy); and A/CONF.13/C.2/L.93 (1958), *Ibid.* 141 (France)."

[33]See A/CONF.62/L.57/Rev.1 (1980), section XIII, XIV Off. Rec. 114, 123 (Chairman Drafting Committee).

[34]A minor amendment to the first word of article 91.2 from "each" to "every" was approved at the tenth session in 1981.

[35]LOSC Article 92 (1) & (2) Status of ships: (1) Ships shall sail under the flag of one State only and, save in exceptional cases expressly provided for in international treaties or in **this Convention**, shall be subject to its exclusive jurisdiction on the high seas. A ship may not change its flag during a voyage or while in a port of call, save in the case of a real transfer of ownership or change of registry. (2) A ship which sails under the flags of two or more States, using them according to convenience, may not claim any of the nationalities in question with respect to any other State, and may be assimilated to a ship without nationality.

[36]HSC Article 6 (1)(2) (Corresponding to Articles 30 and 31 of the ILC's draft Articles): (1) Ships shall sail under the flag of one State only and, save in exceptional cases expressly provided for in international treaties or in **these articles**, shall be subject to its exclusive jurisdiction on the high seas. A ship may not change its flag during a voyage or while in a port of call, save in the case of a real transfer or ownership or change of registry. (2) A ship which sails under the flags of two or more States; using them according to convenience, may not claim any of the nationalities in question with respect to any other State, and may be assimilated to a ship without nationality.

'on the high seas' from article 92[37] on the grounds that the article states: "save in exceptional cases provided for in international treaties *'or in the present convention'*". A further argument by Peru was that, according to the provisions of the Convention, ships are subject to the exclusive jurisdiction of the flag State not only on the high seas or in the exclusive economic zone but also in the territorial sea, except in the cases expressly provided for."

The ILC, in commenting upon its draft articles (ILC, A/3159) in the mid-1950s, stressed the importance of a ship sailing under the flag of only one State as follows:

> The absence of any authority over ships sailing the high seas would lead to chaos. One of the essential adjuncts to the principle of the freedom of the seas is that a ship must fly the flag of a single State and that it is subject to the jurisdiction of that State. (And with reference to their draft article 31 noted that) [d]ouble nationality may give rise to serious abuse by a ship using one or another flag during the same voyage, according to convenience. (Nordquist 1995, p. 123)

The ILC would have been conscious in forming this opinion of the decision in Molvan v Attorney General for Palestine (1948, A.C. 351, 369) in which the Judicial Committee of the Privy Council found that:

> … the freedom of the open sea, whatever those words may connote, is a freedom of ships which fly, and are entitled to fly, the flag of a state which is within the comity of nations. The *Asya* did not satisfy these elementary conditions. No question of comity nor any breach of international law can arise if there is no state under whose flag a vessel sails… Having no usual ship's papers which would serve to identify her, flying the Turkish flag, to which there was no evidence she had a right, hauling it down on the arrival of a boarding party and later hoisting a flag which was not the flag of any state in being, the *Asya* could not claim the protection of any state nor could any state claim that any principle of international law was broken by her seizure (Brown 1994, p. 292).

In the same year as the LOSC was adopted, the United States Appeal Court, in United States v Marino-Gracia (1982, 679 F.2d 1373 at 1382, paras [18] and [19]) strongly reinforced this view (and that of the newly adopted Article 92 of the LOSC):

> Vessels without nationality are international pariahs. They have no internationally recognised right to navigate freely upon the high seas … Moreover flagless vessels are frequently not subject to the laws of a flag-state. As such they represent 'floating sanctuaries from authority' and constitute a potential threat to the order and stability of navigation on the high seas … The absence of any right to navigate freely on the high seas coupled with the potential threat to order on international waterways has lead various courts to conclude that international law places no restrictions upon a nations right to subject stateless vessels to its jurisdiction … Thus the assertion of jurisdiction over stateless vessels on the high seas in no way transgresses recognised principles of international law (Brown 1994, p. 292).

The importance of the nationality conferred upon a vessel by registration in a State, and flying only the flag of that State, was thus firmly established in international law.

---

[37]'This suggestion was consistent with Peru's effort to place articles 91–96, and 98, in a separate Part of the Convention on general provisions concerning ships. Peru renewed its proposal to delete the words "on the high seas" from Article 92, and to restructure the articles on the high seas, at the resumed ninth session (1980) and at the eleventh session (1982)'. (Nordquist 1995, p. 125).

5.4.3 Duties of the Flag State

Having established the freedom of the high seas (LOSC, Article 87), the right of navigation (LOSC, Article 90), the conditions for the grant of nationality of ships (LOSC, Article 91), and the status of ships (LOSC, Article 92), Article 94 of the LOSC, "Duties of the flag State", is central and pivotal to good order on the high seas in clearly defining the matters over which "every State shall effectively exercise its jurisdiction and control in administrative, technical and social matters over ships flying its flag."

Article 94[38] of the LOSC, greatly expanded to be more prescriptive than Article 10[39] of the HSC, was agreed upon at a surprisingly early stage of the deliberations of UNCLOS III. A number of West European States submitted to the second session of UNCLOS III in 1974 a paper that laid out the duties and rights of flag States,

---

[38]LOSC Articles 94.3 (a) (b) (c); 94.4 (a) (b) (c); 94.5; 94.6; 94.7, *Duties of the flag State*. 94.3, (additional text above that contained in the HSC is shown in bold): Every State shall take such measures for ships flying its flag as are necessary to ensure safety at sea with regard, inter alia, to, 94.3(a) The construction, equipment and seaworthiness of ships,94.3(b) The manning of ships, labour conditions **and the training of crews**, taking into account the applicable international instruments, 94.3(c) The use of signals, the maintenance of communications and the prevention of collision. **94.4 Such measures shall include those necessary to ensure: 94.4(a) that each ship, before registration and thereafter at appropriate intervals, is surveyed by a qualified surveyor of ships, and has on board such charts, nautical publications and navigational equipment and instruments as are appropriate for the safe navigation of the ship; 94.4 (b) that each ship is in the charge of a master and officers who possess appropriate qualifications, in particular in seamanship, navigation, communications and marine engineering, and that the crew is appropriate in qualifications and numbers for the type, size, machinery and equipment of the ship; 94.4 (c) that the master, officers and, to the extent appropriate, the crew are fully conversant with and required to observe the applicable international regulations concerning the safety of life at sea, the prevention of collisions, the prevention, reduction and control of marine pollution, and the maintenance of communications by radio.** 94.5 In taking the measures **called for in paragraphs 3 and 4** each State is required to conform to generally accepted international **regulations, procedures and practices** and to take any steps which may be necessary to secure their observance. **94.6 A State which has clear grounds to believe that proper jurisdiction and control with respect to a ship has not been exercised may report the fact to the flag State. Upon receiving such a report, the flag State shall investigate the matter and, if appropriate, take any action necessary to remedy the situation. 94.7 Each State shall cause an inquiry to be held by or before a suitably qualified person or persons into every marine casualty or incident of navigation on the high seas involving a ship flying its flag and causing loss of life or serious injury to nationals of another State or serious damage to ships or installations of another State or to the marine environment. The flag State and the other State shall cooperate in the conduct of any inquiry held by that State into any such marine casualty or incident of navigation.**

[39]HSC Articles 10 (1) (a) (b) (c) (2). (1) Every State shall take such measures for ships under its flag as are necessary to ensure safety at sea with regard inter alia to: (a) The use of signals, the maintenance of communications and the prevention of collisions. (b) The manning of ships and labour conditions for crews taking into account the applicable international labour instruments. (c) The construction, equipment and seaworthiness of ships. (2) In taking such measures each State is required to conform to generally accepted international **standards** and to take any steps which may be necessary to ensure their observance.

stating that the principles and provisions of the HSC might need modification but were "otherwise valid, must remain in force for areas beyond the territorial sea, and should be incorporated in any new comprehensive convention on the law of the sea" (Nordquist 1995, p. 138). There was a clear implication that firm customary law existed on the matter of flag State duties but that there was a need to provide more detail on these duties than was thought necessary in 1958. The proposed Articles 6 *bis* and 10 contained most of the essential final wording that was adopted by UNCLOS III. In its introduction of these amendments, France declared that it was "necessary to state precisely the obligations of the flag State since the relevant articles of the Geneva Convention were incomplete" (Nordquist 1995, p. 125) Article 6 *bis* made Article 5 of the Geneva Convention more explicit with respect to the responsibilities of the flag State: Article 10 "...was intended to ensure safety at sea."[40] (Nordquist 1995, pp. 139, 140) It was recognised that Articles 6 *bis* and 10 were complementary and that they might be merged at a later date.

The International Maritime Consultative Organization (IMCO), which participated at UNCLOS III, influenced the debate[41] at the second session (Nordquist 1995, p. 140) which reflected a prevailing tendency in the Conference to improve upon the HSC by defining the responsibilities of the flag State in administrative, technical, and social matters.[42] Between 1973 and 1982 IMCO was engaged in drafting of a number of important Conventions (SOLAS, MARPOL and STCW[43]) at the same time as UNCLOS III was developing the LOSC that would provide a "jurisdictional framework for the enforcement of IMCO treaties." (IMO Interface with the LOSC, p. 2). Temporary clauses were inserted into IMCO Conventions during UNCLOS III to indicate that "these instruments should not be interpreted as prejudicing the codification and development of the law of the sea" (IMO Interface with LOSC). Other provisions in IMCO instruments were designed to avoid jurisdictional conflicts between them and the LOSC, and to ensure that their requirements would not prejudice any claims or legal views of any State concerning the nature and extent of coastal and flag State jurisdiction (IMO Interface with LOSC).

---

[40]"Second Committee, 42nd meeting (1974), para 2, II Off. Rec. 292. The representative of the U.K. had earlier referred to flag State jurisdiction and control in administrative, technical and social matters as part of the duties of the flag State vis-à-vis the international community." Second Committee, 31st meeting (1974), para. 69, *Ibid.* 237.

[41]See the statement by the representative of IMCO at the 22nd plenary meeting (1974), para. 8, I Off. Rec. 65. See also "The activities of [IMCO] in relation to shipping and related maritime matters," A/CONF.62/27 (1974), III Off. Rec. 43; and UN Office for Ocean Affairs and the Law of the Sea, Navigation on the High Seas, paras. 54–56, at 52.

[42]"[This] requirement was originally adopted in the Second Committee at UNCLOS I for the purpose of strengthening the concept of 'genuine link' with regard to the nationality of a ship ... by indicating matters over which the coastal State should exercise its jurisdiction." (Nordquist

[43]International Convention on Standards of Training, Certification and Watchkeeping for Seafarers. London, 1 December 1978. 1984 *UKTS* 50.1995, p. 144)

Work progressed apace in 1975 at the third session of UNCLOS III, when an informal consultative group merged Articles 6 *bis* and 10 to produce a text that, with minor amendments to five words, was finally adopted as Article 94 of the LOSC (Nordquist 1995, pp. 142, 143). The extent of the broadening of the scope of a flag State's duties in social matters is reflected by the decision taken at the fourth session in 1976 (when the title to Article 94 was added) to replace the draft phrase "applicable international instruments" with "applicable international labour instruments" (IMO Interface with LOSC). This amendment recognised the importance of inclusion of working and social standards, as well as those for safety of navigation, within the framework of the general law of the sea under the auspices of the ILO and the IMO (IMO Interface with LOSC).

A large number of instruments have been put in place to codify the "generally accepted international regulations"[44] that flag States and the crews of their ships are required to meet and understand under Article 94. Most of these instruments were adopted between the HSC and the LOSC to address the issues that arose in the operation of ships in that turbulent quarter century. These instruments have been developed by the Member States of the "competent international organisations"[45] charged by the LOSC with development of "generally accepted standards"[46] for the safety of ships and their crews, and protection of the marine environment; the IMO and the ILO. The various component parts of Article 94 of the LOSC are identified in Table 5.1 along with their associated extant instruments and the international organisation responsible.

The qualified requirement that "every State shall take such measures for ships flying its flag as are necessary to ensure safety at sea with regard, *inter alia*, to 'the following matters'" would indicate that there may well be other instruments which impose duties upon the flag State. Article 94, therefore, defines the administrative, technical, and social duties of a flag State, and the non-exhaustive measures it must take to ensure safety at sea. The Article also requires conformity with generally accepted international regulations, and allows a State (port/coastal State control) that is unhappy with the jurisdiction and control exercised by a flag State to report their concern to that State. A flag State is also required to investigate every serious

---

[44]The "generally accepted international regulations" referred to in Article 94(2)(a) and 94(5) dealing respectively with ship registration criteria and to the detailed requirements of Articles 94(3) and (4) are echoed in Articles 21(4), Innocent Passage, 39(2), Transit Passage, 41(3), Sea Lanes and Traffic Separation Schemes in International Straits, and 53(8) Archipelagic Sea Lanes Passage. An indication of the coverage of the expression is given in Article 39(2) by reference to the International Regulations for Preventing Collision at Sea, a regulation made by the IMO.

[45]See for example LOSC Annex IX, Article 1: "For the purposes of article 305 and of this Annex, 'international organization' means an intergovernmental organization constituted by States to which its member States have transferred competence over matters governed by this Convention, including the competence to enter into treaties in respect of those matters."

[46]See for example LOSC, Article 94.2(a): "In particular every State shall maintain a register of ships containing the names and particulars of ships flying its flag, except those which are excluded from generally accepted international regulations on account of their small size."

Table 5.1 Relationship between the LOSC requirements and IMO and ILO instruments

LOSC Article	Requirement	Instrument	Org.
94.3 (c)	Use of signals	SOLAS	IMO
94.3 (c)	Prevention of collision	SOLAS	IMO
94.3 (c)	Maintenance of communication	SOLAS	IMO
94.3 (b)	Manning of ships	SOLAS	IMO
94.3 (b)	Labour conditions	Various	ILO
94.3 (b)	Training of crew	STCW	IMO
94.3 (a)	Construction, Equipment and Seaworthiness	SOLAS, LOAD LINE	
94.4 (a)	Survey before registration*		
	Survey at regular intervals	SOLAS	IMO
	Charts, nautical publications, navigational equipment and instruments	SOLAS	IMO
94.4 (b)	Qualified master and officers	STCW	IMO
	Appropriate number of qualified crew	SOLAS	IMO
94.4 (c)	Crew who know and observe applicable instruments	SOLAS, STCW	IMO
94.6	Response to Port State Control	SOLAS, MARPOL, STCW	IMO
94.7	Accident Investigation	SOLAS, MARPOL	IMO

NB There is no requirement under any IMO instrument for a safety/structural and safety survey before registration

casualty involving a ship flying its flag that causes loss of life or serious injury to nationals of another State, or causes damage to the marine environment.

5.5 Prevention, Reduction and Control of Marine Pollution

In recognition of widespread environmental pollution from the operation of rapidly increasing numbers and sizes of oil tankers in the 1960s and 1970s, UNCLOS III placed a great deal more emphasis upon prevention of marine pollution from the operation of ships than had been undertaken by UNCLOS I in 1958. Buried in the heart of the HSC, in Article 24, is the sole, and brief, reference to prevention of marine pollution:

> Every State shall draw up regulations to prevent pollution of the seas by the discharge of oil from ships or pipelines or resulting from the exploitation and exploration of the seabed and its subsoil, taking account of existing treaty provision on the subject.

The reference to "existing treaty provisions" included the recently negotiated OILPOL Convention that had come into force immediately prior to adoption of the HSC in 1958.[47] OILPOL focussed upon the issues of the day which were "pollution

---

[47]In force 12 May 1958.

resulting from routine tanker operations and from the discharge of oily wastes from machinery spaces – regarded as the major causes of oil pollution from ships" (IMO, History of MARPOL 73/78). Environmental consciousness amongst seafarers was not high at this time, and the values of the day saw little wrong in pumping tank cleanings and oily bilge water "over the side" along with all rubbish from hold cleaning, and from the operation of the ship itself. As the average sized tanker in the 1950s was 12,000 deadweight (dwt),[48] the consequences of a collision or grounding were minimal compared to that from a Very Large Crude Carrier (VLCC) of the 1970s when one single cargo tank could carry far more cargo than an entire ship of the 1950s.

The consequences of major pollution disasters dating from the late 1960s, consequential adoption of the MARPOL Convention at the very time that UNCLOS III got underway, and increased environmental awareness had a clear impact upon the negotiators of the LOSC as evinced by the extensive consideration given by the treaty to protection and preservation of the marine environment.[49]

Included in this comprehensive suite of measures for protection of the marine environment are specific duties and responsibilities for flag States. There is a general obligation for States, including flag States, to protect and preserve the marine environment (LOSC, Article 192) and to *inter alia* "take … all measures consistent with this Convention that are necessary to prevent, reduce and control pollution of the marine environment from any source (LOSC, Article 194(1)) … [including] pollution from vessels" (LOSC, Article 194 (3)(b)). States are required by Article 211 to "… adopt laws and regulations for the prevention, reduction and control of pollution of the marine environment from vessels flying their flag", and, if the State has established particular requirements for the prevention, reduction, and control of pollution as a condition of entry of foreign vessels to that State's ports, to advise vessels of these requirements and communicate them to the IMO (LOSC, Article 211(3)). A prescient requirement,[50] which has only very recently been addressed by the competent international organisation, the IMO, and for which flag States are required to adopt laws and regulations, is that of prevention, reduction and control of pollution of the marine environment from or through the atmosphere (LOSC, Article 212).

Flag States are required by Part XII of the LOSC to ensure that vessels flying their flag comply with applicable pollution prevention laws and regulations, to provide effective enforcement (LOSC, Article 217(1)), and to prevent such vessels

---

[48]Tanker tonnages are usually referred to in tons deadweight (dwt); a measure of the carrying capacity of the ship at her summer loadline including fuel and stores expressed in long, or metric, tons weight.

[49]LOSC, Part XII, Protection and preservation of the Marine Environment, Articles 192–237. 45 comprehensive articles as compared with one in the HSC 24 years earlier.

[50]MARPOL 73/78, Annex VI. Regulations for the Prevention of Air Pollution from Ships. Entered into force on 19 May 2005.

from sailing if they are not in compliance with such rules (LOSC, Article 217 (2)). Flag States must also ensure that their ships carry statutory certificates attesting to their compliance with such pollution prevention rules and carry out periodic inspections to "verify that such certificates are in conformity with the actual condition of the vessels" (LOSC, Article 217 (3)).

Flag States are, further, compelled to investigate any violations of pollution prevention standards and to institute proceedings irrespective of the location of the pollution incident (LOSC, Article 217 (4)), as well as being obliged to investigate allegations of pollution incidents from other States (LOSC, Article 217 (6)), and to advise the complainant State and the IMO of the outcome of the investigation (LOSC, Article 217 (7)). The efficacy of flag State jurisdiction and control in these matters of prevention, reduction, and control of pollution of the marine environment, is examined in more detail in Chap. 9.

References

Brown ED (1994) The International Law of the Sea. Vol I. Dartmouth Publishing Company Ltd, United Kingdom
Nordquist MH (ed) (1995) The United Nations Convention on the Law of the Sea 1982: A Commentary. Vol III. Martinus Nijhoff Publishers, The Netherlands
Oxford English Dictionary (1989) Second edn. Vol XIV
Singh N (1963) British Shipping Laws. Volume 8. International Conventions of Merchant Shipping. Stevens and Sons, London

Documents

Convention on the High Seas, Geneva, 29 April 1958. In force 30 September 1962. 450 UNTS 11
IMO. Interface with the Law of the Sea Convention. http://www.imo.org/InfoResource/mainframe. asp?topic_id = 406&doc_id = 1077
IMO. History of MARPOL 73/78. http://www.imo.org/Conventions/contents.asp?doc_id + 678&topic_id = 258
International Convention for the Unification of Certain Rules relating to Assistance and Salvage at Sea, Brussels, 23 September 1910. In force 01 March 1913. British and Foreign State Papers, Vol 103
International Convention for the Unification of Certain Rules of Law with respect to Collisions between Vessels, Brussels, 23 September 1910
International Law Commission. Law of the Sea: Regime of the High Seas. http://untreaty.un.org/ ilc/summaries/8_1.htm
International Law Commission. Report covering the work of its eighth session (A/3159)
International Tanker Owners Pollution Federation Ltd (2003) Oil Tanker Spill Statistics

Chapter 6
The Changing World Map of Flag States

Abstract A sea change took place in development of the global shipping industry during the second half of the twentieth century. These developments led to a proliferation of new flag States, and to emerging issues with the effectiveness of flag State jurisdiction and control. The starting point for an analysis of these issues is 1958; a significant year in international maritime law during which the High Seas Convention (HSC) was adopted and the Inter-governmental Maritime Consultative Organization (IMCO) received a mandate to begin its work of updating and developing standards for ships. Another milestone in this half-century of rapid change was adoption of the United Nations Convention on the Law of the Sea in 1982. The state of health of the shipping industry in 1958, 1982, and the present day is determined, as are drivers for the economic and technical revolution that took place during this period and their cumulative effect upon ships, seafarers, the distribution of flag States, and the nature of flag State jurisdiction and control. Developments in the tonnage and types of ships, economics of shipping, and changing patterns in employment of seafarers, are identified as drivers for the burgeoning growth of flag States, particularly in the last quarter of the twentieth century.

6.1 The Very Best of Times

1958 was a watershed year in the history of regulation, control, and standards of shipping.[1] In March, the Convention on the Intergovernmental Maritime Consultative Organization (IMCO) came into effect, establishing for the first time an international body for the regulation of ships. The following month, the High Seas Convention (HSC) was adopted in Geneva, codifying, *inter alia*, the customary right of a State to grant its nationality to ships and to exercise jurisdiction and control over those ships flying its flag (HSC, Article V). For those at sea, it was the very best of times

---

[1] 1958 was also, coincidentally, the year of build of the supertanker *Torrey Canyon* whose loss in 1967 was to have a dramatic effect upon the development of international maritime law for prevention of pollution from ships and oil spill compensation and liability standards.

J.N.K. Mansell, *Flag State Responsibility,*
DOI: 10.1007/978-3-540-92933-8_6, © Springer-Verlag Berlin Heidelberg 2009

in terms of lifestyle, job satisfaction, professionalism, and quality in the management and operation of ships; times that were already under unseen threat on a number of fronts.

The ships of 1958[2] were a mixture of pre-war, wartime built and modern post-war replacement tonnage built by long established, largely European shipyards. They were owned and directly managed by companies with long and proud histories in the shipping industry; many dating back well into the days of sail. Their ships were manned by crews who would often serve their entire seafaring career with the same shipping company, and were proud to be known as "company men".[3]

Ships undertook long international voyages with leisurely sojourns in port allowing ample time for enjoyment of all local attractions. The captain was still largely "Master under God", as in the days of sail, with the only communication with the company being via Morse code or through contact with agents in far-flung ports. Many of the masters, chief engineers, senior officers, and crew had survived the very hard times of the Great Depression and also the perils and rigours of the still recent Second World War. They had been brought up when celestial navigation was largely unchanged from the days of Cook and Nelson, and when a hard-won respect for the sea, and for the centuries old traditions and values of seafaring and seamanship, was paramount.

The officers had probably attended Victorian style pre-sea schools in England or Europe and had undergone 4 years of practical, theoretical and technical training, often aboard cadet ships operated by the major shipping lines as nurseries for their own staff and those of the shipping industry in general. The seamen, stewards, firemen, stokers, motormen, cooks, carpenters, lamp-trimmers, and boatswains were capable and practical seafarers, bought up in the school of hard knocks and members of a unique subculture of society that worked hard and played hard.

The British Merchant Shipping Act 1894 (57 & 58 Vict. c. 60) had set the standard for British ships and was the almost universal model for national maritime law of the many traditional flag States. Ships were surveyed by their flag States, who employed highly qualified and experienced ex-seafarers to carry out this vital task. Long established Classification Societies operating to high standards, such as Lloyd's Register, specialised in surveys of hull, machinery, and certain equipment in order that the owner could assure his insurers that his ship was fundamentally seaworthy. The statutory construction, safety and equipment certificates required by a ship for worldwide trading were issued by the flag State upon successful completion of all surveys. The State also carried out effective administrative, technical,

---

[2]The information on ships of 1958 is from the author's personal experience as someone who went to sea as an apprenticed cadet in November of that year.

[3]Availability and Training of Seafarers. Prepared for the OECD Maritime Transport Committee, Precious Associates Limited, January 2003, p.12: "International shipping has been through phases of considerable change during the last 50 years. In the middle of the twentieth century, there was a period of stability and growth, with the industry being dominated by large, integrated, international companies, many being well known household names. The shipping companies, a considerable of whom were based in OECD countries, were all-embracing; owner, charterer, ship's husband, employer of staff and provider of finance."

and social oversight of the ships flying its flag through a well resourced maritime administration that was usually embedded in the Government structure.

All of this is not to say that the well-found ships of 1958 did not become casualties. The major causes of casualties at this time were collisions and groundings[4] reflecting the greatly increased number of ships that were operating worldwide, and the relatively primitive navigation equipment installed aboard many of them. The only modern electronic device often fitted was a radio direction finder, that was of limited value when requiring a precise position in overcast weather or fog. The ancient tenet of "log, lead and lookout" still prevailed aboard the many ships not fitted with radar; some companies even refusing to fit it to their ships, or removing it, through a belief that it could contribute to collisions.[5] When vessels did have radar fitted, many traditional masters, through a mixture of ignorance and lack of training, would not allow it to be used in clear weather for fear it may wear out.[6] Vessel traffic services and separation schemes did not exist, although large numbers of ships converged at choke points such as the English Channel and the Straits of Malacca; their safety and collision avoidance dependent upon the professionalism of their well-trained watch-keeping officers.

6.2   The Shipping Industry in 1958

It is instructive to document the state of the shipping industry in the mid-twentieth century, and its growth during the first half of the century, in order to establish a benchmark against which significant changes over the succeeding half century, and the effects of future developments in international law for jurisdiction and control of ships, can be measured. In spite of the appalling casualties to seafarers and their ships during both World Wars,[7] and effects of the Great Depression of the 1930s, the number and size of ships had remained remarkably constant throughout the first half of the twentieth century until the 1950s. Table 6.1 illustrates the stable number

---

[4]Focus on IMO: IMO and the safety of navigation., January 1998: "The Lloyd's Register of Shipping Casualty Returns for 1958 – the year before the IMO Assembly met for the first time – showed that 16% of the merchant shipping tonnage lost that year (56,000 gt) resulted from collisions and a further 32% (115,000 gt) from groundings or striking wrecks. The vast majority of these casualties – nearly half the total for the year – were thus caused or contributed to by navigational error or deficiency."

[5]Radar had been developed and fitted to many ships during and after the Second World War. Its misuse lead to phenomena known as "radar assisted collisions" where, through misunderstanding of this aid to navigation collisions occurred that would probably not have happened without 6radar. This was particularly the case when ships were meeting "end-on or nearly end-on" in fog, as in the *Andrea Doria/Stockholm* collison of 1958.

[6]From author's own experience as a watchkeeping officer in the 1960s.

[7]It is generally accepted that about 5,000 ships totalling 21,000,000 tons, and more than 60,000 merchant seamen, were lost during the Second World War.

Table 6.1 Development of the world shipping fleet: 1922–1958

	1922	1948	1958
Number of ships > 100 gross tons (GT)	29,000	29,000	35,202
Number of ships 100 – 499 GT	–	–	13,278
Number of ships > 500 GT	–	–	21,924
Average GT of ships > 100 GT	2,096	2,736	3,353
Average GT of ships > 500 GT	–	–	5,231

Source: Lloyd's Register of Shipping, Statistical Tables 1958

and average size of ships over the decades from the early 1920s to 1948 and the dramatic growth in post-war tonnage of the world fleet.

The following conclusions can be presented from the statistics presented in Table 6.1. The number of ships greater than 100 GT in the world fleet had remained static from 1922 until 1948, although a modest increase in size of ships is reflected in an average gross tonnage (GT)[8] of 2,096 in 1922 compared with 2,736 in 1948 (Lloyd's Register of Shipping 1958). By 1958 both the numbers of ships, and the tonnage of those ships, had increased significantly. The average size of ships built since the war, 74% of which were tankers, had increased to 10,000–15,000 GT and there had been a noticeable increase in the number of tankers of more than 25,000 GT (Lloyd's Register of Shipping 1958).

Ships of between 6,000 GT and 8,000 GT represented 23.6% of total world tonnage. The long-standing predominance of British shipping establishments at this time can be measured by the fact that, at the end of June 1958, the number of British merchant ships worldwide entered in Lloyd's Register Book totalled 10,820 and their total tonnage (50,147,000 GT) represented nearly half of effective world tonnage at that date.[9] Traditional[10] flags predominated. Ships had large crews and there were few large ships. The established flags of convenience[11] of Panama, Honduras, and Liberia represented a significant minority share of total world tonnage at 14,774,000 GT (12.9%), with Liberia having the lion's share at 10,078,000 GT (Lloyd's Register of Shipping 1958). The world fleet contained a large number of very small ships with 37.7% of the total being less than 500 GT, and very few large ships; only 75 having a tonnage larger than 25,000 GT. Of the world fleet of 35,202 ships larger than 100 GT, 15% (5,417 ships) were registered under the British flag and a total of 187,270 seafarers were employed upon these ships.[12]

---

[8]Unless otherwise stated all tonnages refer to Gross Tonnage (GT); a measure of the moulded volume of all enclosed spaces of the ship measured at 100 cubic feet to the ton.

[9]*Ibid.* The average gross tonnage of these ships was 4,635.

[10]The term "traditional" in the sense of flag States refers to those countries with a long history of shipping and a register restricted to nationals of that State.

[11]For a detailed analysis of the term "flag of convenience", see Chapter Seven.

[12]The total tonnage of the 5,417 ships > 100 GT under the British flag was 20,282,028,600an average tonnage of 3,745 GT. British tonnage represented 17% of world tonnage.

6.2.1   *Population and Distribution of Seafarers: 1958*

In order to assess the average number of seafarers serving aboard the typical ship of the day, and provide a benchmark for the dramatic changes in crewing over the next half-century, it is necessary to make certain assumptions borne out by personal experience.[13] Recalling the minimal annual leave of the time, about 90% of seafarers would have been serving aboard ships at any one time, giving an average complement aboard the 5,417 British ships > 100 GT of 31.[14] As the average British ship was a very similar size to the worldwide average of 3,353 GT, and represented a large proportion of world tonnage, it is reasonable to assume, for statistical purposes, that a typical ship in 1958 was 3,500 GT with a crew of 30. These ships were, by today's standards, very small and were operated by numbers of crew that seem very generous by the minimal standards prevailing today.[15]

6.3   Flags of Discrimination and Flags of Convenience

The halcyon days of shipping and seafaring continued throughout the 1960s but the alarm bells had already been rung. The 1958 Annual Report on Maritime Transport by the Organization for European Economic Co-operation (OEEC),[16] in identifying new developments, was quite wide of the mark with predictions of nuclear-powered submarine tankers, and was rightly sceptical about the future of nuclear propulsion for merchant ships. However, the report was right on target in its identification of carriage of liquefied natural gas and new designs in general cargo vessels that were aimed at reducing turnaround times in port, reducing costs, and expediting the movement of cargo from shipper to consignee.

---

[13]For example, the author served aboard ships of 3,500 GT with an average crew of 36 between 1958 and 1962. Crew were entitled to between 3 and 4 weeks annual leave.

[14]The large number (1,833) of very small ships < 500 GT with a crew of about five is offset by the British flagged ships operating exclusively in the Far East, employing very large crews of Asian ratings: 44,000 out of the total of 187,270 seafarers.

[15]For example, when serving as a junior officer aboard refrigerated cargo liners from 1963–1966 of 12,000 GT operated by Shaw Savill and Albion Ltd it was not unusual to have a crew of 75. Similar sized ships today would carry a crew of 15–20 and ships specifically designed for minimum manning could have as few as seven total crew.

[16]*Trends in Economic Sectors, Maritime Transport*, The Organization for European Economic Co-Operation, Paris, 1958, pp. 67–68. The OEEC came into existence on 16 April 1948, comprising 16 European countries, and emerging from the Marshall Plan. In September 1961 the OEEC was superseded by the Organization for Economic Development and Co-operation; (OECD), a world-wide body. http://www.oecd.org/document/48/0,2340,en_2649_201185_1876912_1_1_1_1,00.html.

These were, specifically, the first portents of the forthcoming revolution in the carriage of cargo through roll-on roll-off ships, and particularly container ships,[17] which were also to have a dramatic effect upon the livelihoods of many seafarers. Ironically, the main concern at this time regarding flag States was not about 'flags of convenience' but about 'flags of discrimination', brought about by the discrimination by governments in the attainment of effective and cheap shipping services through a proliferation of subsidised national shipping lines.

The issue of flags of discrimination was to be short lived as the national shipping lines of many of these newly emergent ex-colonial States[18] were, in spite of subsidies, to prove uneconomic as a result of the huge cost increases of the 1970s and emergence of many flags of convenience (FOC)[19] in the 1980s. FOCs accept vessels for registration that are owned by the nationals of any other State with very few restrictions. FOCs have no requirement for crewing of their ships by nationals of the flag State, offer very low registration fees, low annual tonnage fees, relief from taxation of earnings, and a more relaxed scrutiny of international regulatory safety and crewing requirements, often through lack of administrative resources and expertise.

The 1958 OEEC report had few concerns about FOCs but did note that the International Law Commission had stressed the need for a "genuine link" between the ship and the flag she flies, and noted that this principle had been adopted unanimously at UNCLOS I[20] in Geneva in 1958. The report also commented that countries "must exercise effective jurisdiction and control over the ships under its flag" (OEEC 1958, pp. 63–64). At the same time the first rumblings of international concern echoed from the halls of the International Labour Organization, whose 50 adhering members adopted resolutions indicating their concerns with the development of FOCs (ILO 1958). These concerns were reinforced by the International Transport Workers' Federation (ITF), whose Congress decided in 1958 to commence a worldwide boycott of FOC ships (http://www.offshoregate.com/foc.html). This decision was supported statistically by a record increase in world tonnage – 7,788,000 GT in 1958 – coming mainly from ships flagged in Liberia (an increase of 261,200 GT),

---

[17]In 1957–1958 the "father of containerisation", American Malcolm MacLean, converted six wartime-built C2 freighters to carry containers. Matson Navigation, after carrying out a detailed study into containers in 1956, converted one of their C3 freighters in 1958, the *Hawaiian Merchant,* to carry containers between California and Hawaii. The *Hawaiian Citizen* became their first full container ship in 1960. Also, in 1960, another converted C2 cargo ship, the *Santa Eliana* of Grace lines, became the first container ship to trade internationally when she sailed from New York to Venezuela. The first exclusive container terminal was constructed by the Port of New York Authority at Port Newark in 1960. http://amchouston.home.att.net/containers.htm

[18]"Over ninety States have achieved independence since 1945, of which the large proportion are coastal States." (Brown 1994, p. 8)

[19]Sometimes euphemistically called "Open Registers", as against the perceived "Closed Registers" of States which require ships to be owned by nationals. The *Report of the Committee of Inquiry into Shipping* (London, May 1970, p.51), chaired by Lord Rochdale, provides a more detailed definition of an international open register.

[20]The First United Nations Conference on the Law of the Sea.

which replaced Norway as the third largest flag (Lloyd's Register of Shipping, Statistical Tables 1958). World shipping began a major alteration of course in 1958; one of which most seafarers were blissfully unaware as they went about their everyday duties in a time-honoured manner, enjoying their relaxed lifestyle of long passages and equally long sojourns in port.[21]

6.4   The Second Shipping Revolution

A number of significant and related events came together in global shipping during the 1960s and 1970s to cause a revolution in the industry that rivalled the shift from sail to steam in the second half of the nineteenth century. These developments were to have a cumulative and largely negative impact upon the quality of shipping and seafaring, and gave rise to a dramatic increase in the numbers of flag States. The developments can be summarised as: changes in the traditional sources of seafarers; improvements in working and living conditions for seafarers with consequential cost increases for shipowners; the advent of containerisation and its effect upon the size and crewing of ships; the increase in oil prices in the early 1970s and resultant impacts upon the design, size, and crewing of tankers; and the fragility of ship financing arrangements of this era.

6.4.1   Sources of Seafarers

From the late 1960s there was a gradual change in the sources of seafarers; the great majority of whom had traditionally come from OEEC countries and worked aboard ships owned, and usually flagged, in traditional maritime countries. Of the world total of 114,556,700 GT of ships > 100 GT in mid-1958, almost half (56,606,800 GT) were registered in the 15 OEEC countries, with a further 25,675,000 GT in the traditional maritime nations of Canada, Spain, United States of America (23,084,000 GT) and Yugoslavia (Lloyd's Register of Shipping, Statistical Tables 1958). The remaining 28% of total world tonnage was principally apportioned between Japan (5.5 mil.); Liberia (10 mil.); Panama (4.35 mil.); USSR, (2.96 mil.); and Argentina, Brazil, Costa Rica, Finland, Honduras, India and the rest of the world at 5 million GT (OEEC 1958, pp. 10–12). A total of 458,477 seafarers were employed in the merchant fleets of the 15 OEEC countries,[22] with the overwhelming majority being nationals of those countries.

---

[21]For example, a 12,000 ton deadweight cargo liner in the New Zealand/UK trade in 1958 would typically take up to six weeks to discharge a full general cargo and a further six weeks to load a full cargo of frozen produce. The same 24,000 ton of cargo could now be discharged and loaded in less than a day of non-stop cargo work at a modern container terminal.

[22]Belgium, Denmark, France, Germany, Greece, Iceland, Ireland, Italy, Netherlands, Norway, Portugal, Sweden, Switzerland, Turkey, United Kingdom.

The OEEC report for 1958 further records that the total of 41,143 seafarers for Germany included 297 foreigners; Turkey's total of 37,477 included 323 foreigners and that of Greece (10,321) excluded 26,258 Greeks serving under foreign flags. The predominant total of 139,979 seafarers working aboard British ships excluded "some 44,000 Indians, Pakistanis, Chinese, etc. serving on United Kingdom registered ships on articles opened and closed outside the United Kingdom" (OEEC 1958, p. 29, Table X) i.e. the British flagged ships, predominantly trading in the Far East, that never returned to the UK. Nationals clearly served aboard their national ships at this time and foreign nationals were very much in the minority. This situation was brought about by a combination of national ship registration requirements and the sheer impracticality of replacing crews in foreign ports in the days before jet air travel. Most crews signed ship's articles of agreement for 2 years and could well be away from their home port for this entire time. Crew recruitment and replacement therefore took place at the beginning and end of the voyage, which were invariably at a port in the flag State.

6.4.2   Effects of Containerisation and Economies of Scale

During the late 1960s and early 1970s, newly-built, large container ships were making a significant impact, with each one replacing a number of conventional ships. New companies were formed to manage these ships and long established shipping companies disappeared from the world shipping scene virtually overnight. There were considerable job losses amongst the predominantly national crews of these conventional ships, particularly amongst ratings. Qualified officers had an advantage in that they could usually obtain senior positions with the national shipping lines of developing nations; companies that employed their own nationals as ratings.

A similar and parallel development was taking place in the world tanker fleet, as ships increased rapidly in size requiring proportionately less crew. As early as 1959 a tanker of 100,000 ton dwt had been constructed (Couper 1992, p. 65), which was too large to transit the Suez Canal.[23] Although the canal had been deepened following the Second World War, its development lagged behind that of tankers (Couper 1992, p. 66). Even before the canal closed during the 1967 Israel-Egypt war, shipowners were ordering larger tankers designed to economically navigate the extra 5,000 miles from the Persian Gulf to Europe around the Cape of Good Hope. Economies of scale for ships trading this route, and that from the Gulf to Japan, could be obtained from ever larger ships and, by the mid-1960s, the Very Large Crude Carrier (VLCC)[24] had been developed.

---

[23]In the mid-1960s the largest fully laden tanker that could transit the Suez Canal was about 70,000 ton.

[24]Ships larger than 200,000 tons deadweight.

The average size of tankers increased from 200,000 to 250,000 dwt by 1973 (Couper 1992, p. 69), at which time there was a dramatic increase in freight rates; resulting in a trend towards Ultra Large Crude Carriers (ULCC) – ships of 300,000 dwt and over.[25] One of the decisive economies of scale for large tankers (and other vessel types) was reduction in crew costs, as the ratio of cargo carried per crew member increases with size of vessel. Between the 1960s and 1980s the average crew numbers aboard tankers decreased from about 45 to 24 (Couper 1992, p. 66), at the same time that the average size of crude oil carriers had increased considerably (ILO 2004, p. 58). Smaller product tankers delivering refined products from oil refineries also increased in size from about 12,000 dwt in the 1950s to 24,000 dwt in the 1970s (Couper 1992, p. 64).

At the same time as the average size of crews was decreasing aboard all types of ships in the early 1970s due to economies of scale and automation, highly unionised seafarers were flexing their industrial muscle and gaining improved living and working conditions, including extra leave. These two imperatives, of increases in the size of ships and increased leave ratios, collided with the result that the employment of national crews became increasingly expensive and unattractive at exactly the time that air travel made it possible to recruit crews from any part of the world. A decline in employment of seafarers from OECD[26] countries from 1974 was still due partly to productivity gains in all sectors and especially in the container and bulk tramp trades, but by the 1980s the decline was due to "flagging out[27]" to FOCs by OECD shipowners and the recruitment of lower cost seafarers from developing countries and, later in the 1990s, from Eastern Europe (ILO 2004, p. 58).

6.4.3   Economic Issues and Their Impact upon Shipping

Another factor during this period from 1958 to 1982 was the increase in oil prices in 1973, which came at a time when many shipyards had large order books for new vessels, driven in part by ready access to finance for shipowners and by subsidies to shipyards by shipbuilding nations. The lending practices of banks in the heady days of the 1960s led to questionable financing of ships with the often inevitable consequence for those living and working aboard them: job losses when the venture failed (ILO 2004, p. 14). In the 1960s time charters from major oil companies were so lucrative that a bank loan of 90% of the ship's value could be paid off in 5 years (ILO 2004, p. 15). As the ownership, financing, and management of ships moved steadily away from the traditional shipping company model that historically

---

[25]The largest ULCC to enter service was *Seawise Giant*, built in 1979 and enlarged to 564,000 dwt in 1980.

[26]Organization for Economic Co-operation and Development.

[27]A term commonly used when a shipowner changes flag from a national flag to one that offer economic advantages.

financed its ships out of earnings, banks themselves sometimes became shipowners due to failures of mortgages and associated repossession of ships, or by becoming institutional shareholders when debt was turned into equity. At the time of the collapse of the third-largest shipping company in Hong Kong in 1986[28] one commentator[29] said publicly that: "to order a new ship, other than in the liner trades, without contractual employment [that is, without a time charter] is total speculation. To finance that speculation with borrowed funds is an irresponsible gamble, and those banks who provide funds for such gambles and describe them as loans are guilty of gross deception." (ILO 2004, p.15) The cavalier attitude of some banks in financing speculative shipbuilding and purchase at this time inevitably led to an excess of supply over demand in ships, low freight rates, and unfortunate fallout for the crews of many of these ships through job losses. Many of those financial institutions became shipowners by default, and their total lack of operational management experience of ships led to the growth of ship management companies and a consequential, and largely detrimental, distancing of the beneficial owner from the daily management of the ship (ILO 2004, p. 20).

The inevitable massive oversupply of tonnage, coupled with increased fuel and crew costs, encouraged shipowners to economise in the areas that they had most control over: compliance, maintenance, and crew costs. The benefits of this economising were often only to be obtained by "flagging out". These imperatives also led to a drive by shipowners for increased efficiencies in ship operation through automation; for example, unmanned engine-rooms, and more efficient and less labour-intensive cargo equipment.

The workhorses of the sea, bulk carriers, followed the trend of tankers and increasingly sought economies of scale and simplicity, with associated financial benefits of decreased crew sizes (Couper et al 1992, pp. 30, 31). Their development was analogous to that of tankers, in that the market required essentially two types of vessel: very large bulk carriers without cargo gear (gearless) dedicated to certain trades such as grain, iron ore and coal, and even combinations of oil and bulk cargoes; and smaller, handier ships with "tween decks and cargo gear that could handle any number of trades and types of cargo" (Couper et al 1992, pp. 20–31). The same problem of an oversupply of these ships as existed in the tanker fleet, coupled with the shipping recession of the 1970s, resulted in similar issues[30] regarding cost saving measures including flagging out.

---

[28]"Wah Kwong Shipping and Investment, owed more than $850 million to 46 creditors who eventually agreed to reschedule the debt as equity".

[29]P Slater, a prominent shipowner/financier.

[30]"From 1958 on through the early 1970s there was a dramatic rise in the world fleet of ore carriers and great increases in individual vessel size ... The energy crisis and world recession in the mid-1970s, coupled with a peaking of shipyard deliveries of 'supercarriers', created a catastrophic glut of shipping space. Steel industry production, hence raw material and shipping needs, faltered. Shipowners became much more cautious about ordering new ships, especially the very large, therefore very inflexible, single-purpose bulk carriers. This caution persisted throughout the 1980s". (Couper et al 1992, p. 20)

Lower freight rates and the above factors all came together in the mid-1970s, providing an incentive for shipowners to seek means of lowering steadily rising crew costs. This made the employment of crews from traditional maritime nations increasingly unattractive. The result was a rapid increase in flags of convenience whose registers could offer shipowners considerable savings in compliance and crewing costs. Ship management companies could also, amongst other services, supply low cost crews from developing nations – 'crews of convenience' – and also shield the beneficial owner from liability and public exposure through the practice of flagging out. In 1950 Liberia and Panama accounted for 6% of world tonnage; this figure had increased to 27% by 1975 (ILO 2004, p. 28).

The combination of inevitable and largely negative factors (such as oversupply of ships, economies of scale, automation, unwise financing of ships, the oil crisis and containerisation, and better welfare standards for seafarers) that came together in the 1960s and 1970s caused a revolution in the nature of the world shipping industry and the lives of those living and working aboard ships. These factors spelt the beginning of the end of the traditional flag State and, due to an increase in the numbers of flag States, the end of the beginning of issues of effective jurisdiction and control of ships. It was entirely coincidental that the Third United Nations Conference on the Law of the Sea (UNCLOS III) was convened at a time when containerisation and the 1973 oil shock were having a huge impact upon the nature of world shipping. UNCLOS III carried out its lengthy deliberations parallel to the turbulent times in world shipping of the 1970s.

6.5   The Shipping Industry: 1982

By 1982 the quantum and seascape of the world fleet had undergone the most dramatic change since the transition from sail to steam in the mid-nineteenth century. The large increase in numbers of ships, brought about by the buoyant world economy of the 1960s and technological developments in ship design and capacity was eclipsed by the increase in total world tonnage and the enormous increase in the size of many ships[31] as presented in Table 6.2 below:

Of this total of 37,534 ocean-going ships in 1982 the largest percentage (17.8%) were between 10,000 GT and 14,999 GT. The average size of ships of > 500 GT had more than doubled and within this total were some huge increases in the size of ships in 1958.[32] Entrants in the statistical tables of ship types that didn't exist in 1958

---

[31]Numbers of ships > 100 GT increased by 113.5% between 1958 with their average gross tonnage increasing by 68.6%.

[32]Lloyd's Register of Shipping, Notes on Statistical Tables 1982, p. 3: "the number of ships over 100,000 GT (approximately 200,000 dwt) has fallen slightly from 691 in 1981 to the present total of 663. Of this total 146 ships are over 140,000 GT (approximately 275,000 dwt) including three ore/bulk/oil carriers. (In 1958 only 75 ships had a tonnage greater than 25,000 GT including 22 > 30,000 GT)."

Table 6.2 Development of world shipping fleet: 1958–1982

	1958	1982
Number of all ships > 100 GT	35,202	75,151
Number of ships 100 GT–499GT	13,278	37,617
Number of all ships > 500 GT	21,924	37,534
Average GT of all ships > 100 GT	3,353	5,652
Average GT of ships > 500GT	5,231	11,066

Source: Lloyd's Register of Shipping, Notes on Statistical Tables 1982

illustrate the significant changes in technology and transport efficiencies that had taken place and developed very rapidly over this quarter century: 12.9 million GT of cellular container ships and 722 liquefied gas carriers totalling 13.6 million cubic metres capacity (Lloyd's Register of Shipping, Notes on Statistical Tables 1982).

6.5.1 Redistribution of Flag States

The balance between registration in traditional maritime nations and newly emergent flag States changed considerably between 1958 and 1982, as illustrated in Table 6.3 of principal[33] merchant fleets of the world in 1958 and 1982. Net percentage changes indicated take into account the 359% increase in world tonnage: from 118,033 to 424,741 thousand gross tons, between 1958 and 1982.

Table 6.3 Principal merchant fleets: 1958 and 1982

Flag	1958 Tonnage	1982 Tonnage	% Change
USA[34]	25,589	19,111	– 384%
United Kingdom	20,286	22,505	– 348%
Liberia	10,079	70,718	+ 243%
Norway	9,385	21,862	– 226%
Japan	5,465	41,594	+ 302%
Italy	4,900	10,375	– 248%
Netherlands	4,600	5,393	– 376%
Panama	4,358	32,600	+ 289%
France	4,338	10,771	– 211%
Germany	4,007	7,707	– 267%
Sweden	3,303	3,788	– 344%
Russia	2,966	23,789	+ 343%
Denmark	2,035	5,214	– 203%
Greece	1,611	40,035	+ 2,026%
Spain	1,607	8,311	+ 58%
Canada	1,516	3,159	– 251%
Argentina	1,029	2,309	– 235%

Source: Lloyd's Register of Shipping, Notes on Statistical Tables 1982

---

[33] Flags having more than 1,000,000 GT on their register in 1958.

[34] Including USA Reserve Fleet estimated at 14 million GT in 1958 and 2.1 million GT in 1982.

Table 6.4 Growth of newly emergent flag States: 1958–1982

Flag	1958 Tonnage (,000)	1982 Tonnage(,000)	Increase (,000)
China	410	7,653	7,243
Singapore	–	6,889	6,889
India	–	6,020	6,020
South Korea	–	5,142	5,142
Hong Kong	318	2,580	2,262
Indonesia	14	1,745	1,731
Iran	–	1,202	1,202
Iraq	–	1,492	1,492
Kuwait	–	2,317	2,317
Mexico	98	1,135	1,037
Philippines	17	2,540	2,527
Poland	220	3,579	3,359
Romania	–	2,032	2,032
Saudi Arabia	–	3,121	3,121
Taiwan	–	1,888	1,888
Yugoslavia	233	2,541	2,308

Source: Lloyd's Register Shipping, Statistical Tables 1958 and Notes on Statistical Tables 1982

The large percentage increases over and above the worldwide growth of 359 per cent went to the flags of convenience of Liberia and Panama, with the national flags of Greece, Japan, and Russia also showing large net gains of tonnage. Most of the OECD countries, except Spain, suffered large net losses of tonnage. The numbers of flags of convenience remained small, with Liberia and Panama having by far the bulk of world fleet tonnage at a combined total of 102,562,00 GT (24 per cent of world tonnage) and the newly established Cypriot (1,819,000 GT) and Bermudan (499,000 GT) flags beginning to make their presence felt.

The most dramatic increases in registered tonnage between 1958 and 1982 went to flag States that had very little or no tonnage in 1958 as indicated in Table 6.4.

6.5.2   Redistribution of Seafarers

Whilst no statistic is available for total world seafarers in 1982, an indication can be extrapolated from the figures for the United Kingdom, as can an estimate of the average crew size at this time. In 1982 a total of 53,772 seafarers (ILO 2004, p. 59) were employed aboard the 2,826 ships > 100 GT under the British flag.[35] These ships had an average tonnage of 7,964 GT and, with an estimated 60%[36] of seafarers at sea at

[35] There were 187,270 seafarers aboard 5,417 ships > 100 GT in 1958.

[36] Lloyd's Register of Shipping, Notes on Statistical Tables 1982 notes that 45% of Australian seafarers are aboard at any time (footnote p.157) and that for accurate figures for the United States, including personnel absent because of illness, holidays, etc., the figure should be multiplied by two. As these countries had significantly higher leave ratios than most, a more conservative indicative figure of 60% has been used for the British fleet.

any one time, had an average seagoing crew of 11.4. This figure is distorted by the large worldwide percentage (50%) of ships < 500 GT with an average tonnage of 250 GT and, most probably, a crew of about four. Removing this group results in figures for the British flag of 1,413 ships of an average 15,677 GT with a crew of 18.8.[37]

These indicative statistics confirm that the average size of ships worldwide had more than doubled over the quarter century from 1958, at the same time as the average crew size had almost halved due to efficiencies, automation, and economies of scale. This trend has continued from the 1970s to the present day as echoed by the ILO publication *The Global Seafarer*:

> ... during the past 20 years or so, there has been a reduction in the size of crews. In the early 1970s, a typical 10,000 grt bulk carrier would have had approximately 40 crew members. Today, a much larger (that is, 30,000 grt) bulk carrier is likely to have only 18 to 25 crew members on board. The same crew-size pattern applies to cargo carrying ships of all kinds.

6.6   Further Developments in the Shipping Industry

The major changes in shipping during the third quarter of the twentieth century were driven by economic booms, advances in technology, efficiencies, and cost savings brought about by previously unimaginable economies of scale. The average size of ships had more than doubled between 1958 and 1982 and the total world fleet tonnage had almost quadrupled, whilst average crew sizes had halved. Flags of convenience, although very small in number, had attracted almost a quarter of world tonnage by 1982, mostly from traditional maritime nations who were still a dominant presence, and a large number of national shipping lines had come into existence. The main drivers for further dramatic changes during the remaining two decades and into the twenty-first century were the decline in trade[38] in the 1980s and the ongoing economic influence and impact of the shipbuilding industry.

The 1980s were a desperate time for the many shipowners who had over-ordered tonnage from subsidised and protected shipyards during the good times of the 1970s, and were then hit by structural adjustments in the world economy and the worldwide economic recession of the early eighties. The ability of the shipbuilding industry to affect the world shipping economy was pronounced;[39] particularly at a

---

[37]Compared with 5,417 ships of average 3,744 tons and a crew of 31 in 1958.

[38]"Aggregate seaborne trade fell by 400 million tonnes in 1981 and did not return to 1980s levels until 1988, reflecting the fact that the 1980s was the worst decade experienced by the shipping industry since the 1920s and 1930s; the investment bank Warburg Dillon Read described it as a period of 'valiant but mutually destructive competition'." (ILO 2004, p. 6)

[39]"A flood of new and cheap ships launched from the subsidized and protected yards of the world in the late 1970s and onwards into the mid-1980s undoubtably helped to make a bad trading period worse." (ILO 2004, p. 7) ... "It seems that as long as there are developing countries with industrializing ambitions and an active international market enabling the transfer of technical shipbuilding knowledge and ship's ancillary equipment, the shipbuilding industry will be in a position to destabilize shipping." (ILO 2004, p. 9)

time when many shipyards in the Far East were heavily subsidised and engaged in a competition, driven more by national pride than economics, to become the most dominant shipbuilding nation. The level of world shipbuilding activity, in an industry where the lead time for a ship could be as much as 3 years, increased steadily from the late 1960s to reach a zenith of 34 million tons in 1975. From then the annual totals declined steadily, by 34% in 1978, until only 21 million gross ton of ships were built in 1980 (Couper et al 1992, p. 188). However, by the mid-1990s the shipbuilding industry was rampant with *Lloyd's List* commenting in 1996 that "there is now more than adequate capacity in the Far East to build every ship the world needs and more."

In the late 1990s attempts by the General Agreement on Tariffs and Trade (GATT), followed by the World Trade Organization (WTO), to manage capacity in the world shipbuilding industry were unsuccessful and as recently as 2004 disputes still existed between the Republic of Korea and the European Union (EU) over government subsidies to shipyards (ILO 2004, p. 9). The glut of ships from the order books of the 1970s and into the 1980s resulted in over-tonnaged shipowners seeking cost savings during the economic downturn of the 1980s and, along with increased costs of new builds, contributed in the longer term to an ever-aging world fleet with associated problems.[40] Coupled with higher fuel costs and falling freight rates, savings were sought by shipowners through re-engining of ships to obtain greater fuel efficiencies, deferral of essential maintenance, increased use of automation, economies of scale, more efficient turn rounds in port through more efficient cargo handling techniques, and, inevitably, transferral of ships to FOCs to achieve taxation advantages and cheaper compliance and crew costs.

6.6.1   Development of New Flag States from 1982

In 1947, only 2% of total world tonnage was registered with flags of convenience; this figure had increased to 13% by 1958, and 24% by 1982. It has already been noted that there were two predominant FOCs in 1982; Liberia with 16.7% of world tonnage and Panama with 7.6%. Bermuda and Cyprus were emerging FOCs. By 1990 42% of the world's tonnage was registered under FOCs, a figure which had increased to 53% by 2001 (ILO 2004, p. 30). Between 1990 and 2001 the world fleet tonnage had increased by 16% but, over the same period, the numbers of ships under FOCs increased by 70%. Even more dramatically, while world tonnage increased by 106% over this same period, the overwhelming majority of this tonnage was "flagged out", as indicated by the total tonnage under FOCs increasing by 90% (ILO 2004, pp. 28, 29).

This trend is verified when deadweight (dwt) tonnage is compared. The world total of dwt tonnage increased by 58.3% from 1990 to 2007 whilst that of what the

---

[40] See Chapter Ten for statistics supporting the correlation between age and substandard ships.

UNCTAD Secretariat euphemistically refers to as "major open-registry countries" increased by 110.1%.[41] The gains by new flag States were achieved at the expense of "developed market-economy countries" whose percentage share of world dwt tonnage decreased over the same period from 33.3 to 18.9%. A host of new flags had entered the lexicon of the shipping world; flags that did not exist in 1982 and many of which had little or no historical or physical connection with shipping and the sea.

The world fleet of the top 38 flags by tonnage on 1 January 2007 highlights these changes in distribution of the nationalities of ships, as compared with 1982 and 1958. Tonnage of the world fleet of vessels > 100 GT totalled 774.9 million GT as at 1 January 2007, an increase of 82.5% from the total tonnage of 424.7 million GT in 1982. Net gains or losses in tonnage between 1982 and 2007 are shown in Table A.1,[42] Appendix A.

Panama remains the largest FOC at 165.3 million GT (21.3% of the world total) followed by Liberia, 75.3 million GT (9.7%); Bahamas, 41.3 (5.3); Hong Kong China, 35.8 (4.6); Greece, 35.6 (4.6); Marshall Islands, 35.1 (4.5); Singapore, 35.0 (4.5); Malta, 27.5 (3.6); and Cyprus, 18.8 (2.4). The top two FOCs, Panama and Liberia, maintained their dominance with 31% of world tonnage (24% in 1982); the next largest fleets were made of the established and newly emergent flag States of the Bahamas, Hong Kong, Greece, Marshall Islands, Singapore, Malta, and Cyprus, collectively making up a further 229.1 million GT or 29.6% of total world tonnage. Many traditional registers still feature, but with relatively modest increases or decreases in tonnage. The new flag States of Singapore and Hong Kong show huge increases against relatively low bases in 1982. Most FOCs made significant gains, sometimes of volumes massively above the 82.5% increase in world tonnage over this quarter century.[43]

Flags not included in Table A.1, but identified as FOCs as at 1 January 2004 by the International Transport Workers' Federation (ITF), with fleets of less than 700,000 GT, were: Mongolia, Barbados, Bolivia, Burma/Myanmar, Cambodia, Cayman Islands, Comoros, Equatorial Guinea, Germany (Second Register), Gibraltar, Jamaica, Lebanon, Mauritius, Netherlands Antilles, Sao Tome and Principe, Sri Lanka, and Tonga (ITF 2004).

There were, in 2005, 191 independent sovereign States[44] and 166 of these were flag States (Tokyo MOU Port State Control Manual 2005); a number out of all proportion to the dependency of States on shipping. In 1958 membership of the UN stood at 82 States and membership of the IMO in its first year of 1959 totalled 31

---

[41] UNCTAD Reviews of Maritime Transport, 2004 and 2007. Reports by the UNCTAD Secretariat.

[42] Figures are indicated in million gross tons in descending order of tonnage as at 2005. Where no figures are shown the flag either did not exist or had less than 0.7 million ton registered at the time. FOCs in italics.

[43] The total tonnage of the large fleets of Japan, Russia, United States, Philippines, and South Korea include large numbers of small vessels engaged in coastal or short international voyages.

[44] Excluding the Vatican.

flag States. The huge growth in the number of States registering ships over the second half of the twentieth century has been driven by the nationalism of newly independent States, economic pressures upon shipowners, and the opportunity for States to form registers to attract shipowners seeking lower taxation, compliance, and crewing costs, and to earn revenue from the registration of ships.

6.7 Ongoing Development of the World Fleet

Concurrent with this redistribution of tonnage amongst flag States from 1982, the total world fleet increased by 29.7% from 1982–2007, whilst the average GT of these ships over the same period increased by 29.3%; significant reductions in the exponential growth achieved in the previous quarter century of 113.6 and 68.9% respectively. Table 6.5 illustrates this growth:

Table 6.5 Development of the world merchant fleet: 1982–2007

	1982	2007
Number of all ships > 100 GT	75,151	97,504
Number of ships 100 GT–499 GT	37,617	45,966
Number of all ships > 500 GT	37,534	51,538
Average tonnage of all ships > 100 GT	5,652	7,948
Average tonnage of ships > 500 GT	11,066	14,306

Source for 2007 data: Lloyd's Register – Fairplay, World Fleet Statistics 2007

A large component of this growth, particularly over the period from 1990–2005, has been amongst tankers larger than 150,000 GT and dry cargo ships larger than 25,000 GT – reflecting the economies of scale to be gained from larger ships (Warwick Institute 2005). It is anticipated by informed industry sources[45] that numbers of ships in the world fleet will continue to grow at the rate of 1% per annum for the next 10 years but that the size of those ships will steadily increase (Warwick Institute 2005, pp. 19–20). In predicting future growth it is also assumed that, for the next decade, all flag States will benefit equally (Warwick Institute 2005, p. 19).

6.7.1 The Worldwide Demand For, and Supply of, Seafarers

The scale and speed of fundamental changes in the nationalities of crews between 1982 and 2005 was dramatic. In 1987 an extra 14,157 Filipinos were employed on European ships, equating to an increase of 930 ships with a large Filipino compo-

[45]BIMCO/ISF data and predictions for growth of the world fleet are based upon information from Lloyd's Register – *Fairplay*.

nent (Tokyo MOU Annual Report 2005), coupled inevitably with an associated decrease in employment of seafarers from OECD countries. Although this could be seen as the marketplace at work and shipowners legitimately seeking means to reduce their crewing costs[46] it is an inescapable fact that most of these seafarers had not previously worked on ocean-going ships and might accordingly have less-developed skills and experience than those from the traditional maritime States of OECD members.

India had been providing seafarers for European shipowners from the middle of the nineteenth century but now faced competition from new labour supplying countries[47] such as the Philippines, Korea, and Indonesia. In many cases these seafarers were sailing aboard a ship registered in a newly emergent FOC country different to their nationality, and one which often did not have the technical abilities and resources to effectively "take such measures for ships under its flag as are necessary to ensure safety at sea with regard *inter alia* to ... the manning of ships and labour conditions for crews taking into account the applicable international labour instruments." (HSC, Article 10 (1)(b))

The centre of gravity of labour supply for seafarers has continued to shift from OECD countries towards the Far East, the Indian sub-continent, and East Europe. Thirty percent of a rapidly aging supply of senior officers still originates from OECD countries along with 10% of ratings. The demand for seafarers in 2005 was 476,000 officers and 586,000 ratings, against a supply of 466,000 officers and 721,000 ratings (Warwick Institute 2005, p. 8). According to a joint Baltic and International Maritime Council/International Shipping Federation report (Warwick Institute 2005, pp. 35–36) there is no scope for further reductions in crewing of ships. The report predicts that annual increases of 0.5% for both officers and ratings will be required to crew the expected 1% annual increase in ships, due to technology and proportionately reduced crewing for newer and larger ships (Warwick Institute 2005, p. 24).

---

[46] "Shipowners are attracted to foreign flags because of the economic advantages afforded by lenient tax requirements, relief from the submission of tax returns and flexible insurance, maintenance and repair standards. If one was only to consider crewing requirements, the absence of high crew standards and the consequent operating costs, the use of flags of convenience clearly provides a crucial edge in the highly competitive international shipping industry. As a result of the growth of open registers, a huge market of so called 'crews of convenience' has developed made up of mainly nationals of developing countries." (Couper et al 1992, p. 194)

[47] "In the ILO's report to its second Asian Maritime Conference in 1965, Korean seafarers received no mention whatsoever, although Indonesians and Filipinos were reported as working on small inter-island ships. Small numbers of the latter two nationalities had, in fact, worked on a few Dutch and American owned ships but not on a scale sufficient to provide the basis for a rapid and large expansion into international shipping. A similar situation applied to Koreans: small numbers domiciled in Japan had been sailing on Japanese ships for many years. And yet by 1988 there were estimated to be 50,000 Korean seafarers, half of them working aboard Japanese-owned ships flagged mainly in Panama." (Couper et al 1992, p. 60)

The average size of crew across all categories of ships larger than 500 GT in 2005 is 16.57, made up of 6.38 officers and 10.19 ratings. The back-up ratios for these crews is an average of 1.82 for officers and 1.67 for ratings.[48] Ships within the range of the averaged sized ship in 2007 of 14,306 GT (dry cargo 5,000–25,000 GT) would require 7.83 officers and 11.5 ratings at any one time. The average size of crew has not, therefore, changed significantly over the quarter century under review although statistics confirm that smaller crews are being carried aboard larger ships than in 1982.[49]

References

Brown ED (1994) The International Law of the Sea. Vol I. Dartmouth Publishing Company Ltd, United Kingdom
Couper A (ed) (1992) The Shipping Revolution: The Modern Merchant Ship. Conway Maritime Press Ltd, London
International Labour Organization Office (1958). Conventions, Recommendations and Resolutions Adopted by the International Labour Conference at Its 41st Session and Composition of the Joint Maritime Commission (Geneva, 29 April–14 May 1958). Official Bulletin, Vol XLI, No 1
International Labour Organization Office (2004) The Global Seafarer: Living and working conditions in a globalised industry. Geneva
International Transport Workers' Federation (2004) Campaign against flags of convenience and substandard shipping. Annual Report
Lloyd's Register of Shipping (1958) Notes on Statistical Tables
Lloyd's Register of Shipping (1982) Notes on Statistical Tables
The Organization for European Economic Co-Operation (1958) Trends in Economic Sectors, Maritime Transport. Paris
Warwick Institute for Employment Research (2005) BIMCO/ISF Manpower 2005 Update: The worldwide demand for and supply of seafarers.

Documents

Tokyo MOU (2005) Port State Control Manual

---

[48]*Ibid*, pp.61–68. (1) Manning levels relate to seven typical flags (China, Denmark, Greece, Hong Kong, India, Japan, United Kingdom). All other countries have been allocated to one of three broad manning levels: high, standard and low. (A standard level of manning has been used in these figures.) (2) The ratios used are obtained by dividing the total manning requirements including back-up crews for leave, sickness, etc., by the number of crew actually required on board at any one time. For example, a ship with a crew on board of 6.38 officers and 10.19 ratings would need a total pool of 11.6 officers and 17 ratings for continuous operation.

[49]*Ibid*. For example total standard crew size for a dry cargo ship > 25,000 GT is only one rating more than for the same type of ship between 5,000–25,000 GT. A tanker between 10,000–150,000 GT will have an average crew of 8.7 officers and 14 ratings, whilst one > 150,000 GT will have an average of 10.2 officers and 17 ratings.

Chapter 7
Choice of Flag State

Abstract The flag is an enduring symbol of the nationality of a ship but although this nationality is conferred upon a ship under international law as the sovereign right of a State, in many cases it has very little relevance, significance, or association from a nationality or patriotic perspective to the owners and crew of the ship. There is, in today's global shipping world, very often no contact at all between the flag State, the shipowner, and polyglot crews of modern merchant ships, and their ship will normally never trade to that State. This discussion on choice of flag State commences with an examination of the motives of shipowners in making the decision to flag out. The history of the pejorative term "flag of convenience" is then recalled and is supported by a case study of the economic and political factors that played a leading role in the development of Panama as a flag State. The beneficial ownership of ships and linkages to flags of convenience, both in definition of the term and in practice, is identified and analysed to demonstrate that the majority of ships registered under flags of convenience are owned by residents of OECD countries that are themselves flag States. In order to provide a framework for analysis of flag State responsibility issues, flag States are identified and are categorised into four main groups: National, Quasi-National, International, and Pseudo-National flag States. All active flag States are identified and grouped into these four categories. A case study of the influence of the Singapore Government in the nature and category of that flag State is presented. The different types of Classification Society (Recognized Organization) are also identified and categorised into Conventional and Convenient. The starting point in the discussion on choice of flag State is an examination of the motives of shipowners for "flagging out".

7.1 "Flagging Out"

Shipowners have, for economic or political convenience, used the device of flying the flag of another country for centuries: "flagging out" (Bergantino and Marlow 1998, p. 157). British ships improperly flew the Spanish flag to avoid trade restrictions in the West Indies in the sixteenth century, and flew the French flag in the seventeenth century on ships fishing on the Grand Banks to avoid restrictions on fishing imposed by Great Britain. The practice became widespread in the Mediterranean in the eighteenth century due to a myriad of trade and political restrictions. For example, Genoese ships carrying goods to France registered under the French flag; when France increased taxes and fees, the Genoese ships transferred to the Austrian flag. Neapolitan ships trading to Greek ports also registered under the Austrian flag. (Montero Lacer 2002, pp. 2, 3)

Genoese shipowners used the British flag when trading in the Gulf of Corinth to counteract French supremacy in that area, and Greek ships utilised either the Turkish or Russian flag. Irish shipowners who had British homeports took advantage of French registration for more than 20 years from 1760, and, to avoid restrictions imposed by the British, many American owned ships were registered in Portugal during the 1812 war. In order to avoid British surveillance of slave traders upon the high seas from 1830 to 1850 many North and South American countries registered their ships under other flags (Montero Lacer 2002, pp. 2, 3).

The flag is an unmistakable symbol of the motives, values, and intent of the shipowner. In the truly global business of international shipping most owners have absolute freedom of choice as to the flag their ship will fly and the concomitant standards that the ship will be required to meet. The flag State has freedom to determine the "conditions for grant of its nationality to ships"[1] but this is not an absolute freedom and is fettered by the very clear responsibilities placed upon flag States. The administrative, technical, and social responsibilities of the flag State, of whatever ilk, are clearly enunciated in Article 94 of the LOSC. It is the delivery, oversight, and enforcement of these responsibilities that can vary greatly between different types of flag State; some of the factors relevant in the decision of shipowners whether or not to flag out.

It has been demonstrated[2] that the percentage of world tonnage that is registered under FOCs has steadily increased from 2% in 1947 to more than 50% by the turn of the century. By 2003 almost two thirds of world gross tonnage was registered under a flag foreign to that of the beneficial owner (Hoffman et al, p. 5).[3] There are significant differences between States of registration of ships remaining under national flags, with Iran (96%) and India (88%) being markedly different to Belgium (9%), Switzerland (7%), and Monaco (1%) (Hoffman et al, p. 5). It has been established that the probability of flagging out is significantly higher for

---

[1]A freedom that recalls the decision of the Hague Court of Permanent Arbitration in the *Muscat Dhows Case, France v Great Britain* in which the Court stated: "generally speaking it belongs to every sovereign to decide to whom he will accord the right to fly his flag and to prescribe the rules governing such grants". See http://www.pca-cpa.org/upload/files/Muscat%20Dhows%20English%20 Award.pdf for the full text of this award. This principle was reinforced by *Lauritzen v Larsen* (345 U.S. 571 (1953)) and restated in the Convention on the High Seas, 1958.

[2]See Chap. 6.

[3]See more detailed statistics for beneficial ownership in section 7.4.

operators of ships domiciled in developed countries, due to the less liberalised markets and high proportion of State ownership of vessels in developing countries (Hoffman et al, p. 10).

A number of factors affect the decision of an owner to flag out, such as: quality and source of labour, reduction in management costs, minimisation of taxes on profits, and the degree of control exercised by the flag State. In the entrepreneurial world of global shipping, these factors can generally be merged into "the need to reduce overall costs" (Bergantino and Marlow 1998, p. 158). While cost reduction remains the predominant driver, other drivers have been identified such as age, type, and size of the ship, type of trade in which the ship is engaged, the geographical coverage of that trade, and directives from financial institutions (Bergantino and Marlow 1998, p. 159).[4] It has also been determined that whereas previously mainly vessels engaged in lower value trades – dry bulk and tankers – were flagged out, there has been an increasing trend for flagging out of container vessels (Bergantino and Marlow 1998, p. 159). Almost 62% of container vessels by tonnage were flagged in foreign registries in 2003 (Hoffman et al, p. 5); many of them comprising major fleets owned in developed nations and operated by well-established and reputable shipping companies. Other influential factors in the decision to flag out have been identified as avoidance of bureaucratic control and costs of compliance with higher standards under the national flag, the unavailability and need for ongoing supply of skilled labour, and fiscal costs generally (Bergantino and Marlow 1998, p. 165).

Reasons given for not flagging out (and sometimes a portion of a fleet would be flagged out with the remainder staying under the national flag) include the type of ship and trade routes, reputational risk, the value of the national flag in promotion of services, and reasons of historical importance. There are also significant differences in flagging out between types of ships, and ships engaged in coastal and deep sea trades. It has been demonstrated within the British shipping industry that a tanker is nineteen times less likely to be flagged out than a general cargo ship, and a ship trading deep sea is 88 times more likely to be flagged out than one engaged in coastal trades (Bergantino and Marlow 1998, pp. 165, 167). It is postulated by Bergantino and Marlow that factors such as availability of local crews, a far greater number and frequency of port calls, and heightened environmental protection considerations might contribute to these decisions.

Hoffman et al have determined that operators of younger vessels are more likely to choose a foreign flag. This apparently counter-intuitive conclusion is borne out by the statistics analysed in this study for International flags[5] but is a

---

[4]Bergantino and Malow included the following factors in their mixture of qualitative and quantitative questions to obtain data from the British shipping industry: crew costs, other costs, labour productivity, manning rules, profitability, fiscal factors, control, economic/political considerations, and the attitude of financial institutions. The sample included 186 ships connected with 51 British shipping companies. 65% of the ships of these companies had been flagged out. 39%of tankers and 52% of general cargo ships had remained with the national flag.

[5]See Chap. 10.

marked point of difference for Pseudo-National flags where the average age of vessels is considerably higher than both National and International flags. It is also demonstrated in this study that the average tonnage of ships under International flags is greater than National flags,[6] and considerably greater than ships under Pseudo-National flags.

One of the most significant factors in the decision to flag out, crewing costs, is proportional to the vessel's size. There is less likelihood, by a small margin, that vessels with a large dwt tonnage will be flagged out, due to the proportionately smaller number of crew required per ton of cargo carried (Hoffman et al, p. 9). Crew costs in general, regardless of the size of the vessel, have always been a major driver in the decision to flag out.[7] A study of decisions to flag out established that labour and crewing costs for ships registered in the United Kingdom accounted for 39% of the factors taken into account when making the decision to flag out (Bergantino and Marlow 1999, p. 30),[8] with another study determining that manning costs relative to total operational costs, for all ships, have invariably been between nine and fifteen% (Thanopolous 1998, p. 368).

Another driver for shipowners operating in a globally competitive market is to reduce taxation costs to the minimum; this incentive is offered by all FOCs and to a greater or lesser degree by second and dependent territory registers. This can extend to discounts on registration fees, tax incentives for newer ships to improve the age profile of the FOC fleet, tax exemptions for persons financing ships in their territory, and zero taxation on profits.[9] As similar incentives are offered by most

---

[6]"The likelihood that a foreign flag will be chosen versus a national flag increases with the size of the vessel, but decreases with the cargo carrying capacity, all else held constant." Hoffman J, Sanchez R, and Talley W, Determinants of vessel flag. P. 9 of internet version.

[7]"The annual cost of a 32 man American maritime union labour crew aboard a US registered 50,000 ton tanker of US$1.7 million in 1977 could be reduced by as much as US$1.35 million using a Filipino crew under the Liberian flag, and a further reduction of US$50,000 using "a motley crew made up of various nationalities". (Kifner J. Liberia: A Phantom Maritime Power Whose Fleet is Steered by Big Business. New York Times, February 14, 1977, p. 14 c).

According to *Lloyd's Shipping Economist*, the going rate for Filipino seamen was $276 per month, Bangladeshi seamen $140 per month, and for Chinese seamen, $50 per month. The Basic ITF rate for seamen at the time was $821 per month. (Lohr S. Tanker in Big Spill Typifies Freewheeling Industry. New York Times, July 3, 1989, p. 30).

[8]Bergantino and Marlow, however, deduced from a survey in 1998 that the difference in basic salary is inversely related to the likelihood of the ship being flagged out. "What this actually implies is that an increase in the differences in basic salary decreases the probability that the ship is flagged out. This, even if it initially appears to be counter intuitive, seems on a deeper analysis to be logical since flags of convenience crews generally receive a 'consolidated' wage which includes sums towards pension provision and other allowances. The average base salary of seafarers employed on the sampled ships is higher than that of seafarers employed on national flagged ships."

[9]Panama has announced in January 2006 that a new law will promise up to 75% reductions for registration fees for modern liquefied natural gas vessels, tax incentives for container newbuilds, a loosening of immigration restrictions on seafarers and shipowners alike and tax exemptions for ship financiers placing their loan portfolios in Panama. The Panama Maritime Authority deputy administrator, Carlos Raul Moreno, stated to *Lloyd's List* that: "We want to attract ship finance to

FOCs, including Quasi-National flags, there are only matters of degree in competitive advantages between individual registers.

In summary, there are a number of complex factors taken into account by shipowners in making the decision whether to remain under their national flag, or register under a FOC, with the predominant factor being to reduce costs.[10]

7.2 Flag of Convenience

The term "flag of convenience"[11] (FOC) was first popularised by the ITF through its Campaign Against Flags of convenience, begun in 1948. It could be said, as does the ITF, that any flag State that does not require the beneficial owner of a ship to be resident and subject to the same laws as any other company in that country is, by definition, a flag of convenience, however the nuances between some States and their requirements for registration do not allow for such a simple distinction.

There are many definitions of "flag of convenience" with some used by scholars as follows:

The flag of any country allowing the registration of foreign-owned and foreign controlled vessels under conditions which, for whatever reasons, are convenient and opportune for the persons who are registering the vessels. (Li and Wonham 1999, p. 140, citing Bozcek 1962)

The national flags of those states with whom shipowners register their vessels in order to avoid the fiscal obligations and the conditions and the terms of employment of factors of production, that would have been applicable if their ships were registered in their own countries. (Metaxas and Doganis 1976)

The country of registry allows non-citizens to own and control its merchant ships. Access to the registry is easy, as well as the transfer from it. Both transactions can usually be handled by the country's consulate abroad. A ships income is taxed at low rates or is tax exempt. A registry fee and an annual tonnage fee are normally the only charges made. Managing by non-nationals is freely permitted. (Abrahamsson 1980, p. 133)

In 1958 the OECD defined FOC as:

The flags of such countries as Panama, Liberia, Honduras and Costa Rica whose laws allow – and, indeed, make it easy for – ships owned by foreign nationals or companies to

---

Panama so for any ship finance line which is administered from Panama or issued from Panama all the income tax will be free, it can be repatriated to whichever country, tax free, no problem". *Lloyd's List*, 27 January 2006.

[10]"While it is widely recognised that the flagging out phenomenon is primarily fuelled by the desire of the shipowner to minimize both costs and restrictions on his operating freedom, this research has pointed out a multitude of other factors which may have a role in the decision making process" (Bergantino and Marlow 1998, p. 172).

[11]For the purposes of the analysis carried out in this study any flag State that is not a National Flag State is deemed to be a flag of convenience. The terms Closed Register and Open Register are in common usage as synonyms for National flag State and flag of convenience respectively. The terms "flag State" and "register" are also synonymous in everyday usage, as in International Flag State or International Register.

fly those flags. This is in contrast to the practice in the maritime countries (and in many others) where the right to fly the national flag is subject to strict conditions and involves far reaching obligations. (ICFTU et al 2002, p. 7)

The term flag of convenience was codified by the ILO in the introduction to the Convention Concerning Minimum Standards in Merchant Ships (Convention No 147) (International Journal of Marine and Coastal Law 1999, p. 139).

7.3 The Panamanian Register

Flags of convenience, in their twentieth-century guise, came about largely as a result of the political and economic influence of the United States of America (Vorbach 2001, p. 28) and became an attractive option to many nations[12] in the 1930s, due to the desire of nations to obtain neutrality during a time of political unrest and pending hostilities. The development of the small but strategic coastal State of Panama into what has become the world's largest flag State is a classic illustration of the political and economic motivations behind the creation of FOCs.[13]

The fledgling[14] national Panamanian register was opened in 1916 to allow for registration of ship-owning companies owned by foreigners, particularly Americans. At this time American political interests were encouraging Panama to become an independent republic to facilitate the Panama Canal's construction and operation, and American shipowners were suffering under legislative restrictions introduced between 1915 and 1920.[15] These shipowners received official encouragement to register under a less restrictive flag[16] and Panama's official creation of an open register in 1925[17] was a direct result of these drivers (Montero Llacer 2003, p. 3).

---

[12]"In addition to the Basque, Greek, Norwegian, Danzig and British fleets that entered Panamanian registry ... [d]ocumented references to Panamanian registry by owners in Sweden, Germany, Denmark, Holland, France, Algeria, Egypt, Turkey, Rumania, Bulgaria, China, and Japan can be found in the period from 1935 through 1939 ... the variety of registries does demonstrate that the efforts of the Panamanian government to develop a tax haven and a no-questions asked system won quiet recognition all over the globe." (Carlisle 1981, p. 65)

[13]The effects of intervention by the USA in creation of the large flag of convenience of Liberia, and political influences upon Liberia and Panama, and competition between these two flag States, are also emphasised.

[14]During the period between its independence in 1903 and 1915, according to limited documentary sources, the Panamanian merchant fleet was owned by nationals and made up of 26 fishing vessels and coasters of no more than 50 grt each. An exception was its leader, the 451 grt steamship *Panama*.

[15]"in order to reform certain social aspects and for merchant fleet consolidation as a naval auxiliary branch during the First World War" (Montero Lacer 2003, p. 4)

[16]*Ibid*: "as stated by Admiral W. Benson, President of the Shipping Board between 1920 and 1921."

[17]*Ibid*, p. 5: Prior to this, an event which reinforced the Panama register was the transfer in 1922 of two large American passenger ships, the *Reliance* and *Resolute*, after the Shipping Board had stated, "after analysing some countries without aspirations to compete with the USA to develop its merchant fleet and naval power legislations ... Panama is the most suitable for our needs and, we consider it the most acceptable for USA's interests, either for its trading development or its

In 1925, Panama's Legislative Assembly amended their registration requirements through Law 8 to allow ships of any nationality to register, at which time the register contained 14 ships totalling 83,776 gross tons. Law 8 allowed foreign owned vessels to be registered without any restrictions regarding the shipowner's residence or nationality[18] and there was a requirement for the company to be represented by Panamanian domiciled lawyers (Montero Llacer 2003, p. 3). Twenty-four ships owned by Aristotle Onassis were transferred to the Panama flag between 1932 and 1941 and, as early as 1939, the Panamanian register was being referred to as "convenient" (Alderton and Winchester, 2002, p. 1).

With the advent of the Second World War, Panama gained considerable tonnage with the transfer to its register of 63 American ships totalling 359,000 GT, while at the same time the American State Department insisted that Panama not register German or Japanese ships. The carriage of Jews to Israel by Greek-owned, but Panamanian-registered, ships also incurred the wrath of the USA and Great Britain. This led to further political pressure upon the Panamanian administration and resulted in the Greek government declaring the use of Panamanian registration by its nationals to be illegal. Further political influence during the period of the Second World War in which America was neutral, from the USA supported by Great Britain, resulted in the American Maritime Commission taking control of all Panamanian ships trading with the Axis. After America entered the war, the American War Shipping Administration took control of Panamanian registered ships; 158 of which, totalling 736,000 GT, were lost along with 1,500 killed or missing seamen. Post war, the Panamanian fleet benefited from the sale of 1,113 wartime-built Liberty ships by the Americans to European owners to replace tonnage lost during the war,[19] many of which were registered in Panama.

---

availability in periods of war ..." The extent of American commercial and political influence in this decision is highlighted by the facts that Averell Harriman (future Secretary of Commerce from 1946–1948, and Presidential candidate in 1952 and 1956) owned the American Ship and Commerce Corporation, which had bought these two ex-German ships, and Harriman's law firm was the same company that had drafted documents for the independence of Panama from Colombia, and were also Panama's legal representative in America.

[18]The attraction of this concept to foreign shipowners is evident from the fact that, by 1939, the register had increased to 159 ships totalling 717,500 GT. These registrations were motivated by a number of different circumstances during this politically unstable decade. Over 100 European ships, previously registered in Spain, Greece, United Kingdom, and Norway, re-flagged to Panama during the 1930s, 30 of which were owned by Americans. It is believed that these re-registrations were to obtain neutrality. The American owned United Fruit Company transferred 13 vessels totalling 48,000 GT between 1928 and 1931, and the Standard Oil Company of New Jersey added 25 ships totalling 230,000 GT to the Panamanian register in 1935. Basque shipping companies transferred their ships to the Panamanian flag to avoid their ships being confiscated during the Spanish Civil War (1936–1939). The remarkable growth of Greek ownership of oil tankers was facilitated by the benefits to be attained by Panamanian registry.

[19]"In 1945, the Panamanian fleet was made up of 268 units and in 1946 it had reached 406 ... Between 1946 and 1948 American tanker owners took advantage of the Panamanian flag to consolidate their position in the international trade, taking advantage of the imposed restriction by the Maritime Commission in order for T-2 tankers to be sold only to American shipowners." (Montero Llacer 2003, p. 7)

The Panama register doubled its tonnage from the beginning of the war to 1947. This – along with views that, as Panama was not a maritime country, a fleet of this size could not be justified, and concerns about cheap crews, tax advantages, and lower standards of safety – resulted in 1947 in the first demonstrations and boycotts associated with FOC ships, led by the International Transport Workers Federation (ITF) (Montero Llacer 2003, p. 8). The first serious competition to the Panama register came about in 1948, when the Liberian Maritime Act came into effect and created the Liberian register, aimed at encouraging cooperation between the USA and Liberia and offering an alternative flag to Panama. The view of shipowners of the day is summarised in a statement[20] published in the London *Times* in 1958 by the Greek tanker owner Stavros Niarchos, who highlighted the international nature of shipping and defended the right of a shipowner to register his ships wherever he desired.

Over the next 20 years Panama and Liberia competed as the world's largest flag States, with Liberia taking the lead in 1955. Panama's register increased from 515 vessels totalling 2.7 million GT in 1958, to 823 totalling 5.4 million GT in 1969, whilst, over the same period the Liberian register increased from zero to 1,731 ships totalling 29.2 million GT; the very large tonnage resulting from a specialisation in large tankers. Growth continued rapidly in both registers over the next 20 years by the end of which, in 1988, Panama had more than three times the number of ships as Liberia and a similar gross tonnage[21] (Montero Llacer 2003, p. 9). Liberia was shortly to gain a large windfall of Panamanian tonnage as a result of the American invasion of Panama in 1989 and an Executive Order [12635] issued by the President of the United States of America in October that year which closed American ports and territorial waters to Panamanian-registered ships. Nine million gross tons was lost from the Panamanian register but was swiftly recouped by 1991, when Liberia was itself having serious political problems.

In 2007 Panama remained by far the most dominant register with 6,450 ships totalling 165 million GT (Lloyd's Register of Shipping, World Fleet Statistics 2007) generating more than US$50,000,000 per year for the Panamanian Government from its register, which is based in the United States of America. The Panamanian register is still controversial, with much criticism being directed at it for its statutory role on behalf of the flag State in the Red Sea disaster of 2006, when more than one thousand persons were lost in the foundering of the Egyptian registered ferry *al Salam Boccaccio 98*. It became apparent that the flag State duties of Panama had been sub-delegated to a body over which Panama had no interest, oversight, or control. The Vice President of Panama, and head of the maritime administration, Arosemena Valdes, stated that Panama needs to update its standards, introduce programmes to modernise its register, including annual maritime safety inspections on ships registered in Panama, and draw

---

[20]"A ship owned by a national from a particular country, loads in a second one, unloads in a third country and finally trades with a fourth. I must confess I do not believe in any valid reason to justify that this ship must have one flag rather than another. Maritime trade has always been, and must carry on being, an international business." London *Times* 1958

[21]Panama, 5,022 ships totalling 44.6 million GT; Liberia, 1507 ships totalling 49.7 million GT.

up the first maritime code in Panama[22]; frank admissions from a flag State that has been in operation for 80 years and administers more than 20% of world tonnage.

7.4 Beneficial Ownership

Beneficial ownership, and the lack of a "genuine link" between the owner and the flag State, is inherent in all definitions of FOC. The country of residence of the beneficial owner is indicative of the attraction and widespread use of flags of convenience by nationals of the leading ship-owning nations of the world. In 1974 the ITF defined an FOC as:

> Where beneficial ownership and control of a vessel is found to lie elsewhere than in the country of the flag the vessel is flying, the vessel is considered as sailing under a flag of convenience.

This definition recalled the requirements of Article 5 of the HSC,[23] and pre-dated both Article 91 of the LOSC,[24] and the intent of Article 1 of the United Nations Convention on Conditions for Registration of Ships[25] that "there must exist a genuine link between the State and the ship." The ITF undertook a political campaign designed to promote the negotiation of an international agreement on ship registration that would codify a genuine link between the ship, the flag flown, and the nationality or residence of its owners (ITF Flags of convenience Campaign). This instrument, the Convention on Conditions for the Registration of Ships (1986, 7 LOSB 87), was adopted in 1986 but has singly failed to attract any significant support. In spite of the current reality of beneficial ownership, the ITF's present definition of a FOC still harks back to their original concern about lack of a genuine link: "A flag of convenience is one that flies the flag of a country other than the country of ownership" (ITF Flags of convenience Campaign, p. 4).

---

[22]From notes taken by the author during an address by Panama to the ILO Maritime Labour Conference, 2006.

[23]HSC, Article 5(1): "Each State shall fix the conditions for the grant of its nationality to ships, for the registration of ships in its territory, and for the right to fly its flag. Ships shall have the nationality of the State whose flag they are entitled to fly. *There must exist a genuine link between the State and the ship;* (own emphasis) in particular, the State must effectively exercise its jurisdiction and control in administrative, technical and social matters over ships flying its flag."

[24]LOSC, Article 91(1): "Every State shall fix the conditions for the grant of its nationality to ships, for the registration of ships in its territory, and for the right to fly its flag. Ships have the nationality of the State whose flag they are entitled to fly. *There must exist a genuine link between the State and the ship.*" (own emphasis)

[25]United Nations Convention on Conditions for Registration of Ships. Geneva, 7 February, 1986, Not in force. 7 *LOSB 87* (1986) Article 1, Objectives: "*For the purpose of ensuring or, as the case may be, strengthening the genuine link between a State and ships flying its flag,* and in order to exercise effectively its jurisdiction and control over such ships with regard to identification and accountability of shipowners and operators as well as with regard to administrative, technical, economic and social matters, a flag State shall apply the provisions contained in the Convention." (own emphasis)

The extent to which the genuine link does not exist is indicated by the statistics in Table A.2, Appendix A, which indicate the true nationality (beneficial ownership) of the major FOC fleets, as defined by UNCTAD, at 1 January 2004.

The statistics reveal that in 2004, well below 10% of tonnage registered under FOCs was owned by nationals of that flag State. This contrasts with figures above 30% and as high as 80% for national (closed) registers, where the tonnage is owned by nationals of that flag State or nationals of countries that have a privileged relationship with that State; for example Denmark, Norway and Hong Kong (China) (UNCTAD 2004, p. 36). Ownership of FOC vessels is concentrated in ten countries, accounting for 75% of total dwt tonnage, with five countries controlling 58%. Greece and Japan dominate ownership of vessels under FOCs, with a combined total of almost 41% of world tonnage under foreign flags (UNCTAD 2004, p. 36). At the beginning of 2004 the six major FOCs – Panama, Liberia, Bahamas, Malta, Cyprus, and Bermuda – accounted for 93.9% of the tonnage owned by nationals of the 35 countries or territories who accounted for 89% of 12 major FOC fleets, with the balance spread amongst the many minor FOCs (UNCTAD 2004, p. 36).

The acceptance of beneficial ownership in the international shipping community is reflected in recognition by the ITF that not all marine accidents involve FOC ships; nor do all cases of exploitation of seafarers, as reflected in their current campaign that now encompasses sub-standard shipping in general, as well as FOCs in particular (ITF Flag of convenience Campaign, Foreword). The ITF recognises that FOCs are an established feature of the international shipping industry and, in an era of economic liberalism, look likely to remain so for the time being (ITF Flag of convenience Campaign, Foreword). The ITF has recognised the fact that pay and conditions for seafarers aboard some nationally flagged ships can be inferior to that on FOC ships and has, accordingly, focussed increasingly upon a wider view including regulation, standards, and enforcement (Alderton and Winchester 2002, pp. 35–43).

In considering and defining FOCs it is argued that, for analytical purposes, practical distinctions can be made within the broad definition of FOC, and that subsets exist, such as second registers, dependent territories, international, registers, and completely open registers.

7.5 Definitions of Flag States

In order to carry out any meaningful analysis of the effectiveness and performance of flag State responsibility, it is necessary and useful to attempt to define and categorise the various types of flag States (registers). A bewildering, and often misleading, array of descriptions of flag States have evolved, including: Traditional Maritime Nation, Embedded Maritime Nation, National flag, Classic Register, Open Register, Opportunist Register, International Open Register, International Register, Closed Register, Second Register, Dependent Territory Register, Offshore Register, Flag of convenience. Other more pejorative definitions include: bogus maritime flags, cheap flags, easy registry, fictitious flags, flags of accommodation, flags of attraction, flags of necessity, flags of opportunity, flags of refuge, freebooters, free flags, free registry, nominal flags, pirate flags, runaway flags, shadow flags, tax-free flags (International Journal of Marine and Coastal Law 1999, p. 139 n15).

Some terms, such as open register and flag of convenience can be used to encompass a number of subsets of registration with their usage often reflecting the political, social, or economic views of the commentator. The ITF implacably uses the term flag of convenience whereas a shipowner, for commercial expediency, may see the same flag as a "flag of necessity" (International Journal of Marine and Coastal Law 1999, p. 139 n15). The IMO diplomatically uses the term "open register" rather than FOC, to avoid offence to many of its larger Member States. Long-established shipping nations such as India, Malaysia, and China take umbrage at their exclusion from the use of the term "traditional maritime nation" which does not recognise their ancient maritime heritages. There is also long-standing tension between developing States and open registers operated by developed States, over what is perceived as unfair competition and disincentives to develop their own fleet whilst at the same time being exploited as labour supply countries for those registers.

These issues make it necessary to attempt to clearly define different types of flag State or register, and it is argued that the many extant terms can be aggregated for analysis and general reference into four categories: National Flag, Quasi-National Flag, International Flag, and Pseudo-National Flag. Each of these categories of flag State is defined, populated, and analysed below.

7.5.1 National Flag State

The term "National flag State" can be broadly assimilated to "closed register", "traditional maritime nation", and "embedded maritime nation". It is generally accepted that a National flag (or register) is a flag State whose register is, by definition, available only to nationals of that State (Ademuni-Odeke 1998, p. 645, 646). A National register will be operated by the maritime administration of the State, and will require owners or demise charterers[26] to be nationals of that State with a body corporate registered, and active, in the State. Very traditional National registers will also require all or some (usually senior officers) of the crew of a ship to be nationals of the State.[27] If these criteria are present, a register can be categorised as a "closed register" thereby relegating all other registers to the status of "open registers"

---

[26]See for example the New Zealand Ship Registration Act 1992, No 89, s.2, Preamble: "'Demise charter', in relation to a ship, means the demise, letting, hire, or delivery of the ship to the charterer, by virtue of which the charterer has whole possession and control of the ship, including the right to appoint its master and crew." Also commonly known as a "bareboat charter".

[27]See Klikauer T and Morris M (2002) "Into Murky Waters, Globalisation and deregulation in Germany's shipping employee relations". Employee Relations, Vol 24, No 1, pp. 12–28, for a discussion of the effect on German senior officers employed under a national flag of establishment of a Second Register.

of one degree or another, including, by definition and aggregation, flags of convenience, second registers, and dependent territories.

National registers are invariably a product of many long years of maritime administration, during which time responsible frameworks have been established for the regulation and administration of ships. These would normally extend to such matters as consultation with all parties in the law-making process, close association with seafarer unions and welfare organisations, provision of training establishments for seafarers, and an agreed commitment between all parties involved in shipping to maintenance of high standards in all respects for the operation of ships flying their flag. National flag States will usually house representatives of other important actors in the shipping industry, such as Classification Societies, insurance companies, ship-brokers, and maritime law firms. They will usually have ratified a high number of important IMO and ILO Conventions and will be prompt in that ratification.[28] In summary, a National flag State can be assimilated to a regulatory efficient State.[29]

Li and Wonham in 1999,[30] using measures such as equity, requirements for national managers, directors, and chairs, national office and national crew, identified at least 41 closed (national) registers. National registers are in the majority in the current world atlas of flag States and are a mixture of OECD members with a long history of ship registration such as Italy, Norway, Germany, the United Kingdom, the Netherlands, Japan, France, Spain, Australia, and New Zealand, and developing nations such as Bangladesh, Ethiopia, Senegal, Gabon, Ghana, Madagascar, the Maldives, Morocco, Nicaragua, Papua New Guinea, Senegal, Suriname, and Togo.[31] For the purpose of this analysis the 95 States listed in Table 7.1 are deemed to be National flag States.[32]

---

[28]See The Global Seafarer: Living and working conditions in a globalised industry, International Labour Organization Office, Geneva, 2004, p. 40, Table 2.6, for a list of ratifications of IMO Conventions by flag States in 2002. Report 1(a), Adoption of an instrument to consolidate maritime labour standards, published by the International Labour Office, Geneva in 2006 (available on the ILO website) has a useful summary of ratification of maritime labour Conventions by ILO Member States in Appendix B.

[29]"Regulatory efficient States [are those] in which the State seeks to regulate the full extent of maritime operations. These flag States are run centrally from within governmental structures. From the initial survey of the ship before its registration to the welfare provisions for seafarers, these States seek to provide an efficient and effective regulatory environment backed up by both the full range of international law and effective political will. Examples of such flag States are Norway and the United Kingdom." *Ibid*, p. 50.

[30]Li KX and Wonham J (1999) Registration of Vessels. The International Journal of Marine and Coastal Law, Vol 14, No 1. The USA and the People's Republic of China were cited by the study as having amongst the most stringent registration requirements in the world.

[31]*Ibid*, pp. 147–148 contains a complete list of Closed Registers in Table 3. The flag States categorised as "national registers" in this study are listed in Chap. 8t.

[32]States are deemed to be national flag States if they are not "flags of convenience". A number of commentators have identified ships registered under the general pejorative term of "flag of convenience". The International Transport Workers Federation maintains a list of such registers; see http://www.itfglobal.org/flags-convenience/flags-convenience-183.cfm. See also Winchester N, Sampson

Table 7.1 National flag states

Albania	Colombia	Iceland	Libya	Poland	Switzerland
Algeria	Croatia	India	Lithuania	Portugal	Syria
Angola	Cuba	Indonesia	Luxembourg	Qatar	Taiwan
Argentina	Denmark	Iran	Malaysia	Romania	Tanzania
Australia	Dominica	Ireland	Mexico	Russia	Thailand
Austria	Dom. Rep.	Israel	Moldova	Samoa	Togo
Azerbaijan	Ecuador	Italy	Morocco	South Africa	Tunisia
Bahrain	Egypt	Jamaica	Burma/Myanmar	Saudi Arabia	Turkey
Bangladesh	Eritrea	Japan	Namibia	Serbia and Montenegro.	UAR
Belgium	Estonia	Jordan	Netherlands	Seychelles	Ukraine
Brazil	Ethiopia	Kazakhstan	New Zealand	Sierra Leone	United Kingdom
Brunei	Finland	South Korea	Nigeria	Slovakia	USA
Bulgaria	France	DPR of Korea	Norway	Solomon Islands	Venezuela
Canada	Georgia	Kuwait	Pakistan	Spain	Vietnam
Chile	Germany	Latvia	Philippines	Sri Lanka	Yemen
China	Greece	Lebanon	Papua New Guinea	Sweden	

All National registers, regardless of their state of economic development, are clearly at a competitive disadvantage with other more open registers. The beneficial shipowners resident in many National flag States are, accordingly, amongst the largest users of non-national registers, through the simple incorporation of body corporates in those States.[33] Many National flag States have, of necessity, watered down their registration requirements by only requiring that an even smaller percentage of the crew, usually senior officers, be nationals, and by allowing companies not domiciled in the flag State to register ships (ILO2004, p. 51). Many have also introduced second registers, or registration in dependent territories, in order to offer their nationals economic advantages,[34] particularly in employment of lower cost crews whilst remaining under the maritime law, and maintaining the higher standards enforced by the mother State.

H, Shelly T (2006) An analysis of Crewing Levels: Findings from the SIRC Global Labour Market Survey, Seafarers International Research Centre, Cardiff University, p. 30; and the International Labour Office, Geneva (2004) The Global Seafarer, Living and Working Conditions in a globalised industry, p. 31. For the purpose of this analysis, this use of the term "flag of convenience" includes all those States identified as Quasi-National, International and Pseudo-National flag States.

[33]Review of Maritime Transport (2005) Report by the UNCTAD secretariat, United Nations, Geneva. The tonnage of major open-registry countries increased marginally in 2004, by 4.5 million dwt to 404 million dwt. Approximately two thirds of these beneficially owned fleets are owned by developed market-economy countries and the rest by developing countries. See also Chap. 8t of this study for detailed comment on beneficial ownership.

[34]"The great difference between the NIS and the traditional national flag fleet lay in its labour supply options. Only the former permitted the employment of non-Norwegian nationals at lower rates of pay." (Klikauer and Morris 2002, pp. 12–28)

7.5.2   Quasi-National Flag States

"Quasi" is defined by the *ConciseOxford Dictionary* as "seemingly, apparently but not really" and also as "being partly or almost". It is argued that certain types of flag States clearly meet this definition and can thus be considered as Quasi-National flag States. These are Second Registers and Dependent Territory Registers.

7.5.2.1   Second Registers

Second Registers were created from the late 1980s by National registers such as France, Norway, Denmark, and Germany, as a reaction to the haemorrhaging of their national fleet to open registers (ILO2004, p. 29). By their nature and relationship with their parent register they can be deemed to be Quasi-National flag States in the sense that are seemingly, apparently, but not really, National flag States. These registers provide expatriate and national shipowners with taxation and crewing advantages and flexibility as an incentive to return to or remain with their Quasi-National flag; pragmatic recognition of the pervasive influence and attraction of open registers and FOCs (ILO2004, p. 29, 32). Twenty-six Second Registers[35] were identified in 2002, a number of which had very little tonnage registered, little growth, and were comprised of mainly very small ships (ILO2004, p. 33).

The following are amongst registers generally accepted to be Second Register: Registro Especial Brasieiro (REB), Danish International Ship Register (DIS), German International Ship Register (GIS), French International Ship Register (FIS), Norwegian International Ship Register (NIS), Turkish International Shipping Register, Italian International Shipping Register. They are deemed to be Second Registers due to their location in a non-metropolitan territory of another State, although their register might have no formal links with that of the primary State. Some of these registers are effectively non-active[36] both operationally and in terms of their international significance.

---

[35]Table 2.3, Second registers, 2002. (Name of "parent" country in bold): **Brazil**, Registro Especial Brasileiro (REB); **China**, Hong Kong, Macao; **Denmark**, DIS, Faeroe Islands, Faeroe Islands (FAS); **Finland**, Aland Islands; **France**, Kerguelen Islands (French Southern and Antarctic territories), Wallis and Futuna Islands; **Germany**, GIS; **Italy**, Second Register; **Netherlands**, Netherlands Antilles; **New Zealand**, Cook Islands; **Norway**, NIS; **Portugal**, Madiera (MAR); **Spain**, Canary Islands (CSR); **Turkey**, International Shipping Register; **United Kingdom**, Anguilla, Bermuda, British Virgin Islands, Cayman Islands, Channel islands, Falkland Islands, Gibraltar, Isle of Man, Turks and Caicos Islands.

[36]"The following registers can be included in this category: Anguilla; British Virgin Islands; Channel Islands; Falkland Islands; Turks and Caicos Islands, and Wallis and Futuna Islands." (ILO 2004, p. 33)

Second Registers, such as the NIS,[37] GIS,[38] and the DIS have achieved their aims and attracted considerable tonnage,[39] even though these registers are hard to distinguish, in terms of their practices and regulation, from the State's National register and are operated by the flag State administration. One of their *raisons d'être* is the preservation of the home State's maritime industry infrastructure (ILO2004, p. 34). There has, however, been a significant human cost in terms of lost employment opportunities to nationals of the flag State, as the main attraction of such registers is the ability of owners to reduce crew costs by employment of foreign nationals whilst retaining the requirement for a cadre of nationals as senior officers.

Between 1991 and 2000, half of German officers and two-thirds of German ratings lost their positions to crews from labour supply countries as a direct result of the creation of the GIS (Klikauer and Morris 2002). Second Registers can also offer very significant financial incentives to shipowners with the Italian International Ship Register (IIS), established in 1998, cutting the tax rate on company profits from 53.2 to 7.5%. By comparison the Luxembourg Second Register, established in 1990 and open to all vessels less than 15 years of age, requires 50% ownership by nationals or companies based and registered in that State. In an effort to offset open registry and bareboat charter competition, Luxembourg registration provides tax incentives for investment, no requirement for local taxation, and low income tax for non-resident seafarers. Command is restricted to European Commission (EC) nationals, and shipowners are offered collective bargaining and the ability to provide minimal social security benefits to all seafarers serving aboard Luxembourg registered vessels (Li and Wonham 1999, p. 151).

The ironic threat to open registers of such incentives from Second Registers is being realised as the share of the world merchant fleet in major open registries[40] increased by only 1.9% in 2004 after a modest increase of 0.5% the previous year (UNCTAD 2005, p. 32). This trend in world tonnage flagged with the major open registers may reflect the increased competitiveness of Second Registers, given the attractive fiscal regimes for shipowners in some traditional maritime countries (UNCTAD 2005, p. 32).

---

[37]"After two years of establishment the NIS had 533 ships with a total of 13,365,793 gross tonnes registered in 1989. In 1996 there were 685 ships with a total of 18,948,844 gross tonnes under its registration, 6.6 times greater than its national register in terms of gross tonnes. The main aim of the NIS was to attract those Norwegian ships registered under open registers. This has certainly been achieved" (Li and Wonham 1999, pp. 150, 151).

[38]See Klikauer and Morris (2002) Into Murky Waters; Globalisation and Deregulation in Germany's shipping employee relations. Employee Relations, Vol 24, No 1, for a case study of how the GIS challenged Germany's traditional system of employment relations and regulatory framework.

[39]"When Germany introduced its second register in 1988, 52% of German tonnage was registered abroad; the figure subsequently fell to 38% but was up to 65% in 1997. According to Germany's Federal Office of Maritime Shipping and Hydrography, 96% of German-registered tonnage appears on this [second] register. The (German International Ship Register) GIS is also unusual in terms of second registers in that only ships acceptable to the primary register may be entered on it" (ILO 2004, p. 34).

[40]UNCTAD identifies the six major Open Registries as being: Panama, Liberia, Bahamas, Malta, Cyprus, and Bermuda.

7.5.2.2 Dependent Territory Registers

Another form of Quasi-National flag State, which sometimes stretches the accepted definition[41] of a State to the limits of credibility, is the "Dependent Territory" or "Offshore Register". The French were amongst the first flurry of traditional maritime States to establish Dependent Territory Registers in the late 1980s with creation of the French Terres Antartiques et Anstrales Francaises (TAAF) register in 1989 (ILO2004, p. 32). This register, ostensibly located in the French territory of the Kerguelen Islands, would not accept non-liner vessels and required the crew to be composed of at least 35% French nationals,[42] including four officers. The use by France of the Kerguelen Islands as a Dependent Territory Register did not attract significant tonnage and was replaced in 2003 by the French International Ship Register (FIR) based in France (ILO 2004, p. 34).

Dependent territories have, by definition, a dependent relationship in law with their mother country and there is always a relationship between the dependent territory and its parent State through the content of maritime legislation. For example, the principal maritime legislation of the British Crown Colonies and Dependent Territories,[43] the Red Ensign Group, is based upon the United Kingdom Merchant Shipping Acts; a model which could previously be assimilated to that of all British Commonwealth countries, and is a point of difference between Dependent and open registers.

Along with Second Registers, Dependent Territory Registers have been defined by one commentator as "Quasi-flags of convenience" (Couper et al 1999, p. 193), in that they offer almost the same financial advantages as FOCs[44] but do not have

---

[41]"A State must satisfy three conditions: (1) It must have territory. But absolute certainty about a State's frontiers is not required; many States have long-standing frontier disputes with their neighbours, (2) A State must have a population, and (3) A State must have a government capable of maintaining effective control over its territory, and of conducting international relations with other States. This requirement is not always applied strictly; thus, a State does not cease to exist when it is temporarily deprived of an effective government as a result of civil war or similar upheavals. Even when all of its territory is occupied by the enemy in wartime, the State continues to exist, provided that its allies continue the struggle against the enemy." (Akehurst 1987, p. 53)

[42]"To underline the rationale for this system of registration, the increased costs arising from raising the percentage of French nationals to 35% is compensated to shipowners by a partial reimbursement of social security charges paid by owners to French Department of Social Security" (Ademuni-Odeke 1997, p. 655).

[43]Anguilla, Bermuda, British Antarctic Territory, British Indian Ocean Territory, British Virgin Islands, Cayman Islands, Falkland Islands, Gibraltar, Guernsey, Isle of Man, Jersey, Montserrat, Pitcairn Islands, St Helena and Dependencies, Sovereign base areas of Akrotiri and Dhekelia, and the Turks and Caicos Islands.

[44]See for example *Fairplay* magazine, 30 March 2006, p. 24: "A generous benefits system has been served up for shipowners by the Rock's taxman. There's no stamp duty, no capital gains tax and no tax on dividends, either. Capital duties are capped at [ten pounds sterling], too. But for owners, the best news is that the 35% tax charge on shipowning companies was repealed just before Christmas and replaced with a zero-rate regime. That's right: no income tax. If an owner registers in Gibraltar but operates its ships wholly outside and does not bank in Gibraltar, then it doesn't pay anything to the taxman. The new regime runs alongside the non-resident tax-exempt regime, which will have to be terminated before the end of the decade, as a result of pressure from the European Commission ..."

the complete freedom to determine conditions for the grant of their nationality as enjoyed by completely open registers. Both the IMO and ILO treat dependent territories as subservient by always associating them with their parent State – for example, Gibraltar and the United Kingdom – as do the various port State control regimes, but separate statistics are sometimes produced for both the dependent and parent flags. Although some of these Dependent Territory Registers would argue long and loud that they are open registers, for the purposes of this analysis they will be classified as Quasi-National flag States, not only because it is often difficult to distinguish between data and statistics for the primary and dependent registers, but also because they are usually subject to the same regulations for crewing, safety and certification as those prescribed for their countries of origin (Couper et al 1992, p. 193).

Dependent Territory, or Offshore Registers, included with their "parent State" in parenthesis: Anguilla, Bermuda, British Virgin Islands, Cayman Islands, Channel Islands, Falkland Islands, Gibraltar, Isle of Man, Turks and Caicos Islands, St Kitts and Nevis (United Kingdom); French Southern Antarctic Territory, Wallis and Futuna Islands (France); Aland Islands (Finland); Madeira (Portugal); Netherlands Antilles (Netherlands); Faroe Islands (Denmark); Macao, Taiwan (China); Canary Islands (Spain).

A further twelve quasi-national flag States have been identified (Tokyo MOU 2004, paper DBM14WP.4) as: Union of Comoros, French Polynesia, Guadeloupe, New Caledonia, Martinique, Mayotte, St Pierre et Miquelon (France); Greenland (Denmark); Virgin Islands, Guam, Northern Mariana Islands, Puerto Rico (USA).

Due to the difficulty, when considering Quasi-National flag States, of statistical differentiation between the parent State and the second, or dependent, flag State, the Paris and Tokyo port State control regimes and the United States Coastguard (USCG) have accepted that most of these registers are part of the parent country and have taken the pragmatic decision, for statistical purposes, of subsuming most of them into the statistics for the parent flag.[45] For this reason, whilst maintaining the argument that a discrete category of Quasi-National flag State exists for the purposes of this analysis of flag State responsibility, only the flag States for which empirical statistics are available will be considered.

7.5.3   *International Flag State*

An International flag State is simply, and by definition, one where registration of ships is open to nationals of any State, and is sometimes referred to as an open register or international open register. "Open register" is an all-encompassing term that has gained currency in many quarters as an alternative to the pejorative term "flag of convenience". UNCTAD's description of "open registry", probably coloured by their mandate for promotion of trade in under-developed countries,

---

[45]Exceptions are Bermuda, the Cayman Islands, Gibraltar, Isle of Man, Hong Kong, Taiwan, Netherlands Antilles, Faroe Islands, and St Kitts and Nevis.

refers to open registration as a device that enabled the traditional maritime countries
to maintain ownership and control over world shipping, despite the fact that they
could not operate ships economically under their own flags (UN 1985, p. 146).

The United Kingdom Committee on Shipping in 1970 (Rochdale report 1970,
p. 51) identified six features common to all "international open registers" that have
withstood the test of time.[46] Some of the criteria identified in the Rochdale report
would place an International flag State at the "convenience" as opposed to the
"international" end of the registration spectrum that has evolved since these features
were identified in 1970. One suggested parameter for the categorisation of flag
States is their degree of regulatory efficiency and, in this respect, International
(Open) Registers could be deemed to be regulatory inefficient States.[47]

UNCTAD identified the six major open registries as Panama, Liberia, Malta,
Cyprus, Bahamas, and Bermuda, a definition supported by the above criteria
(UNCTAD 2005, p. 35). However, they then go on to describe a number of other
registers as "minor open registries".[48] This highlights the difficulty of separating
international (open) registers into clearly defined categories as some of the latter
group could be deemed to be Quasi-National registers and some Pseudo-National
registers (Tenold 2003).

The global nature of the shipping industry, and the economic attraction for
shipowners from developed countries[49] of the major established International registers,

---

[46]*Ibid*: The country of registry allows ownership and/or control of its merchant vessels by non- citizens;
access to the registry is easy. A ship may usually be registered at a consul's office abroad (or, in
the present day, over the Internet). Equally important, transfer from the registry at the owner's
option is not restricted; taxes on the income from the ships are not levied locally, or are low.
A registry fee and an annual fee, based on tonnage, are normally the only charges made. A guarantee
or acceptable understanding regarding the future freedom from taxation may also be given;
the country of registry is a small power with no national requirement under any foreseeable
circumstances for all the shipping registered (but receipts from very small charges on a large
tonnage may produce a substantial effect on its national income and balance of payments);
manning of ships by non-nationals is freely permitted; and the country of registry has neither
the power nor the administrative machinery to effectively impose any government or international
regulations; nor has the country the wish or the power to control the companies themselves.

[47]"Within such States there is generally a somewhat opaque route between the shipowner and the
flag States. Vessel registry tends to be nominally owned and privately operated. The registration
requirements are not negligible but nor are they stringent. The ratification of IMO Conventions tends
to be moderate and responsibility for compliance is passed onto classification societies. The main
distinction between this category and regulatory efficient States (closed registers) lies in the treatment
of labour issues: welfare provision is, at best, moderate, and, at worst, perfunctory, and is reflected in
low ratification levels of international labour Conventions relating to seafarers. Examples of such flag
States are Liberia, Malta and Panama (in general, the established open registers)" (ILO 2004, p. 50).

[48]St Vincent and the Grenadines, Antigua and Barbuda, Cayman Islands, Luxembourg, Vanuatu,
and Gibraltar.

[49]"As has been shown, it is above all operators from developed countries that chose a foreign flag.
This allows them to remain competitive in a business environment where developing countries
might otherwise have a competitive advantage due to lower wages and, perhaps, less stringent
safety and environmental standards." Hoffmann J, Sanchez R and Talley W, (2003) Determinants of
Vessel Flag. Paper presented to IAME, Korea.
http://www.oduport.org/PaperCullinaneBookForeignFlagDRAFT2003-10-31.htm.

is demonstrated by the fact that more than 50% of world tonnage (Lloyd's Register of Shipping, World Fleet Statistics 2007, p. 12) is registered in the following seven States who, for the purposes of this analysis, are deemed to be International flag States: Bahamas, Cyprus, Hong Kong, Liberia, Malta, Panama, and Singapore. The great majority of the tonnage registered with these International flag States is owned by nationals of developed nations.

7.5.4 Pseudo-National Flag State

The *Concise Oxford Dictionary* defines the word pseudo as meaning "supposed or purporting to be but not really so"; "false; not genuine", and also as "resembling or imitating". When used as an adjective, "pseudo" is defined as "sham"; "spurious"; and "insincere". It is argued that the term Pseudo-National flag State can be applied to a group of flag States at the opposite end of the registration continuum from most National flag States.

It is also argued that the following elements, additional to those of the Rochdale Report, are necessary for a flag State to be considered as "Pseudo-National". The elements are: that the register is not situated in the territory of the flag State; it is not administered by the flag State but by a private entity; the flag State delegates all statutory functions to the register; the flag State allows delegation and sub-delegation of statutory functions to non-IACS[50] members; the flag State encourages and facilitates incorporation of "brass plate" companies in its territory; and there is no transparency in the ownership and control of ships.

If all or most of these elements exist, in addition to those in the Rochdale Report, the flag can be categorised as "Pseudo-National", or a flag State which is effectively unregulated.[51]

An examination of the promotional information contained on the websites of Pseudo-National flag States reveals common themes of expedience, low cost, lack of transparency, and ease of incorporation of companies in their territory. Paradoxically, it is the improvement in performance, driven largely by the success of port State control regimes since the 1980s, of the original and predominant FOCs of Liberia, Malta, Cyprus, the Bahamas, and, to a certain extent, Panama, that has

---

[50]The International Association of Classification Societies: a group of ten societies which agrees on standards for the classification and survey of ships and represents over 90% of the world's merchant tonnage.

[51]"The regulatory environment within these registers is almost non-existent. The register is privately operated. The link between the shipowner and the flag State is extremely minimal. The ratification rate of ILO and IMO Conventions is low and there exist few, if any, structures or personnel in both the flag State and the register operator that could enforce these effectively; additionally, there is little political will to enforce these Conventions. These registers provide a regulatory-free environment for ship operators to act in a manner of their choosing with little regard for the consequences. Examples of such registers are Cambodia, Equatorial Guinea and Tonga" (ILO 2004, p. 80).

created a vacuum at the very lower end of the flag State market. This has been filled by Pseudo-National flag States offering largely unregulated benefits to shipowners.

A study by the Maritime Transport Committee of the OECD in March 2003 (OECD 2003) focussed upon one of the critical criteria in defining a Pseudo-National register; that of the issue of transparency in the ownership and control of ships in the context of the potential threats to security that could result from a lack of transparency. The paper noted that:

> All ship registers require some form of information on ownership to be provided when application is made for the registration of a ship. …The principal difference between registers is that while some clearly make some effort to establish the true ownership (but may be thwarted by other mechanisms), others advertise anonymity as a desirable attribute of that register. For example an advertisement for the Anguillan ship register (but there are many others) notes that two key features of the register are the non-disclosure of beneficial owners and the availability of bearer shares which greatly assist owners to ensure anonymity. (OECD 2003, p. 7)

A total of 32 flag States have registration requirements identified in the report that could, amongst other advantages to shipowners, facilitate anonymity.[52] The report notes that such "open" registers are the most accommodating States in which to register vessels if the owner is seeking a complex web of ownership arrangements; the "corporate veil" that the owner can hide behind in case of accidents to his vessel or pollution incidents. The ownership arrangements will almost certainly cover a number of international jurisdictions, which would be much more difficult to untangle; one of the essential criteria for a flag State to be deemed Pseudo-National (OECD 2003, p. 3).

At least the following 17 active flag States with ships trading internationally are considered to meet the criteria argued for the category of Pseudo-National flag State: Antigua and Barbuda, Barbados, Belize, Bolivia, Cambodia, Comoros, Cook Islands, Equatorial Guinea, Honduras, Kiribati, Marshall Islands, Mongolia, St Vincent and the Grenadines, Sao Tome and Principe, Tonga, Tuvalu, and Vanuatu.

7.6 Singapore as a Flag State

The influence a State can bring to bear upon the nature and quality of its flag State activities is illustrated by the development of Singapore as a flag State. Very shortly after the Republic of Singapore gained full independence in 1966 the political decision was taken to create a ship register modelled upon that of the United Kingdom, open only to Singapore nationals and locally registered companies; that is, a National

---

[52]*Ibid*, Appendix B, pp. 23–34: Anguilla, Antigua and Barbuda, Bahamas, Barbados, Belize, Bermuda, Bolivia, Cambodia, Cayman Islands, Costa Rica, Cyprus, Republic of Djibouti, Dominica, Gibraltar, Hong Kong, Honduras, Isle of Man, Jamaica, Latvia, Liberia, Madeira, Malta, Marshall Islands, Mauritius, Panama, Seychelles, Singapore, Sri Lanka, St Kitts and Nevis, St Vincent and the Grenadines, Kingdom of Tonga, Vanuatu.

register. This register, established in 1967, had some success in attracting a large number of domestically-owned vessels from the British and Malaysian registers but the total tonnage was not high: "The Singapore fleet increased from 13 ships at the time of the introduction of the registry, to 354 ships, totalling approximately 244,000 gross tons, by the end of 1968" (Tenold 2003, p. 256). Desiring to increase the total registered tonnage in order to save foreign exchange, create employment opportunities, and exert greater control over foreign trade, the government made a conscious decision to transform the register into a flag of convenience model based openly on the Liberian model.[53] The register was thus opened to non-nationals and low costs were established for ship registration to attract foreign shipowners (Tenold 2003, p. 257) A guarantee was given that the low annual tonnage fee, lower than both Liberia and Panama, would not be increased for 20 years from the time of initial registration and no income tax was to be levied on shipowners' profits.

The establishment and growth of the Singapore open registry – which was one leg of the stool of the port, the fleet, and the local shipbuilding and repair industry, was successful in terms of growth with an annual growth rate of 40% in the first 6 years. By 1972 the Singapore fleet had grown to more than one million gross tons, and the five million mark was reached 3 years later (Tenold 2003, p. 259). By 1979 Singapore was the fifteenth largest flag State with its share of the world fleet having increased from 0.1% in 1969 to 1.9% in 1979. The average size of vessels increased from 1,100 GT in 1969[54] to more than 10,000 GT in 1979, of which a high proportion were newly built vessels. In spite of this remarkable growth the Singapore register attracted considerable criticism as a flag of convenience, both within Singapore and from outside, and the government welcomed initiatives from the Marine Department for stricter and better control. The main reason for this change in policy was the stigma associated with being a flag of convenience and measures were introduced to increase transparency of ownership[55] and improve the standard of ships under the Singapore flag. A justification for this change of policy was that one of the original objectives of the flag of convenience, to solve unemployment for Singaporeans, had long been realised through the economic boom of the 1970s.

Two other distinctions highlight the difference between Singapore and other flag of convenience States. Firstly, the income from the register was, relative to Singapore's role as a regional trading centre, proportionately insignificant and, secondly, the

---

[53]"On 23 December 1968, the Singapore Parliament passed the Merchant Shipping (Amendment Bill, paving the way for the establishment of an open registry. The Merchant Shipping (Amendment) Act came into force on 31 January 1969." (Tenold 2003, p. 257)

[54]"According to figures from Lloyd's Register, the average size of the vessels in the Singapore merchant marine increased by approximately 266% from mid-1969 to mid-1979. This can be compared with an increase for the world fleet of less than 38%" (Tenold 2003, p. 262).

[55]"With the introduction of the *Merchant Shipping (Registration of Ships) Regulations* in 1981, registration was limited to Singapore citizens, permanent residents and companies incorporated in Singapore. Moreover, the companies had to provide information on shareholders, directors, board members and capital. Second, the authorities sought to improve the standards of the vessels in the fleet by introducing age restrictions enhancing the modernisation of the fleet." (Tenold 2003, p. 264)

very young age profile of ships on the register differed significantly from the fleets of other FOCs. It was relatively easy for Singapore to tighten age requirements as a large proportion of its ships, and particularly the larger foreign-owned ships, were relatively young. The focus upon improving the overall quality of the fleet was upon the two-thirds of vessels that were domestically owned, relatively small, and trading regionally. It was thus easy for the administration to focus upon these vessels without disadvantaging the larger vessels on the register. This change in policy from a completely open FOC to an International register has not disadvantaged the Singapore register, which has enjoyed continuing growth, and in 2007, as the worlds fourth largest flag State, comprised 2,257 vessels with a total 36.3 million gross tons (Lloyd's Register of Shipping, World Fleet Statistics 2007, p. 12), two-thirds of which is still domestically-owned small vessels trading regionally. The register, which defines itself as a "quality register", is actively promoted as a device to attract business to Singapore and accordingly, companies registering their ships are required to have an office and a presence in Singapore. Applications for registration are vetted by a quality committee and the administration employs five flag State inspectors to carry out inspections aboard approximately 25% of their 1,200 larger internationally-trading vessels per annum. Statutory survey and certification functions are only delegated to International Association of Classification Society (IACS) members.[56] In summary, after 10 years as a completely open register, "the authorities found the benefits of the arrangement less weighty than the odium associated with being seen as a Flag of convenience" (Fairplay 2006, p. 256) and Singapore had used political expediency to cover the full gamut of ship registration arrangements over the relatively brief period from 1967 to 1979.

7.7 Categories of Recognized Organization

It is not possible to consider flag State responsibilities without also considering the role and performance of the Recognized Organizations (RO) that, in the majority of cases, implement many of the technical, but increasingly administrative, operational, and social, duties of flag States. Flag States have the ability under the SOLAS, MARPOL, Load Line, and Tonnage Conventions to entrust their survey, inspection and certification functions to ROs in accordance with the guidelines[57] provided in IMO resolutions, which have mandatory effect through the SOLAS Convention

---

[56]From discussion with Chandru Sirumal Rajwani, Assistant Director, Registry and Manning of Ships, Shipping Division, Singapore Maritime and Port Authority, at Geneva, 7 February 2006. One IACS member that Singapore does not delegate statutory functions to is the Russian Register.
[57]IMO Resolution A.739(18), Guidelines for the Authorisation of Organizations acting on behalf of the Administration, adopted 4 November 1993; and A.789(19), Specifications on the Survey and Certification functions of recognised Organizations acting on behalf of the Administration, adopted 23 November 1995.

(regulation I/6). Although the RO then exercises control in these matters over ships registered in that State, the flag State retains responsibility for "taking necessary measures to ensure that ships flying their State's flags comply with the provisions of such Conventions, including surveys and certification" (SOLAS I/6, Preamble), and for the reporting that is required under various instruments to the IMO. The flag State is also required to monitor the activities of the RO to ensure that they are effective (IMO Resolution A.739(18), para. 3).

The effectiveness of the control exercised by the RO on behalf of the flag State depends upon that organisation meeting the standards laid down in the IMO Resolutions A.739(18) and A.789(19). Effective verification and monitoring by the flag State through audits of ROs, and independent flag State inspections of ships flying its flag, are also required. In order to analyse and measure the performance of ROs it is necessary to determine who they are and what categories they might fall into.

Member States of IMO have been requested to provide details of the organisations they have recognised to carry out survey, inspection, and certification functions, to the IMO for inclusion on the newly established GISIS[58] database in order that port State control officers have a means of verifying the information they are presented with aboard ships. Analysis of information available to Member States on the IMO website[59] reveals that IMO has been notified of a total of 86 individual ROs, nine of which have not received delegated authority from any flag State, as listed in Table A.3, Appendix A.

Not all flag States notify the IMO of this information. Records of inspections of ships by the Tokyo and Paris MOU and the USCG on port State control identify a further 17 ROs from evidence obtained directly from ships during port State control inspections (Tokyo MOU Annual Report 2005; Paris MOU Annual Report 2004; USCG Annual Report 2004). There is, therefore, firm evidence of the existence of at least[60] 103 ROs, all of which fall clearly into two categories.

The ten members and three associate members of the International Association of Classification Societies (IACS)[61] with well-established and uniform standards, systems, and procedures, and consultative status at the IMO since 1969, could justifiably be categorised as Conventional ROs. At least 90 other non-IACS Classification Societies and survey organisations, which scramble in the margins in an attempt to represent the 5–8% of world tonnage not covered by IACS members,

---

[58]Global Integrated Ship Information System.

[59]The IMO GISIS database records information provided by flag States, as required by resolution A.739(18)(4) and MSC/Circ.1010/MEPC/Circ.382 of 10 July 2001. Not all flag States provide this information. http://gisis.imo.org/Public

[60]An analysis of Recognized Organization records in the database of the Tokyo MOU from January 2004 to September 2005, (Fourteenth Meeting of the Regional Database Managers, paper DBM14/WP.3 dated 4 November 2005), revealed a large number of other recognized organizations that fell outside the PSC coding system for known recognised organisations.

[61]IACS abandoned the concept of Associate Membership in 2006.

and have no uniformity, consistency of standards, or common policies, could be categorised as Convenient ROs and be assimilated to flags of convenience. For the purpose of this analysis of flag State control it is not necessary to list all of these Recognized Organizations[62] but it is necessary to identify whether the RO is either Conventional or Convenient. This identification is also necessary to establish whether there is a causal link between the flag State/RO association and the safety performance of ships administered by that alliance.[63]

References

Abrahamsson BJ (1980) International Ocean Shipping: Current Concepts and Principles. Westview Press, Colorado

Ademuni-Odeke (1997) Evolution and Development of Ship Registration. Il Diritto Marittomo, Italy

Ademuni-Odeke (1998) Bareboat Charter (Ship) Registration. Martinus Nijhoff Publishers, The Netherlands

Akehurst M (1987) A Modern Introduction to International Law, 6th edn. Unwin Hyman Ltd, London

Alderton T, Winchester N (2001) Globalisation and de-regulation in the maritime industry. Marine Policy. Vol 26, Issue 1

Bergantino A, Marlow P (1998) Factors affecting the choice of flag: empirical evidence. Maritime Policy and Management. Vol 25, Issue 2

Bergantino A, Marlow P (1999) An Econometric Analysis of the Decision to Flag Out. SIRC, Cardiff

Boczek BA (1962) Flags of convenience: An International legal Study. Harvard University Press, Cambridge, MA

Carlisle R (1981) Sovereignty for Sale: The Origins and Evolution of the Panamanian and Liberian Flags. Naval Institute Press, Annapolis

Couper A, ed (1992) Bentley, Ship Registers and the Use of Flags, in The Shipping Revolution. Conway Maritime Press, London

Hoffman J, Sanchez R, and Talley W., Determinants of vessel flag. http://www.oduport.org/ PaperCullinaneBookForeignFlagDRAFT2003–10–31.htm

International Labour Organization (2004) The Global Seafarer: Living and working conditions in a globalised industry. Geneva

International Transport Workers' Foundation (2004) Campaign against flags of convenience and substandard shipping. Annual Report, Foreword.

Klikauer T, Morris R (2002) Into Murky Waters: Globalisation and Deregulation in Germany's shipping employee relations. Employee Relations. Vol 24, No 1

Li KX, Wonham J (1999) Registration of Vessels. The International Journal of Marine and Coastal Law. Vol 14, No 1

Lloyd's Register of Shipping – Fairplay (2007) World Fleet Statistics

Lloyd's Register of Shipping – Fairplay (2006) 9 March

---

[62]A full list of all Recognized Organizations on the IMO GISIS database is contained in Table 7.3, Appendix I.

[63]See Chap. 10 for detailed analysis of the performance of Convenient and Conventional ROs.

Metaxas BN, Doganis RS (1976) The Impact of Flags of convenience. Polytechnic of Central London and Ealing Technical College, London

Montero Llacer F (2003) Open Registers, past, present and future. Marine Policy. Issue 6

Paris MOU (2004) Changing Course. Annual Report

Registration of Vessels (1999) Current Legal Developments. The International Journal of Marine and Coastal Law, Vol 14, No 1. Kluwer Law International

Rochdale, Lord (1970) Report of the Committee of Inquiry into Shipping. HMSO, London.

Tenold S (2003) A most convenient flag: The basis for the expansion of the Singapore fleet, 1969–82. Maritime Policy and Management. Vol 30, No 3

Thanopolous H (1998) What price the flag? The terms of competitiveness in shipping. Marine Policy. Vol 22, No 4

Tokyo MOU (2005) Annual Report on Port State Control in the Asia/Pacific Region

UNCTAD Secretariat (2005) Review of Maritime Transport. United Nations, Geneva

United Nations (1985) The History of UNCTAD (1964–84). New York

United States Coast Guard (2004) Port State Control in the United States. Annual Report. Department of Homeland Security, United States.

World Summit on Sustainable Development (2002) More Troubled Waters, Fishing, Pollution and FOCs: Major Group Submission to the 2002 World Summit on Sustainable Development in Johannesburg, by ICFTU, OECD, ITF and Greenpeace.

Vorbach JE (2001) The Vital Role of Non-Flag State Actors in the Pursuit of Safer Shipping. Ocean Development and International Law, 32:27–42

Documents

IMO (1993) Resolution A.739(18) Guidelines for the Authorization of Organizations acting on behalf of the Administration, adopted 4 November.

IMO Resolution A.789(19), Procedures for Port State Control, as amended by Resoltuion 882(21), adopted 23 November 1995

Tokyo MOU (2004) Fourteenth Meeting of the Regional Database Managers. Paper DBM14WP.4, Bangkok

Chapter 8
The Regulatory Regime for Discharge of Flag State Duties: The Role of Classification Societies

Abstract The two principal actors on the stage of worldwide standards for ships are the International Maritime Organization (IMO) and Classification Societies (Class). Their roles are inextricably entwined and are reflected in the regulatory regime that has evolved over the last two centuries. Flag State issues associated with the creation of an international body to represent shipping, the Intergovernmental Maritime Consultative Organization (IMCO)[1], are recalled. The role of Class in the safety of ships, both historical and topical, and their relationship with the IMO and flag States, is identified as a leading and contentious issue, as is the conflict arising from their private and public roles. The regulatory regime involving Classification Societies, which was codified by the IMO for flag State jurisdiction and control, is analysed to identify issues arising from that framework. The role of the port State, and the development of multilateral port State control initiatives to address the shortcomings of flag State control, is discussed. The evolving concerns of the IMO regarding flag State jurisdiction and the measures they have taken to address these concerns are summarised and analysed. The starting point is to recall development of the two UN agencies that oversee maritime safety and working and living conditions for seafarers, the IMO and ILO, and the commonality of membership of the these organisations and with the UN.

8.1 Member States of International Organisations

When considering flag State responsibility and performance in general it is useful to also consider nation States and their membership of the United Nations (UN) and associated agencies such as the International Maritime Organization (IMO) and the International Labour Organization (ILO), with particular regard to the

---

[1] The Intergovernmental Maritime Consultative Organization's title was changed by an amendment to the Convention on the Intergovernmental Maritime Consultative Organization, 1948, in 1982. Under this amendment the Organization became known as the International Maritime Organization from 22 May 1982. *See* IMCO Res. A.358 (IX) (1975), as amended by IMCO Res. (X) (1977). Unless otherwise stated, the IMO Convention is quoted in the version amended by these Resolutions and the term IMO or the Organization is used throughout this chapter.

J.N.K. Mansell, *Flag State Responsibility,*
DOI: 10.1007/978-3-540-92933-8_8, © Springer-Verlag Berlin Heidelberg 2009

commonality and concurrent growth of membership of these organisations and the involvement of States in their capacity as flag States.

8.1.1   The UN and IMO

When the UN arose from the ashes of the Second World War in 1945 there were 51 original member States[2] This was at a time when the administration of world shipping was dominated by traditional maritime nations with long established maritime administrations. The majority of these nations were founding members of the UN. At the time of adoption of the IMCO Convention, which established an international body for the regulation of ships in 1948, a further seven States[3] had become members of the UN. Over the period between 1948 and 1958, during which gradual acceptance by States of the IMCO Convention brought this instrument into force, a further 25 States[4] joined the UN, including the flag States of Finland, Ireland, Italy, Spain, Japan, and Malaysia, bringing the total membership of the UN to 82.

The IMCO Convention provided that Member States of the UN have automatic membership of the IMCO.[5] If a State is not a UN member it must receive support from two-thirds of Member States of IMCO to become a Member State of IMCO.[6] The original membership of the IMCO, when the IMCO Convention attracted enough support with ratification by Egypt to enter into force in 1958, was made

---

[2] Argentina, Australia, Belgium, Bolivia, Brazil, Belarus, Canada, Chile, China, Colombia, Costa Rica, Cuba, Czechoslovakia, Denmark, Dominican Republic, Ecuador, Egypt, El Salvador, Ethiopia, France, Greece, Guatemala, Haiti, Honduras, India, Iran, Iraq, Lebanon, Liberia, Luxembourg, Mexico, Netherlands, New Zealand, Nicaragua, Norway, Panama, Paraguay, Peru, Philippines, Poland, Russian Federation, Saudi Arabia, South Africa, Syrian Arab Republic, Turkey, Ukraine, United Kingdom of Great Britain and Northern Ireland, United States of America, Uruguay, Bolivarian Republic of Venezuela, Yugoslavia. http://www.un.org/Overview/growth.htm

[3] Afghanistan, Iceland, Sweden, Thailand, Pakistan, Yemen, Myanmar.

[4] Israel, Indonesia, Albania, Austria, Bulgaria, Cambodia, Finland, Hungary, Ireland, Italy, Jordan, Laos (People's Democratic Republic), Libya, Nepal, Portugal, Romania, Spain, Sri Lanka, Japan, Morocco, Sudan, Tunisia, Ghana, Malaysia, Guinea. http://www.un.org/.

[5] "Members of the United Nations may become Members of the Organization by becoming parties to the Convention in accordance with the provisions of Article 57". IMCO Convention, Article 6.

[6] "States not members of the United Nations which have been invited to send representatives to the United Nations Maritime Conference convened in Geneva on 19 February 1948, may become Members by becoming parties to the Convention in accordance with the provisions of Article 57". *Ibid*, Article 7; "Any State not entitled to become a Member under Article 6 or 7 may apply through the Secretary-General of the Organization to become a member and shall be admitted as a Member upon its becoming party to the Convention in accordance with the provisions of Article 57 provided that, upon recommendation of the Council, its application has been approved by two-thirds of the members other than Associate members." *Ibid*, Article 8.

up of States all of which, with the exception of Switzerland,[7] were Member States of the UN.[8] A further 15 States, of which the majority were traditional maritime nations, came aboard the IMCO later in 1958 and in 1959, the year of the IMCO's first Assembly.[9]

The growth of both IMCO and the UN in the period from the establishment of IMCO, and the first United Nations Conference on Law of the Sea (UNCLOS I) in 1958, until the third United Nations Conference on the Law of the Sea (UNCLOS III) a quarter of a century later in 1973, was very similar. Their growth reflected the emergence of many newly independent States in the post-colonisation period following the Second World War.[10] Many of these States became flag States during this period. At the present day (2008) there are 192 member States of the UN (http://www. un.org/), and 168 member States[11] of the IMO plus three Associate members.[12] Not all IMO Member States are flag States and, conversely, not all flag States are members of the IMO. An analysis of the annual reports of inspections carried out by the Paris and Tokyo MOUs on port State Control, and the USCG, along with information from the IMO[13] and the ILO (ILO 2006, Appendix B, pp. 75–79) indicate that there are currently at least 160 active flag States with ships trading internationally.[14]

8.1.2   The UN and ILO

The other United Nations agency that historically had, and continues to have, a leading role in setting international standards for working, living, and welfare conditions for seafarers is the International Labour Organization (ILO), which emerged in 1919

---

[7] Switzerland became the 191st Member State of the UN in 2002. http://www.un.org/.

[8] Original Member States of the IMCO were: Argentina, Australia, Belgium, Canada, Dominican Republic, Ecuador, Egypt, France, Haiti, Honduras, Ireland, Israel, Italy, Mexico, Myanmar, Netherlands, Switzerland, United Kingdom, and United States of America

[9] *Ibid*, Denmark, Finland, Germany, Ghana, Greece, India, Iran, Japan, Liberia, Norway, Pakistan, Panama, Russian Federation, Sweden and Turkey.

[10] The membership of the UN increased by 52 States between 1958 and 1973. http://www.un.org/ overview/growth.htm/. 60 States became members of IMO between 1958 and 1973. http://www. imo.org/About/mainframe.asp?topic_id = 315&doc_id = 840.

[11] The Cook Islands became the 168th Member State of the IMO in July 2008.

[12] Associate members are Hong Kong, China; Macao, China; and the Faroe Islands, Denmark. http://imo.org/.

[13] IMO Member States with year of joining, IMO website at: http://www.imo.org/About/mainframe. asp?topic_id = 315&doc_id = 840.

[14] Lloyd's Register – Fairplay, World Fleet Statistics 2005, pp. 21–27, lists 181 countries of registration for "the propelled sea-going merchant fleet of 100 GT and above. Many of these countries have very small numbers of ships registered and very small total tonnages such as Benin, 6 ships totalling 1,003 GT, Grenada, 11 ships totalling 2,821 GT, Haiti, 5 ships totalling 1,286 GT, Macao, 2 ships totalling 2,321 GT, Djibouti, 14 ships totalling 4,847 GT, Aruba, 2 ships totalling 400 GT, Slovenia, 5 ships totalling 1,130 GT, St Helena, 2 ships totalling 1,818 GT, Anguilla, 3 ships totalling 701 GT, Turks and Caicos Islands, 5 ships totalling 975 GT".

from the peace process at the end of the First World War. Over the remainder of the twentieth century the ILO adopted 40 Maritime Labour Conventions and 29 Recommendations for SOLAS ships, on matters such as recruitment and placement of seafarers and their minimum age. The recommendations also covered hours of work, health and safety, welfare, repatriation, social security and labour inspection for seafarers aboard merchant vessels trading internationally.[15] The extent of ratification of these instruments is a measure of the responsibility a State takes for the social administration of ships flying its flag under article 94 of the LOSC.[16]

The great majority of these Conventions and Recommendations have been consolidated into the Maritime Labour Convention (MLC), adopted in Geneva in February 2006. There was unanimous support from the 106 Member States present for adoption of this groundbreaking convention and it is to be hoped that a sufficient number of these States will ratify the Convention to ensure its early entry into force.[17] The Maritime Labour Convention 2006, provides for port State control and for the "no more favourable treatment" principles of its sister Conventions: SOLAS, STCW, and MARPOL. This provision of port State control did not exist in most of the many instruments it replaces.[18] There are currently 192 Member States of ILO; all of whom, except one,[19] are Member States of the UN. Almost all of the 168 Member States of the IMO are also Member States of the ILO with the exceptions of Brunei Darussalam, the Maldives, the Marshall Islands, Monaco, the Republic of Moldova, Tonga, Tuvalu, and the Union of Comoros. The IMO and ILO work closely together and have joint working groups on a range of matters of mutual interest.[20]

---

[15] International Labour Organization Office (2006) Adoption of an instrument to consolidate maritime labour standards. Report I(1A), International Maritime Labour Conference, 94th Maritime Session. p. 4.

[16] This measure of flag State performance is analysed in Chap. 9.

[17] The Maritime Labour Convention 2006 enters into force 12 months after the date on which there have been registered ratifications by at least 30 Members with a total share in the world gross tonnage of ships of 33%. Liberia was the first Member State to ratify the MLC in June 2006. As at September 2008 the Marshall Islands and the Bahamas had also ratified the MLC 2006 (http://www.ilo.org/global/lang-en/index.htm, September 2008). These three large flag States collectively represent 20% of total world tonnage as at 31 December 2007. (Lloyd's Register – *Fairplay, World Fleet Statistics 2007* p. 12)

[18] The Merchant Shipping (Mininum Standards) Convention, 1976 (ILO 147) and the protocol of 1996 are mandatory instruments under the Paris and Tokyo MOUs on port State control.

[19] The Republic of Moldova. http://www.ilo.org/public/english/standards/relm/country.htm.

[20] For example: the Joint IMO/ILO Ad Hoc Expert Working Group on the Fair Treatment of Seafarers in the Event of a Maritime Accident; the Joint IMO/ILO/BG Working Group on Ship Scrapping; the Joint IMO/ILO Ad Hoc Expert Working Group on Liability and Compensation regarding Claims for Death, Personal Injury and Abandonment of Seafarers; the UNEP/IItalyMO/ILO International programme on Chemical Safety; and the Joint ILO/IMO Working Group on Port Security.

8.2 An International Maritime Organization

The concept of a permanent international body to implement and oversee uniform international standards for the safety of ships has been discussed since the nineteenth century. An International Maritime Conference held in Washington in 1889 recommended the creation of such a body but the concept was not considered expedient and the idea was rejected (IMO 1998, p. 1). The implicit reason was that the shipping industry of the day would not countenance the restriction of its activities and commercial freedom, which, it was perceived, could result from the mandated activities of an international regulatory organisation.

This view was to linger well into the twentieth century and cause protracted delays in the ratification of the founding instrument for the eventual international body, the IMCO Convention. Regardless of the absence of a single international body to oversee maritime safety, the dual drivers of shipping disasters and cooperation amongst maritime States had ensured that a number of important Conventions relating to the safety of ships, tonnage measurement, signalling, and prevention of collisions had been adopted in the first half of the twentieth century.[21] However, these Conventions were not widely accepted or implemented by all maritime countries with the result that international standards were not uniformly applied and could even be contradictory (IMO 2003, paper J/8351, p. 2).

Even before cessation of hostilities in 1945 the idealists who were to establish the UN to ensure there would never again be global warfare, were planning the creation of separate UN organisations that could deal with various matters, both humanitarian and technical.[22] Discussions at this time on the formation of the UN included the concept of an international organisation for shipping; the need for which was taken as self-evident as there was no discussion as to whether or not the cooperation that could be gained would be suitable and useful (IMO 1998, p. 1–2). The modern foundations of organised international cooperation in standards for the safety of shipping were laid during the Second World War when ten of the Allies[23] formed the United Maritime Authority in 1944. This body continued its work immediately after the war as the United Maritime Consultative Council (Lampe 1983, p. 311).

---

[21] The Unification of Certain Rules of Law with respect to Collisions between Vessels. Brussels, 23 September 1910; International Convention on the Safety of life at Sea. London, 31 May 1929; International Convention Respecting Load Lines. London, 5 July 1930; and the Convention Relating to the Tonnage Measurement of Merchant Ships. Warsaw, 1934.

[22] Focus on IMO: IMO 1948–1998: a process of change. International Maritime Organization, London, September 1998, pp. 1–2. The Civil Aviation Organization (ICAO) was founded only 41 years after the first powered flight by the Wright Brothers, in 1944. The Food and Agriculture Organization (FAO) was founded in 1945, and both the United Nations Educational, Scientific and Cultural Organization (UNESCO) and the World Health Organization (WHO) in 1947.

[23] "The original members were Belgium, Canada, France (Exile Government), Greece, the Netherlands, Norway, Poland, the United Kingdom, and the United States of America. In 1946, the following countries joined the group: Australia, Brazil, Chile, India, Yugoslavia, New Zealand, Sweden, and South Africa." (Lampe 1983, p. 311)

Eventually, in February 1948, a conference in Geneva resulted in the adoption of the
Convention on the Intergovernmental Maritime Consultative Organization 1948 and
the Intergovernmental Maritime Consultative Organization (IMCO) was conceived.
However due to the wording of its principal articles IMCO was to experience a very
long and difficult gestation.

8.2.1 Issues of IMCO Mandate

The aims of IMCO, captured in Article 1[24] of the IMCO Convention, made no
reference to marine pollution[25] and only a passing reference to safety. A dominant
emphasis in the IMCO Convention was upon economic action for the promotion of
"freedom" and to "end discrimination", which, along with references to a "world
without discrimination" and action against "unfair restrictive practices" caused a
number of States to enter reservation[26] when they signed the Convention.

Article 2 of the IMCO Convention, which dealt with the functions of the
Organization, limited it to a consultative and advisory role. Further, Article 3, in
stating that the Organization should "provide for the drafting of conventions,
agreements, or other suitable instruments, and to recommend these to Governments
and to international organisations, and to convene such conferences as may be

---

[24]IMCO Convention, Article 1: (a) To provide machinery for co-operation among Governments
in the field of governmental regulation and practices relating to technical matters of all kinds
affecting shipping engaged in international trade, and to encourage the general adoption of the
highest practical standards in matters concerning maritime safety and efficiency of navigation; (b)
To encourage the removal of discriminatory action and unnecessary restrictions by Governments
affecting shipping engaged in international trade so as to promote the availability of shipping
services to the commerce of the world without discrimination; assistance and encouragement
given by a Government for the development of its national shipping and for the purposes of
security does not in itself constitute discrimination, provided that such assistance and encouragement
is not based on measures designed to restrict the freedom of shipping of all flags to take part in
international trade; (c) To provide for the consideration by the Organization of matters concerning
unfair restrictive practices by shipping concerns in accordance with Part II; (d) To provide for the
consideration by the Organization of any matters concerning shipping that may be referred to it
by any organ or specialised agency of the United Nations; (e) To provide for the exchange of
information among Governments on matters under consideration by the Organization.
[25]Article I (a) of the IMCO Convention was amended by Res. A.358 (IX) in 1975 to add the words
"and the prevention and control of marine pollution from ships; and to deal with legal matters
related to the purposes set out in this Article".
[26]"It was no coincidence that all the Scandinavian countries made a statement – and an unusually
strong one – to the effect that they would consider a renunciation of the Convention if IMCO were
to assume competence in matters of the kind mentioned in Articles 1(b) and (c). The Scandinavian
countries (led by Norway), as well as Greece, have always been strong supporters of the principle
of the freedom of international shipping, which according to their philosophy, should be upheld
through virtually unrestricted maritime shipping regulated by nothing but free and fair competition." (Lampe 1983, p. 312)

necessary" made it clear that IMCO did not have the authority to adopt or amend treaties.[27] This restrictive mandate, and a focus upon matters of trade and discrimination rather than safety, was compounded by Article 4 which placed IMCO in the role of mediator in matters of "restrictive practices by shipping concerns".[28]

The focus in Article 1 of the IMCO Convention upon matters unrelated to the safety of ships or protection of the marine environment caused a great deal of suspicion in the maritime community about the role of the new Organization and resulted in very slow entry into force of the IMCO Convention (IMO 1998, p. 4). There was a prevailing belief amongst many potential members of the Organization that the Convention was constructed largely for the benefit of the dominant shipping nations of the time (IMO 1998, p. 4). Many of the 18 States[29] that did ratify the Convention during the 1950s registered declarations or reservations[30] that resulted in a very limited scope for the Organization when the IMCO Convention finally received the necessary number of ratifications to enter into force in 1958; 10 years after its adoption.[31] It was, therefore, very clear from the large number of reservations that had been submitted that, when the Organization commenced its work in January 1959, economic and commercial matters were not part of its mandate.

8.2.2   IMCO, Flag States, and Issues of Governance

IMCO soon became embroiled in a dispute over the status of traditional flag States vs. newly emergent "flags of convenience". A decision was made at the First Assembly of IMCO in January 1959 that the Organization would be funded by a

---

[27] Focus on IMO: IMO 1948–1998: a process of change. International Maritime Organization, London, September 1998, p. 2. It is necessary for the IMO to convene a Diplomatic Conference in order to formally adopt or amend a draft Convention that has been approved by the Council and Assembly. Invitations to such conferences are sent to all member States of the Organization and also to all member States of the United Nations or any of its specialised agencies.

[28] IMCO Convention, Article IV: "When, in the opinion of the Organization, any matter concerning unfair restrictive practices by shipping concerns is incapable of settlement through the normal processes of international shipping business, or has in fact so proved, and provided it shall first have been the subject of direct negotiations between the Members concerned, the Organization shall, at the request of those Members, consider the matter."

[29] Argentina, Australia, Belgium, Canada, Dominican Republic, Ecuador, Egypt, France, Haiti, Honduras, Ireland, Italy, Mexico, Myanmar, Netherlands, Switzerland, United Kingdom, United States of America. http://www.imo.org/About/mainframe.asp?topic_id = 315&doc_id = 840.

[30] "Several used identical wording stating that 'it is in the field of technical and nautical matters that the Organization can make its contribution towards the development of shipping and seaborne trade throughout the world. If the Organization were to extend its activities to matters of a purely commercial or economic nature, a situation might arise where the Government (of the country concerned) would have to consider resorting to the provisions regarding withdrawal'." Focus on IMO: IMO 1948–1998: a process of change. International Maritime Organization, London, September 1998, p. 4

[31] Ibid, p. 5. The IMCO Convention entered into force on 17 March 1958 when Egypt became the 19th State to accept the Convention.

combination of a capped percentage of each Member State's contribution to the UN, plus an additional amount based upon the total gross tonnage of the vessels registered in the Member State (IMO 1998, p. 5). This latter levy, and its implications under the IMCO Convention for membership of the Organization's main decision-making bodies, caused teething pains amongst the IMCO's founding member States, and demonstrated the early and pervasive influence of non-traditional flag States in the Organization.

The original IMCO Convention provided *inter alia* that the Organization's main committee, the Maritime Safety Committee, should consist of 14 members elected by the Assembly from the members and Governments of those nations having an important interest in maritime safety, of which not less than eight were required to be the largest ship-owning nations.[32] Another provision of the Convention was that the Organization's governing body, the Council, should *inter alia* consist of 16 members, six of whom were required to be governments of the nations with the largest interest in providing international shipping services.[33]

The wording of the Convention had, therefore, the effect of allowing membership of the Council of the Organization and the Maritime Safety Committee to be made up of Member States with similar interests in shipping and trade; the traditional maritime States owning the largest merchant fleets. Liberia and Panama, as perceived flags of conveniences were not deemed to be shipowning countries even though, at the time, they ranked third and eighth respectively in world tonnage (Lampe 1983, p. 315).

Panama and Liberia believed that they had exercised their sovereignty in registering ships in accordance with their national law and could therefore be deemed to be ship-owning countries; a view supported by the USA whose shipowners made up the majority of the ships on both the Panamanian and Liberian registers (Lampe 1983, p. 316). The majority of other IMCO Member States took the opposing view that "flags of convenience" could not claim to be shipowning nations under international law as there was no genuine link between the shipowner and the flag State as required by the newly adopted High Seas Convention,[34] a requirement that they deemed necessary to establish nationality.

As the matter could not be resolved at the first IMCO Assembly in January 1959 it was referred to the International Court of Justice (ICJ) for an advisory opinion.[35] The ICJ reformulated the question as: "Has the Assembly, in not electing Liberia and

---

[32]IMCO Convention, Article 28 (a). In force until 1968.

[33]*Ibid*, Article 17 (a). In force until 1967.

[34]Convention on the High Seas, Geneva, 29 April 1958, Article 5(1): "… there must exist a genuine link between the State and the ship"

[35]ICJ, Constitution of the Maritime Safety Committee, Intergovernmental Maritime Consultative Organization, 1960. I.C.J 150, Communique No 60/15, June 8 1960. For further information see International Organizations, Spring 1960 (Vol 14, No2) p. 329.

Panama to the Maritime Safety Committee, exercised its electoral power in a manner in accordance with the provisions of Article 28(a) of the IMCO Convention?"[36] In a majority decision[37] supporting Panama and Liberia, the Court decided that the term "registered tonnage" could not be applied in different ways depending on the context (Lampe 1983, p. 316). Panama and Liberia were thus, due to their burgeoning and predominant roles as flag States, assured of long-term seats on the Maritime Safety Committee and the Council, and their status in the Organization was given equal weight to that of the traditional maritime nations.

Considerable efforts were made by the Member States of IMCO over the next two decades to both update and introduce instruments for maritime safety, prevention of marine pollution, and a number of other matters, with the major safety Conventions achieving almost universal acceptance.[38] A total of 21 Conventions were adopted between 1960 and 1980, the great majority of which have entered into force.[39] One, the International Convention for the Prevention of Pollution of the Sea by Oil (OILPOL) 1954, was adopted during the period when the IMCO Convention was awaiting sufficient ratifications. However, by the 1980s, there was growing concern as to the effectiveness of the implementation and enforcement of these instruments

---

[36]*Ibid.* "The court has to give an 'advisory opinion' in accordance with Article 96 of the Charter of the United Nations. The Assembly acted in accordance with Article 56 of the IMCO Convention, according to which the ICJ should decide upon legal points in the interpretation and application of the provisions of the IMCO Convention." See IMCO Res.A.12(1) (1959) First Assembly Resolutions, London, 1959.

[37]In coming to this decision the Court took into account repeated use of the term "registered tonnage" as the criteria for matters such as the entry into force of Convention amendments and as a basis for apportionment of member State contributions to IMCO.

[38]IMO document MSC84/INF.13 Percentages as at 29 February 2008 were: SOLAS 74, 98.8%; Load Line 66, 98.77%; STCW 78, 98.77%; Tonnage 69, 98.80%; COLREG 72, 98.05%.

[39]International Convention for the Safety of Life at Sea (SOLAS) 1960; Convention on Facilitation of International Maritime Traffic (FAL) 1965; International Convention on Load Lines (LL) 1966; International Convention Relating to Intervention on the High Seas in Cases of Oil Pollution casualties (INTERVENTION) 1969; International Convention on Civil Liability for Oil Pollution Damage (CLC) 1969; International Convention on Tonnage Measurement of Ships (TONNAGE) 1969; Special Trade Passenger Ships Agreement (STP) 1971; Convention Relating to Civil Liability in the Field of Maritime Carriage of Nuclear Material (NUCLEAR) 1971; International Convention on the Establishment of an International Fund for Compensation for Oil Pollution Damage (FUND) 1971; International Convention for Safe Containers (CSC) 1972; Convention on the International Regulations for Preventing Collisions at Sea (COLREG) 1972; Convention on the Prevention of Marine Pollution by Dumping of Wastes and Other Matter (LC) 1972; International Convention for the Prevention of Pollution from Ships, 1973, as modified by the Protocol of 1978 (MARPOL 73/78); Athens Convention Relating to the Carriage of Passengers and their Luggage by Sea (PAL) 1974; International Convention for the Safety of Life at Sea (SOLAS) 1974; Convention on the International Maritime Satellite Organization, 1976; Torremolinos International Convention for the Safety of Fishing Vessels (SFV) 1977; International Convention on Standards of Training, Certification and Watchkeeping for Seafarers (STCW) 1978; International Convention on Maritime Search and Rescue (SAR) 1979.

by flag States; concerns exacerbated by a succession of major maritime disasters: *Herald of Free Enterprise* (1987),[40] *Dona Paz* (1987),[41] *Exxon Valdez* (1989),[42] and *Scandinavian Star* (1990).[43]

During this same period one of the principal actors on the world maritime stage, Class, was itself undergoing a crisis of credibility and confidence. Owing to the regulatory framework that has evolved and been codified for flag State jurisdiction and control, Class and the IMO are closely associated. It is therefore necessary to explain the role and functions of Class within this framework, with particular attention being paid to the authority Class can obtain from a flag State to carry out statutory functions on its behalf, and associated issues.

8.3   A Matter of Class

To understand how the historic role of Classification Societies (Class) has evolved to its present multifaceted role it is necessary to go back to the beginnings of Class and trace its development to the present day. Class evolved out of a need for merchant shipowners to be able to provide evidence to their insurers and charterers that their ship had been built to a suitable standard. The first society was that of Lloyd's, named after the London coffee house where merchants, marine underwriters and others connected with shipping gathered from the late seventeenth century.[44] The owner of this establishment, Edward Lloyd, published a printed news-sheet, *Lloyd's News*, with information on foreign and war news, trials, executions, parliamentary proceedings, and marine news and gossip (Bell 1995, p. 2). After Lloyd's death in 1713 the business was carried on by relatives who founded *Lloyd's List* in 1734 with a focus upon shipping news, much of which was gathered from correspondents, Lloyd's Agents, around the world (Bell 1995, p. 2). In 1760 a Register Society was incorporated, and by 1764 a Register of Ships was published to give information on the condition of ships to merchants and marine underwriters (Lloyd's Register: A Brief History).

Issues of the secrecy of classification information soon became evident. The ratings provided by Classification Societies became an essential tool for

---

[40] The British-registered ro-ro passenger ferry *Herald of Free Enterprise* capsized off Zeebruge harbour in 1988 with the loss of 198 lives.

[41] The Philippines-registered passenger ferry *Dona Paz*, trading internally in the Philippines archipelago, caught fire and sank after a collision with a small tanker. It is estimated that 4300 persons were lost.

[42] The American-registered oil tanker *Exxon Valdez* grounded in Alaska and spilt 37,000 tons of oil.

[43] The Bahamas-registered ro-ro passenger ferry *Scandinavian Star* caught fire in the Baltic in 1990 with the loss of 160 lives.

[44] Edward Lloyd established a coffee house in Tower Street, London, in 1689. Bell JD, The Role of Classification in Maritime Safety. 9th Chua Chor Teck Annual Memorial Lecture, Singapore, 13 January 1995, IMO Library.

underwriters but were not popular with shipowners and shipbuilders as they discriminated against certain shipbuilding areas and the information was confidential to insurers (Lloyd's Register: A Brief History, p. 365). As a direct result of a Lloyd's Register publication in 1797, which discriminated against any ship not built on the Thames, shipowners formed their own register.[45] This enterprise did not prove successful in the long term and it merged with Lloyd's Register in 1834 as the Lloyd's Register of British and Foreign Shipping (Lloyd's Register: A Brief History). The new organisation, which included merchants, shipowners, and underwriters, published rules at this time for the survey and classification of ships – hence, 'Classification Society' or 'Class'.[46]

8.3.1   Growth of Class

During the early nineteenth century the size and complexity of ships increased rapidly, particularly with the advent of steam propulsion. There were also heavy losses of ships at this time and, with an associated requirement from insurers for standards of construction of these ships, the Class concept proliferated internationally. A critical time for Lloyd's was the winter of 1821, during which 2,000 ships and 20,000 seafarers were lost and several French marine insurance companies were bankrupted (Boisson 1994, p. 365) This cast doubt upon the effectiveness of Lloyd's rating system resulting in the formation in 1829 of a French Classification Society, Bureau Veritas (BV).[47] Other Classification Societies, including the American Bureau of Shipping (ABS), in 1862 and Det Norske Veritas (DNV), in 1864, were established during the nineteenth century in many of the traditional maritime nations.[48]

All of these societies were founded by marine insurers and followed the Lloyd's model of non-profit organisations undertaking surveys of the hull and machinery of ships for the underwriter, in order that the standard of construction could be classified and insurance cover obtained by the shipowner.

In order to ensure complete independence, the original clients of the Classification Societies were marine underwriters, not shipowners (Boisson 1994, p. 366) Payment

---

[45] *Ibid: The New Register of Shipping* or the *Red Book.*

[46] *Ibid*, "63 surveyors were employed in the first year and by 1840 15,000 vessels had been surveyed in accordance with the Rules."

[47] Jenkins WE, *The OCIMF view of recent classification society progress.* Paper to the International Seminar on Tanker Safety, Pollution Prevention, Spill Response and Compensation, Hong Kong, 06 November 2002. The stated purpose of BV was: 'to be of use [for] all maritime professions including ship owners, charterers and mariners, but above all to the insurers by...preserving them from the underwriting risks of bad ships.'

[48] For example Registro Italiano Navale (RINA) in 1861, established by mutual insurance clubs in Italy.

was made to Lloyd's by underwriters through subscriptions for the Registers (Bell 1995, p. 4). This model changed with the reformation of Lloyd's Register of Shipping in 1834, when charges for surveys were levied against shipowners as well as the charges for the purchase of the Register books (Bell 1995, p. 4).

All Classification Societies developed similar methods of evaluating risks through a process of assessing the actual condition of ships and assigning them a 'rating'. This would usually entail a visit to the ship by an experienced captain based in the port. He would assess the constructional quality and state of maintenance of the hull, (important in the days of predominantly wooden ships), state of the rigging, and navigational categories, i.e. the permitted area of operation of the ship. The rating process would also gather and confirm other information such as the name of the builder and year of build, the owner, the master, tonnage and home-port (Boisson 1994, pp. 367, 368) This rating system could result, for example, in the well known highest rating of 100A1 + from Lloyd's Register.

8.3.2 Private and Public Roles of Class

A combination of factors during the second half of the nineteenth century resulted in a movement by all classification societies away from solely ratings, and a fundamental change in the relationship between Class and the shipowner, and eventually, the flag State. Shipowners increasingly wanted more value from Class than just a survey of construction and the occasional rating, and wanted proof, through regular certification, of the ongoing standard of their vessel. Class responded through the concept of a classification certificate that was issued for a number of years dependent upon a regular survey of the ship (Boisson 1994, p. 369). This resulted in a guaranteed and ongoing source of income for Classification Societies, which enabled them to develop their technical resources and international coverage. It also resulted in a need for all societies to produce clearly understood and uniform guidance to their surveyors, who increasingly became technical people such as engineers, rather than the shipmasters used in the rating system. This was the genesis of the "Class Rules" that have become paramount in the regulatory framework for design and construction of ships. Parallel to this system of regular Class surveys, as national law evolved for safety of ships from the mid-nineteenth century, flag States began to carry out statutory surveys to verify the condition of the remainder of the ship and its equipment, particularly safety and navigational equipment (Boisson 1994, p. 370).

The surveys of hull and machinery[49] carried out by Classification Societies to Class Rules were increasingly accepted by flag States as verification of the standard

---

[49] Bell JD, The Role of Classification in Maritime Safety. 9th Chua Chor Teck Annual Memorial Lecture, Singapore, 13 July 1995, p. 5. "It was only in 1877 the first Lloyd's register engineering surveyor was appointed and in 1880 the survey of 'machinery installed' began and was considered a part of classification".

of these components of the ship and duplication of surveys was avoided. Flag States also began to delegate their statutory powers to Classification Societies who had the technical expertise and personnel to carry out the increasingly complex task of surveying ships, with Lloyd's and Bureau Veritas being delegated the authority to assign freeboard to British ships in 1890 (Boisson 1994, p. 370).

8.3.3 Issues of Class

A significant change took place in the late nineteenth century in the role of Class and its relationship with the shipowner. To obviate the clear conflict of interest between their public and private roles, Classification Societies drew up detailed regulations regarding complete surveys of the vessel and its equipment, including their traditional area of hull and machinery. This led to some flag States delegating all of these responsibilities to Class who, as a result, decided to sever their traditional ties with marine underwriters and offer their services directly to shipowners (Boisson 1994, p. 370). Classification Societies could then be carrying out regular surveys to ensure the vessel remained "in Class" for insurance purposes (private services), whilst at the same time undertaking statutory surveys on behalf of the flag State (public services), with clear issues of conflict of interest.

An additional issue, which continues to the present day, is that information regarding classification is the property of the shipowner and deemed to be commercially confidential between the shipowner, who is paying the bills, and the Classification Society.[50] Classification Societies take the view that information obtained by a surveyor, in either a Class or flag State role, belongs to the person to whom the information is being provided, with an associated obligation to keep that information confidential (Hidaka 2001). They further maintain that such information cannot be passed on to any third party except in response to a legally based order from the flag State, through a court order, or with the owner's consent (Hidaka 2001). This view has come in for criticism from those who consider that the resultant "shroud of secrecy" does not assist in the identification of substandard ships.[51]

---

[50] Hidaka M, Chairman (2001) IACS, The Role of Class in Meeting the Safety Challenge. Seatrade Safe Shipping Conference, 10 April. http://www.iacs.org.uk/seatrade.htm: "Information obtained when performing a class survey or statutory survey on behalf of a flag administration belongs to the person to whom the information is being provided. The Classification Society has a responsibility to maintain the confidentiality of that information. It cannot be passed on to any third party, except in response to a legally based order (with legal authority) from the flag State, or a court order, or the owner's consent."

[51] Ibid, p. 7 A Fairplay editorial commented that "Secrecy breeds suspicion, and there has always been too much of it in our industry. There are instances where it is both necessary and justified, but not half as many as some would have us believe. Take the case of class. Is there any good reason why it should not be public knowledge whether a ship is in class or not, and with whom?"

The ultimate sanction by a Classification Society for non-compliance, acting in its private category, is removal of Class; a move that would render the ship's insurance null and void. However, with the ready ability of shipowners to change Class, and the readiness of Classification Societies to take on new members, this can be an empty threat. The IMO grappled with this issue and, in 2005, produced standard guidelines to ensure the adequacy of transfer of class-related matters between Recognized Organizations (IMO MSC/MEPC 2005,.5/Circ.2).

A further issue is that, as Class is employed by the shipowner, a Class surveyor cannot attend aboard a ship unless invited to do so by the shipowner.[52] This can lead to confusion and conflicts of interest between the public and private roles of Class, with a Class surveyor reluctant to attend a ship on matters that relate to delegated flag State functions in the belief that the problem is strictly one associated with private Class matters. The boundaries between the private and public roles of Class can also result in the master of a ship being aware of matters that are required to be reported to Class, as they could affect the safety or seaworthiness of the ship, but being reluctant to do so for a variety of reasons. The master could be attempting to conceal unauthorised repairs to the ship, which have been undertaken for commercial expediency, or be concealing damage, as it may delay the ship or reflect badly on himself or herself.

If these issues become known to parties in the port such as pilots, harbourmasters or port State control officials they will usually be notified to the local Class surveyor and there are provisions in SOLAS for Class, as the Recognized Organization acting on behalf of the flag State of the ship, to "carry out inspections and surveys if requested by the appropriate authorities of a port State" (SOLAS, Chapter I/6(b)). There are provisions in Class agreements with the shipowner for the surveyor to attend the ship "uninvited" but Class do not have any powers of enforcement.[53]

The coverage and mandate of Class expanded enormously after the Second World War when the flags of convenience of Panama and Liberia attracted considerable tonnage from Greek and American shipowners. These flag States, and those of

---

[52] Organization for Economic Co-operation and Development, Competitive Advantages obtained by some Shipowners as a result of Non-observance of Applicable International Rules and Standards. OECD/GD(96)4, Paris 1996, p. 20. "They [Class] are contracturally bound to the shipowner only in the implementation of their rules and regulations and are only required to survey those parts of the vessel that they are requested to look at. Classification Societies cannot board a vessel without the owner's permission."

[53] Hidaka M, Chairman, IACS, The Role of Class in Meeting the Safety Challenge. Seatrade Safe Shipping Conference, 10 April 2001, http://www.iacs.org.uk/seatrade.htm, p. 3: "There is a common misunderstanding concerning the function of the Classification Society as an RO. While the authority to carry out statutory surveys and inspections on behalf of the flag administrations may be delegated, the RO's powers of enforcement are more limited. In essence, when required repairs or corrective actions are not carried out or a survey is not passed satisfactorily, practically speaking, ROs do not have the police powers needed to detain the ship. The most that the RO can do is attempt to withdraw the statutory certificates, or declare them invalid, and notify the ship's flag State and the port State where the vessel happens to be located of the situation for their further action." See SOLAS 1/6(c).

newly emergent nations, had neither the infrastructure nor the maritime administration, nor any desire to oversee and enforce statutory regulations. By this time Classification Societies had set up worldwide networks to survey the ships in Class with them, and many flag States saw them as the logical organisations to carry out statutory as well as Class surveys and delegated these functions to them accordingly. Currently more than two-thirds of IMO Member States delegate their statutory functions to Classification Societies (Recognized Organizations).[54]

Due to concerns in the 1960s amongst the "traditional" Classification Societies at a proliferation of what were perceived as substandard societies, the International Association of Classification Societies (IACS) was formed in 1969 and now represents ten major societies.[55] Between them, IACS members account for 92–95% of world tonnage.[56] IACS, through the extensive technical and research facilities of its members, and its role as the only Non-Governmental Organization (NGO) at the IMO able to develop Rules, exercises a great deal of influence upon the instruments produced by IMO, where it has held consultative status since 1969. The remaining 5–8% of world tonnage is in Class with a proliferation of Classification Societies and survey companies of dubious provenance, many of whom also carry out the delegated statutory functions of flag States.[57]

The wheel turned full circle in the late 1970s, with the originators of the Classification Society concept, marine insurers in the United Kingdom and Scandinavia, becoming very critical of perceived loopholes in Class rules (Boisson 1994, p. 372). These marine insurers, who operate mutual shipowners' collectives as Protection and Indemnity (P&I) Clubs, recorded wide variations in the delivery of Class services, identified unwarranted extensions of Class for older substandard ships, and criticised the secrecy of information in Class survey reports. They also criticised the lack of access to this critical information due to the contractual arrangements between the shipowner and his Classification Society, and the fact that Class rules paid no attention to the operation of the ship.[58]

This criticism resulted in the formation of inspection teams by P&I Clubs to focus upon matters not covered by Class, in particular hatch covers, cargo holds, navigational aids, and safety equipment. These programmes have been progressively introduced by many P&I Clubs with the resultant inspections reinforcing, in

---

[54]For detailed statistics on delegation of statutory functions by flag States to ROs see Chap. 9.

[55]Members of IACS (2007) are: American Bureau of Shipping (ABS), Bureau Veritas (BV), China Classification Society (CCS), Det Norske Veritas (DNV), Germanischer Lloyd (GL), Korean Register of Shipping (KR), Lloyd's Register of Shipping (LR), Nippon Kaiji Kyokai (Class NK), Registro Italiano Navale (RINA), Russian Maritime Register of Shipping (RS).

[56]Payer HG, Past-Chairman IACS, The Role of Classification Societies: Is it changing? September 2000, p. 2: "But we have to remind ourselves that altogether there are only about 5 to 8% of the world tonnage outside IACS." http://www.iacs.org.uk/role.htm.

[57]See Chap. 9 for detailed statistics on delegation of flag State statutory functions to Recognized Organizations.

[58]See also *Lloyd's List*, Do we need more class distinction? 9 October 1979, p. 9.

many cases, the view that Class was not doing its job properly.[59] One industry commentator observed in 1980 that "it has become generally recognised that a vessel's being validly 'in Class' with one of the major [Class] societies means very little to a potential charterer." (Fairplay 2005, p. 48)

Charterers of oil tankers, usually large oil companies, who also relied upon Class surveys to determine the standard of ships, also began to increasingly question the standards of these surveys in the early 1980s.[60] Claims were made that the surveys were not detecting important safety issues such as deterioration of the ship's hull and this, coupled with a spate of environmental disasters from oil spills, led to establishment of comprehensive independent vetting systems for chartered tankers. Similar initiatives were established for chemical tankers in 1994[61] (Boisson 1994, p. 373).

The credibility of Class was further questioned by other principal actors in the marine insurance market: hull and cargo insurers, the International Union of Marine Insurers, from 1987 (Boisson 1994, p. 372). Their concerns went to the heart of the Class system in their view that the extant model of provision by Class of both private and public services embodied an insoluble conflict of interest.[62] This fundamental issue of conflict of interest can be explained by the example of a Classification Society requiring a shipowner to improve safety, the costs of which will inevitably result in reduced profits and earning capacity. In an effort to keep the shipowner's business the Classification Society may reduce its requirements, or place "conditions of class" on the ship to enable it to continue to trade in a standard of lesser safety. A lesser sanction that is more acceptable to the shipowner is that of Class Recommendations. Class is a very competitive business and efforts by Classification Societies to persuade shipowners with large fleets to transfer Class had resulted in unacceptable flexibility of standards (Boisson 1994, p. 373). Shipowners have the commercial freedom to transfer Class – "class hopping" – a threat that can be perceived to lead to reduced standards from the "losing" society, or a move that can result in lower standards and reduced compliance costs from the "gaining" society (Barchue 2005, p. 2). The absence of clear standards for transfer between classification societies exacerbated this issue.

The overriding concern of the IACS, facing the brunt of this widespread criticism and condemnation, was to restore credibility, which the IACS has attempted to do through a number of initiatives. A permanent secretariat was established in London in

---

[59]See also, Sporie P, Clubs keep an eye on ship standards, *Lloyd's List*, 2 March 1982, p. 8; Norman K, P&I surveys promote shipboard safety, Safety at Sea, December 1982, p. 34.

[60] See also Lloyd's List (1982) Exxon attacks classification surveys rules, 8 November, p. 1.

[61] The initial results of these inspections have proved them to be well worthwhile. Shell found that 20% of the oil fleet was substandard (in respect of cargo worthiness). For BP, the proportion was 30%, and for Mobil it was 35%. See also Shell International Marine, May 1992, *A study of standards in the oil tanker industry*; and Guest A, *Lloyd's List*, 2 February 1993, *Big Oil versus tanker owner*.

[62]See also, Prescott J (1987) Underwriter in attack on class conflicts. Lloyd's List, 24 September; and Prescott J (1987) An unanswerable conflict of interest. Lloyd's List, 15 October, p. 2

1990 and a procedure for transfer of Class was agreed between all IACS members.[63] Quality management systems were introduced and an enhanced survey system was developed for bulk carriers and tankers (Boisson 1994, p. 373).

8.3.4   Codification of Class

There has, traditionally, been no regulatory requirement for a ship to be "in Class", as market forces, such as the requirements of insurers, owners, shippers of cargo, and charterers, have ensured that virtually all ships are Classed. The fact that Class Rules have been adopted by the IMO since 1959 as the standard for design and construction has also reinforced the vital role that Class has long played in international shipping.[64] This role has been codified by an amendment to the SOLAS Convention in July 1998 that states:

> In addition to the requirements contained elsewhere in the (SOLAS) regulations, ships shall be designed, constructed and maintained in compliance with the structural, mechanical and electrical requirements of a classification society which is recognised by the Administration in accordance with the provisions of Chapter XI/1,[65] or with applicable national standards of the Administration which provide an equivalent level of safety. (SOLAS Chapter II-1, Part A-1, Reg. 3–1)

The amendment is restrictive in that it only relates to design, construction, mechanical, and electrical requirements of a Classification Society; the traditional mandate of Class. A weakness in this amendment is that it does not specify the standard of Classification Society. Reference is made in the amendment to two

---

[63]The Sub-Committee on Flag State Implementation of the IMO is currently working on acceptance of IACS transfer of Class rules as a standard for transfer between all classification societies, both IACS and non-IACS.

[64]For example, see Bell JD, The Role of Classification in Maritime Safety. 9th Chua Chor Teck Annual Memorial Lecture, Singapore, 13 July 1995, p. 4: "… there was a Lloyd's Rule as far back as 1835 when the Committee decided that there should be 'a freeboard of 3 inches for foot of depth of hold'. This 'rule of thumb' apparently provided an adequate means of gauging the Loadline until the early 1870's when there was trouble over awning decks being closed in without scuppers by shipowners trying to secure additional cargo capacity in their ships. Two years later Lloyd's Register stated their 'right to enforce those standards it believes desirable' and produced an early form of Loadline mark. … By 1882 Lloyd's Register had developed Rules on behalf of the Board of Trade who accepted as valid all freeboard certificates issued by Lloyd's register. A year later Samuel Plimsoll was instrumental in the passing of the famous Merchant Shipping Act which gave the Board of Trade power to detain overladen ships as unseaworthy."

[65]SOLAS, Chapter XI, Special measures to enhance maritime safety, Regulation 1, Authorization of recognized organization: "Organizations referred to in regulation I/6 shall comply with the guidelines adopted by the Organization by resolution A.739(18), as may be amended by the Organization, and the specifications adopted by the Organization by resolution A.789(19), as may be amended by the Organization, provided that such amendments are adopted, brought into force and take effect in accordance with the provisions of article VIII of the present Convention concerning the amendment procedures applicable to the annex other than Chap. 1."

mandatory Resolutions[66] that are quite prescriptive regarding standards for Recognized Organizations, and IACS firmly believes that only their members will meet these requirements (IACS 1997, p. 4). It is an unfortunate reality that, due to the extant regulatory regime that has evolved and been codified by IMO, the term "Classification Society" in this SOLAS amendment includes all of the many societies that are not IACS members. An analysis of port State control codes for Recognized Organization (RO)[67] indicates that there could be upwards of 160 organisations, including Classification Societies, other than IACS members carrying out statutory functions on behalf of flag States for the very small percentage of world tonnage not covered by IACS.[68]

Broadening of the role of Class with introduction into force of the International Safety Management (ISM) Code (SOLAS reg. IX/1.1) in 1998 and the International Ship and Port Facility Security (ISPS) Code (SOLAS reg. XI-2) in 2004, and the ready delegations of these statutory functions by most flag States to Class, has further blurred the boundaries between their technical, private, and public services. Class was very receptive to, and actively sought, these delegations which took them far beyond their original technical mandate of hull and machinery. This exacerbated existing conflicts of interest as Class was now assuming statutory responsibility under the ISM Code for oversight of the safety management of the ship; a matter inextricably linked with the safety and maintenance of the ship.

The reference in the amendment to SOLAS to the "applicable national standards of the Administration that provide an equivalent level of safety" (SOLAS Chapter II-1, Part A-1, reg. 3–1) has little relevance to a flag State whose sole purpose is to gain revenue and who has no effective national standards or interest in effective administration of the ships under its flag. The broad discretionary powers that many IMO instruments provide to flag States through equivalency and exemption provisions result in a wide variance in national laws and their implementation and enforcement.[69] The statutory

---

[66]For analysis of SOLAS XI/1 and Resolution A.739(19) see under Recognized Organizations, Chap. 8.

[67]The term "Recognized Organization" is used in IMO Resolution A.739(18), Guidelines for the Authorization of Organizations Acting on behalf of the Administration, to denote those survey and classification society organizations "acting on behalf of the Administration (flag State) to perform statutory work on its behalf".

[68]The Tokyo MOU Port State Control Manual, in Section 5, lists codes for 65 Recognized Organizations (RO). Provision is made for a code (999) for other ROs that do not have prescribed codes. In a report (DBM14/WP.3) to the Fourteenth Meeting of Database Managers of the Tokyo MOU in November 2005, a total of 106 names of ROs recorded under code 999 were recorded by port State control officers between January and September 2005.

[69]Barchue LD, Making a case for the Voluntary IMO Member State Audit Scheme, October 2005, p. 1: "Under various treaties, governments/flag States are ultimately responsible for ensuring compliance with the provision of such treaties. However, some of these treaties provide unrestrained powers to flag States to delegate statutory work. They also provide additional latitude for States to determine their own shipping standards through the phrase 'to the satisfaction of the Administration' and equivalency and exemption provisions. As a result, national laws to implement international shipping treaties vary considerably and this leads to: partial or full delegation of statutory work to non-State parties; different degrees of implementation and enforcement; ship registration becoming an attractive and legitimate business in the absence of State accountability; and, some shipowners enjoying considerable economic advantage due to lack of uniform flag State enforcement." www.imo.org/home.asp.

functions of many States will, as a result, inevitably be delegated to a Classification Society of equally dubious provenance; a "class of convenience".

Classification Societies have moved a long way from their original role of determining the standard of construction of ships exclusively for marine underwriters. Class has now attained a dominant, if sometimes confused and contradictory, role in the standards, jurisdiction, and control of all aspects of a ship's design, construction equipment, and safe and secure operation. Class is still the collective depository of technical expertise within the maritime sector, and without Class it is hard to imagine just how the modern shipping industry, or the extant regulatory regime, would survive (Fairplay 2005, p. 2). There is still, however, widespread misunderstanding both inside and outside the shipping industry over the role that Classification Societies play, or should be playing in the market, with associated issues regarding the effective implementation of IMO instruments on behalf of flag States (Barchue 2005, p. 1).

8.4   Issues of Flag State Compliance

At the same time that the IACS was grappling with the issues underlying its tarnished image, the IMO was also coming to grips with an urgent need to improve maritime safety following the maritime disasters of the late 1980s (Marten-Castex 2004, p. 1). In April 1992 the MSC reaffirmed the urgent need to address more strict and uniform application of IMO instruments (Hoppe 2000, p. 3). Submissions calling for development of standards for effective implementation of IMO instruments by flag States were considered from a number of leading maritime nations (Hoppe 2000, p. 2). A Joint MSC/MEPC (Marine Environment Protection Committee) Working Group on Flag State Compliance was established at the 60th session of the Maritime Safety Committee (MSC 60) in 1992 to prepare the groundwork for a new Sub-committee on Flag State Compliance.

The combined oversight of this new committee by the MSC and the MEPC emphasised the importance IMO placed upon wider compliance with IMO instruments on both maritime safety and prevention of marine pollution (Hoppe 2000, p. 2). As a result it was agreed in late 1992 that a new sub-committee would be established under the joint coordination of MSC and MEPC to find ways of assisting Administrations in implementing and, more importantly, enforcing IMO instruments (Hoppe 2000, p. 2). The specific mandate of this body, the Sub-committee on Flag State Implementation (FSI), was to deal with implementation of IMO instruments, port, flag, and coastal State matters, survey and certification, and to analyse casualty statistics. FSI was also to consider the status of the LOSC at every session with a view to determining what impact developments relating to the LOSC could have upon its work.[70]

---

[70]Marten-Castex B, The Work of the Sub-Committee on Flag State Implementation: An Overview, (2003 – up to and including FSI 11), 19 January 2004, p. 8. From FSI 12 in 2003 the committee has extended its terms of reference to include environmental aspects, maritime security, accident investigation, and UN classification of States.

Most of the Sub-committees at the IMO deal solely with matters of a technical nature and are composed of experts in those particular fields. The FSI Sub-committee is unique in that it deals largely with flag, port, and coastal State matters along with the inevitable tensions that arise from the different perspectives of many of the members of the committee, who can be speaking as representatives of each or all of those States in varying degrees of involvement, standing, and repute. FSI is inevitably the most political of all IMO committees. Even the name of the Sub-committee has caused dissension with some of the more sensitive Member States representing open registers claiming that it reflects too much emphasis upon the perceived shortcomings of some flag States.[71] The primary objective of the Sub-committee is the identification of measures necessary to ensure effective and consistent implementation of global instruments, including the consideration of difficulties faced by developing countries, primarily in their capacity as flag States but also as port and coastal States, and this objective has been deemed to accurately reflect its title. FSI itself, and MSC/MEPC, have considered objections to the name and have reaffirmed that it is appropriate to address all of the issues the committee is tasked with (Marten-Castex 2004, p. 8).

One of the most urgent tasks of the first meeting of the Sub-committee, FSI 1 in 1993, and the first Resolution drafted, was a direct reflection of its *raison d'etre*: the development of guidelines and minimum standards for organisations acting on behalf of Administrations. A Correspondence Group, established by FSI 1, prepared draft specifications for Recognized Organizations and these were finalised by FSI 3. The resultant Resolution A.739(18) Guidelines for the Authorization of Organizations acting on behalf of the Administration, approved by the IMO Assembly in November 1993, codifies the longstanding practice of delegation of flag State jurisdiction and control.[72] The resolution notes that: "…Administrations are responsible for taking the necessary measures to ensure that ships flying their State's flag comply with the provisions of such conventions, including surveys and certification" (IMO Resolution A.739(18), Preamble), and recognises that "…many flag States authorize organizations to act on their behalf in the surveys and certification and determination of tonnages as required by [these] conventions" (IMO Resolution A.739(18), Annex, General, para 1). The Resolution also desires to "develop uniform procedures and a mechanism for the delegation of authority to, and the minimum standards for, Recognized Organizations acting on behalf of the Administration, which would assist flag States in the uniform and effective implementation of the relevant IMO conventions" (IMO Resolution A.739(18), Preamble). Appendix 1 to the Resolution details these minimum standards with Appendix 2 spelling out the

---

[71]For example, the original proposed name of the Sub-Committee was Flag State Compliance. This was unacceptable to the Member States of IMO and the word Implementation replaced Compliance.

[72] Through reference in the Resolution to the provisions of regulation I/6 of SOLAS 74; article 13 of Load Lines 66; regulation 4 of Annex I and regulation 10 of Annex II of MARPOL 73/78; and article 6 of Tonnage 69.

elements to be included in an agreement between the Administration and the Recognized Organization.

8.5   Delegation of Flag State Responsibilities

The Secretariat of IMCO was closely involved in the work of UNCLOS III to ensure consistency between IMO instruments and the intent of the LOSC. References to the LOSC were made in several IMO treaty and non-treaty instruments before the entry into force of the LOSC. Under IMO Conventions, which reflect the requirements of the LOSC for safety and prevention of marine pollution, ships are required to be surveyed by the flag State (Administration) at regular intervals and be issued with a suite of statutory certificates as evidence of their full compliance with those regulations. Port States are obliged to accept these certificates as *prima facie* evidence of compliance.[73]

It is possible for the flag State to entrust its inspection, surveying, and certification functions to ROs. This must be done through giving full effect to the requirements and conditions of relevant IMO conventions and resolutions. If delegation of these statutory functions is made, the Administration must retain the capability and resources to monitor and verify the work of the RO, to carry out its own flag State inspections of vessels flying its flag, and maintain an effective Administration for the many other administrative, technical, and social matters required of a properly functioning flag State administration.

It is very clear that the intent of the principal IMO instruments,[74] and the supporting resolutions,[75] is that it is only the inspection, surveying, and certification functions of a flag State that are allowed to be delegated and that granting and enforcement of exemptions cannot be delegated. This view is supported by the wording of SOLAS Chapter I, Regulation 6 (a) which provides that:

> The inspection and survey of ships, so far as regards the enforcement of the provisions of the present regulations and the granting of exemptions therefrom, shall be carried out by the officers of the Administration. The Administration may, however, entrust the inspections and surveys either to surveyors nominated for the purpose or to organizations recognized by it.

SOLAS goes on to express the limitations of this entrustment and recognition in Regulation 6, paragraph (b) as follows:

> An Administration nominating surveyors or recognizing organizations to conduct inspections and surveys as set forth in paragraph (a) shall as a minimum empower any nominated surveyor or recognized organization to:

[73]See for example SOLAS I/19 on acceptance of certificates.
[74]SOLAS 74; LOAD LINES 66; MARPOL 73/78; STCW 78/95; TONNAGE 69.
[75]Resolutions A.739(18) and A.789(19).

i) require repairs to a ship;

ii) carry out inspections and surveys if requested by the appropriate authorities of a port State.

MARPOL, Annex I, regulations 4(a)–(c), and Annex II, regulation 10, contain almost identical provisions and limitations upon surveyors and ROs.

In spite of these clear limitations many governments, particularly Pseudo-National flag States, entrust their entire maritime administrations to ROs, often in distant countries, in the guise of a register that is focused primarily upon attracting tonnage for revenue purposes, and has neither the knowledge nor resources to effectively exercise control over the ships that fly the flag of the distant government.

The implementation and enforcement of IMO instruments, and indirectly the requirements of the LOSC, are the sole responsibility and duty of the flag State and rely heavily upon proper exercise of flag State jurisdiction and control as required by article 94 of the LOSC. However, the majority of the 168 Member States of the IMO have delegated the inspections and surveys, and issuance of all statutory certificates required by IMO instruments, to ROs as provided for by SOLAS (SOLAS Chapter I/6b). The majority of world tonnage is registered in States which are considered to be flags of convenience of one order or another, and the majority of these States delegate their statutory functions to ROs of one order or another. This sometimes unholy alliance, and sometimes total derogation of flag State responsibility, can create fundamental flaws in the international safety regime and result in unsafe ships obtaining the nationality of a State through the registration process.

8.6   Recognized Organizations

If flag States delegate their statutory functions they are required by SOLAS,[76] and IMO Resolution A.739(18), to notify the IMO of the specific responsibilities and conditions of the authority delegated to nominated surveyors or ROs. An important requirement of Resolution A.739(18), and one which is honoured more in the breach by many States, is for the flag State to determine that the RO has adequate resources in terms of technical, managerial, and research capabilities to accomplish the tasks being assigned, in accordance with the Minimum Standards for Recognized Organizations Acting on behalf of the Administration (IMO Resolution A.739(18), Annex. 2.1).

IMO Resolution A.787(19) (Procedures for Port State Control, s.1.6.7) contains a definition of "Recognized Organization" as follows:

---

[76]SOLAS Chapter 1, Part B, Surveys and certificates, Regulation 6 (b)(ii), *Inspection and survey*: "The Administration shall notify the Organization of the specific responsibilities and conditions of the authority delegated to nominated surveyors or recognized organizations."

An organization which meets the relevant conditions set forth by A.739(18) and has been delegated by the flag State Administration to provide the necessary statutory services and certification to ships entitled to fly its flag.

Appendix 1 of Resolution A.739(18) gives some guidance as to the minimum conditions for which an organisation should submit complete information and substantiation to the Administration, to be recognised to perform statutory work on its behalf:

> The relative size, structure, experience and capability of the organization commensurate with the type and degree of authority intended to be delegated thereto should be demonstrated.

The organisation should be able to document extensive experience in assessing the design, construction and equipment of merchant ships and, as applicable, their safety management system.

The organisations that are most likely to satisfy these minimum conditions are the long-established Classification Societies. IACS members would clearly meet this standard but it is questionable whether the dozens of other ROs would also meet this standard as, with all matters to do with international shipping, there are widely varying standards of these organisations. An examination of the annual reports for the Paris MOU (2004), Tokyo MOU (2005), and USCG port State control report for 2004, along with information on the IMOGISIS database, reveals a total of 103 identifiable ROs. If it is borne in mind that the 10 IACS members claim to represent 92–95% of total world tonnage, it can be seen that the remaining small percentage is disproportionately over-represented by ROs. These many Classification Societies and survey organisations are clearly given delegated authority by flag States and are therefore deemed to be ROs, but many do not come anywhere near meeting the minimum conditions of IMO Resolutions. This often results in substandard surveys of substandard ships, and issuance of meaningless statutory certificates on behalf of the flag State, with the associated risks to the lives of crews, and to the marine environment.[77] The primacy of the certification issued either by the flag State, or by the RO under delegated authority from the flag State, must be accepted by other States as provided for by SOLAS Chapter 1, regulation 11:

> Certificates issued under the authority of a Contracting Government shall be accepted by the other Contracting Governments for all purposes covered by the present Convention. They shall be regarded by the other Contracting Governments as having the same force as certificates issued by them.

A flag State must be able to monitor and enforce its requirements anywhere in the world and the ROs carrying out the statutory functions of that State must therefore have a worldwide system of offices and surveyors as well as the technical, managerial,

---

[77]SSY Consultancy & Research Ltd, The cost to users of substandard shipping, OECD Maritime Transport Committee, January 2001, p. 35: "Some flag States disregard their responsibilities to the principle of safe shipping because these, too, are not sufficiently exposed to real liabilities. To some degree, they are able to offload the notional responsibility of enforcing standards by engaging classification societies to perform their ship certification duties. However, there is no guarantee that the societies to which these duites are entrusted are those with the greatest commitment to rigorous enforcement of international requirements."

and research facilities required to support those offices and personnel. These surveyors should be exclusively employed by the RO but, over time, it became obvious that standards were being lowered by the employment of "non-exclusive", or part-time surveyors.[78] The Administration is also required to establish a system to ensure the adequacy of work performed by the organisations authorized to act on its behalf through procedures for communication, reporting from the RO, additional inspections of ships by the Administration, audits of the RO, and monitoring and evaluation of Class-related matters such as deficiencies in a ship's structure or equipment (IMO Circular letter No 2630, Annex 3.1–3.5).

The focus upon effective delegation of flag State jurisdiction to ROs continued at the third meeting of the FSI Sub-Committee in 1995 (FSI 3) with development of a draft resolution containing Specifications on the Survey and Certification Functions of Recognized Organizations acting on behalf of the Administration. This resolution was adopted by the 19th IMO Assembly in 1995 as Resolution A.789(19). Both A.739(18) and A.789(19) were later given mandatory status through regulation 1 of SOLAS Chapter XI-1: Special measures to enhance maritime safety (Barchue 2005, p. 2). The same meeting of the FSI Sub-Committee recognised a need for a model agreement that could be used by flag States when delegating statutory functions and powers to ROs, and drafted appropriate circulars.[79] FSI 3 also started work on amalgamation of all relevant instruments contained in various resolutions and MSC/MEPC circulars relating to ROs for ease of reference and implementation by flag States. A final circular was issued in January 1997.[80]

8.7 Delegation or Derogation of Flag State Responsibilities

An alarming example of irresponsible delegation of inspections, surveys, and statutory functions by a flag State was demonstrated by Cambodia in 2003. Cambodia at that time had one of the worst records of any flag State, as evidenced by their continued

---

[78]Due to the inadequacy of some work being carried out by part-time employees of Recognized Organizations (non-exclusive surveyors) the Guidelines were amended to allow only full-time surveyors and auditors to perform certification functions of a statutory nature. See IMO Circular letter No 2630. New paragraph 2–1 to be added after the existing paragraph 2. "2–1 The organisation should perform survey and certification functions of a statutory nature by the use of only exclusive surveyors and auditors, being persons solely employed by the organisation, duly qualified, trained and authorised to execute all duties and activities incumbent upon their employer, within their level of work responsibility. While still remaining responsible for the certification on behalf of the flag State, the organisation may subcontract radio surveys to non-exclusive surveyors in accordance with the relevant provisions of resolution A.788(19)."

[79]MSC/Circ.710 – MEPC/Circ.307 – Model agreement for the authorisation of organizations acting on behalf of the Administration. See Appendix II.

[80]MSC/Circ.788 – MEPC/Circ.325 – Authorization of recognized organizations acting on behalf of administrations, incorporating resolutions A.739(18) and A.739(19) and MSC/Circ.710 – MEPC/Circ.307 – Communication of information on the authorization of recognized organizations (ROs)

presence on the blacklists of both the Paris and Tokyo MOU port State control regimes and the USCG.[81] Due to international expressions of concern at the alarming casualty and detention rate of Cambodian flagged vessels, the Cambodian Government decided in 2003 to reinvent the register and delegated their administrative duties to a private organisation in North Korea.[82] This company, the International Ship Registry of Cambodia, sub-delegated authority to 15 ROs, one of which is alleged to have further sub-delegated the right to carry out surveys and issue statutory certificates to a shipowner who issued statutory certificates on his own behalf; an action that is far from the intent or requirements of the LOSC, the SOLAS Convention and IMO Resolutions. Yet Cambodia has been a member of the IMO since 1961 and has ratified all of the principal Conventions. Winchester and Alderton's Flag State Audit 2003 comments further on the Cambodian registry as follows:

> The Cambodian administration accepts only the bare minimum of responsibilities for vessels flagged to its register. The register is run purely for profit, with limited interest being shown in issues of vessel safety or crew welfare. There are no restrictions on the ownership of any vessel registered in the Cambodian Ship Registry. Any legal entity capable of owning vessels under the law of the country in which it is established or domiciled may be registered as an owner. Other than the official fees applicable to vessels, non-resident shipping companies/owners are not required to pay corporate/personal taxes of any description. Since its reactivation in 1995 the Cambodian register has exhibited a net increase in tonnage of 3,230% (up from the 1995 level of 59,958 gross tons to 1,996,738 gross tons in 2001). (http://www.sirc.cf.ac.uk/fsa.html)

This not uncommon example of an irresponsible flag State and the vexed question of flags of convenience is exacerbated by widespread delegation of the flag State duties imposed by the LOSC, through SOLAS and MARPOL, to ROs, many of which have similar low standards of professionalism and expertise to the flag State they purport to represent.

8.8   Assistance to Flag States

The early meetings of FSI produced a considerable body of work under the mandate of implementation of instruments, survey, and certification, and assistance to flag States on their implementation of IMO instruments. Resolution A.739(18), was closely followed by Resolution A.740(18), Interim Guidelines to assist flag States,[83] which

---

[81]Paper FSI 14/INF.8IMO Sub-Committee on Flag State Implementation, 14th Session, June 2006. The Blacklists of the Paris and Tokyo MOUs on Port State Control, and the USCG, are based upon the detention rate of vessels under a particular flagged on a three-year rolling average.

[82]Letter of 25 February 2003 from the International Ship Registry of Cambodia to the Director of Maritime Safety, Maritime Safety Authority of New Zealand.

[83]Resolution A.740(18) was revoked in November 1997 by Resolution A.847(20) to take account of some requirements of the 1995 STCW amendments.

included general guidelines for flag States and for the monitoring of bodies acting on their behalf, including minimum training and experience requirements for staff assigned implementation and monitoring duties.[84] A Correspondence Group was established at FSI 3 to work intersessionally on a review of A.740(18) and to develop guidance material for all aspects of a flag State's obligations (Hoppe 2000, p. 3). This resolution was amended by FSI 5 to take account of references in the resolution to the revised STCW[85] Convention and was adopted by the 20th Assembly in 1997 as Resolution A.847(20), Guidelines to assist flag States in the implementation of IMO instruments (Marten-Castex 2004, p. 3).

In spite of all these energetic and proactive efforts of FSI, concerns were expressed at the fourth meeting of FSI that not enough was being done to deal with substandard shipping, and calls were made for development of a new binding instrument on flag State responsibility (Marten-Castex 2004, p. 5). Agreement could not be reached at FSI 4 and this matter was referred to FSI 5 in January 1997 for further consideration. The depth of concern coming out of FSI 4 about ineffective flag State performance is reflected in the following matters that were referred to FSI 5 for consideration by the main committees. These were: examination of possible criteria for assessing flag State performance and possible measures to ensure that States fulfil their responsibilities; preparation of an Assembly resolution on the interpretation of SOLAS regulations I/1 to I/20 and the revision of SOLAS chapter I; compilation of a list of States that have "repeatedly disregarded their obligations", and the study of the provisions of regulation I/7 (Communication of information) of the 1995 amendments to the STCW Convention and the associated STCW Code (Hoppe 2000, pp. 4–5).

Work on resolution of these issues proceeded through to FSI 6, which came to agreement on a Flag State Performance Self Assessment Form (SAF) which was approved by the main IMO Committees in 1998 and issued as a Circular.[86] The Circular invited Member States to utilise the SAF for a voluntary self assessment of their performance as a flag State and, if they wished to do so, to provide the IMO with a copy of the completed SAF. The SAF could also be used to approach IMO for technical assistance to address weaknesses in their discharge of flag State responsibilities. It was intended that the confidential results of the SAF would be placed on an IMO database which would assist the Organization in its efforts to

---

[84]Also approved at the 18th Assembly of the IMO in late 1993 out of the work of FSI 1 were: A.741(18), International Management Code for the Safe operation of Ships and for Pollution Prevention (International Safety Management (ISM) Code); A.742(18) Procedures for the control of operational requirements related to the safety of ships and pollution prevention; A.744(18), Guidelines on the enhanced programme of inspections during surveys of bulk carriers and oil tankers; and A.746(18), Survey guidelines under the harmonised system for survey and certification.

[85]International Convention on Standards of Training, Certification and Watchkeeping for Seafarers. London, 01 December 1978. As amended 1995. # 1984 *UKTS* 50.

[86]MSC/Circ.889-MEPC/Circ.353, Self Assessment of Flag State Performance.

achieve consistent and effective instruments (Hoppe 2000, p. 6). An Assembly Resolution, A.881(21), Self Assessment of flag State Performance, was subsequently adopted (Hoppe 2000, p. 5).

The original intent of the SAF was that it would be mandatory but this was not politically acceptable to many Member States with the result that, regardless of considerably more work, guidance, encouragement, circulars, and resolutions throughout the course of FSI's work until the 11th meeting of the committee in 2002, there was a disappointing uptake of the voluntary SAF process. As at November 2003 53 initial SAFs and 18 updates had been received (Marten-Castex 2004, p. 6) and the process was effectively moribund. Clearly, more robust initiatives were required to address the vexed issue of effective flag State implementation of IMO instruments.

8.9 Issues of Effective Implementation of IMO Instruments

By the turn of the twenty-first century IMO was publicly acknowledging that its efforts to improve the implementation and enforcement of its instruments by flag States had failed and that new and stronger measures needed to be taken, as indicated in an extract from a speech by the Secretary General of the IMO in 2001:

> Is the [international regulatory regime] system working? I believe that the improvements in safety, the reduction in casualties and the record of achievement of IMO over the years would indicate that the answer is yes. If, as a corollary, you asked if it could work better, the answer would also be yes ... I believe that the problems perceived today do not lie basically with shipping's regulatory framework or with the mechanism by which that framework is constructed, but with its implementation. Inherent in a system based on international consensus such as that which is developed through IMO are both rights and responsibilities. All IMO Members have the right to a voice in defining standards and regulations that will be applied to international shipping and that right is equal for all regardless of the size of their fleets, the strength of their economies or the depth of their maritime traditions. But the rights bring with them responsibilities and accountabilities that are commensurate with the rights.

In recognition of ongoing frustrations with ineffective flag State implementation and enforcement of IMO instruments a proposal was tabled at the eleventh session of FSI in 2003 to revise and update Resolution A.847(20), Guidelines to assist flag States in the implementation of IMO instruments, and to introduce a Voluntary flag State Audit Scheme to provide a comprehensive and objective assessment of how effectively flag States administer and implement the key IMO technical treaties.[87] This resulted in a debate led by some large International flag States who collectively questioned why the emphasis was upon only flag States, and why port and coastal States were not included in such an instrument. After

---

[87] Voluntary IMO Member State Audit Scheme,
http://www.imo.org/Safety/mainframe.asp?topic_id = 841.

extensive debate it became clear that a focus solely upon flag States would not be acceptable to the Sub-committee and the decision was made to include port and coastal States in a Code that would provide a framework for, what became known as, the Voluntary IMO Model Audit Scheme.

8.9.1 International Civil Aviation Organization Flag State Audit Model

In its consideration of a system of flag State audits IMO turned to the recent work of its sister United Nations agency, the International Civil Aviation Organization (ICAO) for guidance. Due to the very rapid growth of aviation in the late 1980s and early 1990s some ICAO Member States had difficulty keeping up to date with advances in technological and regulatory developments and ICAO requirements. Lack of proper implementation of regulatory requirements by Member States of ICAO was identified as a causal factor in serious accidents or near misses. This lead to some States, including the United States, taking unilateral action against "black-listed" airlines and banning them from entry into their airspace and airports.[88] ICAO's response was to introduce the Voluntary Safety Oversight Program (SOP) in 1996 which had similarities to the IMO's subsequent Self Assessment of Flag State Performance (SAF) scheme. Both schemes failed due to their voluntary nature and lack of any independent audit. From March 1996 to December 1998 ICAO conducted only 67 assessments of Member States[89] out of 88 requests, with the results confirming that widespread problems existed relating to lack of adequate regulatory frameworks, inadequate administrative structures, lack of appropriate certification and licensing systems, and control and supervision capabilities (Sasamura 2003, p. 5).

A direct parallel can be made between these issues and those current in the maritime sector. In his opening address to the 9th session of the Sub-Committee on Flag State mplementation in February in 2001, the Secretary General, William O'Neill, stated: "So far, we have received 32 completed self-assessment forms, which, 2 years after the forms were first circulated by an MSC Circular, we cannot consider a satisfactory rate of response. I therefore, once again, request those governments which have not yet done so to complete the form in time for your next session" (http://www.imo. org/Newsroom/mainframe.asp?topic_id = 106&doc_id = 2677). In spite of this, and further exhortations at subsequent meetings of FSI, the self assessment scheme was abandoned in favour of the Voluntary Model Audit Scheme, even though by 2004, a total of 54 IMO Members and Associate Members had submitted the initial

---

[88]This situation is analogous to the banning of single hulled tankers to American ports after the *Exxon Valdez* disaster under the 1990 Oil Pollution Act (OPA), and to current EU initiatives after the *Erika* and *Prestige* oil pollution incidents.

[89]Sasamura Y, Development of Audit Scheme in ICAO and IMO. Seminar on Model Audit Scheme, London, 27 May 2003, p. 5. At this time ICAO had 188 Contracting States.

self assessment form with a combined gross tonnage of 79% of the world fleet (http://imo.org/Newsroom/mainframe.asp?topic_id = 106&doc_id = 3351). The original IMO Resolution[90] that had formed the basis of the self assessment process for flag States was incorporated into the Voluntary Audit Scheme.

As a result of the inadequacies of the ICAO SOP scheme, which could be sheeted home directly to its voluntary nature, the ICAO established a mandatory Universal Safety Oversight Audit Program (USOAP) on 1 January 1999 through an ICAO Assembly Resolution (ICAO Resolution A 32–11), and an MOU with each Contracting State (Sasamura 2003, p. 5). During the following 4 years, 181 of the 188 Contracting States were audited at an annual average of 45; far above that of the SOP program (Sasmura 2003, p. 5). The objective of the USOAP program is to increase overall safety with a focus upon identification of weaknesses in a Contracting State's regulatory system and determination of action plans to address those weaknesses. Indirect peer pressure is brought upon other States with non-compliance issues, and transparency is the key element of the programme (Sasmura 2003, p. 5).

All of these factors have been taken into account by the IMO in drafting the Model Audit Scheme, accepting that there are essential differences between the aviation and maritime regulatory regimes that may make the ICAO model more difficult to apply to the safety of ships. Firstly, maritime accidents are sometimes caused by structural failures, whilst this is rare in the aviation industry. Secondly, compliance regimes in the aviation industry are invariably under the direct control of the aviation authority, whilst the statutory functions of a maritime administration are more often than not delegated to a Recognized Organization. And, lastly, although the operators of aircraft are invariably located in the country of registration, the beneficial owners of ships are more often located outside the country of registration (Sasamura 2003, p. 6).

8.9.2   Adoption and implementation of the IMO Model Audit Scheme

In spite of the differences between aviation and shipping the IMO Assembly considered that the preparatory work carried out by FSI in adapting the ICAO model to IMO requirements, albeit on a voluntary basis, was adequate to engender approval at its 23rd meeting in November 2003 as Resolution A.946(23), Voluntary IMO Member State Audit Scheme. The 24th Assembly in November–December 2004 adopted Resolution A.974(24), Framework and Procedures for the Voluntary IMO member State Audit Scheme and A.973(24), Code for the implementation of mandatory IMO instruments, which provides the audit standard.[91]

---

[90]Resolution A.847(20), Guidelines to assist flag States in the implementation of IMO instruments.
[91]A.973(24) revokes resolution A.847(20), Guidelines to assist flag States in the implementation of IMO instruments; the basis for the self assessment scheme.

One of the fundamental principles of the Code for the Implementation of Mandatory IMO Instruments is that:

> Under the provisions of the United Nations Convention on the Law of the Sea 1982 (UNCLOS) and of IMO conventions, Administrations are responsible for promulgating laws and regulations and for taking all other steps which may be necessary to give these instruments full and complete effect so as to ensure that, from the point of view of safety of life at sea and protection of the marine environment, a ship is fit for the service for which it is intended and is manned with competent maritime personnel. (Resolution A.973(24), Code for the Implementation of Mandatory IMO Instruments, Annex, para. 4)

The IMO sees the Voluntary IMO Member State Audit Scheme (VIMSAS) as a means to achieve harmonised and consistent global implementation of IMO standards. The scheme addresses current issues of conformance in enacting appropriate legislation for the IMO instruments to which a Member State is a party, administration and enforcement of national law, delegation of statutory authority, and control and monitoring of Recognized Organizations (VIMSAS, http://www.imo.org/Safety/mainframe.asp?topic_id = 841). Attention is not all upon the effectiveness of flag State implementation but extends, as does the ICAO USOAP scheme, to identification of needs for capacity building of Member States who are struggling to provide a proper Administration, and assistance through technical cooperation where recommended by the IMO appointed auditors. On a wider scale generic feedback from all audits will be provided to the IMO Council and all IMO member States, and may also assist the regulatory process at the IMO ((VIMSAS, http://www.imo.org/Safety/mainframe.asp?topic_id = 841).

A further resolution was approved at the 24th IMO Assembly in 2005, A.975(24), Future development of the Voluntary IMO Member State Audit Scheme, which requests the MSC and the MEPC to review the feasibility of including, within the scope of the audit scheme, other issues which have assumed prominence in the maritime world such as security and other safety functions not presently covered. Consideration is also required of any implications of broadening the scope of the scheme (VIMSAS, http://www.imo.org/Safety/mainframe.asp?topic_id = 841). Due to extreme sensitivity within the corridors of the IMO on the question of the VIMSAS becoming mandatory, the resolution is silent upon this important possible development. Many Member States are closely monitoring the process and effectiveness of the audits before committing themselves to support for a mandatory IMO audit scheme. There is also some cynicism that only member States who are effective Administrations will put their hands up for an audit and those that are most in need of an audit will not.

Many of the LOSC requirements for flag, port, and coastal States are covered by VIMSAS, including: general information on the capacity of the flag State Administration; international instruments and how they have been incorporated into national legislation; enforcement, recruitment, and training of surveyors; investigation and analysis of marine casualties and pollution incidents; port State control and coastal State activities; reporting requirements to the IMO; how evaluation and review is carried out to measure the performance of the maritime administration; and management systems.

A pilot scheme involving six IMO Member States[92] was successfully carried out during development of VIMSAS. Voluntary IMO Member State Audits commenced during the second half of 2006, with the IMO continuing to call for Member States to volunteer for an audit and to also put forward suitably trained and qualified persons as auditors. The initial response as at the March 31 2006 deadline for applications for audits and auditors was disappointing, with only 14 States volunteering for audits and 21 applications as auditors being deemed acceptable. However, by the time of the 96th meeting of the IMO Council in June 2006, numbers had increased to 19 Member States and 45 auditors, and the IMO Secretariat was optimistic of achieving the goal of 25 audits in the first biennium.[93] Industry reaction has been cautiously optimistic with a comment from the leading shipping industry publication, *Fairplay*, expressing the view of many commentators: "It looks like flag State audits will be formally approved this month – with teeth. But will they mean a quality revolution or just another costly paper exercise?" (Fairplay 2005)

8.10 Possible Future Development of VIMSAS

There was extensive debate on the subject of whether VIMSAS should become mandatory at the 100th Session of the IMO Council in June 2008. Support for this concept was given by many Western European and OECD countries with an opposing view coming from some developing countries and International registers. It became clear during the debate that a principal objection centred around the cost to developing countries of rectifying deficiencies found during a mandatory IMO audit. This led to a debate as to whether VIMSAS should be more closely aligned to IMO's technical cooperation programme or whether there should be a different standard for developed and developing countries (IMO Delegate's Report, p. 4).

It was finally agreed that the Secretary General should prepare, for the 101st Session of the Council in November 2008, "an holistic study of possible ways of developing the audit scheme, taking into account the statements made during the debate and containing concrete proposals to stimulate a meaningful discussion on the Scheme's next phase and how to achieve the objectives established when the Scheme was introduced" (IMO Delegate's Report, p. 4).

If the IMO Council eventually votes on whether VIMSAS should become mandatory it may be relevant that, of the 40 Council members for the 2008–2009 biennium, 27 had already volunteered for an audit by December 2007 (IMO 2007, Circular 2830) and there is an overall preponderance of traditional maritime nations amongst Council members.

---

[92]IMO Member States audited in the pilot scheme were Cyprus, the Marshall Islands, the United Kingdom, France, Iran, and Singapore.

[93]The IMO Secretariat reported to the 100th Session of the the IMO Council in June 2008 that 21 audits had been completed, another 21 countries had offered thenselves up for audit, and that a further eight audits were planned for 2008.

8.11   Port State Control as a Response to Ineffective Flag State Control

Another response to ineffective flag State jurisdiction and control, albeit originally as a multi-lateral State initiative outside of IMO, was that of port State control. The LOSC gave States the right to exercise port State control over foreign flagged ships within their jurisdiction but only for matters of environmental pollution (LOSC, Article 218). Various IMO instruments[94] contain control provisions for every ship in matters of environmental protection, safety, and security, when in the port of another Contracting Government: port State control (PSC). The procedures for PSC are contained in an IMO Resolution (Resolution A.787(19)) and are reflected in nine extant regional port State control Memoranda of Understanding, the members of which cover most of the world's trading regions.[95] The reasons for, and functions of, port State control, in particular the "clear grounds" necessary for a detailed inspection of a foreign flagged ship to be carried out, and the place of port State control as a link in the ship regulatory chain, are explained as follows.

In an ideal world there would be no need for port State control. Flag States would take their responsibilities under the LOSC and IMO instruments seriously and would either discharge their duties themselves or delegate them to responsible Recognized Organizations. By the 1970s, the maritime regulatory world was becoming far from ideal, due to a proliferation of flag States of questionable motives, increasing availability of unscrupulous ROs and a distancing by shipowners from their ships, through increased usage of ship management companies. Some significant casualties in European waters (*Torrey Canyon*, 1968; *Amoco Cadiz*, 1979) and widespread resultant pollution of the marine environment brought home to coastal States their vulnerability from foreign flagged ships, over which they had no control, transiting their coastal waters and visiting their ports.

These concerns lead to the signing by 14 European States of a Memorandum of Understanding on port State control in Paris in 1983 (Paris MOU), under which all members undertook to inspect a total of 25% of ships visiting their ports. This MOU has been followed by eight other regional MOUs over the succeeding 20 years, not including the unilateral port State control programme operated by the United States of America. Regional port State control MOUs are increasingly

---

[94]IMO Resolution A.787(19); SOLAS I/19 as modified by the SOLAS Protocol 1988; SOLAS IX/6 and XI/4; article 21 of Load Lines 1966 as modified by the Load Line Protocol 1988; articles 5 and 6, regulation 15 of Annex II, regulation 8 of Annex III and regulation 8 of Annex V of MARPOL 73/78; article X of STCW 78; and article 12 of TONNAGE 69 provide for control procedures to be followed by a Party to a relevant convention with regard to foreign ships visiting their ports. The administrations of port States should make effective use of these provisions for the purposes of identifying deficiencies, if any, in such a ship which may render them substandard, and ensuring that remedial measures are taken.

[95]Paris MOU, 1982; Acuerdo de Vina del Mar, 1992; Tokyo MOU, 1993; Caribbean MOU, 1996; Mediterranean MOU, 1997; Indian Ocean MOU, 1998; West and Central African MOU, 1999; Black Sea MOU, 2000; Riyadh MOU, 2004. The United States of America operates a unilateral PSC regime.

cooperating and exchanging inspection data electronically in a cooperative endeavour to ensure that significantly substandard ships have nowhere left to trade, and are introducing qualitative risk-based inspection programmes, rather than earlier quantitative ones. The IMO is also taking an increasingly proactive role in the global harmonisation of port State control (PSC) through technical assistance to developing PSC MOUs, organisation of technical workshops for secretariats and database managers of regional PSC MOUs, and establishment of an ad hoc working group at FSI on harmonisation of port State control activities.

Port State control procedures under the IMO Resolution and regional MOUs allow for an initial inspection of the ship's relevant certificates and documents to ensure they are valid (IMO Resolution A.787(19), chapter 2.2.3). If the port State control officer's (PSCO) general impression and visual evidence on board confirm a good standard of maintenance, the PSCO should generally confine the inspection to reported or observed deficiencies, if any (IMO Resolution A.787(19), chapter 2.2.4). If, however, the PSCO, from general impressions or observations on board, has clear grounds for believing that the ship, its equipment, or crew do not substantially meet international standards, the PSCO should proceed to a more detailed inspection (IMO Resolution A.787(19), chapter 2.2.5). Ultimately, if the PSCO believes that the ship presents a threat to the safety of the crew or to the marine environment, he/she has the ability under SOLAS, MARPOL and IMO Resolution A.787(19), as reflected in national law of the port State, to detain the ship until the serious deficiencies have been rectified.[96]

If the ship is detained, the fact must be reported to the flag State, the RO if applicable, and the IMO. Under the national law of most port States,[97] detentions are challengeable and both the Paris and Tokyo MOUs have instituted detention review panels that consider objections from the owner or flag State to detentions. In 2007, the average detention rate of ships inspected across the two main regional port State control MOUs, Paris and Tokyo,[98] was almost identical at 5.46 and 5.62% respectively.[99]

The use of the term "clear grounds" has great significance in port State control and is amplified in SOLAS and the IMO Resolution.[100] SOLAS recognises the

---

[96]SOLAS 1/19; Resolution A.787(19) chapter 1.6.3 Detention: "Intervention action taken by a port State when the condition of the ship or its crew do not correspond substantially with the applicable conventions to ensure that the ship will not sail until it can proceed to sea without presenting a danger to the ship or persons on board, or without presenting an unreasonable threat of harm to the marine environment, whether or not such action will affect the normal schedule of the departure of the ship."

[97]For example New Zealand's Maritime Transport Act 1994, s.56/398.

[98]Tokyo MOU Annual Report 2007 (detention rate 5.46%) and Paris MOU Annual Report 2007 (detention rate 5.62%).

[99]Detentions rates in both the Paris and Tokyo MOU regions decreased steadily over the past decade from highs of 9.5% (2000) and 8.49% (2003) respectively to lows of 4.67% (2005) and 5.40% (2006) respectively. There has been a slight increase in detention rates in both regions since 2005–06.

[100]SOLAS 1/19(b): "Such certificates, if valid, shall be accepted unless there are clear grounds for believing that the condition of the ship or of its equipment does not correspond substantially with the particulars of any of the certificates or that the ship and its equipment are not in compliance with the provisions of regulation 11(a) and (b)."

sovereignty of flag States to issue certificates and the obligation of other States to accept these certificates as *prima facie* evidence of the ship's compliance with IMO instruments.[101] The experience and professionalism of the PSCO is a vital element in the assessment of the condition of the ship and its equipment (IMO Resolution A. 787(19), 2.4), and increasingly its safety management system, in determination of whether there are clear grounds for a detailed inspection – which may lead to detention of the ship with consequential delays and costs to the shipowner. Even with the most experienced and professional PSCO, it is not always possible to identify serious structural defects in a ship during a detailed inspection; defects that should be identified during regular statutory surveys by flag States or ROs authorised on their behalf.

8.12 Atlantic Trader

Many of the issues identified within the extant regulatory regime of ineffective registration, flag State control, and RO responsibility are encapsulated in the following case study of the *Atlantic Trader I*.

The *Atlantic Trader I* was one of three small (65 metres) roll on, roll off cargo vessels built in Norway in 1969 for an American company to trade between Florida/ Gulf ports and the Caribbean. Over the next 30 years the ship remained in this trade and underwent a number of changes of name and classification societies until she was bought by a New Zealand citizen in early 2001 for trade between the North and South Islands of New Zealand. At the time of purchase the ship was registered in Panama and was in class with a Taiwanese classification society, the China Corporation Register. The ship had a full set of valid statutory certificates issued by the classification society under authorisation by the flag State. The owner relied upon these certificates as evidence that the ship was sound and seaworthy in all respects, and did not have an out of water pre-purchase survey carried out before proceeding upon a voyage to Wellington with a New Zealand crew. As the ship was owned and operated by a New Zealand citizen it was required to be registered in New Zealand before departure from America (New Zealand Ship Registration Act 1992, s.6). The owner planned to re-flag the vessel upon arrival in New Zealand but could not re-register while the vessel was still registered under Panamaian law.[102]

During the delivery voyage it was found to be impossible to keep the ship's double bottom ballast tanks dry, and difficult for the ship's pumps to cope with the ingress of water. For this reason the owner diverted the ship to Auckland as first port in New Zealand for an out of water inspection. It was discovered that the

---

[101] An obligation which is, for example, reflected in New Zealand through the Maritime Transport Act 1994, s.41.

[102] *Ibid*, s.9. It was not clear what entitlement a New Zealand citizen would have to retain the Panamanian registration

bottom plating was severely corroded and had numerous holes covered illegally by small patches and wooden and rubber plugs. Inspection of the ballast tanks revealed extreme corrosion and wastage of structural members to the extent that the ship was inherently unsafe and unseaworthy. Upon arrival in Auckland the ship was due for her annual classification society survey by China Corporation on behalf of the flag State after which the surveyor refused to issue statutory certificates and recommended that the ship be removed from Class. The Maritime Safety Authority of New Zealand carried out a port State control inspection, discovered 51 deficiencies and detained the ship in June 2001.

If the *Atlantic Trader I* had been re-registered as a New Zealand SOLAS ship at a port in the United States, the New Zealand administration would have appointed a local classification society surveyor to confirm the ship's tonnage for registration purposes, and to carry out an inspection of the safety, lifesaving, and fire-fighting equipment to ensure the ship was adequately equipped and crewed to international standards for the delivery voyage to New Zealand. There would have been no requirement under New Zealand law for a structural survey at this time before registration and it is doubtful whether the classification society would have had a requirement for a full change of flag survey. The ship's extant statutory certificates issued by the RO on behalf of Panama would have had to have been accepted as evidence of the structural integrity of the ship. A flag State inspection would have been carried out upon arrival in New Zealand but this would not have included a survey of the ship's internal structure, nor would it have required an out of water survey, as the ship's certification for its existing survey cycle would have been accepted.

If the ship had arrived in Wellington as first port of call in New Zealand under the Panamanian flag, and no notification had been made of the flooding problems experienced en route, a port State control inspection would have been carried out upon arrival. There would have been clear grounds for a detailed inspection but the ship was in a superficially good condition for her age and most of the 51 deficiencies concerned safety and fire-fighting equipment. As there would have been no indication, with the ship afloat, of the severe corrosion in ballast tanks and hull, the port State control inspection would not have included these spaces. As New Zealand does not recognise the China Corporation classification society the ship would have undergone a change of flag survey by the "gaining" classification society under delegation from New Zealand but this would not have included an internal or out of water survey, again due to the fact that the ship had valid statutory certificates. The *Atlantic Trader 1* would then have been registered as a New Zealand ship and, once the deficiencies had been rectified, allowed to commence carrying cargo in the Cook Strait trade with a New Zealand crew and up to 12 passengers.

A third option, under international and New Zealand law, would have been for the New Zealand owner to register a company in Panama and to operate the ship in New Zealand waters under the Panamanian flag and the China Corporation Register classification society. New Zealand would have been obliged to accept the certificates issued by this classification society on behalf of the Panamanian flag State as *prima facie* evidence of the ship's existing and ongoing compliance with international standards.

Under any of these registration arrangements a significantly substandard ship could have operated on the New Zealand coast, or worldwide if the owner had so required. The *Atlantic Trader 1* was in such a sub-standard condition that she remained under detention from 2001 until being broken up and scrapped in her berth in 2008.

References

Barchue LD (2005) Making a case for the Voluntary IMO Member State Audit Scheme. October. http://www.imo.org/home.asp.

Boisson P (1994) Classification societies and safety at sea: Back to the basics to prepare for the future. Marine Policy. Vol 18, Issue 5

Hidaka M, Chairman (2001) IACS: The Role of Class in Meeting the Safety Challenge. Seatrade Safe Shipping Conference, 10 April. http://www.iacs.org.uk/seatrade.htm.

Hoppe H (2000) IMO: The Work of the Sub-Committee on Flag State Implementation – An Overview. http://www.imo.org/InfoResource/mainframe.asp?topic_id = 406&doc_id = 1080

IACS Briefing (1997) IACS and IMO, The Essential Relationship. No 4. February. International Association of Classification Societies Ltd.

IMO (1998) Focus on IMO. IMO 1948–1998: a process of change. International Maritime Organization, London

IMO (2008) Delegate's Report to Maritime New Zealand on the 100th Session of the IMO Council

Lampe WH (1983) The "New" International Maritime Organization And Its Place In Development of International Maritime Law. Journal of Maritime Law and Commerce. Vol 14, No 3

Lloyd's Register of Shipping. A Brief History. http://www.lr.org/corporate_information/brief_history.htm.

Lloyd's Register of Shipping – Fairplay (2005) Opinion. 18 August

Lloyd's Register of Shipping – Fairplay (2005) 25 Years Ago in Fairplay. 13 October

Lloyd's Register of Shipping – Fairplay (2005) November

Marten-Castex B (2004) The Work of the Sub-Committee on Flag State Implementation: An Overview, (2003 – up to and including FSI 11). 19 January. http://www.imo.org/home.asp.

O'Neill W (2001) Raising the Safety Bar – Improving Marine Safety in the 21st Century. Speech to the Seatrade Safe Shipping Conference, Royal College of Surgeons, London, 10 April. http://www.imo.org.org/Safety/mainframe.asp?topic_id = 82&doc_id = 703.

Sasamura Y (2003) Development of Audit Scheme in ICAO and IMO. Seminar on Model Audit Scheme. London, 27 May

Documents

IMO (2003) IMO: Committed people working for Safe, Secure and Clean Seas. Paper J/8351, World Maritime Day 2003, Background paper

IMO (2005) MSC/MEPC.5/Circ.2. Survey and Certification-related Matters, Guidelines for Administrations to ensure the adequacy of transfer of class-related matters between recognized organizations. 26 September.

IMO (2007) Circular letter No.2830. 6 December

International Labour Organization Office (2006) International Labour Conference, 94th (Maritime) Session. Report I(1A), Adoption of an instrument to consolidate maritime labour standards. International Labour Office, Geneva

Chapter 9
Measures of Flag State Administrative and Social Performance

Abstract In order to analyse flag State social and administrative performance it is necessary to examine the duties required by the LOSC and principal IMO and ILO instruments. An analysis of flag State performance of administrative and social duties is undertaken to test the hypothesis that International and Pseudo-National flag States have worse records of administrative and social performance than National flag States. The effectiveness of flag State administrative performance is measured through ratification of IMO instruments and analysis of the delivery of various mandatory reports required by the IMO under the principal maritime safety and pollution prevention conventions. The effectiveness of flag State social performance is measured through ratification of ILO maritime labour standards along with an analysis of measures used by the International Transport Workers' Federation, and the results of port State control inspections of seafarers' working and living conditions.

9.1 Measures of Performance of Flag State Administrative Duties

The LOSC requires every State to assume jurisdiction under its internal law over each ship flying its flag and its master, officers, and crew, in respect of administrative, technical, and social matters concerning the ship (LOSC, Article 94(2)(b)). The principal Conventions developed by the Member States of the IMO place a general obligation upon contracting governments to, for example:

> undertake to give effect to the provisions of the present Convention and the Annex thereto, which shall constitute an integral part of the present Convention. Every reference to the present Convention constitutes at the same time a reference to the annex. The Contracting Governments undertake to promulgate all laws, decrees, orders and regulations and to take all other steps which may be necessary to give the present Convention full and complete effect, so as to ensure that, from the point of view of safety of life at sea, a ship is fit for the service for which it is intended. (SOLAS 74, Article 1(a)(b))

There are, therefore, clear and explicit requirements in international law for a contracting Government, in this case a flag State, to ratify a Convention and bring it into full and complete effect through its internal law. A flag State is not under any obligation to implement the provisions of a Convention to which it is not a party.[1] The extent of ratification of maritime Conventions by a flag State is a measure of the commitment of that State to abide by the international standards agreed by the Member States of the IMO, to bring them into effect through their internal law, and to fully and effectively implement and enforce them.

9.1.1   Ratification of IMO Instruments

It has already been determined that the overwhelming majority of flag States are Member States of the IMO and also that it is not necessary for a flag State to belong to that Organization in order to ratify[2] maritime Conventions.[3] Information available on the ratification of IMO maritime safety and security instruments as at 29 February 2008 (IMO 2008, Document MSC 84/INF.13), indicates that out of 194 identified flag States, the majority have ratified the principal safety and pollution prevention Conventions. 158 flag States have accepted SOLAS 74. STCW 78 has also received broad acceptance by 151 flag States, as has the International Regulations for the Prevention of Collisions at Sea, 1972 (COLREG 72) with 151 acceptances (IMO website). Load Line 66 has been accepted by 158 States (IMO website). Statistics for percentages of world tonnage represented by IMO member States' ratification of these instruments confirms the very high levels of acceptance of these IMO instruments.[4]

The high acceptance of IMO Conventions can be explained by the fact that all of the statutory safety and pollution prevention certificates that enable a ship to trade internationally are issued under these particular instruments.[5] Their ratification is necessary for a flag State of any ilk – National, International or Pseudo-National – as the contracting Government to the Convention, to issue certificates under its

---

[1] Vienna Convention on the Law of Treaties, Article 34: A treaty does not create either obligations or rights for a third State without its consent. For example, a port State cannot take enforcement action under Annex VI of MARPOL if its Government has not ratified that instrument and brought it into effect under its national law.

[2] The Vienna Convention on the Law of Treaties states in Article 2(1)(b) that: "'ratification', 'acceptance', 'approval', and 'accession' mean in each case the international act so named, whereby a State establishes on the international plane its consent to be bound by a treaty."

[3] An example is that of the Cook Islands who, when not members of the IMO nor the UN, ratified TONNAGE 69, LOAD LINE 66, SOLAS 74 and the 1988 Protocols. See *Tokyo MOU Port State Control Manual, Section 1–8pp. SI–7–1 to SI–7–4. Revision 1/2006.* (Information supplied to the Tokyo MOU Secretariat by the IMO.) Cook Islands gained membership of the IMO in July 2008.

[4] *Ibid*, and Lloyd's Register of Shipping, World Fleet Statistics, as at 29 February 2008: SOLAS 74, 98.80%; STCW 78, 98.77%; COLREG 72, 98.05%; LOAD LINE 66, 98.77%.

[5] *Ibid*. TONNAGE 69, which does not have any safety or pollution prevention requirements, but which determines the ships tonnage and is necessary for registration, has been accepted by 147 flag States.

internal law. The percentage of acceptance by flag States is increased when it is taken into account that 29 of these 194 flag States, including a high number of developing African States, have not accepted any of the principal maritime Conventions.[6] Most of these flag States have insignificant registered tonnage and only five of them appear in authoritative statistics of world tonnage.[7] Port State inspection statistics confirm that the majority of these flag States are either inactive, or have very small fleets that are not trading internationally.[8]

This very broad acceptance of maritime conventions gives no indication of effective implementation through national law, nor of effective enforcement by the flag State. A better indication of the ongoing commitment of a flag State to its administrative responsibilities is the extent, and speed, to which it has ratified protocols and annexes to maritime conventions such as the 1978 and 1988 Protocols to SOLAS 74, the voluntary annexes to the MARPOL Convention, and the 1988 Protocol to the Load Line Convention. Once again there has been broad acceptance of these instruments,[9] albeit generally lower than the principal instruments, with no clear demarcations between categories of flag State.

Speed of acceptance could be taken as an indication of a flag State's desire to be a responsible international citizen and it could be expected that national flag States would be proactive in ratification of new instruments. This is borne out, for example, by initial acceptance of Annex VI[10] of MARPOL 73/78 that came into force on 19 May 2005. The 29 flag States[11] that had accepted this instrument as of August 2005 were predominantly National and International flag States with a smattering of Pseudo-National flags such as Marshall Islands and Vanuatu. It must, however, be acknowledged that flag States are often constrained in their ability to bring instruments into effect through their national law due to other political priorities, and that Annex VI of MARPOL 73/78 has only been in force for a relatively short time.

---

[6]*Ibid.* Afghanistan, Andorra, Armenia, Bosnia and Herzegovina, Botswana, Burkina Faso, Burundi, Central African Republic, Chad, Costa Rica, Guinea-Bissau, Kyrgyzstan, Laos, Liechtenstein, Mali, Federated States of Micronesia, Nauru, Nepal, Niger, Palau, Rwanda, San Marino, Swaziland, Tajikistan, the former Yugoslav Republic of Macedonia, Turkmenistan, Uganda, Uzbekistan, Zimbabwe.

[7]Lloyd's Register – *Fairplay*, World Fleet Statistics 2005: Costa Rica, 16 ships (4,863 GT); Guinea-Bissau, 25 ships (6,627 GT); Laos, 2 ships (2,853 GT); Micronesia, 21 ships (12,392 GT); Turkmenistan, 45 ships (48,516 GT).

[8] None of these twentynine flag States appear in the lists of flag States inspected by the Paris MOU in 2004 and the Tokyo MOU in 2005. (See Annual Reports).

[9]*Ibid.* SOLAS Protocol 78 (112); SOLAS Protocol 88 (81); MARPOL, Annex III (121), Annex IV (107), Annex V (127), and Annex VI (29).

[10] Regulations for the Prevention of Air Pollution from Ships.

[11]Azerbaijan, Bahamas, Bangladesh, Barbados, Bulgaria, Croatia, Cyprus, Denmark, Estonia, Finland, France, Germany, Greece, Japan, Liberia, Lithuania, Luxembourg, Marshall Islands, Norway, Panama, Poland, St Kitts and Nevis, Samoa, Saudi Arabia, Singapore, Spain, Sweden, United Kingdom, and Vanuatu.

9.2   Mandatory Reporting to the IMO

There are a number of mandatory requirements under IMO instruments for Member States to report the activities they undertake for administration of the ships to which they have granted nationality. The delivery of these reports requires a commitment from the flag State to comply with the mandatory requirements of the particular convention, to record and analyse statistics, and carry out investigations into serious casualties, with the commensurate requirement for skilled and qualified staff to carry out these administrative functions. These mandatory IMO reporting requirements are examined to determine whether the degree of their support and compliance can indicate the effectiveness of the various categories of flag States in fully implementing their administrative duties.

9.2.1   MARPOL Mandatory Reporting Requirements

MARPOL 73/78 requires a number of reports to be made by Member States of the IMO to that Organization. These reports include: notification to IMO of the appropriate officer or agency to receive and process all reports received from Masters of ships on pollution incidents (MARPOL 73/78, Article 8(2)); communication of information on the text of any national law promulgated on the various matters within the scope of MARPOL (MARPOL, Article 11(1)(a)); a list of nominated surveyors or Recognized Organizations which are authorised to act on their behalf in the administration of matters relating to the design, construction, equipment and operation of ships carrying harmful substances (MARPOL, 11(1)(b)); a sufficient number of specimens of their certificates issued under the provisions of the regulations (MARPOL, 11(1)(c)); a list of reception facilities (MARPOL, 11(1)(d)); official reports so far as they show the results of application of MARPOL (MARPOL, 11(1)(e)), and an annual statistical report, in a form standardised by IMO, of penalties actually imposed for infringements of MARPOL (MARPOL, 11(1)(f)). Casualties to ships which might be deleterious to the marine environment are required by MARPOL to be investigated and reported to the IMO if such information might assist the Organization in determining what changes to the Convention might be desirable (MARPOL, Article 12(1) and (2)).

These mandatory reports are required by an IMO Circular[12] to be reported in a particular format to the FSI Sub-committee as a standing agenda item. The report for 2004 (IMO 2004, Document FSI 14/4) recorded that the rate of reporting "has also been consistently low (20%), as also was in the past 5 years".[13] An analysis of the levels of reporting by category of flag State revealed that of the 28 Member

---

[12] MEPC/Circ.318, Formats for a mandatory reporting system under MARPOL 73/78.

[13] *Ibid*, Reporting percentages were: 1999 – 16.1%; 2000 – 16.0%; 2001 – 20.8%; 2002 – 16.8%; 2003 – 23.8%; 2004 – 20.8%.

States that reported in 2004, 24 were National flag States, three International and one Pseudo-National. Of a total of 137 reporting and non-reporting parties to MARPOL, as identified by the IMO (IMO 2004, Document FSI 14/4/1), a total of 19 (13.9%) submitted their mandatory reports every year over the 5 years from 1999–2004 (IMO 2004, Document FSI 14/4/1). Sixteen of these were submitted by National flag States, two by International flag States and one by a Pseudo-National flag State. Over the same period eight parties to MARPOL submitted four out of five reports: seven National flag States and one Pseudo-National flag State.

Of the 72 parties to MARPOL that failed to submit any reports over this 5 year period the majority were National flag States (58) followed by Pseudo-National (11) and International (3). A small percentage of predominantly National flag States fully meet, or almost meet, their mandatory reporting requirements under MARPOL 73/78 and a very large percentage of all three categories of flag State do not, including the large International flag States of Panama, Malta, and Cyprus, and the majority of Pseudo-National flag States.

The report for 2006 (IMO 2006, Document FSI 16/4) notes that the rate of reporting is still very low and noted that this had been the comment on the report for the previous five meetings of the FSI Sub-committee. Of the 120 Member States of IMO that were Party to MARPOL over the 5 year period from 2002–2006 inclusive, 19 had reported every year. Seventeen of these States were National, with one each International and Pseudo-National flag States. Thirty-four member States reported for the 2006 year, comprising 27 National, 3 International and 4 Pseudo-National flag States.

9.2.2   SOLAS Mandatory Casualty Reports

One of the administrative duties of a flag State under the LOSC is for a State to hold inquiries into serious casualties involving vessels flying its flag upon the high seas, and to cooperate with other States in the conduct of such inquiries[14] This requirement is brought into effect in international maritime law through SOLAS 74 which requires that:

> Each Administration undertakes to conduct an investigation of any casualty occurring to any of its ships subject to the provision of the present Convention when it judges that such an investigation may assist in determining what changes in the present regulations might be desirable.

> Each Contracting Government undertakes to supply the Organization with pertinent information concerning the findings of such investigations. No reports or recommendations of the Organization based upon such information shall disclose the identity or nationality of the ships concerned or in any manner fix or imply responsibility upon any ship or person. (SOLAS 74, Chapter I, Part C, Regulation 21(a) and (b))

---

[14]LOSC, Article 94(7). Similar casualty reporting requirements are contained in Article 23 of the International Convention on Load Lines, London, 5 April 1966. #640 *UNTS* 133.

The IMO has produced guidelines for the conduct of investigations by flag States into marine casualties and incidents.[15] The resultant reports by flag States of serious casualties are required to be made to FSI and are analysed by a Correspondence Group and Working Group on Casualty Analysis (http://www.imo.org/Safety/ mainframe.asp?topic_id = 799). A total of 74 casualty reports that had been analysed by the Correspondence Group were reported to the fifteenth meeting of FSI in June 2006 (IMO 2006, Document FSI 14/5). Three of these casualties dated back to 2002, with the balance spread evenly between 2003 and 2004. It is not proposed to analyse the causes of these casualties, but rather to determine the categories of flag States that fulfil their administrative requirements to investigate serious casualties affecting their ships and report the results to the IMO for analysis.

The 74 casualties between 2002 and 2004 were reported by a total of 29 flag States in 2006, with almost half of the reports being made by two National flag States – Germany and the United Kingdom, with 11 reports each – and the International flag States of Panama and the Bahamas with six reports each. The total of six reports from the Bahamas of serious casualties involving ships flying its flag were misleading, as two of these casualties[16] were investigated by the coastal State, New Zealand, as was one casualty under the Singapore flag to another ship suffering a serious structural failure in a New Zealand port.[17] In all three casualties the flag States were notified of the casualties but did not wish to undertake investigations.[18]

It is not unusual for a coastal State to be vitally interested in determining the cause of a casualty to a foreign flagged ship in its waters, as the casualty may be the result of a failure of the port entry or departure systems, such as vessel traffic services, pilotage, or aids to navigation, rather than any fault of the foreign flagged ship. That coastal State may well advise the flag State of the casualty and enquire as to whether they will be carrying out an investigation. This is entirely consistent with the LOSC, which requires cooperation between the flag State and the other State in the conduct of any inquiry held by that State into any [such] marine casualty or incident of navigation (LOSC, Article 94(7)). Sometimes the flag State will request the coastal State to carry out the casualty investigation on its behalf, but it is not uncommon for there to be no response from the flag State.

The relatively large number of reports from Germany and the United Kingdom are disproportionate when it is taken into account that, in 2005, there were 894 and 1,563 ships respectively registered under these flags, compared with 6,838 under the Panamanian flag and 1,361 registered in the Bahamas (Fairplay 2005, p. 10). The remaining 41 reports were received from 14 National, five International and four Pseudo-National flag States.[19] The fact that the numbers of ships registered in

---

[15] Resolution A.849(20), Code for the investigation of marine casualties and incidents, as amended by Resolution A.884(21).27 November 1997.

[16] *Eastern Honour* and *Capella Voyager*.

[17] *Perla*.

[18] IMO has amended the reporting form for casulaties to identify the Flag Administration and the Reporting Administration. See IMO document FSI 16/6/1, Casualty Statistics and Investigations, List of reports of investigations into casualties, Note by the Secretariat, 17 March 2008.

[19] Antigua and Barbada (2), Marshall Islands (1), Vanuatu (2) and St Vincent and the Grenadines (2).

these four States totalled 1,030; 853; 409; and 1,044 respectively in 2005 (Fairplay 2005, pp. 10, 21, 26, 27) would indicate significant under reporting.

The majority of the 24 flag States that reported a total of 54 very serious and serious casualties were National[20] (13) followed by International[21] (7) and Pseudo-National[22] (4), with 39% of reports coming from two National and two International flag States. The above statistics indicate that there is a marked lack of reporting by the majority of National and Pseudo-National flag States and that reporting by all flag States may be misleading, in that the flag State may not have carried out the casualty investigation. Of the Member States that do consistently meet their reporting requirements under various IMO instruments, the great majority are National flag States. All International flag States reported serious casualties over this 3 year period, but the numbers of reports were minimal compared with the total number of ships on their registers and the probable percentage of casualties experienced by those ships. The majority of Pseudo-National flag States do not report and, of those few that do, there appears to be significant under-reporting.

9.2.3 Mandatory Reporting by Flag States of Delegations to Recognized Organizations

The delegation of statutory functions by a flag State to ROs, and the category of those ROs – Conventional or Convenient – is a measure of the administrative responsibility and ability of a flag State. It is argued that a flag State that only delegates the functions prescribed by IMO instruments – survey, certification, and determination of tonnage – to Conventional ROs is clearly exercising its administrative duties more responsibly than one that delegates all, or some, of its maritime administration to Convenient ROs, or to a mixture of Conventional and Convenient ROs. An examination of information contained on the IMO's GISIS database[23] supports this hypothesis. As at September 2006, a total of 90 National, International and Pseudo-National flag States had met the request of the Secretary-General to collect information on the implementation of the applicable resolution and had reported (IMO Resolution A.739(18)(4)) to the IMO on the ROs acting on their behalf. A large number of States listed by the IMO as flag States had either not reported or had not delegated any functions to ROs, although the very large number of these supposed flag States, at 232, is not supported by previously identified figures of active flag States of 160. A little more than half of active flag States have therefore reported to the IMO on the identity of the organisations they have recognised. Of the 90 reporting States, 73 can be categorised as National, seven as International and ten as Pseudo-National flag States.

---

[20] Netherlands, North Korea, France, Germany, United Kingdom, Denmark, Norway, Turkey, Italy, Sweden, Egypt, Philippines, and Japan.

[21] Panama, Hong Kong, Bahamas, Liberia, Singapore, Malta, and Cyprus.

[22] Vanuatu, St Vincent and the Grenadines, Antigua and Barbuda, and the Marshall Islands.

[23] http://gisis.imo.org/Public/RO/BrowseOrganisation.aspx?oid = 47. See Table 9.1, Appendix I, for a list of the 85 recognized organizations listed on the GISIS database.

A little under half, a total of 44 flag States, have delegated only to Conventional ROs. The great majority of these 44 flag States are National[24] (39), followed by four International[25] and one Pseudo-National flag State.[26] Some National flag States[27] restrict delegation to only one RO; often the national Classification Society.[28] A further 25 flag States have delegated their statutory functions to conventional ROs plus one other; usually an associate member of IACS[29] or a national Classification Society.[30] Of these 25 flag States, 21 are National,[31] one International,[32] and three Pseudo-National.[33]

A striking feature of the GISIS database in 2006 was the large number of delegations to ROs by some flag States. The largest flag State, Panama, led this list with a total of 28 delegations, including all IACS and (previously) associate IACS members. Panama was followed by the Pseudo-National flag State of Belize with 24 delegations including ten Conventional ROs, and the National flag State of Georgia with 22 ROs; evenly split between Conventional and Convenient. The Pseudo-National flag State of Honduras was close behind Georgia with 20 delegations including nine Conventional ROs. Other Pseudo-National flag States of Saint Vincent and the Grenadines with 17 delegations, Comoros (16), and Cambodia (14) also stood out, along with the International flag of Cyprus (15); not only for large numbers of delegations. Of these eight flag States with large numbers of Convenient as well as Conventional ROs, four – Cambodia, Saint Vincent and the Grenadines, Honduras and Belize – appeared on the Black Lists of both the Paris and Tokyo port State control regimes in 2004; and in the same year, Georgia and Panama were on the Paris MOU Black List, and Cyprus on the Grey List, of both port State control regimes.

This evidence may not be a conclusive indication of a causal link between a regulatory inefficient administration that has delegated to a large numbers of ROs, and the safety record of their ships, as other flag States on these Black Lists with equally bad safety records have delegated their statutory functions to relatively few ROs.[34]

---

[24] Algeria, Australia, Austria, Azerbaijan, Bangladesh, Barbados, Belgium, Chile, Denmark, Djibouti, Ecuador, Estonia, Ethiopia, Finland, France, Germany, Iceland, Israel, Italy, Kuwait, Luxembourg, Malaysia, Maldives, Mexico, Netherlands, New Zealand, Norway, Pakistan, Papua New Guinea, Republic of Korea, Russian Federation, Saudi Arabia, Somalia, Sweden, Switzerland, Thailand, Trinidad and Tobago, Tunisia, and United States of America.

[25] Bahamas, Hong Kong, Liberia, and Singapore.

[26] Antigua and Barbuda.

[27] Germany, Japan, Azerbaijan, Chile, the Republic of Korea, and the Russian Federation.

[28] For example, Germanischer Lloyd by the German flag State.

[29] Croation Register of Shipping, Indian Register of Shipping, Polski Regestr Statkow.

[30] For example, Turkish Lloyd by the Turkish flag State.

[31] Brazil, Bulgaria, Colombia, Cuba, Egypt, Greece, Hungary, India, Indonesia, Iran, Latvia, Libya, Lithuania, Oman, Philippines, Poland, Portugal, Romania, Slovenia, South Africa, and Turkey.

[32] Malta.

[33] Marshall Islands, Tuvalu, and Vanuatu.

[34] For example, the pseudo-national flag State of Bolivia has delegated to three convenient ROs, and the national flag State of the Democratic Republic of Korea to one convenient RO.

There are also National flag States on both Black Lists who have delegated their statutory functions exclusively to conventional ROs, although they are a minority.[35]

9.3   Performance Measures for Flag State Social Duties

Every State is required by the LOSC to effectively exercise its jurisdiction and control in social matters over ships flying its flag (LOSC, Article 94(1)). The LOSC also requires every State to assume jurisdiction under its internal law over each ship flying its flag and its master, officers, and crew in respect of social matters concerning the ship (LOSC, Article 94(2)(b)). The LOSC goes on to require each State to take such measures for ships flying its flag as are necessary to ensure safety at sea with regard, *inter alia,* to: "...the manning of ships, labour conditions and the training of crews, taking into account the applicable international instruments." (LOSC, Article 94(3)(b)) In taking these measures States are required to conform to generally accepted international regulations, procedures, and practices and to take any steps which may be necessary to secure their observance (LOSC, Article 94(5)).

9.4   ILO Instruments

The generally accepted international regulations for social matters aboard ships are the 40 Conventions and 29 Recommendations developed by the International Labour Organization from shortly after its creation under the Treaty of Versailles in 1919 (ILO 1998, Annex 1, pp. 153–154) to the present day. From its foundation the ILO gave particular attention to working and living conditions aboard ships, with the first Maritime Session of the International Labour Conference being held in 1920. The National Seamen's Codes Recommendations (ILO 9), which was adopted that year, referred to the concept of an international seamen's code that would ensure that all seafarers of the world "whether engaged on ships of their own or foreign countries, may have a better comprehension of their rights and obligations." (ILO 2006, p. 2) The wide-ranging ILO Conventions for SOLAS vessels have not all received the requisite number of ratifications to come into force[36] and many of them, such as the Minimum Age (Trimmers and Stokers) Convention 1921, have been overtaken by time and technology.[37]

---

[35] Four out of a combined total of 28 flag States: Egypt, Thailand, Bangladesh, and Algeria.

[36] *Ibid*: "Thirteen Conventions have not received the required number of ratifications for entry into force or are no longer open to ratification as a result of entry into force of a revising Convention".

[37] For example, trimmers and stokers were required for coal burning steam engines, which have long since been replaced as a means of propulsion for ships.

Four other Conventions, which apply to all workers, are also considered by the ILO to be of relevance to minimum maritime standards.[38]

A weakness in the effectiveness and widespread acceptance of ILO instruments is the very low level of ratifications necessary for their entry into force. Even with these low thresholds, the Social Security (Seafarers) Convention 1946 (ILO Convention C70), with a requirement for only seven ratifications, did not receive enough support to enter into force. The revised Convention, 1987, has two ratifications. Regarding accommodation standards for seafarers, the Accommodation of Crews Convention 1946 (ILO 92), never received enough support to enter into force and was replaced with a revised Convention in 1949 that, in 2005, had been ratified by only 42 of the 178 ILO Member States.[39] The ILO acknowledges this issue and claims that low levels of ratification of maritime Conventions can be explained by the fact that a number of ILO Member States do not have a strong interest in maritime affairs (ILO 2006, p. 3). This claim can be disputed by an analysis that identifies that 160 of ILO's Members States have been identified as flag States and Member States of the IMO.[40] Further, an analysis of annual ratifications of IMO maritime labour standards between 1970 and 2005 (ILO 2006, pp. 6–7) reveals an average of 12.5 ratifications per year; a figure which has been inflated by the advent of new States[41] following the fall of the Berlin Wall in 1991 and by a large number of ratifications of maritime Conventions by Serbia and Montenegro in 2000.[42] Most of these new ILO Member States are members of both the ILO and IMO, and half are active flag States.[43]

9.4.1 ILO Merchant Shipping (Minimum Standards) Convention, 1976 (ILO 147)

In an effort to obtain more universal acceptance of maritime labour standards the decision was made by the ILO in 1976 to consolidate a number of important maritime instruments into one Convention: the Merchant Shipping (Minimum Standards)

---

[38]Freedom of Association and protection of the Right to Organise Convention, 1948 (No 87); the Right to Organise and Collective Bargaining Convention, 1949 (No 198); the Medical Care and Sickness Benefits Convention, 1969 (No 130); and the Minimum Age Convention, 1973 (No 138). Other ILO instruments of general scope which are of importance to seafarers include the Forced Labour Convention, 1930 (No 29); the Abolition of Forced Labour Convention, 1973 (No 138); and the Discrimination (Employment and Occupation) Convention, 1958 (No 111).

[39]Number of ILO Member States as at 30 September, 2005.

[40]See Table 9.1, Appendix I, for a list of States that have ratified both IMO and ILO instruments.

[41]Ibid. Croatia, The Former Yugoslav Republic of Macedonia, Azerbaijan, Kyrgyzstan, Slovenia, Tajikistan, Bosnia and Herzegovina.

[42]Ibid.

[43]The exceptions are Kyrgyzstan and Tajikistan both of which are neither members of IMO nor flag States, and Macedonia and Bosnia and Herzegovina, which are not known to be flag States.

Convention 1976 (ILO 147).[44] This Convention, which has been subsequently updated through a Protocol of 1996,[45] came into force in 1981 and has since been ratified by 51 States. ILO 147 incorporates nine seafarer welfare Conventions[46] and two other core ILO Conventions applicable to all workers.[47] However, ratification of ILO 147 by many States has been slow[48] and the ILO in 1997 commented that:

> Convention No 147 has become the basic point of reference in the maritime industry for minimal acceptable standards on living and working conditions of seafarers. Although more than 50 per cent of the world fleet is now covered by this instrument, six of the top 15 shipping countries have still not ratified it: Panama, Bahamas, Malta, China, Singapore and the Philippines. (ILO Focus 1997, Vol. 10, No. 1)

ILO 147, and its Protocol, has been given added weight by its inclusion as a relevant instrument for all members of the Paris and Tokyo MOUs on port State control, enabling them to utilise the "no more favourable treatment" principle to encourage recalcitrant States to ratify ILO 147. Ratification of ILO 147 is a condition of membership of the Paris MOU,[49] but that is not the case for the Tokyo MOU. Many States in the Asia-Pacific region do not find the inclusion of ILO 87 and ILO 98 politically acceptable as they are perceived to legitimise labour strikes over economic and social issues, sympathy strikes and secondary boycotts. Only four of the 18 members of the Tokyo MOU have ratified ILO 147.[50] One of the features of

---

[44]ILO Convention No 147 concerning Minimum Standards in Merchant Ships, Geneva, 29 October 1976. ND IV.

[45]P147 Protocol of 1996 to the Merchant Shipping (Minimum Standards) Convention, 1975, Geneva, 22 October 1996.

[46]Minimum Age Convention 1973 (N0. 138), or Minimum Age (Sea) Convention (Revised) 1936 (No 58), or Minimum Wage (Sea) Convention 1920 (No7); Shipowners' Liability (Sick and Injured Seamen) Convention 1936 (No 56), or Medical Care and Sickness Benefits Convention, 1969 (No 130); Medical Examination (Seafarers) Convention 1946 (No 73); Prevention of Accidents (Seafarers) Convention 1970 (No 134) (Articles 4 and 7); Accommodation of Crews Convention (Revised) 1949 (No 92); Food and Catering (Ships' Crews) Convention 1946 (N0. 68) (Article 5); Officers' Competency Certificates Convention 1936 (No 53) (Articles 3 and 4); Repatriation of Seamen Convention 1926 (No 23).

[47]Freedom of Association and Protection of the Right to Organize Convention 1948 (No 87); and the Right to Organise and Collective Bargaining Convention 1949 (No 98).

[48]The Global Seafarer: Living and working conditions in a globalised industry, International Labour Organization Office, Geneva, 2004, pp. 39–40. For example: "Convention No 147 is dated 1976, yet the Bahamas did not ratify it until 2001, Cyprus in 1995 and Barbados in 1994 (a notable exception is Liberia, which ratified this instrument in 1981). By contrast, embedded maritime States have tended to ratify the Convention with greater speed, for example France ratified it in 1978, Norway in 1979 and Greece in 1979. This also applies to international labour Conventions in general: open registers ratify fewer Conventions and do so more slowly than embedded maritime nations. In fact, both Vanuatu and the Marshall islands are not even ILO members."

[49]Paris MOU, Changing Course, Annual Report 2004, p. 13: "Convention 147 is a relevant instrument applied by the Paris MOU as well as the EC Directive on Port State Control."

[50]Tokyo MOU Annual Report, 2007, p. 17. The members that have ratified ILO 147 are Canada, Hong Kong, Japan, and the Russian Federation. (Canada and the Russian Federation are also members of the Paris MOU under which ratification is a pre-requisite for membership).

this Convention is that its component instruments can be ratified individually under internal law and this is the case for many States. A port State can therefore enforce requirements of the component Conventions if they have been brought into effect in internal law and this is the case for many members of the Tokyo MOU (Tokyo Annual Report 2007, p. 17).

9.4.2   Flag State Ratification of ILO Maritime Labour Standards

A measure of the social responsibility of a flag State is the extent to which it has ratified ILO maritime labour Conventions. It could reasonably be expected that National flag States that, by definition, require some or all of the crew to be nationals of the State would have a higher commitment to decent working and living conditions for seafarers than either International or Pseudo-National flag States. Further, developed National flags could be expected to have a higher rate of ratification than the average for all National flags. This commitment, or lack of same, would be expressed through the number and scope of ratifications of important ILO maritime labour Conventions; in particular ILO 147. Table A.4, Appendix A, summarises memberships by maritime States of both the IMO and ILO, total numbers of ratifications of ILO maritime labour standards, and those States that have ratified ILO 147 and its Protocol of 1996. This analysis includes the 166 Member States of the IMO at 2006 plus one associate member (Hong Kong, China), and the 117 maritime States identified by the ILO,[51] out of the total ILO membership in 2006 of 178 States.[52] Inactive flag States, those operating domestically, or those not operating in the Paris or Tokyo MOU port State control regions are in parentheses.

9.4.3   Member States of the ILO and IMO and Ratifications of Maritime Labour Standards: National Flag States

The data in Table A.4 for National flag States demonstrates that 30% of active and inactive National flag States have ratified ILO 147 and 10% have also ratified the 1996 Protocol to ILO 147 (P147). The average number of ratifications for all National flag States is 6.44. If the 51 inactive flag States[53] are removed the figures become 46.3%, 15.4%, and 6.9%, respectively. The argument that developed National flags could be expected to have a higher rate of ratification of ILO maritime labour

---

[51] ILO Member States that have ratified maritime labour standards.
[52] Tuvalu has become the 182nd Member State of ILO on 2 June 2008. www.ilo.org.
[53] Indicated in Table 9.1 in parentheses.

standards than the average of all active National flags is confirmed by the rate for OECD countries,[54] all of which have, to some extent, a maritime infrastructure that depends upon national seafarers and mostly national flag vessels (Precious Associates 2003, p. 11). These ratios are 67% for ratification of ILO 147 and 33% for ratification of the 1996 Protocol to ILO 147. The average number of ratifications per OECD country at 13.93 is more than double that of all National flag States and almost double that of active National flag States, confirming that developed economies have the economic ability to have a social conscience.

9.4.4   Member States of ILO and IMO and Ratifications of Maritime Labour Standards: International Flag States

The data for the seven International flag States in Table 9.1 demonstrates that four (57%) have ratified ILO 147 and one (14.28%) has ratified the 1996 Protocol to ILO 147. The average number of ratifications (6.86) is slightly higher than that of all National flag States.[55] If figures for numbers of ratifications by China (4) are

Table 9.1 Member States of ILO and IMO and ratifications of maritime labour standards; 2006: International flag States

Flag	ILO	IMO	No	147	P147
Bahamas	Yes	Yes	3	Yes	No
Cyprus	Yes	Yes	5	Yes	No
Hong Kong	No	Yes	–	No	No
Liberia	Yes	Yes	9	Yes	No
Malta	Yes	Yes	11	Yes	Yes
Panama	Yes	Yes	16	No	No
Singapore	Yes	Yes	4	No	No

Source Member States of the ILO and ratification of ILO maritime labour instruments, including ILO 147, from Report 1(1A), *Adoption of an instrument to consolidate maritime labour standards,* International Labour Conference, 94th (Maritime) Session, 2006. International Labour Office, Geneva. Data for Member States of the IMO as at 2006 from file://F:\International Maritime Organization_files\mainframe.htm

---

[54]Precious Associates Ltd., for the OECD Maritime Transport Committee, Availability and Training of Seafarers, January 2003, p. 11. OECD countries as at 2003 were: Australia, Austria, Belgium, Canada, Czech Republic, Denmark, Finland, France, Germany, Greece, Hungary, Iceland, Ireland, Italy, Japan, Republic of Korea, Luxembourg, Mexico, Netherlands, New Zealand, Norway, Poland, Portugal, Slovak Republic, Spain, Sweden, Switzerland, Turkey, United Kingdom, and United States of America.

[55]Hong Kong, by reason of its relationship with China, cannot be a separate Member State of the ILO.

included as being representative of Hong Kong, the average number of ratifications for International flag States increases to 7.42. All International flag States are Member States of both the ILO and IMO.

9.4.5   Member States of ILO and IMO and Ratifications of Maritime Labour Standards: Pseudo-National Flag States

With the exception of Belize, the data on Pseudo-National flag State ratification of maritime labour standards demonstrates a singular lack of commitment to the social welfare of crews of ships flying their flags, and to support for ILO instruments. Their average rate of support for ILO 147 (12.5%) and for the 1996 Protocol to ILO 147 (6.25%) is well below the rates for both National and International flag States, as is the average number (1.63) of ratifications of ILO instruments, as indicated in Table 9.2.

The data presented in Tables A1, 9.1 and 9.2 also demonstrates that two-thirds of ILO Member States are maritime States and that the great majority of these maritime States (95%) are also member States of the IMO.

Table 9.2 Member States of ILO and IMO and ratifications of maritime labour standards; 2006: Pseudo-National flag States

FLAG	ILO	IMO	NO	147	P147
Antigua and Barbuda	Yes	Yes	1	No	No
Barbados	Yes	Yes	5	Yes	No
Belize	Yes	Yes	13	Yes	Yes
Bolivia	No	Yes	–	No	No
Cambodia	No	Yes	–	No	No
Comoros	No	Yes	–	No	No
Cook Islands	No	No	–	No	No
Equatorial Guinea	Yes	Yes	2	No	No
Honduras	Yes	Yes	1	No	No
Marshall Is	No	Yes	–	No	No
Mongolia	No	Yes	–	No	No
St Vincent and the Grenadines	Yes	Yes	4	No	No
Sao Tome and Principe	No	Yes	–	No	No
Tonga	No	Yes	–	No	No
Tuvalu	No	Yes	–	No	No
Vanuatu	No	Yes	–	No	No

Source Member States of the ILO and ratification of ILO maritime labour instruments, including ILO 147, from Report 1(1A), Adoption of an instrument to consolidate maritime labour standards, International Labour Conference, 94th (Maritime) Session, 2006. International Labour Office, Geneva. Data for member States of the IMO as at 2006 from file://F:\International Maritime Organization_files\mainframe.htm

9.5   International Transport Workers' Federation (ITF)

Another measure of flag State social performance is that determined by the International Transport Workers' Federation (ITF) which has been campaigning for the rights of seafarers in its present form since 1919.[56] The ITF, which includes 624 trade unions in 142 countries representing 4,400,000 transport workers (ILO 2006, p. 23), has waged a campaign since 1948 aimed at the elimination of FOC vessels, ensuring that seafarers employed on FOC ships are not exploited, and, increasingly, campaigning for the establishment of a proper regulatory framework for global shipping. The ITF organises seafarer representation at the tripartite negotiations at ILO Maritime Sessions and meetings in the ILO Joint Maritime Commission (ILO 2006, p. 23), and is a non-Governmental organisation at the IMO.

Recognition is made by the ITF that not all FOC ships are involved in maritime casualties or in all cases of exploitation of seafarers (ITF Annual Report 2004, p. 2) and the focus of the organisation has gradually shifted away from the elimination of FOCs to a recognition that there are substandard ships under all types of flag States, and upon attainment of better working and living conditions and wages for all seafarers through their ITFStandard Collective Agreement.[57]

As a global organisation devoted to the welfare of seafarers on ships of all nationalities, the ITF is in a unique position, through its worldwide network of ITF inspectors, to determine those flag States that do not have a genuine commitment to their social duties and responsibilities under the LOSC and ILO maritime labour standards. When the ITF declares a flag State to be a FOC it takes into account that State's ability and willingness to effectively implement and enforce minimum international social standards, which include the universal ILO Conventions covering respect for basic human and trade union rights, freedom of association, and collective bargaining rights through genuine trade unions (ITF Annual Report 2004, p. 4). Ratification and enforcement of ILO maritime labour standards and IMO safety and pollution prevention instruments is also taken into account, along with records of port State control deficiencies and detentions. Their resultant determination of substandard ships, regardless of the flag they fly, is a comprehensive measure of the performance of flag States in their social duties and responsibilities.

---

[56] International Labour Office, Geneva, Report II, Report of the Director General on developments in the maritime sector, International Labour Conference, 94th (Maritime) Session, 2006, p. 23: "The ITF was founded in 1896 as the International Federation of Ship, Dock and River Workers. In 1898 it expanded to include transport workers in non-maritime industries. The organisation had its roots in various special conferences and federations of European seafarers and railway workers in the early 1890s, and in the international cooperation of European transport unionists during the 1896–97 dock strikes in Rotterdam and Hamburg. Following disruptions caused by the First World War, the federation was re-established in 1919 as the International Transport Workers' Federation."

[57] Flags of convenience Campaign, http://www.itfglobal.org/flags-convenience/index.cfm.

In their 2004 Annual Report the ITF determined that 29 flag States were FOCs,[58] whilst recognizing that some ship registers that are not designated as FOCs share the same tax avoidance and minimal enforcement of safety and employment standards characteristics as FOCs and can be designated as operating substandard ships.

The ITF determination of flag States with substandard fleets closely relates to the flag State categories postulated in this study, in that there are five National, five Quasi-National, five International, and 14 Pseudo-National flag States. National flag States as a percentage of all National flags, even combined with Quasi-National flags, are significantly under-represented (12.5%), International flags are over-represented (71%) and almost all Pseudo-National flags (87.5%) are included in the ITF designation of FOCs. The greatest percentage (66%) of the ITF-designated FOCs are International and Pseudo-National flag States but, as indicated through previous analysis, there are also National flag States with questionable standards.[59]

9.6   Port State Control as a Measure of Performance for Flag State Social Duties

The monitoring of working and living conditions is a vital component of port State control inspections as, along with inspections by ITF inspectors, there are no other objective measures of, or data on, maritime labour standards aboard ships. The most reliable data is that published by the Paris MOU, as ILO 147 is not only a relevant instrument under that regional memorandum of understanding but is also a pre-requisite for membership. In addition to routine port State control inspections the members of the Paris MOU have carried out two Concentrated Inspection Campaigns (CIC) on working and living conditions over the past 10 years. These campaigns concentrated, in the course of routine inspections over a three-month period, upon matters covered by a number of the component Conventions of ILO 147: crew, accommodation, food and catering, working space,[60] accident prevention, and mooring arrangements. The serious concern of the Paris MOU was expressed midway between these CICs in its 2001 Annual Report:

---

[58]The following flag States were identified as ITF-designated FOCs in July 2004: Antigua and Barbuda, Bahamas, Barbados, Belize, Bermuda, Burma/Myanmar, Cambodia, Cayman Islands, Comoros, Cyprus, Equatorial Guinea, Germany (second register), Gibraltar, Honduras, Jamaica, Lebanon, Liberia, Malta, Marshall Islands, Mauritius, Mongolia, Netherlands Antilles, Panama, Sao Tome and Principe, Sri Lanka, St Vincent and the Grenadines, Tonga, and Vanuatu.

[59]Quasi-National flag States are not considered in this study due to the lack of empirical evidence. Data on Quasi-National flag State performance is usually subsumed into that of their parent flag State.

[60]Paris MOU Annual Report 1999, p. 27. "Crew" includes Certificate of Competency, Number/ Composition of crew, Medical Certificate, Other; "Accommodation" includes Cleanliness of Accommodation/Parasites, Ventilation/Heating, Sanitary facilities, Drainage, Lighting, Pipes/ Wires/Insulation, Sick Bay, Medical equipment; "Food and Catering" includes Galley/Handling spaces, Provisions, Fresh water/Piping/Tanks, Other; "Working Spaces" includes Ventilation/ Heating/Work Spaces, Lighting – work spaces, Other.

> It is widely recognized that there is a close correlation between safety and working and living conditions (ILO Convention 147). Deficiency rates have increased over many years. In particular older bulk carriers and general dry cargo ships are sometimes found in appalling condition for the crew. Combined with contracts of long service on board and extensive working hours there is no room for a safety culture on board these ships. Unfortunately many flag States and classification societies take no interest or deny their competence and leave it to port States to pick up the pieces. (Paris MOU Annual Report 2000, p. 5)

The percentage of working and living condition deficiencies to the total number of port State control inspections carried out by members of the Paris MOU from 1997 to 2005 is summarised in Table 9.3:

The data in Table 9.3 clearly indicates that the percentage deficiency rate for working and living conditions has been significant throughout the period from 1997 to 2005; in some cases has not improved and is, in 2003–2005, higher than the average for the entire period. The average rate for all types of working and living condition deficiencies is higher in 2005 than it was in 1997 in spite of the best efforts of port State control officers and ITF inspectors. Percentages of working and living condition deficiencies against total deficiencies over this period have increased with the average percentage in 2005 (12.6%) being higher than that in 1997 (10.3%) and significantly higher than the average for the entire period (10.2%). These statistics corroborate the ineffectiveness of extant ILO maritime labour standards, many of which have not been ratified by flag States, and the ineffectiveness of port State control as a means to improve working and living conditions for seafarers on a long-term basis.

A Concentrated Inspection Campaign (CIC) on Working and Living conditions, carried out by members of the Paris MOU in 2004, provided a more detailed insight into labour standards aboard the 4,555 ships inspected in the course of the three-month campaign and provided an indication of trends since the previous CIC in 1997 (Paris MOU Annual Report 2004, p. 13). More than 40% of the ships inspected (total 1,345) had deficiencies compared with 25% in 1997. Twenty one ships were detained for ILO 147 deficiencies. Most deficiencies were related to food storage, galley conditions, sanitary facilities, and sick bays. The master was required to remedy most deficiencies without the ship being detained. Tellingly, ships registered with flag States that were already targeted by the Paris MOU for

Table 9.3 Percentage of working and living condition deficiencies; Paris MOU 1997–2005

Year	97	98	99	00	01	02	03	04	05	Ave. %
ILO 147 Category										
Crew and Accommodation	20.4	17.3	16.8	17.5	18.1	15.7	17.3	17.2	13.2	17.1
Food/catering	14.1	9.9	8.5	9.2	7.5	5.6	9.3	15.4	12.6	10.2
Working spaces	4.7	4.6	4.5	6.0	6.0	5.1	27.5	22.8	19.7	11.2
Accident prevention	8.5	9.0	11.9	13.4	13.6	12.1	0.9	5.4	8.1	9.2
Mooring arrange.	3.7	4.9	5.4	7.8	9.5	9.0	9.1	8.4	7.1	7.2
Averages	10.3	9.1	9.4	10.8	10.9	9.5	12.8	13.8	12.1	10.9
% all deficiencies	10.3	8.8	8.7	8.9	9.3	8.2	11.2	13.5	12.6	10.2

Source Annual Reports of the Paris MOU, 1997–2005

poor safety and environmental protection standards were also found to be deficient in their working and living conditions.[61]

The vital relationship between maritime safety and environmental protection and the human element in ship operation was underscored by the fact that ships detained for serious ILO 147 deficiencies were also detained for safety and pollution prevention deficiencies. This trend confirms the importance of safety management in ship operations; a concept that had been progressively introduced throughout the period from 1998 to 2002 through the International Safety Management (ISM) Code. The link between safety, environmental protection, and working and living conditions is confirmed by the fact that in 1999, Albania, Algeria, Georgia, Libya, Morocco, Romania, and Syria featured on the Paris MOU Black List of flag States and Tuvalu was on the Grey List.[62] In 2005 Albania, Algeria, Georgia, and Syria were still on the Paris MOU Black List whilst Morocco and Romania had graduated to the Grey List.[63]

Data from port State control inspections carried out by the 18 members of the Tokyo MOU throughout the Asia-Pacific region is not as comprehensive as that from the Paris MOU. Records are kept of inspections of the same aspects of ILO 147 as for the Paris MOU, and Table 9.4 summarises this data for the years from 1997 to 2005:

These statistics confirm that there is a far lower level of port State control exercised in the Asia-Pacific region on working and living conditions than in the region covered by the Paris MOU; by a factor of approximately 1:10. Even with these lower percentages, the trend for particular categories under ILO 147 is similar to those of the Paris MOU with some being higher in 2005 than 1997, and the remainder only marginally better. The percentage of ILO 147 deficiencies against total deficiencies has steadily decreased over the period under review. In the absence of more detailed statistics it is not possible to determine whether this is due

Table 9.4 Percentage of working and living condition deficiencies: Tokyo MOU 1997–2005

Year	97	98	99	00	01	02	03	04	05	Ave. %
ILO category										
Crew/Accom.	2.7	1.8	1.4	1.2	1.4	0.8	0.5	0.7	0.5	1.2
Food/Catering	1.3	0.7	0.9	0.7	0.6	0.3	0.2	0.2	0.2	0.6
Working spaces	0.7	0.5	0.5	0.4	0.5	0.5	0.5	0.5	0.7	0.5
Accident prevent.	0.7	0.7	1.0	0.8	0.9	0.8	0.8	0.8	0.8	0.8
Mooring arrange.	1.0	1.2	1.3	1.0	0.9	1.0	1.0	1.1	1.1	1.1
Averages	1.3	1.0	1.0	0.8	0.9	0.7	0.6	0.7	0.7	0.9
% all deficiencies	6.3	4.9	5.2	4.2	4.3	3.3	2.9	3.2	3.3	4.2

Source Annual reports of the Tokyo MOU, 1997–2005

---

[61] Flag States with the highest deficiency ratio during the campaign were: Albania, Algeria, Georgia, Libya, Morocco, Romania, Syria, Togo, and Tuvalu. Ships flying the flag of Algeria, Morocco, Romania, and Syria also scored the highest deficiency ratio per flag during the CIC in 1997. General cargo ships were the worst performing ship type (57%), followed by bulk carriers (21%).

[62] Paris MOU Annual Reports 1999–2005. Togo did not undergo sufficient port State control inspections (30) to be included.

[63] *Ibid*. Libya, Togo,and Tuvalu underwent fewer than 30 inspections.

to an improvement in working and living conditions or a decreasing effort by port States in this area. Statistics for individual categories would indicate the latter.

Although ILO 147 is a relevant instrument for members of the Paris MOU, its ratification is not compulsory for membership of the Tokyo MOU and at 2005 only four of the 18 members had ratified ILO 147. Many members have ratified a number of the component Conventions of ILO 147 and have the ability to inspect the working and living conditions relevant under those instruments. It might reasonably be expected that the four members of the Tokyo MOU that have ratified ILO 147 – Canada, Hong Kong, Japan, and the Russian Federation – would have a higher level of activity in the monitoring of working and living conditions, and this is partially borne out by detailed port State control statistics for 2004 (Tokyo MOU, Paper DBM14/07A, Annex 1, p. 71). Of the 2,374 deficiencies issued under ILO 147 during that year, Japan (439) and Russia (435) had the highest number, closely followed by Australia (412). Canada (221) was behind China (262), and Hong Kong (76) issued a lower number of deficiencies than Korea (160), Philippines (138), and New Zealand (102). A number of Asian members of the MOU issued very low numbers of working and living condition deficiencies; for example, Malaysia (28), Singapore (42), Thailand (1), and Vietnam (40).

However, when working and living condition deficiencies under ILO 147 are considered as a percentage of all deficiencies issued by these port States a different picture emerges. Canada had the highest percentage (21.8%), followed by New Zealand (10.6%), the Philippines (9.9%), Russia (7.8%), and Australia (5.5%). Hong Kong and Singapore who have ratified ILO 147 had low rates of ILO 147 deficiencies of 2.3 and 0.8% respectively. No statistics are available over the period from 1997 to 2005 for ILO 147 deficiencies per flag State in the Asia-Pacific region.

9.7   Academic and Industry-Based Measures of flag State Performance

Two academic and industry-based standards have been developed in an effort to develop all-encompassing measures of flag State performance that might also result in more targeted and coordinated approaches by both Government and industry parties to inspections of ships. These measures are analysed to test their veracity, and their alignment with the results of analysis undertaken in this study.

9.7.1   Flag State Conformance Index

The first comprehensive academic study into measurement of the ability of a flag State to both enact, and effectively enforce, maritime legislation resulted in the Flag State Conformance Index (FLASCI) developed by the Seafarers' International Research Centre at Cardiff University (Alderton and Winchester 2002, pp. 35–43). FLASCI was developed over a 3 year period, taking into account trends over the previous 10 years, through analysis of 37 National, Open and Second Registers. The performance index is designed to measure the regulatory efficiency of the flag State and take into account a wide range of relevant factors such as: responsibilities for vessels on the register, restrictions on nationality of crewing, location of the register, certification/training of seafarers, eligibility for registration, registration fees, taxation of shipowners, average age of fleet, casualty rate, beneficial ownership of fleet, growth trends of the fleet, port State control detention rates from the Paris and Tokyo MOUs and the USCG, crew complaints to the ITF and Missions to Seamen, composition of the labour force, abandonment of seafarers, deaths, labour force records/statistics, health screening of seafarers, welfare provisions, and maritime interest groups representing seafarers.

Labour laws are taken into account through inclusion or otherwise of rights of association/recognition, the right to strike, access to arbitration and existence of ITF agreements. Company law is also included through examination of provisions for transparency of beneficial ownership, speed of incorporation of companies for ship registration purposes, cost of company incorporation, taxation level on offshore earnings, requirement for annual audited accounts, and required presence of incorporated companies in the jurisdiction. Elements of politico-economic risk, corruption, harmful tax regime, and anti-money laundering legislation are used to measure the standard of governance by the flag State.

FLASCI aims to produce an index that can be used to measure the effectiveness of enactment and enforcement of maritime legislation based on a wide range of variables. The range of scores are grouped into flag States having similar characteristics in the Table 9.5.

The FLASCI model was used to produce the Flag State Audit 2003 report. This report used the same factors to measure the effectiveness of flag State jurisdiction but modified the FLASCI rating system into five ratings from A–E (where A equals best practice) for Performance, Procedures, State Participation, Legal, and Welfare/Rights.[64] Flag States were then grouped into four categories from high to poor regulatory capacity. The Flag State Audit in 2003 ranked flag States as follows (Table 9.6):

Table 9.5 Grouped FLASCI scores and characteristics of those groups

Category	Range of scores	General characteristics
High	72–84	Traditional maritime nation and second registers that are closely controlled
Med.–high	58–64	Semi-autonomous second registers
Medium	41–50	More established open registers with higher scores with EU membership. National registers.
Low–med.	35–36	Newer open registers
Low	19–30	New entrants to the open register market.

Source Alderton T and Winchester N (2002) Globalisation and de-regulation of the maritime industry. Marine Policy, Vol 26, Issue 1, January

---

[64]For example Cambodia has ratings of D,D,E,D,D and Cyprus, C,B,C,C,D.

Table 9.6 Grouped flag state rankings

Regulatory Capacity	Flag
High	Danish Second Register, German Second Register, Kerguelen Islands, Netherlands, Norwegian Second Register, Norway, Philippines, United Kingdom.
Good	Bermuda, Canary Islands, Cayman Islands, Cyprus, Estonia, Hong Kong, Isle of Man, Latvia, Madeira, Netherlands Antilles, Russia, Singapore, Turkey, Ukraine.
Modest	Antigua and Barbuda, Bahamas, Barbados, Belize, Bolivia, Equatorial Guinea, Liberia, Malta, Marshall Islands, Panama, Vanuatu.
Poor	Cambodia, St Vincent and the Grenadines.

Source Flag State Audit 2003, p. 3. http://www.sirc.cf.ac.uk/fsa.html

Alderton and Winchester identify Cambodia and Equatorial Guinea, for example, as super unregulated flag States that register vessels deemed to be too risky by Open registers such as Panama and Liberia. This enables owners of these ships to extend their working life in an almost regulatory free environment (Alderton and Winchester 2002, p. 3). It is not clear how the 37 flag States were selected for this analysis, apart from there being a mixture of what are deemed by the authors to be National, Open and Second registers. The study supports the hypotheses in this study that high performing flag States are either National or their closely associated Second Registers (National and Quasi-National flag States). The seven International flag States are scattered through the rankings with good to modest performance. 11 of the 15 flag States with modest to poor rankings are Pseudo-National flag States.

9.7.2 Shipping Industry Guidelines on Flag State Performance

With the stated belief that maintenance and enforcement of safety, environmental, and social standards by flag States, in full compliance with IMO regulations, is essential (Shipping Industry Guidelines, p. 3), the "Round Table" of shipping industry organisations[65] has developed Shipping Industry Guidelines on Flag State Performance (the Guidelines) that are updated and published annually. The Guidelines are intended to advise shipowners of the effectiveness and regulatory efficiency of flag States and also to inform maritime administrations and policy makers. They are also aimed at providing information that shipowners may use to bring pressure to bear on regulatory inefficient flag States in matters of safety of life, environmental protection, and provision of decent working and living conditions for seafarers (Shipping Industry Guidelines, p. 3).

The Guidelines summarise flag State responsibilities as: sufficient maritime administration infrastructure, ratification of maritime treaties, implementation and enforcement of maritime treaties, supervision of surveys of ships, effective

---

[65] BIMCO, INTERCARGO, International Chamber of Shipping, International Shipping Federation and INTERTANKO.

implementation of the International Safety Management (ISM) Code, demonstrated compliance with seafarers' competency standards, safe manning and hours of work for seafarers, undertaking casualty investigations, standards for transferral of flag, having arrangements for repatriation of seafarers, completion of the IMO's self-assessment form, and participation at IMO and ILO meetings.

Data for measurement of implementation of these responsibilities is obtained from port State control records, information on ratification of maritime treaties, use by flag States of Recognized Organizations, age of flag State fleets, mandatory reporting requirements to the IMO and ILO, and attendance at the major IMO meetings. The results of this annual analysis, which are reported in a tabular form, summarise 18 of these performance indicators under the main headings of port State control, Non-Ratification of Conventions, IACS or non-IACS, flag State delegations to Recognized Organizations, average age of fleet, completion of mandatory reports to the IMO and ILO, and attendance at major IMO meetings. Possible negative indicators are shown and flag States with 12 or more negative performance indicators are identified.

As at the end of June 2003 a number of flag States[66] were identified as having 12 or more negative performance indicators and the majority of these still featured in June 2005.[67] Whilst the results in 2003 and 2005 of this laudable attempt to take all relevant factors required of a regulatory efficient flag State into account would appear to reflect the results of other research and analysis, there are some fundamental flaws in the process of arriving at these conclusions.

Possible negative indicators are included if a flag State does not appear on the Paris MOU White List and the Tokyo MOU White List, and does not appear in the USCG Qualship 21[68] Programme. The guidelines acknowledge that some poorly performing flag States may be omitted owing to the small number of their ships trading in particular PSC regions. In order to be statistically sound the Black/Grey/White Lists of the Paris and Tokyo MOUs require at least 30 port State control inspections to be carried out over a 3 year period in their respective regions. The ships registered under many flag States either do not undergo this number of inspections per year, or do not trade in these regions, and may receive negative performance indicators if they are not on the respective PSC Lists or do not trade to the United States.[69]

---

[66] Albania, Belize, Bolivia, Cambodia, Costa Rica, Democratic Republic of Congo, Honduras, Jordan, Madagascar, Sao Tome and Principe, Suriname, and the Syrian Arab Republic.

[67] Albania, Bolivia, Cambodia, Costa Rica, Democratic Republic of Congo, Georgia, Honduras, Indonesia, Kenya, Madagascar, Mongolia, Sao Tome and Principe, Suriname, and the Syrian Arab Republic.

[68] USCG, Port State Control in the United States, Annual Report 2004, p. 21: "The Quality Shipping for the twenty first Century (Qualship 21) programme recognises and rewards vessels that demonstrate a commitment to safety and environmental compliance."

[69] For example New Zealand, with a very small fleet trading internationally, receives three negative performance indicators as it does not feature on the Paris and Tokyo MOUs and Qualship 21.

Non-ratification of the principal IMO Conventions[70] and ILO 147 results in negative performance indicators. The guidelines indicate, quite correctly, that ratification does not necessarily indicate effective implementation and enforcement of a Convention, but notes that a flag State should be able to explain non-ratification, and to implement and enforce national regulations that comply with the vast majority of their requirements (Shipping Industry Guidelines, pp. 6 and 10). However, having said this, the negative performance indicators used in the guidelines for non-ratification by flag States of these instruments do not reflect the ability of States to, for example, ratify and enforce the component Conventions of ILO 147, or the ability to gradually bring into effect the non-mandatory Annexes to MARPOL. It has been demonstrated in this study that the majority of flag States have not brought both of these instruments into full effect, for either political or timing reasons,[71] and the table of negative indicators reflects this reality.

Compliance with the requirements of IMO Resolution A.739(18), Guidelines for the authorization of organizations acting on behalf of the administration, is measured by whether the flag State has recognised a large number of non-IACS Classification Societies to carry out statutory work on its behalf. It is assumed in the guidelines that IACS members meet the requirements of the Resolution but it is also recognised that non-IACS members may also meet these requirements (Shipping Industry Guidelines, pp. 7, 10, 11). Negative indicators are shown if the flag State has delegated to a large number of non-IACS ROs, or if no report has been made to the IMO on ROs. These indicators are considered to be valid and have been used in measures of performance of both flag States and ROs in this study.

The association of age with substandard ships that is demonstrated in this study[72] is used as a performance measure in the Guidelines and whilst giving recognition that age is not necessarily synonymous with poor quality, certain flag States attract older tonnage of questionable quality (Shipping Industry Guidelines, p. 11). The suggestion is made that flag States with a very high age profile may be worthy of more detailed analysis. The performance measure used in the Guidelines is for flag States with the highest average age in terms of both numbers of ships and total gross tonnage (Shipping Industry Guidelines, p. 11).

Reporting requirements to international organisations are deemed by the Round Table to be a pertinent measure of performance of flag States. The two reporting requirements used in the Guidelines are whether sufficient information on compliance with the STCW Convention has been supplied to the IMO for inclusion on the IMO STCW "White List" of approved Member States, and whether mandatory compliance and practice reports have been submitted to the ILO (Shipping Industry Guidelines, p. 11). The great majority of Member States of the IMO have achieved

---

[70] SOLAS 74; MARPOL 73/78 (and Annexes 1 – VI); LOAD LINE 66 (and the 88 Protocol), STCW 78; CLC/FUND 92.

[71] For example, Annex VI of MARPOL came into force relatively recently in May 2005 but a negative indicator is given if a flag State has not ratified all six Annexes.

[72] See Chapter Nine.

White List status, as evidenced by the Flag State Performance Table for 2005, so it is questionable how effective this measure is (Shipping Industry Guidelines, Flag State Performance Table, p. 2). However, those few States that have not – Albania, Bolivia, Costa Rica, Democratic People's Republic of Congo, Kenya, Libya, Mongolia, Sao Tome and Principe, and Suriname – fall clearly into the category of very poorly performing flag States under the various measures postulated in this study.

The performance measure of compliance with mandatory ILO reporting reveals a higher level of compliance overall than the STCW White List measure and a similar clear demarcation between developed and developing countries. Both of these measures require an efficient level of maritime administration to record, analyse and aggregate statistics, along with effective implementation of international instruments. It is clear from the Guidelines that the States that have not met these standards[73] have regulatory deficient and inefficient administrations, and many of them do not also meet the IMO White List standards and have been identified as poorly performing flag States in this study.

The last of the 18 measures of flag State performance used by the Round Table is that of attendance at the main IMO committees.[74] The argument is made that attendance at these committees is important in order for flag States to keep up-to-date with regulatory requirements. The measure used is attendance at these three main committees or the biennial meeting of the IMO Assembly during the previous 2 years. Evidence is obtained from IMO meeting reports. It is notable that 52 of the 106 flag States on the table do not achieve this level of meeting attendance, and this very high percentage must call into question the effectiveness of this measure. It is also notable that the great majority of these countries are developing States; a possible indication of the high costs of travel and accommodation associated with attendance at IMO meetings which some developed countries struggle to meet.

However, in spite of the deficiencies identified with these various performance measures, the Flag State Performance Table is a useful indicator of flag State performance and has identified most of the factors necessary for effective flag State jurisdiction and control. The high threshold of non-compliance with 12 of the 18 measures, necessary for identification as an insubstantial or substandard flag State, confirms the conclusions demonstrated in this study, but also allows more than a few regulatory inefficient flag States to remain unidentified by the performance measures.

Of these two attempts to produce reliable measures of the effectiveness of flag State jurisdiction and control, FLASCI is more all-encompassing and uses more objective and robust criteria, although it has been applied to a limited number of flag States. The Round Table measurement of flag State performance includes the

---

[73] *Ibid.* Bahrain, Belize, Brunei Darussalam, Cambodia, Cayman Islands, Chile, Cuba, Democratic People's Republic of Korea, Democratic Republic of Congo, Dominica, Georgia, Gibraltar, Jamaica, Jordan, Kuwait, Liberia, Luxembourg, Madagascar, Marshall Islands, Mongolia, Netherlands Antilles, Sao Tome and Principe, Saudi Arabia, South Africa, Spain, Suriname, Thailand, Tunisia, Turkey, Ukraine, Vanuatu, and Vietnam.

[74] *Ibid*, pp. 11–12. The main committees are identified as the Maritime Safety Committee, Marine Environmental Protection Committee, Legal Committee and Assembly.

great majority of active flag States, but is more subjective and inaccurate in some of its measures. However, both systems of measurement of flag State performance confirm the conclusions drawn in this study from a range of other analyses, that International and Pseudo-National flag States have less effective administrative and social regulatory regimes than most National flag States.

References

Alderton T, Winchester N (2002) Globalization and de-regulation in the maritime industry. Marine Policy. Vol 26, Issue 1
International Labour Organization Office (1997) Maritime conference adopts better conditions for seafarers. ILO Focus, Winter/Spring, Vol 10, No 1. Geneva
International Transport Workers' Federation (2004) Campaign against flags of convenience and substandard shipping. Annual Report
Lloyd's Register – Fairplay (2005) World Fleet Statistics
Precious Associates Ltd., for the OECD Maritime Transport Committee (2003) Availability and Training of Seafarers
Shipping Industry Guidelines on Flag State Performance. http://www.marisec.org/flag-performance

Documents

IMO (2006) Analysis and evaluation of deficiency reports and mandatory reports under MARPOL 73/78 for 2004. Document FSI 14/4
IMO (2006) Report of Correspondence Group on Casualty Analysis. Document FSI 14/5
IMO (2008) Analysis and evaluation of deficiency reports and mandatory reports under MARPOL for 2006. Document FSI 16/4
IMO (2008) Summary of the Present Status of Conventions related to Maritime Safety and Security (as of 29 February 2008). Document MSC 84/INF.13
International Labour Organization Office (1976) Convention No 147 concerning Minimum Standards in Merchant Ships. Geneva, 29 October. ND IV
International Labour Organization Office (1998) Maritime Labour Conventions and Recommendations including standards relating to fishing, dock work and inland navigation, 4th edn, rev. Geneva time Session on developments in the maritime sector. International Labour Conference, 94th (Mari International Labour Organization Office (2006) Report II: Report of the Director General
Tokyo MOU (2004) Detailed Statistics on Port State Control Inspections for 2004. Paper DBM14/07A. Shanghai, November.

Chapter 10
Measures of Flag State Technical Performance

Abstract In order to analyse flag State technical performance it is necessary to determine, examine, and measure the technical duties of flag States under the LOSC and IMO instruments. These technical duties are essential to ensure that the design, construction, equipment, maintenance, and operation of ships are adequate to withstand the perils of the sea. The safety records of ships, as established by port State control inspections, are analysed as a measure of flag State technical performance, along with targeting mechanisms such as Black/Grey/White lists of flag States. Combinations of causal factors in substandard ships such as age, tonnage and detention record are identified and analysed. The performance of Recognized Organizations (ROs) in delivery of technical functions on behalf of flag States is also analysed along with linkages between ROs and particular categories of flag States. The hypothesis that certain flag States attract older and smaller general cargo ships and that these ships are more prone to detention or casualty regardless of category of flag State is tested. Data on serious and non-serious casualties, total losses, and associated loss of life is analysed to determine whether there are correlations with the technical performance of particular categories of flag State, as is technical oversight of ships on behalf of flag States by Recognized Organizations. The ultimate sanction available to coastal States of refusal of access to proven substandard ships is considered.

10.1 Flag State Technical Duties

The LOSC requires every flag State to take such measures for ships flying its flag as are necessary to ensure safety at sea with regard to, at least, construction, equipment, and seaworthiness; manning of ships; training of crews; use of signals; the maintenance of communication by radio; prevention of collisions; and the prevention, reduction, and control of marine pollution (LOSC, Article 94(3)(a)(b)(c), and (4)(c)). In taking these measures each State is required to conform to generally accepted international regulations, procedures, and practices and to take any steps that may be necessary to secure their observance (LOSC, Article 94(5)). The technical aspects of these

J.N.K. Mansell, *Flag State Responsibility,*
DOI: 10.1007/978-3-540-92933-8_10, © Springer-Verlag Berlin Heidelberg 2009

duties and responsibilities of flag States are specified in detail in the regulations of SOLAS 74, MARPOL 73/78, Load Line 66, STCW 95, and COLREG 72. The flag State may elect to exercise its duty and carry out technical administration, such as surveys and flag State inspections and audits, itself or it may elect to entrust some or all of these duties to Recognized Organizations (ROs) as allowed by IMO instruments. If statutory duties are delegated to ROs the flag State must ensure that audits and independent flag State inspections are carried out to ensure that these duties are being effectively carried out by the RO (IMO Resolution A.739(18)).

Regardless of the administrative structure of the flag State a well-found and seaworthy[1] ship that complies with all of the requirements of these Conventions, and is administered by a regulatory efficient flag State, should meet the expectations of the LOSC and the principal IMO instruments regarding safety at sea. Conversely, it might be expected that a substandard ship, operated by a regulatory inefficient flag State, would be less safe. "Substandard" is defined in IMO Resolution A.787(19)[2] as:

> A ship whose hull, machinery, equipment or operational safety is substantially below the standard required by the relevant convention or whose crew is not in conformancy with the safe manning document.[3]

10.2   Port State Control as a Measure of Flag State Technical Performance

The most reliable evidence of the standard of a ship and its operation is derived from the objective opinion of qualified and trained mariners exercising their authority under port State control. The two leading regional port State control regimes[4] have developed measures for identifying substandard ships, regulatory inefficient flag States, and poorly performing Recognized Organizations, from the experience of undertaking many hundreds of thousands of port State control inspections since 1983. Measures have also been developed to recognise ships and flag States that are performing to a satisfactory level. Some of the measures have been developed relatively recently but, as they are based upon the cumulative experience and wisdom of many years evidence from port State control inspections, they are statistically sound.

---

[1] Seaworthy, "Fit to put to sea", The Concise Oxford Dictionary.

[2] Resolution A.787(19) Procedures for Port State Control, 23 November 1995, s.1.6.9.

[3] Another definition of the term "substandard" is found in the Australian Navigation Act 1912, s.207A(1), which states that "a ship is substandard if it is seaworthy but conditions on board the ship are clearly hazardous to safety or health". S.207A(2) of the Act provides that, "in determining whether a ship is substandard, regard shall be paid to such matters as are prescribed". Such matters are prescribed in Marine Order – Part 11: Substandard ships. Issue 2 (Order No 14 of 2002).

[4] The Paris MOU on port State control consisting in 2005 of 24 European States plus Canada, and the Tokyo MOU on port State control consisting of 18 Asia Pacific States.

10.2.1   *Flag State Performance and Detentions Under Port State Control*

The port State control detention rate of ships has been established and analysed for many years to measure the performance of flag States[5] This statistic is compared with the detention rate across the entire port State control regime, thus enabling flag States with a higher than average detention rate to be clearly identified and targeted. The resultant information is published in the annual reports of the respective port State control regimes.[6] An analysis of information on average detention rates from inspections carried out by members of the Paris MOU from 1999 to 2005 reveals that a total of 43 flag States had higher than average detention rates over this period.[7] The regional average detention rate for all flag States inspected by the members of the Paris MOU over this 7 year period was 7.9%. The 43 flag States with detention rates above this average are listed in Table A.5, Appendix A.[8]

Ten of these flag States had higher than average detention rates every year from 1999–2005 inclusive.[9] Of these, three – Honduras, Cambodia and Belize – are Pseudo-National flag States with the remainder being National flag States. It has been argued in Chapter Seven that there are 95 National, seven International and 17 Pseudo-National active flag States, representing approximately 80%, 6%, and 14% respectively of total flag States.[10] Of the 43 flag States with higher than average detention rates in Paris MOU records for 1999–2005 inclusive, 29 were National flag States, equating to 67.4% of the forty-six flag States; three (7%) were International; and eleven (25.6%) were Pseudo-National flag States. In spite of the abysmally poor and ongoing detention records of five national flag States in the top ten – Albania, DPR of Korea, Libya, Lebanon, and Algeria – the detention rate of National flag States was below average. International flag States were marginally above average representation and Pseudo-National were over-represented by a factor of almost two with countries such as Bolivia, Tonga, Sao Tome and Principe, Comoros, and

---

[5] The three main PSC regimes – Paris MOU, Tokyo MOU and the United States Coastguard – have published Annual Reports from their inceptions that contain statistics on the performance of flag States and Recognized Organizations. Developing PSC regimes such as the Indian Ocean MOU, and the Black Sea MOU, also produce Annual Reports containing the same statistics.

[6] Only flag States with more than 20 port State control inspections are included in statistics on detentions produced by the Paris MOU.

[7] Paris MOU Annual Report, 2005, p. 28. Over the period from 1996–2005, when a three-year rolling average calculation of total numbers of inspections was carried out, the members of the Paris MOU carried out a total of 187,858 inspections of 116,174 individual ships.

[8] The remaining three flag States out of the total of 43 were Quasi-National.

[9] Paris MOU Port State Control Annual Reports 1999–2005. The ten States were: Honduras, Algeria, Syrian Arab Republic, Cambodia, Lebanon, Belize, Turkey, Egypt, St Vincent and the Grenadines, and the Ukraine.

[10] Actual percentages are 79.8%, 5.9%, and 14.3%. See Chapter Seven for definitions, categorisations, and listings of National, Quasi-National, International and Pseudo-National flag States.

Honduras making major contributions to the Paris MOU's determination of the top ten worst performing flag States (Paris MOU Annual Report 2007).

An update of these statistics from the 2007 Annual Report of the Paris MOU has 28 flag States with above average (5.48%) detention rates ranging from DPR of Korea at 28.79% to the United States of America at 5.56%. Eleven[11] of these States has above average detention rates in 1999.

The Tokyo MOU has also produced statistics in annual reports over the same period of 1999–2005[12] for flag States with above-average detention rates as collated and summarised in Table A.6, Appendix A.[13] A total of 27 flag States[14] appear on this list of higher than average detention rates, with exactly two-thirds also appearing on the comparable Paris MOU list. Of these 27 States, 17 (60.70%) are National, one (3.57%) International and ten (35.71%) Pseudo-National flag States. Against the overall proportion of categories of flag States, National and International flags are under represented and Pseudo-National flags significantly over represented.

Of the top ten worst performing flag States in 2005,[15] five are National and five Pseudo-National; figures identical to those of the Paris MOU. Regional influences are clearly present in this top ten, with Indonesia and Vietnam not undergoing sufficient inspections by the Paris MOU to be eligible for their detention list. The remaining eight poorly performing flag States in the Asia-Pacific region also feature on the excessive detention list of the Paris MOU. Seven flag States[16] have featured on the above average detention list of the Tokyo MOU every year from 1999–2005 inclusive, although, with the exception of Indonesia, all have improved their detention rates over this period, consistent with the trends for all flag States in the region.

An update of these statistics from the 2007 Annual Report of the Tokyo MOU has 19 flag States with detention rates higher than the regional average of 5.62%, ranging from Kiribati at 44.12% to Malaysia at 5.64%. Nine of these States had higher than average detention rates in 1999.[17] Three flag States – Kiribati, Mongolia, and Tuvalu – did not exist in 1999.

---

[11] Algeria, Syria, Cambodia, Lebanon, Belize, Turkey, Egypt, St Vincent and the Grenadines, Ukraine, Malaysia, and Panama.

[12] As detention rates are based upon a three-year rolling average the collated statistics represent records from port State control inspections carried out from 1996–2005. Over this period members of the Tokyo MOU carried out 170,259 port State control inspections. Tokyo MOU Annual Report, 2005, p. 16.

[13] Some flag States either do not have ships trading in other port State control regimes or ships under their flag have been inspected less than 20 times and are not included in the statistics.

[14] One Quasi-National flag State, Netherlands Antilles, is excluded from the list.

[15] DPR of Korea, Bolivia, Mongolia, Cambodia, Indonesia, Honduras, Vietnam, Belize, Tuvalu, and Egypt.

[16] DPR of Korea, Cambodia, Belize, Vietnam, Indonesia, St Vincent and the Grenadines, and Thailand.

[17] DPR of Korea, Cambodia, Vietnam, St Vincent and the Grenadines, Belize, Taiwan, Indonesia, Thailand, and Malaysia.

In comparing the Paris and Tokyo MOU lists of above-average detention rates there are clear parallels and consistent trends. There are a number of National flag States in each region with very poor performances. DPR of Korea, Albania, Libya, Algeria, Georgia, and Lebanon have averaged more than three times the overall average for the Paris MOU, of 7.9% detentions for the period 1999–2005. Slovakia, Syria, Romania, Turkey, and Morocco have consistently maintained detention rates of more than double the regional average. Most of these flag States are on the Paris MOU Black List or high on the Grey List.[18] It is notable that none of these flag States are members of the OECD, the EU, or the Paris MOU on port State control, and this points towards issues of resources, capacity, and administrative ability in developing States and ex-Communist States. There are no developed countries on the Paris MOU list of above-average detentions, except for Ireland (8.57%).

In considering the 2005 Tokyo MOU list of flag States with above-average detention rates there are also a number of National flag States with very poor performances. DPR of Korea and Indonesia have averaged detention rates more than three times the regional average of 6.89%. Vietnam and Egypt have consistently had detention rates more than double the regional rate, and Georgia has recently entered the list at 13.04% closely followed by Myanmar at 12.13%.[19] As with the Paris MOU region none of these countries belong to the OECD although two of them, Indonesia and Vietnam, are members of the Tokyo MOU. It is to be hoped that these flag States with very high detention rates, some of which are economically disadvantaged, will volunteer for an IMO Audit, which would serve to identify shortcomings in their flag State jurisdiction and control, and may serve to trigger technical cooperation in the form of financial or expert assistance from the IMO.[20]

The trend in detention rates for both the Tokyo MOU and Paris MOU regions is similar with a recent noticeable reduction in average rates after an increase since 1999. Although detention rates in the Paris MOU region have been consistently higher than in the Asia-Pacific region, average rates over the period 1999–2007 are very similar at 7.14 and 6.63% respectively, with rates increasing slightly in both regions from 2005 to the almost identical figures in 2007 of 5.46 and 5.62% for the Paris and Tokyo MOUs respectively. This is not surprising given the close cooperation between these two leading port State control regimes and the number of joint Concentrated Inspection Campaigns (CIC)[21] over this

---

[18]Paris MOU Annual Report 2005, pp. 35, 37, Black List: Korea, (DPR), Albania, Algeria, Georgia, Lebanon, Slovakia, Turkey, Syria; Grey List: Morocco and Romania.

[19]Tokyo MOU Annual Report 2007. Georgia's detention rate was 31.25% in 2007 but Myanmar's had reduced to 5.88%.

[20]Resolution A.974(24), Preamble: "Being desirous to assist Governments to improve their capabilities and overall performance in order to comply with the IMO instruments to which they are party."

[21]Both the Paris and Tokyo MOUs carry out Concentrated Inspection Campaigns (CIC) from time to time; often coordinated, during which time in the course of normal port State control inspections a particular issue is focussed upon. These issues are often associated with the introduction of new maritime instruments; e.g. GMDSS, STCW, ISM Code to measure compliance and effectiveness. The results of CICs are analysed and published on PSC websites and are submitted to the IMO.

period, particularly when new statutory requirements, such as the International Safety Management (ISM) Code,[22] the Global Maritime Distress and Safety System[23] (GMDSS), and revised Standards of Training, Certification and Watchkeeping[24] (STCW), have entered into force; all initiatives which may have contributed to safer operation of ships and the overall trend to reduced detentions over the period under review. A harmonised system of survey and certification was also introduced during this period.[25]

In 2007 a total of 28 and 19 countries respectively had higher than average detention rates in the Paris and Tokyo MOU regions; this compares with 21 and 19 respectively in 1999.[26] The annual average detention rate for these poorly performing flag States in the Paris MOU region has, however, decreased over this 9 year period from 21.23% in 1999 to 13.93% in 2007. That of the Tokyo MOU has followed an opposite trend with the average detention rate for poorly performing flag States increasing from 13.59% in 1999 to 16.21% in 2007; verification of the effects of some consistently very poorly performing flag States in this region over this 9 year period and the impact of new Pseudo-National flag States.[27]

10.2.2 Paris MOU Black/Grey/White List of Flag States

The Paris MOU instituted a Black List in 1992 to identify flag States with a consistently poor safety record (Paris MOU Port State Control Report 1999, p. 9). In 1999 a Black/Grey/White List was introduced, based upon a 3 year rolling average of inspection and detention records, to identify respectively flag States with poor, average, and high performance.[28] The Tokyo MOU followed suit in 2002 (Tokyo MOU Port State Control 2004, p. 13). The Black Lists of both port State control regimes separate ships on the Black List into Very High Risk, High Risk, Medium to High Risk, and

---

[22] Entered into force through Chapter IX of the SOLAS Convention on 1 July 1998 for passenger ships, tankers, gas carriers, bulk carriers, and high speed craft. All other cargo ships and mobile offshore drilling units of 500 GT and upwards were required to comply not later than 1 July 2002.

[23] Entered into force on 1 February 1999 through Chapter IV of the SOLAS Convention.

[24] Entered into force through the 1995 STCW Convention on 1 February 2002.

[25] Entered into force under the 1988 Protocols to the SOLAS and Load Lines Conventions and under amendments to the MARPOL 73/78 Convention on 3 February 2000.

[26] Paris MOU Annual Report 1999 and 2007 and Tokyo MOU Annual Report 1999 and 2007. Average detention rates for 2007 were 5.46% and 5.62%.

[27] For example the DPR of Korea had an average detention rate of 30.68% in 1999 and 42.31% in 2007. The new flag State of Kiribati entered the top of the table in 2007 at 44.12% in its first year of operation. Mongolia achieved a detention rate of 48.48% upon its entry into the table in 2003, the same year that Korea DPR's detention rate was 58.17% from 203 detentions.

[28] See Paris and Tokyo MOU Annual Reports for a copy of detailed explanatory note on the calculation of the Black/Grey/White list, which is identical for both the Paris and Tokyo MOU port State control regimes.

Medium Risk. Recent port State control Annual Reports describe those flag States consistently in the Very High Risk category, along with new flag States that have featured immediately on the Black List as follows.

A "hard core" of flag States reappear on the "Black List". Most flags that were considered "very high risk" in 2002 remain so in 2003. The poorest performing flags are still Albania, Sao Tome and Principe, DPR of Korea, Tonga and Bolivia. The flag of Comoros has managed to jump to 6th place in the "very high risk" sector (Paris MOU Annual Report 2003, p. 15)

The "Black List" is composed of 21 flag States, 5 less than last year. A "hard core" of flag States reappear on the "Black List". Most flags that were considered "very high risk" in 2003 remain so in 2004. The poorest performing flags are still Albania, DPR of Korea, Tonga and Bolivia. The flag of Sao Tome and Principe has disappeared from the Black List. However this is due to insufficient inspections being carried out on ships flying this flag in the period 2002–2004 (Paris MOU Annual Report 2004, p. 16)

The poorest performing flags are still DPR of Korea, Albania, Tonga and Honduras. There are no new flag States on the "Black List". Belize, Panama and Romania have moved from the Black List to the Grey List and will hopefully maintain this trend (Paris MOU Annual Report 2005, p. 23).

Although much has been accomplished in the past 25 years, there are still some shipowners who manage to operate unsafe ships, thereby endangering the crew and the environment. Unfortunately they are assisted by poorly performing flag States and fly-by-night recognized organisations (Paris MOU Annual Report 2007, p. 5).

The flag States referred to in these reports that featured on the Paris MOU Black List in 1999 were: Albania, Honduras, Belize, Lebanon, Syrian Arab Republic, Romania, Cambodia, Turkey, Georgia, Algeria, Libya, St Vincent and the Grenadines (Very High Risk); Egypt, Morocco, Mauritius, Bangladesh (High Risk); Ukraine, Malta, Pakistan, Cyprus (Medium to High Risk); Panama, Malaysia, Cuba, Russian Federation, Bulgaria, Thailand, Latvia, Croatia and Azerbaijan (Medium Risk).

As highlighted in comments in the Paris MOU Annual Reports for intervening years some flag States still feature on the Black List 9 years later in 2007 as follows: Albania, Georgia, Syrian Arab Republic, Honduras, Cambodia, St Vincent and the Grenadines, Belize, Egypt, Panama, Lebanon, and Ukraine. Six of the 11 flag States on both the 1999 and 2005 lists are National and four are Pseudo-National flag States with one International flag. Of the 19 flag States appearing on the 2007 Paris MOU Black List, 9 (47.37%) can be categorised as National, and seven (36.84%) as Pseudo-National flag States and one (5.26%) International.[29] Panama remains on the Paris MOU Black List for 2007 as medium risk with all other International flags on the Paris MOU White List.[30]

---

[29] One flag State, St Kitts and Nevis, is categorised as Quasi-National in this study.

[30] Panama was on the Paris 2005 MOU Black List and Malta on the 2005 Tokyo MOU Blacklist.

10.2.3   Tokyo MOU Black/Grey/White List of Flag States

An analysis of the Black/Grey/White list for the Tokyo MOU[31] on port State control, established in 2002, reveals similar membership and trends to that of the Paris MOU, taking into account the fact that there are ships that do not trade in both regions.[32]

Flag States on the 2007 Black List of the Tokyo MOU on port State control were, in descending order of risk: Kiribati, Georgia, *Sierra Leone*, Indonesia, *Mongolia*, (Very High Risk); *DPR of Korea*, *Cambodia*, Tuvalu, (High Risk); Vietnam, (Medium to High Risk); *Belize*, Dominica, Taiwan, China, and Thailand (Medium Risk).[33] Eight of these 13 flag States are National (61.5%) and five (38.5%) Pseudo-National flag States. No International flags appear on the Tokyo MOU Black or Grey List for 2007 (Tokyo MOU Annual Report 2007, p. 28).

Some new flag States, for example Tonga, Mongolia, and Tuvalu, entered the Black Lists of both the Paris and Tokyo MOUs immediately after they were established. Other flag States have significantly improved their performance over time for a variety of motives. The National flag of the Republic of Korea, embarrassed within the Tokyo MOU membership by an average detention rate of 9.27% in 2000,[34] managed to reduce this rate through more effective flag State jurisdiction and control over its ships to 0.23% within 4 years (Tokyo MOU Annual Reports 2000–2004). The International flags of Malta and Cyprus were required and encouraged to improve the performance of ships on their registers by the European Union as a condition of membership. With this motivation, and the active cooperation of experts from the Paris MOU, organised by the European Maritime Safety Agency (EMSA) and sponsored by the European Union (Paris MOU Annual Report 2005, p. 7), both flag States lowered their detention rate to well below the regional average for the Paris MOU, moving from the Paris MOU Black List to the Grey List in 2004, and to the White List in 2005. Both Malta and Cyprus became full members of the Paris MOU in 2006 (Paris MOU Annual Report 2005, p. 18).

---

[31] Flags listed on the Tokyo MOU Black/Grey/White list are those of ships which were involved in 30 or more port State control inspections over a three-year period.

[32] Tokyo MOU Port State Control Report, 2007, p. 10: "The black-grey-white list for 2005–2007 consists of 60 flags, whose ships were involved in 30 or more inspections during the period. There are 13 flags in the black list. Kiribati and Sierra Leone take the positions as the first and third worst flags respectively although it is their first time to be shown in the list. With its effort to improve its performance, Comoros changes position from the black list to the grey list. The grey list still has 17 flags. It is remarkable that the number of flags appearing in the white list continues to be increasing. This year, the white list comprises 30 flags that maintain good performance at the high level".

[33] The five flag States in italics are those with common membership of the 2007 Paris MOU Black List.

[34] Tokyo MOU, Annual Report, 2000, p. 14. The average detention rate within the Tokyo MOU in 2000 was 7.18%.

10.2.4   Paris Mou White List

An analysis of the 38 flag States appearing on the White List of "quality flags" in the 2007 Paris MOU Annual Report (p. 35) shows 24 National (63.15%), three Quasi-National (7.89%), six International (15.78%), and five Pseudo-National flag States (13.15%). National and Quasi-National flags combined are marginally under-represented, with the six International flags slightly over-represented and the five Pseudo-National flags almost on par. In 1999 there were only 20 flag States on the Paris MOU White List comprising 13 National, one Quasi-National, three International, and two Pseudo-National flag States (Paris MOU Annual Report 1999, p. 18).

The single most notable change in the intervening 9 year period is the inclusion on the White List in 2007 of almost all International flag States.[35] The commendable and steadily increasing respectability of International flag States has paradoxically created opportunities for Pseudo-National flag States eager to attract the older vessels that have either been rejected from International flags as substandard, excluded by way of age restrictions upon new vessels imposed by most Conventional Recognized Organizations,[36] or are more attractive to unscrupulous owners seeking a flag that offers minimal regulatory scrutiny and compliance. Alderton and Winchester (2002, pp. 151–162) have identified this phenomenon, and also the paradox that stricter and more effective port State control encourages the growth of poorly performing flag States, who depend upon their ability to offer an increasingly ineffective and relaxed regulatory regime.

10.2.5   Tokyo Mou White List

The Tokyo MOU commenced collation of a Black/Grey/White List in 2002 from information on detentions dating back to 2000. An analysis of the 23 counties on the first White List in 2002 indicates 12 National flag States (52.1%), two Quasi-National (8.70%), six International (26.09%), and three Pseudo-National flag States (13.04%). National and Quasi-National flags combined were under-represented, International flags significantly over-represented and Pseudo-National flag States almost exactly on par with category totals for all 119 flag States under consideration. It is notable, particularly as they collectively represent 51% of world tonnage, that six of the seven International flag States were on the White List in 2002 with the remaining one of Malta midway up the Grey List.

---

[35] *Ibid*, p. 18. In 1999 Bahamas, Liberia and Singapore were on the Paris MOU White List, Hong Kong on the Grey List and Panama, Cyprus and Malta on the Black List.

[36] Discussion with Mr Tateo Kaji, Managing Director, Nippon Kaiji Kyokai, (Class NK) Friday 13 September 2006. Class NK will accept vessels older than 15 years if they have been continuously in Class with NKK from new. Class NK will not accept new vessels older than 15 years.

Five years later, in 2007 (Tokyo MOU Annual Report 2007, pp. 28–29), the number of flag States on the Tokyo MOU White List had increased by seven to thirty. All countries on the White List in 2002 remained with the addition of Australia, Kuwait, Iran, Sweden, Malta, Russian Federation, and the United States of America. 17 of these 30 flags were National and two Quasi-National representing a combined percentage very similar to that of 2002 at 63%. All seven International flags were present, representing 23% of the total as opposed to 26% in 2002. The same three Pseudo-National flag States on the White List in 2007 – Vanuatu, Antigua and Barbuda, and the Marshall Islands – represented 10% of flag States on the White List.

10.2.6   Proposed Tokyo MOU Ship Black List

Preliminary work within the Tokyo MOU in 2006 on development, and possible publication, of a Ship Blacklist[37] revealed that 125 ships met the criteria of having been detained three times or more within the previous 3 years, having a very high target factor, and being registered with a flag State that was on the Tokyo MOU Blacklist. The majority, 48, of these ships were registered in Cambodia, followed closely by 34 ships registered in the DPR of Korea; a National flag State that has consistently featured high on the black lists of both the Paris and Tokyo MOU. Other National flag States that featured were Indonesia (11), Vietnam (5), Thailand (2), and Taiwan, China (1). Ships registered in Pseudo-National flag States on the list were from Mongolia (12), Belize (7), Tuvalu (4), and Bolivia (1).

Out of the total of ten flags eligible for a Ship Black List, five (50%) were National flags and five (50%) were Pseudo-National flag States. No ships registered in International flag States were identified. National flags were thus under-represented and Pseudo-National flags significantly over-represented. Three of the flag States – Vietnam, Indonesia and Thailand – are members of the Tokyo MOU. A striking feature of the ships eligible for the proposed Black List was that only two of the ships were in Class with Conventional ROs. The remaining 123 ships were associated with a wide variety of Convenient ROs.

Another notable feature of ships eligible for the Tokyo MOU Blacklist was the very small size of some of the ships trading internationally and subject to port State control. Twenty-two of the ships were less than 500 GT with the smallest, a 30 year old refrigerated cargo carrier registered in Cambodia, being only 122 GT. The oldest ship was another small refrigerated cargo carrier of 298 GT, built in 1961 and registered in DPR of Korea, that had been detained six times in the previous 3 years (Tokyo MOU Port State Control Committee 2006, Document PSCC 16/07.4A). The dubious honour for most detentions in a 3 year period went to a relatively new (built 1986) 999 GT oil tanker registered in DPR of Korea that had been detained 13 times. The average size was relatively small with only two of the 125 ships being

---

[37]Sixteenth meeting of the Tokyo MOU Port State Control Committee, 25–28 September 2006, Document PSCC 16/07.4A. The analysis is for the three years preceding May 2006.

greater than 10,000 GT; a probable reflection of the short international trades prevalent between many Asian countries.[38]

10.2.7   Paris MOU Banning of Ships

The Paris MOU has not developed a Black List of ships but, in 1999, with the support of a directive from the European Union,[39] made the decision to restrict access to European ports for ships that had been detained more than three times in 3 years, had "jumped" detention, had not proceeded to an agreed repair port, or did not carry a valid Safety Management Certificate under the International Safety Management (ISM) Code. The possibility of "banning" has been discussed in the Tokyo MOU but, without an umbrella political organisation such as the EU, it was felt that it would not be possible to achieve the agreement of all 18 politically, economically, and geographically diverse members of the MOU. Another political and economic obstacle to "banning" in the Asia-Pacific region is the inclusion in the Tokyo MOU of members such as Singapore and Hong Kong, who are in the unique position of being a one port country, where the maritime administration operates the port infrastructure as well as carrying out port State control. It is unlikely that such States would agree to the exclusion of ships from their ports. On the other hand, the Transport Ministers of all members of the Tokyo and Paris MOUs, including those of Hong Kong and Singapore, signed a Joint Ministerial Declaration in Vancouver in November 2004 that invited the Paris and Tokyo port State control committees to:

> ...develop criteria for the identification of the flag States and their Recognized Organizations that jointly have poor performance and to investigate options, including the possibility of changing the relevant Conventions so that the certificates issued by these recognized organizations on behalf of these flag States are not recognized as valid. (Vancouver Declaration 2004)

An analysis of the flag States and ROs of 53 ships[40] banned from European ports in 2005 reveals that almost half, 24, are from National flag States. The ROs that issued certificates to these ships on behalf of the flag State comprised ten

---

[38] A summary of ships in class with the three predominant classification societies in the east Asian region – Nippon Kaiji Kyokai (NKK) of Japan, the Korean Register of Shipping (KRS) and the China Classification Society (CCS) – shows that they collectively represent 9,511 ships. Of these 925 are <500 GT; 2,005 are 500–3,000 GT; 1,060 are 3,000–5,000 GT; 2,520 are 5,000–20,000 GT; 2,087 are 20,000–50,000 GT; 914 are >50,000 GT. Thus 42% of ships classed with these three societies are less than 5,000 GT. Document DBM 15/04A, Tokyo MOU on Port State Control, Database Managers' Meeting, Victoria, British Colombia, September 2006, p. 3.

[39] Article 7b(1) of Directive 95/21/EC http://www.emsa.europa.eu/end185d007d002d001d001.html.

[40] As at 6 October 2006 there were 57 banned ships, but port State control databases did not include information on flag State or recognised organisation for four ships. http://www.parismou.org/ParisMOU/Banned±Ships/xp/menu.3971/default.aspx.

Conventional ROs and 14 Convenient ROs. There were ten ships under International flags; evenly split between Conventional and Convenient ROs. Eighteen ships registered in Pseudo-National flag States were included in association with four Conventional and 14 Convenient ROs.[41] When the proportion of these categories of flag State is compared with total flag States a different picture emerges. (Of total active flag States National flags comprise approximately 80%, International 6%, and Pseudo-National 14%). Percentages for the flags of the 53 ships banned by the Paris MOU are National (45.2%), International (18.9%), and Pseudo-National flag States (34%). National flags are significantly under-represented whilst those of International and Pseudo-National flag States are significantly over-represented. An examination of data for 56 ships banned by members of the Paris MOU for 2007 (Paris MOU Annual Report, p. 44) shows similar trends with 38.18% of ships flying the flags of National flag States, 23.64% International flags, and 38.18% Pseudo-National flags.

When considering the ROs associated with these high risk ships, Convenient ROs were in the majority with 33 (62.26%) as opposed to 20 (37.74%) Conventional ROs. Notable features of the banned ships were their high average age of more than 34 years[42] and relatively small average size of 5,194 GT,[43] with seven of the ships banned from European ports less than 500 GT. These features, along with the distribution of flag States and ROs are similar to those of ships that would be eligible for the proposed Tokyo MOU Black List, many of which would meet the criteria for banning by the Paris MOU.

10.3   Performance of Recognized Organizations

Private organisations recognised by flag States to carry out inspection, survey, and certification functions are leading actors on the worldwide stage of flag State juris-diction and control. The majority of flag States entrust these important technical functions to Recognized Organizations (ROs) as provided for by the SOLAS Convention[44] and associated IMO resolutions.[45] Flag States are reminded by the IMO of the possible consequences of ineffective delegation to ROs when ships flying their flag are in foreign ports as follows:

> Whereas Parties may entrust surveys and inspections of ships entitled to fly their own flag either to inspectors nominated for that purpose or to recognized organizations, they should be made aware that under the applicable conventions, foreign ships are subject to port State

---

[41] One Quasi-National flag State was included in conjunction with a Convenient RO.

[42] The oldest was built in 1938 and the newest in 1984.

[43] The smallest ship was 148 GT and the largest 16,754 GT. Only nine of the ships were >10,000 GT.

[44] SOLAS, Chapter 1 Part B Regulation 6(a).

[45] IMO Resolutions A.739(18), Guidelines for the Authorzsation of Organizations acting on behalf of the Administration; and A.789(19), Specifications on the Survey and certification functions of recognized Organizations acting on behalf of the Administration.

control, including boarding, inspection, remedial action, and possible detention, only by officers duly authorized by the port State. This authorization of these PSCOs may be a general grant of authority or may be specific on a case-by-case basis. (IMO Resolution 787(19), Procedures for port State control, Chapter 2.1.3)

Recognizing the increasing criticality of the association of flag States and ROs in the delivery of effective flag State jurisdiction and control, and the need to measure the performance of ROs, the Paris and Tokyo MOUs have, since 1999, applied guidelines to assess the responsibility of ROs for deficiencies and associated detentions.[46] Those detainable deficiencies discovered during port State control inspections that can be directly attributed to a failure of the inspection, survey, and certification functions of the RO are tabulated in the annual reports of port State control regimes, with the Paris MOU going further and tabulating detentions of ships with RO-related detainable deficiencies per flag State.[47]

The argument is recalled[48] that there are two categories of RO; the ten long-standing and well-resourced members of the International Association of Classification Societies (IACS), who can be deemed to be Conventional ROs, and the dozens of other private survey and "classification society" organisations, the Convenient ROs, that have no cohesion or uniform professional standards. Statistics from inspections carried out by members of the Paris MOU from 1999 to 2005 are analysed in Table A.8, Appendix A, to demonstrate that Convenient ROs are associated with more detentions than Conventional ROs.

Trends for detention of ships with RO related deficiencies per RO[49] are very similar to those for detainable deficiencies (Table A.7, Appendix A), with annual average rates increasing from 1999 then reducing considerably by 2005. By 2005 almost all ROs were below the total average for all ROs over the period from 1999–2005 of 10.42%. It is notable that ten of the 12 best-performing ROs are Conventional ones, all with consistently low detention rates well below total averages and, without exception, steadily decreasing over the 7 years from 1999 to 2005. This decreasing trend in RO-related detentions is also evident across all the 28 ROs identified resulting in the remarkable average in 2005 of 2.64% detentions of individual ships inspected; a rate equivalent to that of the Conventional ROs in 1999, at a time when the Convenient ROs averaged 18.76%. This positive trend would have continued into 2007 were it not for the Register of Shipping (Albania) having a detention rate of 21.43%. The average of the remaining 19 ROs for 2007 is 2.27% detentions of ships inspected. (3.27 if the Register of Shipping is included) (Paris MOU Annual Report 2007, p. 44).

---

[46] See for example the Tokyo MOU Port State Control Manual, Section 6–4, p. S6–4–1, Guidelines for the responsibility assessment of the recognised Organization.

[47] See for example Paris MOU Annual Report 2005, p. 50. http://www.paris.mou.org.

[48] See Chapter Seven.

[49] For details of trends in detentions of ships with RO-related deficiencies per RO see Table 10.4, Appendix I.

10.4   Combined Performance of Flag States and Recognized Organizations[50]

It will be recalled that the extant international regulatory regime allows for a flag State to entrust its inspection, survey and certification functions to ROs. Recognizing the importance of this relationship in effective flag State technical jurisdiction, port State regimes are increasingly monitoring the outcomes of this alliance through collation of data on detentions with RO related deficiencies per flag State, as shown in Table A.7, Appendix A, for the years 1999–2005.[51]

Forty eight National, International and Pseudo-National flag States[52] had class-related detainable deficiencies above the regional average of 2.39% from inspections carried out by members of the Paris MOU on port State control, for the 7 year period from 1999 to 2005 inclusive. Of the 48 flag States and associated ROs, 36 (75%) were National, three (6.25%) International, and nine (18.75%) Pseudo-National. These percentages are very close to the overall percentage of these three categories of flag State at 80%, 6%, and 14% respectively, with National flag States being marginally under-represented, International flag States marginally over-represented and Pseudo-National flag States 25% over-represented. Of the 14 worst performing flag States and associated ROs, with average detention rates above the average for all 48 flag States of 9.01%, ten (71.42%) were National and four (28.57%) Pseudo-National. There were no International flag States represented in this group. The increasing respectability of International flag States and their associated ROs is reflected in the relatively low detention rates for Panama (3.34%), Malta, (3.35%), and Cyprus (3.47%).

An analysis of the categories of ROs – Conventional and Convenient – that have been entrusted with survey, inspection, and certification by the 14 worst performing flag States[53] supports the hypothesis that poorly performing flag States are often associated with Convenient and/or multiple ROs. Five of these 14 poorly performing flag States[54] had not reported to the IMO and it was not possible to determine what delegations they had made to ROs. Of the remaining 10 flag States, one, Saudi Arabia, had only delegated to Conventional ROs, and two, Bolivia and the DPR of

---

[50] Paris MOU Annual Report 2005, p. 48. The recognized organization is related to the detention if at least one deficiency is identified as being the responsibility of the RO.

[51] *Ibid*, p. 46: "The information contained in the statistical material of Models 1–4 concerning recognised Organizations were collected during the calendar year 2005 on the basis of provisional criteria for the assessment of RO responsibility. Due to updating anomalies the figures may include a small margin of error. This margin is not greater than 1.5 percent to either side".

[52] The Quasi-National flag States of Bermuda, Netherlands Antilles, and the Faroe Islands are included in Table 10.3 but are not included in statistical calculations due to the lack of empirical evidence.

[53] Information from the IMO GISIS database as at October 2006. http://gisis.imo.org/Public/RO/BrowseCountry.aspix?cid=110

[54] Sao Tome and Principe, Albania, Tonga, Qatar and Slovakia

Korea, only to Convenient ROs. Romania and Libya had delegated statutory functions to a number of Conventional ROs plus one Convenient national RO based in their country. The United Arab Emirates (UAE) had delegated to six Conventional and two Convenient ROs. The remaining three flag States had delegated to multiple Conventional and Convenient ROs; Honduras (9 and 11), Comoros (7 and 9), Georgia (10 and 11). Twelve of the 16 flag States appeared on the Paris or Tokyo MOU Blacklists for 2005, with the remaining four of Sao Tome and Principe, Libya, Qatar, and the UAE undergoing less than the ten inspections required during the year to be included in statistical tables for ROs.

Although the Paris MOU has ceased to tabulate detentions of ships with RO-related deficiencies per flag State they have introduced a ranking for performance of ROs based on the same formula as for the Black/Grey/White List for flag States.[55] The table shows that all Conventional ROs (IACS members) had high performance[56] with very low performance attributed to the Korean Classification Society (Korea DPR) and International Register of Shipping (USA).

10.5 Ship Age, Tonnage, and Detention Rates per Flag State

Consideration of percentages of ships per flag State and/or RO with poor perform-ance records does not take into account the size of the fleets registered in those countries in either numbers of ships or total registered tonnage. In order to establish the full impact of poor flag State performance it is necessary to determine the numbers of ships, their size, and age, and the total tonnages registered in the three categories of flag State under consideration: National, International and Pseudo-National. These totals need to be considered in the context of the size of the total world fleet of merchant ships of not less than 100 GT that, as at 31 December 2007, stood at 97,504 ships totalling 774.9 million GT, with an average age of 22 years and average tonnage of 7,948 GT. The world's cargo carrying fleet[57] stood at 51,538 ships of 737.3 million GT, with an average age of 20 years and average GT of 14,306.

Table 10.1 summarises the numbers, tonnage and age of ships registered in the 119 flag States identified in this study as National, International and Pseudo-National.

The 119 active flag States under these three categories represent 89.9% of ships and 92.4% of total world tonnage. The balance is made up of Quasi-National flag States and small flag States not active internationally.

There has been a considerable change in age profiles of groupings of flag States over the past decade. A study of flag States and safety between 1997 and 1999

---

[55] Paris MOU Annual Report 2007, p. 46: "Only ROs that had [undertaken] more than 60 inspections are taken into account. The formula is identical to the one used for the Black Grey White list. However, the values for P and Q are adjusted to P=0,02 and Q=0,01"

[56] *Ibid*, p. 12: "Among the best performing recognozed organisations were Det Norske Veritas (Norway), Germanischer Lloyd (Germany) and Registro Italiano Navale (Italy)"

[57] Ships greater than 500 GT

Table 10.1 Aggregated tonnage and age by flag State category; all ships >100 GT

Flag State	Ships	%	Total GT	%	Age	Ave. GT
National	63,382	72.31	248,715,099	34.73	25.17	3924.07
International	17,111	19.52	407,253,979	56.88	14.00	23,800.71
Pseudo-National	7,160	8.17	60,071,163	8.39	25.24	8,389.83
Totals	87,653		716,040,241			

Source Lloyd's register – Fairplay, World Fleet Statistics 2007

(Alderton and Wichester 2002, pp. 155, 156) established that the average age of the groupings of flag States that suffered casualties under that study[58] were 21.7 years for National flags, 19.1 years for FOCs and 18.2 years for second/international registers. The most notable change is that, in 2007, the seven International flag States not only have by far the largest ships registered but that those ships have average ages well below the world average, and other groupings of flag States, ranging from Singapore at 10 years to Panama at 19 years. Hong Kong and Liberia are both at 12 years average. Ships registered in Cyprus and the Bahamas have an average ages of 14 and 15 years respectively, and those registered in Malta, 16 years. The only comparable average fleet ages amongst all 119 flag States under consideration are as listed in Table 10.2:

The flag State with the youngest fleet is Switzerland at five years whilst the most elderly ships in this study are registered in the Dominican Republic (41 years) closely followed by Togo at 39 years.

The direct correlation between age and ship safety standards, which many Classification Societies recognise by refusing to accept new entrants greater than 14 or 15 years, is validated by the safety records of these flag States with fleets of relatively low age. None of 18 abovementioned flag States are on the Black List of the Paris MOU in 2007, three[59] are on the Grey List and nine[60] on the White List. The remaining six[61] did not undergo sufficient inspections (30 over a 3 year rolling average period) to determine their Black/Grey/White List status, largely for reasons of either geographical location of fleets or their very small size. Of these 18 flag States with lower than average fleet ages, 11 had undergone sufficient inspections from 2005 to 2007 to feature on the Tokyo MOU Black/Grey/White List. Two countries[62] remained on the Black List from 2005, three[63] remained on the Grey List with the same[64] six on the White List.[65]

---

[58] *Ibid*, pp. 151–152. Groupings were: "old" FOCs, "new" FOCs, second or international ship registers, traditional national flags, emerging national flags10.2

[59] Japan, Malaysia, and Austria

[60] Switzerland, Israel, India, Vanuatu, Belgium, Luxembourg, Netherlands, Antigua and Barbuda, and the Marshall Islands

[61] Eritrea, Ethiopia, Kazakhstan, Qatar, Tuvalu, Vietnam.

[62] Tuvalu and Vietnam.

[63] Malaysia, Israel, and India.

[64] Japan, Netherlands, Switzerland, Antigua and Barbuda, Marshall Islands, and Vanuatu.

[65] Due to the small numbers of vessels registered in these nine flag States and their trading patterns only Tonga features in Tokyo MOU Black/White/Grey List statistics for 2007; on the Grey List.

Table 10.2 Number of ships >100 GT, total tonnage and average age of fleets equal to or below average age of International ships

Flag state	No of ships	Total gross tons	Average age
National			
Austria	4	14,014	8
Belgium	243	4,091,292	17
Israel	51	741,431	18
Eritrea	14	14,478	19
Ethiopia	10	122,729	17
India	1,417	9,168,046	18
Japan	6,519	12,787,968	15
Kazakhstan	63	54,291	17
Luxembourg	75	883,524	8
Malaysia	1,151	6,139,392	17
Netherlands	1,258	5,669,041	17
Qatar	84	619,535	15
Switzerland	32	588,622	5
Vietnam	1,235	2,529,619	15
Pseudo-National			
Antigua and Barbuda	1,130	8,634,620	11
Marshall Islands	1,099	35,964,159	10
Tuvalu	155	857,338	18
Vanuatu	433	1,955,413	17

Source Lloyd's Register – Fairplay, World fleet statistics 2007

Table 10.3 Number of ships, total tonnage and average age of fleets with highest average age

Flag state	No of ships	Total gross tons	Ave. age
National			
Albania	73	67,455	35
Dominican Rep.	23	9,678	41
Rep. Of Moldova	21	50,110	35
Lebanon	58	135,904	39
Syria	139	360,990	35
Togo	28	19,274	39
Pseudo-National			
Bolivia	75	102,851	39
Sao Tome and Principe	30	29,588	38
Tonga	48	66,744	36

Source Lloyd's register – Fairplay, World fleet statistics 2007

It is perhaps fortunate for the flag States with the oldest registered ships that they have relatively few ships on their register, which not only lessens the risk but also means that many of these ships do not acquire sufficient port State control inspections to feature on the Black/Grey/White lists. Flag States in this study with ships averaging 35 or more years old and the total number of ships on their register are listed in Table 10.3.

The 495 ships registered in these nine States are not only old but relatively small at an average size of 1,812 GT. Of these flags with very elderly fleets, Albania, Bolivia, Lebanon, and Syria featured on the Black List of the Paris MOU in 2007.[66] In contrast, of the seven International flag States representing the second largest category of ships (17,111), the largest tonnage (407,253,979 GT), the largest average size of ship (23,800 gt), and lower than average fleet ages, all feature on the White Lists of both the Paris and Tokyo port State control regimes with the sole exception of Panama which remains on the Paris MOU Blacklist (Paris and Tokyo MOU Annual Reports 2007).

An analysis of the age and tonnage profiles for ships registered in all 26 flag States featuring commonly on the Black Lists of both the Tokyo and Paris MOUs for 2007 reveals that the average age of the ships is 27.12 years, with the oldest fleets (Bolivia) averaging 39 years, and the youngest (Vietnam) averaging 15 years. This compares with an average age for all ships in the world fleet >100 GT of 22 years (Fairplay 2007, p. 12). The average size of the total 21,648 ships >100 GT represented by the 26 flag States on the combined Black Lists is 3,800 GT, as opposed to the worldwide average for all ships greater than 100 GT of 7,947 GT, supporting the hypothesis that older smaller ships are more prone to detention. The flag States with the equal oldest fleets, at 39 years (Bolivia and Lebanon), also have relatively small ships at an average of 1,371 and 2,343 GT respectively, closely followed by Honduras at 34 years and the smallest average tonnage of 677 GT. Albania, amongst the top three flag States on the Paris MOU Blacklist since 1999, has ships of an average age of 35 years and tonnage of 924 GT. Statistics compiled by the Tokyo MOU (Tokyo MOU 2004, Document DBM14/07A, p. 13) support the hypothesis that smaller and older ships are more prone to detention showing that 24.76% of inspections of ships between 100 and 500 GT resulted in detentions, as did 15.01% of inspections of ships between 500 and 2,000 GT. This compares with the regional average for all 21,401 inspections carried out in 2004 by the 18 members of the Tokyo MOU of 6.51% (Tokyo MOU 2004, Document DBM14/07A, p. 69). The detention percentage per inspection for larger ships steadily decreased with size from 7.96% for ships between 2,001 and 5,000 GT to 2.35% for ships larger than 50,001 GT, as illustrated by Table 10.4, which demonstrates the close relationship between size, age, and detention rates for 2004.[67]

It could reasonably be expected that these statistics would enable the detention rate of National, International and Pseudo-National flag States to be predicted for

---

[66] Tokyo MOU Annual Report 2007, pp. 21–23. Ships registered with these flag States were either not inspected in the Tokyo MOU region or underwent insufficient inspections (30 or more over a three-year period) to feature in the Tokyo MOU Black/Grey/White List.

[67] Updated statistics from the Tokyo MOU for 2006 confirm the trend for smaller older ships to have higher detention rates with 33.3% of ships between 100 and 500 GT, and between 21 and 25 years old, being detained. Ships between 26 and 35 years of age from 500 to 2,000 GT record a detention rate averaging 16.7%; both rates against a regional average for all ships for 2006 of 5.40%.

Table 10.4 Detention percentages against age and tonnage; Tokyo MOU 2004

Age (years)	0–5	6–10	11–15	16–20	21–25	26–30	31–35	36–40	41+	Det. %
GT x 100										
1–5	8.3	13.5	7.7	22.8	24.7	32.7	28.2	41.9	63.6	27.0
5–20	8.6	6.3	8.6	12.8	17.9	23.0	18.6	29.2	16.7	15.7
20–50	4.4	2.9	5.0	7.1	9.1	18.0	11.7	16.5	00.0	8.3
50–100	0.8	2.5	4.1	7.4	7.1	16.6	16.9	00.0	00.0	6.2
100–200	0.9	3.2	1.9	7.8	6.9	10.8	8.7	00.0	00.0	4.5
200–300	0.7	1.3	3.3	4.4	6.4	7.9	00.0	00.0	33.3	6.4
300–500	1.0	2.1	2.8	4.1	6.0	4.3	27.3	00.0	00.0	5.3
500 +	0.7	1.1	1.8	5.3	10.3	00.0	00.0	00.0	00.0	2.1
Average	3.2	4.1	4.4	9.0	11.1	14.2	13.9	10.9	14.2	9.4

Source Database Managers' Meeting, Tokyo MOU, Bangkok, November 2005, DBM14/07A, Detailed Statistics on Port State Control Inspections for 2004. p. 13

the following year (2005) from the detentions rate from the 21,401 inspections across all flag States inspected in the Asia-Pacific region in 2004. National flags (3,738 GT and 24.53 years) could be expected to have a detention rate of 9.1%, International flags (23,248 GT and 14.29 years) would be 3.3% and Pseudo-National (7,637 GT and 24.81 years) would have a detention rate of 7.1%. This postulated correlation between tonnage, age, and detention is tested as follows.

10.5.1   Correlation Between Tonnage, Age, Detention and Category of Ships: National Flag States

A very close correlation for National (9.7%) flag State detention rates was obtained from the actual detention percentages per inspection for 2005.[68] The smaller average size of ships under National flags and relatively high average age are causal factors in the above-average detention rate of National flag States. A common factor amongst the worst performing National flag States is the relatively small size of their fleets and the lower than average tonnage of the ships in those fleets. Data on size of fleet and average tonnage and age of ships for the worst performing National flag States in both the Tokyo and Paris MOU regimes is summarised below in Table 10.5 for the years 1999–2005. These figures should be considered against the average tonnage in 2005 for all National flag States of 3,752.01 GT, average age of 24.53 years, and an average detention rate for all national ships of 9.72%.

Ships with the worst detention records in the Paris MOU region were 27% smaller than average tonnage for ships of all national flags, and 11% older. They were only

---

[68] Detention rates taken from the Tokyo and Paris MOU Annual Reports for 2005 in order to obtain the greatest spread of flag States. A total of 42,360 inspections used. (Paris MOU 21,302; Tokyo MOU, 21,058). Where a flag State featured in both reports the detention percentage for the greatest number of inspections was used. Flag States with no detentions were included. There were no minimum inspections, thus, one detention out of two inspections is rated at 50%.

37% the size of the average for world totals for all ships greater than 100 GT
(7,330.25 GT) and were more than 5 years older (22 years). When compared to totals
for "cargo-carrying ships" the figures reduce to 21% of average world GT (13,268
GT) and more than 7 years older. Taking world average tonnages and ages for bulk
carriers (32,184 GT and 11 years) and tankers (75,989 GT and 15 years) into account
(Fairplay 2005) it is clear that there would not be many of these classes of ship in the
above-listed national fleets. (Table 10.5)

Very similar results to those from the Paris MOU are obtained from consideration
of the ten worst performing National flag States in the Asia-Pacific region, as summarised in Table 10.6, with almost identical average tonnages and average ages above
the world average for all ships (22 years) and 18% above that for cargo carrying
ships. Average detention rates are lower than in the Paris MOU region.

Table 10.5 Average tonnage and age of National flag States with highest detention
rates; Paris MOU: 1999–2005

Flag	Ships	Total GT	Ave. GT	Ave. Age	Ave. Det. Rate (%)
Albania	77	74,793	971.34	33	42.92
DPR of Korea	445	1,257,818	2,826.55	30	35.97
Comoros	205	608,544	2,968.51	31	27.26
Lebanon	73	177,918	2,437.23	36	26.10
Libya	140	117,349	838.20	22	26.01
Algeria	129	809,006	6,271.36	25	25.83
Georgia	376	1,091,859	2,903.88	28	24.76
Syria	162	412,495	2,546.27	34	22.34
Slovakia	47	211,219	4,494.02	26	21.87
Romania	209	336,533	1,610.21	26	21.03
Total/Average	1,863	5,097,534	2,786.80	29.1	27.41

Source Tonnage and age data from Lloyd's Register – Fairplay, World Fleet Statistics
2005. Detention rates calculated from Paris and Tokyo MOU Annual Reports,
1999–2005

Table 10.6 Average tonnage and age of National flag States with highest detention rates; Tokyo
MOU: 1999–2005

Flag	Ships	Total GT	Ave. GT	Ave. Age	Detention %
DPR of Korea	445	1,257,818	2,826.55	30	49.90
Indonesia	3,214	4,330,407	1,347.36	25	23.55
Vietnam	883	1,677,876	1,900.20	17	21.76
Georgia	376	1,091,859	2,903.88	28	13.04
Myanmar	125	435,540	3,484.32	24	12.13
Turkey	1,156	5,044,703	4,363.93	25	11.34
Taiwan	636	3,226,277	5,072.76	24	10.66
Russia	3722	8,334,455	2,239.24	22	9.57
Thailand	789	3,025,332	3,934.39	25	9.34
Malaysia	1,052	5,758,729	5,474.08	16	9.23
Totals/Averages	12,398	34,182,996	3354.67	23.6	17.05%

Source Tonnage and age data from Lloyd's Register – Fairplay, World Fleet Statistics 2005.
Detention rates calculated from Paris and Tokyo MOU Annual Reports, 1999–2005. Flag States
featuring on the Paris MOU list, Table 10.4, not included

10.5.2   *Correlation Between Tonnage, Age, Detention and Category of Ship: International Flag States*

International flag States were under-represented in this correlation of tonnage, age, and detention rate of categories of flag State with an average detention rate of 3.1%; remarkably close to the prediction of 3.3%. International flag States do not feature on the Black Lists of either the Paris or Tokyo MOUs, with the exception of Panama on the Paris MOU Blacklist, but is worthy of note that comparable statistics in 2005 for these seven flag States are an average of 23,248.11 GT and an average age of 14.29 years.[69]

10.5.3   *Correlation Between Tonnage, Age, Detention and Category of Ships: Pseudo-National Flag States*

The actual detention rate for Pseudo-National flag States for 2005 at 9.43% was 33% higher than predicted, in spite of two flag States (Comoros and Cook Islands) having no detentions and Barbados (0.84%), the Marshall Islands (1.86%), and Vanuatu (2.17%) having low detention rates. The ships of these particular flag States have an almost identical average age to those of National flags, but are more than twice their average tonnage, which should lead to a lower detention rate (7.1%) as evidenced by the overall statistics for 2004. However, the detention rates for some Pseudo-National flag States such as Cambodia (14.72%), Comoros (20.0%), Honduras (16.67%), Mongolia (22.67%), and Tonga (16.67%), which are well above both the Paris and Tokyo MOU regional averages, offset the relatively good performance of other Pseudo-National flags as indicated in Table 10.7:

These figures should be considered in relation to an average of 6,597 GT in 2005 for all Pseudo-National ships, an average age of 24.81 years, and average detention rate of 9.43%. Average tonnage of the ten worst performing Pseudo-National flags is almost identical to that of the worst ten National flag States, from both the Paris and Tokyo MOU regions. Average age is considerably higher, with an almost linear decrease against performance, while average detention rates are significantly lower than those of poorly performing National flag States.

---

[69] *Ibid*, pp. 22–27. Comparable statistics for 2007 are 23,801 GT and 14 years. (*Lloyd's Register – Fairplay, World Fleet Statistics 2007*, p. 12)

Table 10.7 Average tonnage and age of Pseudo- national flag States with highest detention rates; Paris and Tokyo MOU combined: 1999–2005

Flag	Ships	Total GT	Ave. GT	Ave. Age	Detention %
Mongolia	106	301,526	2,844.59	24	22.67
Comoros	205	608,544	2,698.51	31	20.00
Honduras	1,093	793,232	725.74	32	16.67
Tonga	61	85,509	1,401.79	34	16.67
Cambodia	732	1,876,437	2,563.34	27	14.72
Tuvalu	96	211,155	2,209.94	16	11.27
Belize	667	1,585,225	2,376.65	23	10.77
St Vincent and the Grenadines	1,044	5,904,826	5,655.96	24	10.76
Bolivia	68	153,140	2,376.65	35	10.00
Sao Tome and Principe	37	46,697	1,262.08	38	-
Totals/averages	4109	11,566,291	2411.52	28.4	14.84

Source Tonnage and age data from Lloyd's Register – Fairplay, World Fleet Statistics 2005. Detention rates calculated from Paris and Tokyo MOU Annual Reports 1999–2005

10.6   Correlation Between General Cargo Ships, Detentions, and Flag States

Many of the ships detained under all categories of flag State are smaller and older general cargo ships. The correlation between age, tonnage, and detention has been demonstrated. The correlation between general cargo ships (which are on average older and smaller), detentions, and flag States is demonstrated in Table A.9, Appendix A, from detailed statistics from the Tokyo MOU for general cargo ships undergoing more than 20 port State control inspections during 2004 (Tokyo MOU, Document DBM14/07A, pp. 31–37). Statistics are included for total inspections per flag State to present an indication of the proportion of general cargo ships against total ships inspected per flag State.[70]

These statistics represent the great bulk of the total of 6,277 port State control inspections of general cargo ships carried out by members of the Tokyo MOU. These resulted in 705 detentions with an average detention rate of 11.3% during 2004 (Tokyo MOU Annual Report, p. 26). Only refrigerated cargo ships had a higher detention rate at 12.31%. The statistics for general cargo ships should be considered against a Tokyo MOU regional detention rate for all ships that year of 6.51%. As a total of 21,400 inspections were carried out by members of the Tokyo

---

[70] It is acknowledged that some ships may have undergone more than one inspection but, as data is not available for general cargo ships per flag State, this calculation is considered to be statistically sound as an indication of the percentage of general cargo ships per flag State.

MOU in 2004 resulting in 1,393 detentions, general cargo ships represented 29.6% of total inspections but represented 50.6% of detentions.[71]

There was a direct correlation between flag States on the Black or Grey List of the Tokyo MOU in 2004, high detention rates, and high proportions of general cargo ships registered under a particular flag State. Nine of the 11 flag States with the highest detention rates were on the Black List, with the remaining two high on the Grey List. These 11 flag States had an average detention rate of 20%, compared with an average for all general cargo ships of 11.3% and for all ships inspected in the region of 6.5%.

The average percentage of general cargo ships registered under these particular flags is very high at 65.5% compared with a worldwide average for general cargo ships of 24%, and an average for all flag States undergoing more than 20 inspections by the Tokyo MOU during 2004 of 40.6%. The 13 flag States with detention rates below the regional average of 6.5% for all ships had fleets with an average (25.9%) closer to the world-wide average for general cargo ships (17%). The data in Table A.9 on detention rates, port State control records, and very high fleet proportions of general cargo ships demonstrates that there is a direct correlation between these factors and certain Pseudo-National and National flag States with very poor safety records.

Statistics for general cargo/multi-purpose ships in 2007 (Tokyo MOU Annual Report, p. 35) confirm the disproportionate level of detention for this class of, generally, older and smaller ship. 31.53% (6,949) of the 22,039 ships inspected in the Tokyo MOU region in 2007 were general cargo/multi-purpose ships. 690 (9.26% of these ships) were detained against a regional average of 5.41%. General cargo/multi-purpose ships represented 55.69% of the 1,239 detentions in the Tokyo MOU region during 2007 although they comprised 31.53% of the total ships inspected.

Data from the Tokyo MOU for 2004 on detentions of general cargo ships in the Asia-Pacific region was very similar to that derived from port State control inspections carried out by members of the Paris MOU for the same year. Sixty% of general cargo ships inspected had deficiencies compared with 54% for all types of ships and 8% were detained against a regional average of 6%. 43% of all inspections were of general cargo ships and these inspections resulted in 57% of all detentions.[72] Statistics from the Paris MOU for 2007 confirm these trends. 40.61% (9,292) of total inspections (22,877) were carried out on general cargo ships and 8.20 of these ships were detained against a regional average detention rate of 5.46%. 745 (59.6%) of total detentions (1,250) in the Paris MOU region were of general cargo ships.

---

[71] By comparison detention rates for all other ship types were below the regional average at; Passenger (1.2%), Ro-ro cargo (3.6%), Livestock Carriers (3.0%), Tanker (3.7%), Combination Carrier (7.8%), Oil Tanker (5.7%), Gas Carrier (4.4%), Chemical Tanker (1.9%), Bulk Carrier (4.2%), Vehicle Carrier (2.3%), Container Ship (3.5%).

[72] All data from IMO document MSC 82/21/19, General Cargo Ship Safety, 29 August 2006, submitted by the Russian Federation to the 82nd session of the Maritime Safety Committee, p. 2. Sources of data: Lloyd's Register – *Fairplay, World Fleet Statistics 2005* and *World Casualty Statistics, 1999–2004*; IMO GISIS module on casualties; Annual reports of the Indian Ocean, Paris and Tokyo MOUs and the United States Coastguard.

The disproportionate nature of these deficiency and detention statistics for general cargo ships is emphasised by the fact that, in 2005, general cargo ships made up 17% of world tonnage by number, of ships greater than 100 GT, and 8% by tonnage.[73]

10.7   Casualties as a Measure of Flag State Performance

The IMO has classified casualties (IMO 2000, MSC Circular 953) into three categories: Very Serious,[74] Serious,[75] and Less Serious.[76] Lloyd's Register – *Fairplay*, in their annual report on world casualty statistics for 2004 (Fairplay 2004, p. 10), group casualties into the categories of: Foundered, Fire/Explosion, Collision, Contact, Wrecked/Stranded, Missing, and Hull/Machinery. Mendiola et al,[77] in a study of total loss accidents of ships under 15 flags, over a 25 year period determined that stranding was the predominant cause of very serious casualties (total losses) followed by fire, ingress of water, weather, and collisions. If explosions are included with fire, this category would make up 25% of all total losses while stranding and fire combined represent 50% (Mendiola et al, p. 1).

Regardless of definitions, categories, and frequency, most seafarers who have spent a significant time at sea will have experienced some of these multifarious calamities in their career, regardless of how professionally the ship was operated or which particular flag it sailed under. They will also, in most cases, have utilised their professionalism and accumulated wisdom and experience to extricate themselves and the ship from the particular peril. Joseph Conrad, Master Mariner and shipmaster, was well acquainted with the perils of the sea when he commented; "And yet I have known the sea too long to believe in its respect for decency" (Conrad, Chapter 2, p. 1).

---

[73] *Ibid.*

[74] *Ibid*, "Casualties to ships which involve total loss of the ship, loss of life or serious pollution." Definition of Severe pollution as agreed by the Marine Environment Protection Committee at its 37th session is: "a case of pollution which, as evaluated by the coastal State(s) affected or the flag State, as appropriate, produces a major deleterious effect upon the environment, or which would have produced such an effect without preventative action."

[75] *Ibid*: "casualties to ships which do not qualify as 'very serious casualties' and which involve fire, explosion, collision, grounding, contact, heavy weather damage, ice damage, hull cracking or suspected hull defect, etc. resulting in distortion, immobilization of main engines, extensive accommodation damage, severe structural damage such as penetration of the hull underwater etc. rendering the ship unfit to proceed, or pollution (regardless of quantity); and/or a breakdown necessitating towage or shore assistance."

[76] *Ibid*: "casualties to ships which do not qualify as 'very serious casualties' or 'serious casualties' and for the purpose of recording useful information also include 'marine incidents' which themselves include 'hazardous incidents' and 'near misses'."

[77] Mendiola S, Achutegui JJ and De la Roas MA, Fire Ranks Second in Maritime Casualties. FireNet (Maritime), International Maritime Fire and Rescue Information, http://www.fire.org.uk/marine/papers/marinecasu.htm. The study looked at a sample sizes of 500 to 1,500 ships greater than 500 gross tons.

And, it is correct that even a well-found ship can be overwhelmed, but it is less likely to meet this fate than a ship that has been badly maintained and has undergone superficial, if any, independent scrutiny and control by its flag State. It is argued that it is more likely to succumb to the perils of the sea if it is an older and smaller ship. It is also postulated that vessel type, flag State, and Recognized Organization are also, to varying degrees, causal factors in one ultimate outcome of ineffective flag State responsibility; vessel casualties. Linkages between these causal factors and the probability of casualty are examined, with statistics for the years 1999–2007 being analysed to test this hypothesis.

10.7.1   Probability of Casualty

A recent study[78] into the effect of port State control inspections on the probability of casualty confirms the links between ship type, age, tonnage, flag State, and Recognized Organization, and the probability of very serious casualties. General cargo ships are identified as having the highest probability of both detention and very serious casualty. The risks associated with age are demonstrated to increase by 0.35% per year, with general cargo ships showing the highest risks from increasing age. The study confirms that smaller ships are at greatest risk, with associated risks to general cargo ships that, on average, have smaller tonnages.[79] Ships on the Paris MOU Black List are demonstrated to have higher probability of a very serious casualty than those on the Grey and White Lists.

Ships with Conventional ROs have lower casualty rates and less chance of detention than those with Convenient ROs. This very comprehensive and detailed analysis of port State control statistics also demonstrates that ships registered with Black Listed flag States have a higher number of deficiencies when inspected at least six months before a casualty (4.3) compared with flag States on the Grey List (2.7) and the White List (1.7) (Knapp 2006, p. 131). For very serious casualties, vessels that have been detained have a significantly greater number of deficiencies (17) than vessels that have not been detained (3) (Knapp 2006, p. 131). Knapp and Franses confirm the conclusion in this study that general cargo ships have the highest probability

---

[78] Knapp S and Franses PH, The Overall View of the Effect of Inspections and Evaluation of the Target Factor to target substandard vessels. Econometric Institute Report 2006–31, Econometric Institute, Erasmus University, Rotterdam. The study is based upon data from 183,000 port State control inspections, predominantly those of the Paris MOU but including the Indian Ocean MOU, Vina del Mar Agreement, Caribbean MOU, and the United States Coastguard. Data from inspections carried out by the Australian Maritime Safety Authority are also included. A full electronic version of the thesis can be found at http:///hdl.handle.net/1765/7913.

[79] Ibid, p. 132: "Tonnage is also only significant for very serious casualties but is negative indicating that a smaller vessel seems to be at higher risk than larger vessels which goes in line with the general cargo vessels being more high risk prone".

of a very serious (1%) or serious (2%) casualty compared to tankers at 0.5% and 1% respectively (Knapp 2006, p. 132).

10.7.2 Casualty Rate of Flag States

Alderton and Winchester (2002, pp. 152–154) examined casualty rates[80] of flag States between 1997 and 1999 to determine whether the safety record of flags of convenience[81] was worse than other types of flag State. The authors deemed that serious and non-serious casualties were a more reliable and comprehensive source of data on vessel safety and seaworthiness, than total losses, although it has been demonstrated in this study that there is significant under-reporting in these areas, as opposed to the empirical evidence from total losses. Nevertheless, the results of their study merit consideration as a measure of flag State performance of technical duties.

Alderton and Winchester's initial findings were that flags of convenience (FOC) had a mean casualty rate of 3.58 per 1,000 ships, second/international registers 2.11, and national flags 1.36. However, as only the difference between the rates for FOC and national flags was considered to be statistically significant[82] the view was put that very small fleets skewed the results. The example is given that the top five flag States with highest average casualty rates had average fleets of less than 17 vessels and suffered two or less casualties over the 3 year period. Taking this into account the calculations were re-worked excluding fleets of less than 100 ships, producing casualty rates for FOCs of 2.91, for second/registers/international flags of 2.33 and for national flags of 1.29 (Alderton and Winchester 2002, pp. 153, 154).

When the size of Pseudo-National fleets, as categorised in this study, are taken into account, a number of such States would be excluded such as Bolivia (75), Cook Islands (93), Equatorial Guinea (39), Kiribait (62), Sao Tome and Principe (30 ships), and Tonga (48 ships) (Fairplay 2007). Further, a number of National flag States that have demonstrated very poor safety performance through port State control and casualty data would also be excluded, such as: Albania (73 ships), Kazakhstan (63), Lebanon (58), Moldova (21), Seychelles (54), and Slovakia (57 ships) (Fairplay 2007). It is argued that, as casualties and total losses are infrequent happenings, and to the seafarers and their families involved are hugely significant, it serves no purpose to exclude small fleets from the analysis, and that the large numbers of national flag States with very low casualty rates skews Alderton and Winchester's results in their favour. Very small National and Pseudo-National flag States registering smaller than

---

[80] The study examines 3194 serious and non-serious casualties from the Lloyd's casualty database for the years 1997–1999 rather than just total losses.

[81] The term "flag of convenience" is as defined by the ITF, 1999, Flag of convenience Campaign Report, London UK: International Transport Workers' Federation, p. 3.

[82] The 0.05 level of statistical significance was used.

average ships contribute disproportionately to detentions, casualties and total losses and their exclusion does not alter the ratio of casualty rates identified by Alderton and Winchester for their three categories of flag State.

A closer examination of actual, as opposed to overall average, serious and non-serious casualty rates presents a different ranking of flag State categories, as Table 10.8 of rank-ordered average casualty rates for the top ten National, International and Pseudo-National flag States illustrates.

It is clear from this analysis of all fleets that, regardless of fleet numbers, the worst National flag states had more than twice the casualty rate of Pseudo-National flag States between 1997 and 1999, and that International flag States had the lowest average casualty rate.

Table 10.8 Rank-ordered average serious and non-serious casualty rates for flag States: 1997–1999

National	Rate	International	Rate	Pseudo-Nat	Rate
Dominica	23.33	Cyprus	5.03	Tuvalu	10.87
Hungary	22.22	Malta	4.05	Eq. Guinea	9.69
Congo	11.11	Liberia	3.73	Barbados	4.78
Jamaica	8.33	Bahamas	3.44	Cook Is.	4.17
Ethiopia	7.78	Panama	2.31	St Vincent and the Grenadines	3.19
Mozambique	7.02	Hong Kong	1.55	Belize	2.65
Sierra Leone	5.81	Singapore	1.26	Marshall Is.	2.50
Canada	5.76			Honduras	1.74
Jordan	3.33			Cambodia	1.54
Switzerland	3.25			Bolivia	0.60
Averages	9.79		3.05		4.17

Source Table 1, p.153 in Alderton and Winchester (2002) Flag States and Safety: 1997–1999. Maritime Policy and Management. Vo. 29, No 2, pp. 153–154

Table 10.9 Rank-ordered average serious and non-serious casualty rates for Flag State categories: 2000–2002

National	Rate	International	Rate	Pseudo-Nat	Rate
Canada	11.4 (5.8)	Bahamas	5.1 (3.4)	Antigua. & Barbuda.	8.9 (4.4)
Greece	6.7 (2.5)	Liberia	4.1 (3.7)	St V & G	2.9 (3.2)
UK	5.6 (1.6)	Cyprus	3.4 (5.0)	Marshall Is	2.6 (2.5)
Netherlands	4.2 (2.0)	Malta	3.1 (4.1)	Belize	1.5 (2.7)
Finland	3.6 (1.3)	Panama	2.8 (2.3)	Vanuatu	1.3 (0.4)
Sweden	3.2 (2.9)	Hong Kong	2.6 (1.6)	Honduras	1.0 (1.7)
Turkey	3.1 (2.6)	Singapore	1.0 (1.3)		
Norway	2.8 (1.3)				
Germany	2.7 (1.6)				
USA	2.4 (1.1)				
Averages	4.6 (2.1)		3.2 (3.1)		3.0 (2.5)

Source Lloyd's Casualty Yearbook 2003, Lloyd's Maritime Intelligence Unit, Colchester

It has been demonstrated that there have been significant improvements in the performance of most flag States and ROs recently even though a number of poorly performing Pseudo-National flag States have entered the market. An analysis of a rank-ordered sampling of flag State serious and non-serious casualty rates has been carried out for 2002, (Table 10.9), to establish whether the same ranking of flag State categories continued into the twenty-first century. Rankings for countries with fleets larger than 100 vessels are included in parentheses for comparison with Alderton and Winchester's statistics from 1997–1999.

The increase in casualty rates for all flag States could be attributed to better reporting of non-serious casualties, many of which do not involve damage to the ship but are, for example, casualties to crew members, loss of cargo overboard in heavy weather or even, in one instance, the discovery of drugs in a container before discharge from the ship. Even taking these ameliorating factors into account, it is worthy of note that there has been a doubling in rates of serious and non-serious casualties for the National flag States sampled from 1997–1999 to 2002, and marginal increases for International and pseudo-national flag States.

10.7.3   Ships and Lives Lost: 1989–2007

Over the period from 1989 to 2007 the number and annual tonnage of total losses of ships slightly diminished. However, the same cannot be said for numbers of seafarers and passengers lost, or persons reported missing, as a result of these total losses[83] as summarised in Table 10.10 for total losses of ships greater than 100 gross tons, and lives lost as a consequence, between 1989 and 2007.

The lives of 644 seafarers and passengers were lost on average every year over this 19 year period as the direct result of the yearly total loss of an average of 209 ships >100 GT.

A study carried out for the OECD (SSY Consultancy and Research Ltd 2001, p. 41) confirmed that the great majority (42.6%) of the ships lost from 1985 to 1999 were small (average 2,583 GT) general cargo ships. The total tonnage of tankers and bulk carriers lost during this period was similar to that for general cargo ships,[84] but there was a striking difference in average tonnages for tankers (29,338 GT) and bulk carriers (18,209 GT) and numbers of ships lost between tankers (198), dry bulk carriers (263), and general cargo ships (1,570). These figures indicate that total gross tonnage lost is an inadequate measure for the number of seafarers placed at risk

---

[83] *Ibid*, p. 8: "The year's most notable confirmed total loss in terms of lives lost, was the Philippines registered passenger/roro/cargo/ferry *Superferry 14* (built 1981, 10,181 GT) which caught fire after an explosion in the engine room off Corregidor Island, Manila Bay, Philippines on 27/02/04. 194 passengers and crew lost their lives."

[84] For example there were a total of 198 tankers lost totalling 5,809,000 GT and 263 bulk carriers totalling 4,789,000 GT.

Table 10.10 Statistics on total losses of ships 100 GT and above and losses of lives as a consequence to the total loss: 1989–2007[85]

Year	Lives lost	Ships lost
1989	688	244
1990	389	244
1991	1,204	321
1992	246	266
1993	504	278
1994	1,552	240
1995	419	254
1996	710	257
1997	257	219
1998	566	263
1999	439	220
2000	373	206
2001[86]	346	155
2002	1,242	144
2003	198	144
2004	606	113
2005	424	149
2006	1,767	120
2007	299	135
Total	12,229	3,972
Averages p.a.	644	209

Source IMO documents FSI.3/Circ.5 Annex 2 and CWGSP 8/5

through total losses. Regardless of the small average size of general cargo ships, the proportionately high ratio of crew members to tonnage aboard these ships clearly means that they are at greater risk than those aboard larger tankers and bulk carriers.

10.7.4 Ships, Tonnage and Lives Lost: 1989–2007

A summary of numbers of ships, tonnage, average tonnages of ships lost, and lives of seafarers and passengers lost over the most recent 9 years is given in Table 10.11:

---

[85] IMO document FSI.3/Circ.5 Annex 2. As compiled on the basis of data available at the time of issuance of the circular and, in particular, on the basis of the World Casualty Statistics (LRF) and the Lloyd's Casualty Week publication (LMIU). In its World Casualty Statistics report for 2007 Lloyd's Register – *Fairplay* updated figures for previous years from 2002. These updated figures have been used. Although from the same source (IMO) it will be noted that some statistics in Table 10.15 do not tally with those in other tables but the statistical inaccuracies are not considered sufficient to affect the conclusions drawn in this study.

[86] IMO doc. CWGSP 8/5 Analysis of data measured against the performance indicators, p. 17.

Table 10.11 Ships, Tonnage and Lives lost: 1999–2007

Year	No Ships lost	GT	Ave. Tonnage	Lives lost
1999	222	1,290,000	5,810	439
2000	215	1,200,000	5,581	373
2001	182	1,080,000	5,934	346
2002	149	770,000	5,168	1,242
2003	163	570,000	3,497	198
2004	134	450,000	3,358	606
2005	155	470,000	3,032	424
2006	128	710,000	5,547	1,767
2007	135	570,000	4,222	299
Averages	165	790,000	4,683	633

Source IMO documents FSI 3/Circ.5 Annex 2, p. 8, and Lloyd's Register – Fairplay, World Casualty Statistics 2004 and 2007 (Propelled sea-going ships of not less than 100 tons gross

These figures represent all ships greater than 100 GT, almost 46,000 of which are small and not seagoing cargo-carrying ships.[87] To obtain a more accurate picture of the risks to crews and passengers from casualties, it is necessary to consider the ships that are subject to the IMO Conventions and other instruments that have been adopted to ensure the safety of ships, seafarers and passengers; cargo carrying ships.[88]

10.7.5 Ships Subject to IMO Regulations and Lives Lost: 2000–2007

The Secretary-General of the IMO reports every year to the IMO Council on the Organization's performance as measured against certain performance indicators. Table 10.12 represents information reported to the Council for the years 2000 to 2007 on ships >100 GT lost, and ratios of ships lost and lives lost:

Most lives lost in 2007, for example, were through casualties involving anchor handling/supply tugs (16), bulk carriers (39), chemical tankers (14), general cargo ships (166), passenger/ro-ro/vehicle ships (22), and ro-ro cargo ships (10) (Fairplay 2007, p. 10). The IMO reports note that the ratio of lives lost to estimated total number of seafarers and passengers is "infinitesimally small" when it could be considered significant and of concern that an average of almost three ships and 15 seafarers or passengers were lost or went missing every week over this 7 year period. The human face of raw casualty statistics is graphically illustrated by the

---

[87] Lloyd's Register – Fairplay, World Fleet Statistics 2007. There were 45,966 non cargo carrying ships totalling 37.6 million gross tons in 2007 for an average tonnage of 818 GT.

[88] Cargo ships of 500 GT or more trading internationally, and passenger ships (ships carrying more than 12 passengers) of any tonnage trading internationally.

Table 10.12   Ships >100 GT lost; ratio of ships lost; lives lost: 2001–2007

	Ships Lost[89]	People carried[90]	Lives lost[91]	Ratio[92]
2001	155	811,802,100	448	.0000005
2002	144	855,668,842	1,308	.0000015
2003	144	1,089,606,604	248	.0000003
2004	113	1,088,606,004	664	.0000006
2005	149	1,413,212,471	470	.0000003
2006	120	1,647,687,090	1,825	.0000011
2007	135	1,885,726,039	525	.0000002
Total	960	8,792,309,150	5,488	
Average	137	1,256,044,164	784	.0000006

Source IMO documents C97/3(a) 29 September 2006; FSI.3/Circ.6; and CWGSP 8/5 13 August 2008

following report on a typical high-risk older general cargo ship, registered in a Pseudo-National flag State, that foundered with loss of life in heavy weather in the Black Sea in October 2006.

> London, October 14 – A press report, dated today, states: A cargo ship sank in the Black Sea, killing three crew members, a Turkish naval rescue centre reported today. General cargo *Magic* (Comoros) sank Friday night about two miles south of the Turkish coastal town of Igneada, near the Bulgarian border, the centre said. The ship had 10 crew members on board, including Turks, a Georgian, a Ukrainian and an Azeri, the private Dogan news agency said. Seven crew members were rescued. Dogan did not give the nationalities of the dead. The vessel was carrying 1,500 tons of cement from the Romanian port of Constanta towards Istanbul when it hit a storm and began to take on water, Dogan reported, citing crew members. Survivors gave a harrowing account of being thrown about in waves up to 15 feet high while riding in a small rubber lifeboat as the larger ship sank. One of the survivors was rescued with a broken arm. The bodies of the dead could not be found and recovered until morning, Dogan said. ... *Magic*, which has also traded in recent years as *Audacious*, *Dacio* and *Precious*, is of 2,239 dwt and was built in 1969. The vessel has been detained five times since 2003. Most recently it was held for 134 days from Mar 25 last year, after a port State control inspection recorded 34 deficiencies, many of them major. Industry databases give the beneficial owner as a single ship company based in Istanbul. (Lloyd's Maritime Intelligence Unit. http://www.Lloydsmiu.com/lmiu/casualties/details.htm?casualtyID=357702&mid=40226)

---

[89] IMO document C94/3(e)/1, FSI.3/Circ.6 and preliminary IMO Secretariat data for 2005. Number of ships subject to IMO conventions lost for safety-related reason other than those declared constructive total losses for insurance purposes. i.e. not accidents and incidents which are due to security failures, acts of piracy and armed robbery or whose prevention is addressed by international conventions.

[90] *Ibid.* Estimated total number of seafarers and passengers (approx.).

[91] *Ibid.* p. 3. Number of lives lost (seafarers and passengers) due to safety-related accidents and incidents on ships subject to IMO conventions and other instruments. The higher incidence of lives lost in 2002, shown in the table, may be ascribed to two casualties namely, the passenger ferries *Le Joola* and *Salahuddin-2*, which sank off the Gambia and Bangladesh respectively, with over 1,500 lives lost between them.

[92] *Ibid.* Ratio of ships subject to IMO conventions lost for safety-related reason, other than those declared constructive total losses for insurance purposes, to total number of ships subject to IMO conventions.

The statistics above are for casualties from total losses of all ships greater than 100 GT, almost 46,000 of which are small and not seagoing cargo carrying ships.[93] To obtain a more accurate picture of the risks to crews and passengers from casualties to larger ships, it is necessary to consider the ships that are subject to the majority of IMO Conventions and other instruments that have been adopted to ensure the safety of ships, seafarers and passengers; cargo carrying ships >500 GT,[94] as indicated in Table 10.13.

Table 10.13 Ships >500 GT lost with Loss Rate; 2001–2007

	2001	2002	2003	2004	2005	2006	2007
>500GT	104	95	97	75	96	88	91
Loss rate	0.17%	0.19%	0.25%	0.19%	0.21%	0.18%	0.17%

Source: IMO document CWGSP 8/5 from Lloyd's Register – Fairplay, World Casualty Statistics 2007

Risks solely to seafarers in the course of their duties, as opposed to seafarers and passengers combined, are greatest when they are serving aboard general cargo ships and passenger/ro-ro cargo ships. For the period from 1989 to 1999, during which 6,892 seafarers were lost worldwide aboard all classes of ship, general cargo ships (28.1%) and passenger/ro-ro cargo ships (29.5%) accounted for more than half of all lives lost (SSY Consultancy and Research Ltd 2001, p. 56).

For the period 2001–2007, during which 4,536 lives of passengers and seafarers were lost, the overwhelming majority (62.33%) were lost aboard passenger/ro-ro/vehicle ships with most of the balance (19.33%) being the crews of general cargo ships (Fairplay 2007, p. 10).

10.7.6 Causes of Total Losses of Ships: 2007

A breakdown of the causes of total losses and associated tonnages and ages of ships lost in 2007, as shown in Table 10.14, indicates that most ships lost were relatively small and old, and that more than 50% foundered. These figures should be considered against the 2007 figures for the total worldwide fleet greater than 100 GT of 97,504 ships, averaging 7,947 GT, with an average age of 22 years. Cargo carrying ships >500 GT totalled 51,538, with an average gross tonnage of 14,306, and average age of 20 years (Fairplay 2007, p. 12).

Of the 135 ships lost 106 (78.5%) were 20 years old or more and 19 (14.1%) were between 10 and 19 years old. The remaining ten ships (7.4%) were less than 10 years old. The greatest number (48) of ships lost more than 20 years old were general cargo ships.

---

[93] Lloyd's Register – Fairplay, World Fleet Statistics 2007. There were 45,966 non cargo carrying ships totalling 37.6 million gross tons in 2007 for an average tonnage of 818 GT.

[94] Cargo ships of 500 GT or more trading internationally, and passenger ships (ships carrying more than 12 passengers) of any tonnage trading internationally.

Table 10.14   Types of incident leading to total loss; 2007

Cause of loss	Ships	Total GT	Average GT	Age
Foundered	70	217,157	3,102	27
Fire/explosion	16	37,557	2,347	27
Collision	17	144,677	8,510	22
Contact	4	6,827	1,707	38
Wrecked/stranded	25	158,384	6,335	27
Hull/Machinery	2	7,161	3,581	32
Other	1	387	387	27
Total	135	413,555		
Average			3063	28.6

Source Lloyd's Register – Fairplay, World Casualty Statistics 2007, p. 12

10.7.7   Tonnage, Age and Total Losses as Measures of Flag State Performance: 2000–2004

Over the period between 2000 and 2004 a total of 470 ships of 500 GT or more, totalling 3,444,000 GT, were lost. The correlation between age and tonnage, as summarised in Table 10.15, clearly supports the argument that the greatest number of total losses were older and smaller ships, with (as the size of crew reduces proportionately with increasing tonnage) significantly greater risks to the crews of smaller vessels.

The numbers of ships lost as a percentage of fleet, or world numbers of ships, is a more accurate determinate than gross tonnage of the risk to seafarers and passengers, as a large number of the ships lost are relatively small but have a proportionately large crew compared with larger ships. This argument is supported[95] (Li and Wonham

Table 10.15   Reported world total losses by age at time of loss, and tonnage: 2000–2004

Age (years)	0–4	5–9	10–14	15–19	20–24	25+	Total
Gross tons							
500–1,000	2	8	2	6	8	52	78
1,001–2,000	1	-	4	16	19	70	110
2,001–4,000	1	1	4	20	16	53	95
4,001–6,000	2	2	7	15	15	22	63
6,001–10,000	3	-	1	7	12	15	38
10,001–15,000	-	-	-	3	10	10	23
15,001–20,000	-	1	-	2	11	10	24
20,001–30,000	-	1	-	4	3	5	13
30,001–100,000	2	2	2	8	5	6	25
100,001+	-	-	-	-	-	1	1
TOTALS	11	15	20	81	99	244	470

Source Lloyd's Register – Fairplay, World Casualty Statistics 2004

---

[95] The example is given to support the argument that: "it is not always true that the bigger (in terms of gt, nt and dwt) the ship the more seamen work on it. For operational and economic reasons, the number of seafarers on board ships does not constantly increase relative to the tonnage of the ship, rather it maintains at a certain level, which, however, differs for ship types."

1996, p. 138) who state that "it was proved that accidental deaths of seamen has stronger correlation with the 'number of total loss ships' than 'ship total losses in gross tons'." Alderton and Winchester (2002, p. 152), in a detailed analysis of loss rates of 121 flag States, confirm that it is pointless comparing loss rates of flag States in terms of numbers of ships or tonnage lost, and emphasise the importance of using a rate per size of fleet.

These views are supported by an examination of the 470 total losses by flag State from 2000 to 2004 (Shipping Statistics Yearbook 2005, p. 44), expressed as a percentage of total tonnage lost. Panama suffered the total loss of 62 ships greater than 500 GT, totalling 679,000 GT, during this 5 year period; by far the greatest percentage of tonnage lost at 14.9%. Over this 5 year period the total Panamanian fleet averaged 6,291 ships totalling 123,727,300 GT representing 20.92% of world tonnage (Fairplay 2000–2004). The losses therefore equated to 0.99% of ships under the Panamanian flag and 0.55% of total tonnage registered. By contrast Singapore, which lost the second largest percentage of tonnage (11.2%) from the loss of eight ships totalling 196,000 GT, had a loss rate for its average fleet of 1,766 ships of 0.45%, representing 0.008% of the total tonnage registered under the Singaporean flag. With an average size of ship lost for the 62 Panamanian ships of 10,952 GT, the total number of seafarers put at risk from these casualties was significantly higher than for those seafarers aboard the eight Singapore flagged ships averaging 24,600 GT.

10.7.8   Loss Rates for Ship Types: 1996–2004

Data for the period from 1996 to 2004, as shown in Table A.10, Appendix A, indicates that the majority of ships that become total losses are not tankers, bulk carriers, or combination carriers, but other categories of ships, and that older ships of all types are at greater risk of total loss. Ships of all types, including tankers and bulk carriers, that are older than the worldwide average of about 20 years for all types of ships, are also at greater risk.

These statistics are supported by figures produced by Lloyd's Register – *Fairplay* (Fairplay 2004, p. 13) for the years 1999–2007 on loss rates per 1,000 ships at risk for the main ship type categories. Table 10.16 reflects a steady reduction in risk to tankers (crude oil) and bulk carriers and emphasises the higher risk to general cargo ships, as previously demonstrated from the results of port State control inspections.

Table 10.16   Loss rates for ship types per 1,000 ships at risk: 1999–2007

Ship type	1999	2000	2001	2002	2003	2004	2005	2006	2007	Average
Crude oil	0.56	2.24	1.67	0.90	0.98	1.05	0.93	0.90	0.48	1.08
Bulk Dry	3.89	4.30	2.60	1.39	1.08	0.90	0.86	1.11	1.34	1.94
General cargo	5.92	5.31	4.98	3.28	4.25	3.35	4.04	2.91	3.44	4.16
Other ships	3.39	3.42	2.93	1.35	2.26	1.30	1.54	1.75	0.94	2.10

Source Lloyd's Register – Fairplay, World Casualty Statistics 2007, p. 15

For the majority of this period general cargo ships accounted for 42% of total losses in numbers of ships, 26% by tonnage, and 27% of fatalities against a population of nearly 17% of world numbers and eight% of world tonnage (IMO 2006, Document MSC 82/21/19, p. 2). These losses resulted in 147 fatalities per year between 1999 and 2004, from an annual average of 73 total losses of general cargo ships (IMO 2006, Document MSC 82/21/19, p. 2).

The high proportion of general cargo ship losses continued a trend identified in a study undertaken by the Royal Institution of Naval Architects (RINA) in 2002 (IMO 2003, Document MSC 77/25/4). This study investigated total losses of general cargo ships between 1995 and 2000 against all other categories of ships. Over this period 40% by number of total losses were to general cargo ships. These losses were in a population of general cargo ships making up nearly 20% of total world tonnage greater than 100 GT (IMO 2003, Document MSC 77/25/4). Approximately 90 general cargo ships were lost per year during this period; almost one ship every four days. This equates to a total loss rate of 5.4 per 1,000 ship years (IMO 2003, Document MSC 77/25/4). The comparable loss rate for bulk carriers was 3.3, and for oil tankers, 1.4. (IMO 2003, Document MSC 77/25/4, p. 2)

170 fatalities through total losses of general cargo ships occurred per annum throughout the period from 1995 to 2000, equivalent to 37% of fatalities through total losses of ships greater than 100 GT, and 1.8 deaths per total loss (IMO 2003, Document MSC 77/25/4, p. 2). The study concludes that seafarers aboard general cargo ships face an annual chance of death of 1 in 2,700, which is 50% higher than that aboard bulk carriers, twice as high as tankers, and ten times higher than aboard ro-ro passenger ferries (IMO 2003, Document MSC 77/25/4, p. 4).

10.7.9   Total Losses and Flag State Performance

In a study of total losses per groups of flag State over a 20 year period from 1977 to 1996, Li and Wonham concluded that the safety record of the world fleet had steadily improved over the period and that this improvement might be due to the introduction of safety management, better technology and new safety regulations. The study grouped 36 flag States into three categories[96] according to UNCTAD

---

[96] The first group (Group I) is developed (or traditional) maritime countries, including Australia, Canada, Denmark, France, Germany, Greece, Italy, Japan, Netherlands, Norway, Spain, Sweden, Turkey, UK, and USA. Second group (Group II), developing countries (areas) includes Brazil, China, Hong Kong, India, Indonesia, Korea (South), Malaysia, Mexico, Peru, Philippines, Poland, Russia, Singapore, and Taiwan. The third group (Group III) is open registry countries including Bahamas, Cyprus, Honduras, Liberia, Malta, Panama, and St Vincent and the Grenadines. In the publication of UNCTAD (United Nations Conference on Trade and Development), the Group 1 refers to developed market-economy countries, Group II refers to countries of central and Eastern Europe, socialist countries in Asia and other developed countries. See UNCTAD, Review of Maritime Transport 1995: Report by the UNCTAD Secretariat (New York and Geneva: United Nations), pp. 143–146.

definitions of developed and developing maritime countries, and open registries (Li and Wonham 1999, p. 138) and came to the conclusion that open registry countries had the worst rates of total loss, with the exception of the Bahamas and Liberia. The worst total loss rate was experienced by ships registered in Honduras with an aggregated rate three times that of the average. Flag States with the best records were a mixture from Groups I and II, all of which,[97] with the exception of Hong Kong, would be categorised under this study as National flag States.

The worst safety records were held by a mixture of flag States[98] from all three of Li and Wonham groupings, but including the National flags of South Korea, Greece, and Taiwan; the International flags of Panama, Malta, and Cyprus, and the Pseudo-National flags of St Vincent and the Grenadines, and Honduras. It has been demonstrated that the safety records of South Korea, Panama, Malta, and Cyprus, as evinced by detention records of port State control regimes, have improved significantly since 1997 whilst St Vincent and the Grenadines and Honduras have continued to be consistently poor performers in matters of safety.

An analysis of numbers of total losses as a percentage of flag State fleets for the period from 1998 to 2002, listed by categories of flag State, has been carried out to determine whether these trends extend into the twenty-first century. Table 10.17 demonstrates that Panama, Malta, and Cyprus had a ranking over this period above the average for all International flag States and equal to some of the more poorly performing National flag States. Pseudo-National flag States continued to have the highest rankings.

Table 10.17   Rank-ordered average total loss rates for flag States: 1998–2002

National	Rate	International	Rate	Pseudo-Nat.	Rate
U.K.	0.73	Cyprus	0.37	Vanuatu	1.39
Turkey	0.52	Malta	0.32	St V. & G.	0.70
Canada	0.51	Bahamas	0.31	Belize	0.59
Taiwan	0.44	Panama	0.28	Honduras	0.43
Denmark	0.38	Liberia	0.18	Antigua & B.	0.40
USA	0.37	Singapore	0.16	Marshall Is.	0.07
Egypt	0.32	Hong Kong	0.11		
Romania	0.30				
South Korea	0.28				
Greece	0.26				
Indonesia	0.26				
India	0.26				
Averages	0.41		0.25		0.60

Source Lloyd's Register – Fairplay, World Casualty Statistics 1998–2002

[97] *Ibid,* p. 143. Russia, China, Brazil, Sweden, Hong Kong, Poland, Netherlands, and Australia.
[98] *Ibid.* Korea (South), Panama, Greece, Malta, St Vincent and the Grenadines, Taiwan, Cyprus, and Honduras.

10.7.10   Total Losses of Bulk Carriers, with Flag States: 1963–1996

A large proportion of the numbers of total losses during the period under the study by Li and Wonham were from sudden and usually catastrophic structural failures and resultant founderings of bulk carriers loaded with high density cargoes. A study in 1991 (Roberts and Marlow 2002, pp. 437–450) concluded that the majority of the bulk carriers lost were more than 20 years old and most were carrying iron ore. It was also concluded that if the world fleet of bulk carriers could be maintained at an "under ten year old condition" losses could be reduced by 80%. Significantly, for the question of casualties as a measure of flag State performance, this analysis (Roberts and Marlow 2002, pp. 437–450) of losses of bulk carriers between 1963 and 1996 came to the conclusion that the third most significant risk factor associated with increased risk of loss of bulk carriers was the country of registration, or flag State, behind type of cargo and trading route. During the 1963–1996 period considered by Roberts and Marlow, 125 bulk carriers were lost, resulting in the loss of 2,038 seafarers. With reference to the Australian "Ships of Shame" report (HORSCOTCI 1992), Roberts and Marlow state that "arguments rage over the relevance of the flag but the report notes that a ship registered in a flag State with a high casualty rate had the same risk of failure as a ship 5 years older registered under a flag State with a low casualty rate."

Most of the bulk carriers lost were registered in National or International flag States, with the flags of Panama (25), Greece (17), Liberia (15), South Korea (11), Cyprus (10), and Malta (5) accounting for the majority of the 125 ships lost. A significant number of the 125 ships (40) were more than 20 years old and a large number (45) were less than 14,999 GT. Non-OECD countries such as St Vincent and the Grenadines, Malta, the Bahamas, and South Korea featured prominently in the casualty rate for loss of seafarers through founderings of bulk carriers (per 10,000 ship years) (HORSCOTCI 1992, p. 10). Seafarers sailing under flags other than National accounted for 58% of fatalities.

The Secretary-General of IMO has recently warned of "creeping complacency" regarding increasing casualties to bulk carriers, noting that, in spite of a long-term downward trend since the high rate of casualties in the 1990s, a total of eight ships were lost in 2007 resulting in the loss of 39 seafarers. In noting that statistics from the Union of Marine Insurance Underwriters showed an acceleration in the combination of partial and total ship losses over the past few years he further noted that the loss of life since the start of 2008 "gives rise to serious concern as, in comparison with the average number for recent years, it is worryingly high"[99] (125 lives lost from January to May 2008) (IMO, Document CWGSP 8/5, p. 14).

---

[99]Lloyd's List (2008). Mitropolous warns against complacency. From address to the 84th session of the Maritime Safety Committee of IMO. 8 May.

10.8   Summary

There has been a measured improvement in the general performance of flag State technical responsibilities, and Recognized Organizations, over the period from 1999 to 2007, but there is evidence of an increase in serious and non-serious casualties across all categories of flag State. There is a correlation between the safety record of certain flag States, as evinced by detentions, casualties and total losses, and the age and type of ships. Certain National and Pseudo-National flag States attract and register predominantly older and smaller ships, with ages above the worldwide average for all ships. These ships have high detention, casualty, and total loss rates in both the Paris and Tokyo MOU regions. Some National flag States have very high detention rates, with a direct correlation to the very high age of ships in their fleets. Older and smaller general cargo ships registered in these National and Pseudo-National flag States are more prone to casualty or total loss. Seafarers aboard these particular ships are placed at a disproportionate level of risk. Flag States with fleets of above-average tonnage suffer proportionately fewer casualties and total losses. In contrast to perceived wisdom, International flag States, which individually and collectively have fleets with tonnages well above and ages well below the worldwide average for all ships, have lower than average detention and casualty rates.

References

Alderton T, Winchester N (2002) Flag States and Safety: 1997–1999. Maritime Policy and Management. Vol 29, No 2
Conrad J (1901) Falk – A Reminisce.
HORSCOTCI (1992) Ships of shame: inquiry into ship safety. Australian Government Publishing Service, Canberra
Li KX, Wonham J (1999) Who is safe and who is at risk?: A study of 20 year records on accident total loss in different flags. Maritime Policy and Management. Vol 26, No 2
Lloyd's Register – Fairplay (2004) World Casualty Statistics
Lloyd's Register – Fairplay (2004) World Fleet Statistics
Lloyd's Register – Fairplay (2007) World Fleet Statistics
Mendiola S, Achutegui JJ and De la Roas MA. (1999) Fire Ranks Second in Maritime Casualties. FireNet (Maritime), International Maritime Fire and Rescue Information, http://www.fire.org.uk/marine/papers/marinecasu.htm
Roberts SE, Marlow PB (2002) Casualties in dry bulk shipping (1963–1996). Marine Policy. Vol 26, Issue 6
Shipping Statistics Yearbook (2005) Institute of Shipping Economics and Logistics (ISL) Bremen, Druck & Medien Knotor, Rotenburg/W
SSY Consultancy and Research Ltd (2001) The Cost to Users of Substandard Shipping. Directorate for Science, Technology and Industry, Organization for Economic Co-operation and Development.

Documents

IMO (2000) MSC Circular 953. 14 December

IMO (2006) General Cargo Ship Safety. Submitted by the Russian Federation to the 82nd session of the Maritime Safety Committee. Document MSC 82/21/19

IMO (2003) Comparison of general cargo ship losses and fatalities.Submitted by the Royal Institution of Naval Architects (RINA) to the 77th session of the Maritime Safety Committee. Document MSC 77/25/4

Tokyo MOU (2005) Database Managers' Meeting: Detailed Statistics on Port State Control Inspections for 2004. Document DBM14/07A. Bangkok

Tokyo MOU (2006) Sixteenth meeting of the Tokyo MOU Port State Control Committee, 25–28 September. Document PSCC 16/07.4A.

Vancouver Declaration (2004) Report of the Second Joint Ministerial Conference of the Paris and Tokyo MOUs. http://www.tc.gc.ca/marinesafety/PSCConference/second-jmc.htm.

Chapter 11
Issues of Flag State Responsibility and Proposed Remedies

Abstract The international regulatory framework for ships allows for the existence of regulatory inefficient flag States, delegation of statutory functions, and the registration and operation of substandard ships. It is useful to recall these issues before analyzing them and proposing remedies within international law for effective global governance of ships. Issues can arise from the unfettered right of a State to grant its nationality to ships and continue with widespread dereliction by flag States of their duty to survey a ship before registration. The ability provided by international maritime instruments for a flag State to delegate its duties and responsibilities under the LOSC to private organisations, and the associated issues if this delegation does not meet the standards demanded by those instruments, is discussed. The long-established principle in customary, national, and international law of primacy of the flag State as a means of ensuring good order upon ships is called into question, and the starting point is to examine an alternative model for global governance of ships that does not rely upon this precept. The issues that, individually and collectively, contribute to ineffective flag State jurisdiction are identified as grant of nationality, survey and registration of ships, effective implementation of IMO instruments, delegation of flag State duties, global oversight of flag State implementation, enforcement by flag States of IMO instruments, and the status of the IMO Member State voluntary audit scheme. The need is identified for a comprehensive and coordinated approach to be taken by the IMO in deliverance of a suite of measures to collectively ensure that the intent of the LOSC and IMO instruments is met, the regulatory framework is strengthened, and all flag States exercise effective jurisdiction and control over the ships flying their flag.

11.1 An Alternative Model for Global Governance of Ships

One commentator (Kovats 2006, p. 76) questions the extant model of flag State primacy for governance of ships and proposes that a "regime change in the public law provenance of the industry is overdue". A treaty-based model of sovereignty and public law translating into national law is seen to be an impracticably traditional

J.N.K. Mansell, *Flag State Responsibility,*
DOI: 10.1007/978-3-540-92933-8_11, © Springer-Verlag Berlin Heidelberg 2009

model in the reality of the homogeneously global nature of modern shipping. That very global nature of shipping could suggest that an all-inclusive industry wide body, wider than just flag States, could be an appropriate and relevant model for the twenty-first century to replace flag State jurisdiction. It is argued by Kovats that the juridical independence of flag States implied by the LOSC, which requires every State to effectively exercise its jurisdiction and control in administrative, technical, and social matters over ships flying its flag (LOSC, Article 94(1)), and to assume jurisdiction under its internal law over each ship flying its flag and its master, officers, and crew in respect of administrative, technical, and social matters concerning the ship (LOSC, Article 94(2)(b)), is in effect illusory.

Kovats suggests a radical model of governance in which ships would be the *subjects* of international law operating under legally binding rules made by a democratic legislative forum of all participants in the shipping industry; not just Member States as is the present case through the IMO. This body would reach agreement on standards for ships and their crews superceding or adapting the standards sets by the IMO and ILO. It is proposed that an international maritime judiciary be established independent of State jurisdictions. This would effectively result in shipping's own international public law regime under which those persons directly responsible for the ship, such as owners, master, crew, managers, insurers, and everyone "whose acts or omissions affect the ship's behaviour, would become the *objects* of international (maritime) law" (Kovats 2006, p. 77). The ship would then be directly responsible for ensuring seaworthiness and fitness for purpose under the obligations placed upon it by the international community. The freedom of the seas would thus be guaranteed to the ship directly by the international community, without imposition of a State's national law. Grotius' 500 year old *res communis* would be replaced by the concept of a secular *universitas humana*, a form of governing "in pursuit of a common substantive objective[1]; the ruler being related to this enterprise in some such manner as that of its custodian, guardian, director or manager" (Kovats 2006, p. 78).

The ILO tripartite model of Governments, seafarers, and employers working together to draft international standards goes some way towards Kovats' model but is still dependent upon public international law and sovereign States. It is a more inclusive model than that of the IMO, which allows discussion by non-governmental organisations, ship-owners, seafarers, and industry bodies but does not allow them voting rights. This is of no great importance as IMO largely develops standards through a process of consensus; a process that fully involves non-Governmental organisations, and IMO very seldom puts matters to the vote. The ILO model of a more participatory nature worked extremely well in development of the Maritime Labour Convention 2006, but this treaty must still await ratification by a high percentage of States to come

---

[1]With reference to Loughlin M, (2003) The Idea of Public Law. London, Oxford University Press, p. 17; and quoting from Oakshott M, (1975) On the Civil Condition. In On Human Condition. Oxford, Clarendon Press, p. 218.

into force, and then be brought into effect through national law, with all the associated problems of implementation and enforcement by sovereign States. The voting system of the ILO still pays homage to the primacy of the State (governments) over the votes of the employers (shipowners) and employees (seafarers).

Admirable and original though Kovats' model may be in international law, it ignores the reality that only a very small percentage of the more than 700 million gross ton of world shipping greater than 100 GT operates under the few National and Pseudo-National flag States that are regulatory inefficient.[2] Those same shipowners would take equal advantage of a regime that gave them sole responsibility for the operation of their ships without the oversight, for better or worse, of a flag State. The suggested model of governance for ships also does not recognise the all inclusive industry-wide nature of development of standards at the IMO or the fact that the Organization is well aware of the shortcomings of flag State implementation of IMO standards. There would be huge difficulties in introducing a totally new international system of governance for ships that is not based in international law.

It is concluded that, instead of wholesale change to the existing model for governance of ships, more can be achieved to ensure effective flag State responsibility through enhancement, reinforcement, and empowerment of the current model of flag State jurisdiction and control.

11.2 Global Oversight, Analysis, and Measurement of Flag State Performance

The IMO has, to date, largely addressed issues of effective flag State implementation and enforcement of IMO instruments through the work of the Sub-Committee on Flag State Implementation (FSI). FSI has developed standards for flag States and Recognized Organizations (ROs) and their interaction, and voluntary initiatives to encourage effective flag State performance. It has been demonstrated in this study that, in spite of this work, opportunities still exist within the regulatory framework for exploitation of these standards by unscrupulous flag States, ROs, and shipowners. There is an urgent need for the Member States of IMO to agree that the Organization take a more active role in global oversight of flag State performance.

In order for this to happen the IMO Secretariat must be adequately resourced and have the ability to carry out the collection of data to enable analysis of flag State performance. The results of this analysis need to be publicised for the advice and benefit of all Member States and the wider maritime community.

The IMO has a clear mandate to assume a global oversight role through existing wording on the purpose of the Organization in its parent Convention (IMCO Convention, Article 1(a)):

---

[2] See Chapters Nine and Ten for detailed statistics on flag State performance.

To provide machinery for co-operation among Governments in the field of governmental regulation and practices relating to technical matters of all kinds affecting shipping engaged in international trade, and to encourage the general adoption of the highest standards in matters concerning maritime safety, efficiency of navigation and prevention and control of marine pollution from ships; and to deal with administrative and legal matters related to the purposes set out in this Article. To provide for the exchange of information among Governments on matters under consideration by the Organization. (IMCO Convention, Article 1(e)).

The IMO is increasingly focusing upon particular aspects of State responsibility within the Secretariat. An Implementation and Port State Control Coordination (IPC) Section has recently been created within the Maritime Safety Division of the Secretariat, with a clear mandate for global harmonisation of port State control activities. Along with the standing Working Group on Casualty Analysis under FSI, the first meeting of a Working Group on Harmonisation of Port State Control Activities was held in 2006.[3] This Working Group will be convened on an ad hoc basis at future meetings of FSI.

The IMO acknowledges that the Organization has neither the mandate nor the resources to enforce international safety and environmental standards (United Nations 2004, p. 13), and recognises that, if the Organization is to be further involved in achieving substantive improvements in flag State implementation and enforcements of its instruments, it must be given authority to verify whether this is, or is not, happening (United Nations 2004, p. 13). There has been a suggestion that "performance clauses" should be included in all mandatory instruments, with provision for sanctions or penalties for recalcitrant flag States. The importance of the Voluntary IMO Member State Audit Scheme in verification of flag State compliance is stressed by the IMO (United Nations 2004, p. 13).

It is concluded that the IMO does have a mandate and a burgeoning need to assume a role of global oversight, analysis, measurement, and dissemination of flag State performance. The Secretariat must be adequately resourced to carry out this task on behalf of IMO's Member States.

11.3   Issues of Delegation, or Derogation, of Flag State Responsibilities

The clear intent of the LOSC is that a flag State effectively exercises jurisdiction and control in administrative, technical and social matters over ships flying its flag (LOSC, Article 94(1)). Customary State practice, which has been codified by the IMO, allows flag States to authorise private organisations to act on their behalf in matters of inspection, survey, and certification of ships. The IMO has provided clear standards for this authorisation and for the standards of ROs. Flag States are

---

[3] Fourteenth meeting of the Flag State Implementation Sub-committee (FSI 14), June 2006.

required to establish a system to ensure the adequacy of work performed by the organisations acting on its behalf (IMO Resolution A.739(18), Annex (3)). Some regulatory inefficient flag States have taken advantage of the ability to delegate their statutory functions and a proliferation of substandard ROs have evolved as confirmed by this study.[4] This has resulted in a sometimes unholy alliance of substandard flag States and substandard ROs, with no verification and monitoring carried out by the flag State of the activities of the RO.

Flag States are required by the SOLAS Convention to report to the IMO on the organisations they have authorised to act on their behalf. This information is published by the Organization for the information of port States. The Voluntary IMO Member State Audit Scheme (VIMSAS) examines in some detail the verification and monitoring activities of ROs by flag States but this does not provide a useful indication of the effectiveness of the activities of these private organisations. In order to ensure effective implementation and enforcement by flag States of IMO instruments, and effective jurisdiction and control of ships flying their flags, there is an urgent need to address the issue of authorisation of flag State duties to ROs. The standards provided by the pertinent IMO resolutions, which are mandatory under the SOLAS Convention, are more than adequate but are ignored by a large number of flag States and ROs.

Resolution A.973(24), Code for the Implementation of Mandatory IMO Instruments, pays particular attention to the issue of delegation of flag State authority to ROs.[5] As part of the pre-audit questionnaire (IMO Resolution A.974(24)), flag States are asked to list the ROs and nominated surveyors acting on their behalf, to specify whether there is a written agreement with each RO, and provide copies or, in the absence of a written agreement, to specify scope of authorisations including a matrix indicating which functions (plan approvals, surveys, certification, exemption and equivalent arrangements) have been delegated to ROs. They are also asked to state how they verify and monitor the performance of ROs,[6] and to indicate the resources allocated to verification and monitoring of RO performance. These are all issues at the heart of the delegation/derogation issue of flag State responsibility.

VIMSAS does not require a direct audit of ROs. It relies instead on an indirect audit of the processes required in order for the flag State to delegate inspection, survey, and certification functions to ROs and to monitor their performance. This narrow systems-based approach brings with it the associated risk of a regulatory inefficient flag State either not having these processes in place, or the audit records

---

[4] See Chapter Eight for a detailed analysis of recognized organizations and Chapter Ten for analysis of the relationship between flag States and ROs.

[5] Resolution A.973(24), Annex, Part 2, Flag States, para. 18: "Flag States authorizing recognized organizations on their behalf in conducting the surveys, inspections, the issue of certificates and documents, the marking of ships and other statutory work required under the IMO conventions must regulate such authorisation in accordance with SOLAS regulation XI-1/1".

[6] Details of audits carried out by the flag State to monitor the ROs within the preceding two years should be provided, as well as any planned audits and other oversight and guidance procedures applied by the State to ROs are required.

being a sham. This particular part of the IMO audit draws heavily upon Resolution A.789(19), Specifications on the survey and certification functions of Recognized Organizations acting on behalf of the Administration, which prescribes in detail the minimum technical specifications for ROs. Resolution A.789(19) is complemented by Resolution A.739(18), Guidelines for the authorization of organisations acting on behalf of the administration. This instrument lays down the minimum standards for ROs in terms of technical, managerial, and research capabilities to accomplish the tasks being assigned, along with the verification and monitoring processes that must be put in place by the Administration to ensure that the work is adequate. Both Resolutions, A.739(18) and A.789(19), are given mandatory effect under the SOLAS Convention.[7]

A regulatory efficient flag State will have a signed Memorandum of Agreement in place with ROs, as required by A.739(18),[8] or have equivalent legal provisions in its national law, and will carry out an annual audit of ROs using Resolution A.739(18) and A.789(19)[9] as the audit criteria. The delegation by some regulatory inefficient flag States to ROs that do not meet these criteria, and the resultant derogation of flag State responsibility, allows substandard shipowners and ships to assume a persona of compliance and is central to issues of flag State implementation and enforcement.[10]

A framework is already established through the VIMSAS that could, with not a great deal of amendment, effectively deal with the vexed question of delegation of flag State functions to ROs.[11] An initial step in addressing this weak link in the regulatory chain would be for VIMSAS to be amended to require audits, independent

---

[7] See Annex 5 of IMO Resolution A.974(24) for a list of all instruments made mandatory under IMO instruments.

[8] Resolution A.739(18), Guidelines for the authorization of organizations acting on behalf of the Administration.

[9] Resolution A.789(19), Specifications on the survey and certification functions of recognized organizations acting on behalf of the Administration.

[10] See Chapter Ten for detailed statistics on the relationship between flag States and ROs of different categories.

[11] A paper (MSC 84/22/13) was presented to the 84th meeting of the Maritime Safety Committee (MSC) in May 2008 on behalf of all members of the EU and the European Commission proposing inclusion of a new agenda item – "Development of a Code for Recognized Organizations" – in the work programme of the Sub-committee on Flag State Implementation (FSI). The paper notes that Member States are responsible for ensuring that Recognized Organizations (ROs) comply with their instrument of authorization and their oversight programme, and that IMO requirements are currently scattered in different instruments; some of which are mandatory whilst others remain recommendatory, and that no audit scheme exists to verify that these requirements are effectively and uniformly implemented. The paper proposes that a Code for Recognized Organizations should *inter alia* gather all the applicable RO requirements in a single IMO mandatory instrument and, amend the existing and applicable legal framework to ensure that the ROs are correctly audited by qualified independent auditors with respect to the Code. The paper identifies a compelling need for this initiative. It is identified that the FSI would need two sessions of work to develop the Code with a suggested target completion date of 2010.

of those carried out by the flag State, of ROs to be carried out to the criteria in A.739(18) and A.789(19) and reported directly to the IMO.[12] The information resulting from such audits could be analysed by the IMO on a confidential basis to feed into the debate that will inevitably take place amongst the Member States of the Organization, as it did within the ICAO, as to whether the VIMSAS should be made mandatory. If, or when, that day arrives, the Member States of the IMO could put measures in place through amendments to the principal instruments that would allow a flag State to only delegate statutory functions to ROs that met the requirements of the two pertinent IMO resolutions.

Taking the above issues into account it is concluded that the IMO must seek a means of measuring the performance of ROs, ensuring that ROs meet the standards of the mandatory resolutions, and that the relevant flag States verify and monitor the activities of ROs. Port States should be advised of ROs that do not meet these standards, in order that they could refuse to accept the certificates issued to ships by those particular ROs on behalf of a flag State. This would effectively cull the large number of Convenient ROs that currently carry out statutory functions, mainly on behalf of regulatory inefficient flag States. These measures would be strengthened by extension of the scope of the VIMSAS scheme to include independent audits of ROs against the mandatory standard.

11.4   Issues of Global Oversight of Flag State Implementation of IMO Instruments

The original mandate of the Inter-governmental Maritime Consultative Organization (IMCO) was reflected in its name and in Article 2 of the associated Convention,[13] which stated: "The functions of the Organization shall be consultative and advisory". IMCO was not given the authority to itself adopt treaties (IMO Convention, p. 1). In 1977 the Convention was amended to remove the consultative and advisory functions contained in Article 2 (IMO Convention, p. 3). IMO[14] has no powers of

---

[12] The scope of the ICAO SOAP scheme has been phased in with the original basis of the mandatory audit being safety-related standards and recommended practices (SARPs) and associated procedures covering Personnel Licensing, Operation of Aircraft and Airworthiness of Aircraft. It was envisaged from the beginning that other Annexes to the Chicago Convention would be added in future programmes. The 35th Session of the ICAO Assembly resolved that the SOAP programme be extended to cover all safety-related Annexes and also to transit to a comprehensive systems approach for the conduct of safety oversight programmes. http://www.dotars.gov.au/aviation/international/universal.aspx.

[13] Convention on the Intergovernmental Maritime Consultative Organization, Geneva, March 6 1948, 289 UNTS 3; ND IV.

[14] *Ibid*. The name of the Organization was changed to the International Maritime Organization through an amendment to the IMCO Convention in 1975 that entered into force in 1982.

enforcement of its instruments but "depends upon the Governments of Member States. Contracting Governments enforce the provisions of IMO Conventions as far as their own ships are concerned and also set the penalties for infringements when these are applicable ... in most Conventions the flag State is primarily responsible for enforcing Conventions as far as their own ships and personnel are concerned".[15]

Under this mandate the IMO cannot directly ensure that the provisions of its Conventions are implemented and enforced by Member States. It also has not traditionally carried out any global oversight or audits of Member States, relying instead on flag States and shipowners, who have the ultimate responsibility, to comply with the international safety standards adopted by the IMO (Sasamura 2003, p. 3). This approach changed with revision of the STCW Convention[16] in 1995, when the importance of all parties meeting the requirements of the Convention resulted in the IMO appointing panels of competent persons provided by Member States. These panels assessed applications from Member States for inclusion on the so-called "White List" of approved flag States under the amended Convention. This was the IMO's first tentative foray into the field of increased oversight of Member States, with initial approval for inclusion on the IMO White List being confined to an evaluation of submitted documents. No visits were carried out by IMO-competent persons to Member States and no indication could therefore be gained of the effectiveness of the submitted documents or adequate delivery of training programmes. Initial approvals were for 5 years, with an independent audit required to ensure ongoing inclusion on the White List. Many Member States arranged for other Member States to carry out this audit. This monitoring and compliance role by the IMO was approved by the Member States of the Organization and was clearly a precursor to acceptance by those States of the concept of voluntary audits of flag, port, and coastal State duties under mandatory IMO instruments (Sasamura 2003, p. 3).

As early as 2000, before development of the IMO Model Audit Scheme, FSI agreed on a list of criteria and a series of performance indicators by which flag States could measure their performance.[17] It was agreed that the following criteria were pertinent when flag States chose to assess their performance (Sasamura 2003, pp. 2–3):

- Legal performance and means of promulgating maritime legislation which shall satisfy the international maritime obligations of the State.
- Ability to demonstrate giving full and complete effect to instruments in force to which the State is a party.

---

[15] Conventions, http://www.imo.org/Conventions/mainframe.asp?topic_id = 148.

[16] International Convention on Standards of Training, Certification and Watchkeeping for Seafarers, 1978, as amended in 1995, 1984 *UKTS* 50 269.

[17] Sub-Committee on Flag State Implementation, 8th session: 24–28 January 2000, p. 2. These were included in resolution A.881(21) as a flag State Performance Self-Assessment Form. Intended to be used by flag States on a voluntary basis to obtain a clear picture of how well their maritime administrations are functioning and to make their own assessment of their performance as a flag State. http://www.imo.org/Newsroom/mainframe.asp?topic_id = 106&doc_id = 336.

- Enforcement of maritime legislation.
- Responsibility for any Recognized Organization (RO) acting on behalf of the Administration, including authorization and monitoring of, and any corrective action against, the RO.
- Ability to investigate the causes of personal injuries, non-compliance, casualties, pollution incidents and ability to take appropriate remedial action.
- Ability to ensure that a ship having joined its register does not operate unless it complies with applicable instruments.
- Ability to demonstrate that a policy is in place to promote at all times a safety and environmentally-minded working culture.

A series of performance indicators were also agreed for analysis against these criteria and these were approved as an IMO Circular (MSC/Circ.954 – MEPC/ Circ.373). In November 2001, Resolution A.881(21) was revoked by Resolution A.912(22), which included performance criteria and indicators for self-assessment by flag States of their performance (IMO 2002, p. 4).

These criteria and performance indicators were to feed into a proposed IMO database that would allow analysis by the Organization "in its efforts to achieve consistent and effective implementation of IMO instruments" (IMO 2002, p. 4). This database would contain information on three levels that would allow the Organization to monitor effectiveness and consistency of implementation of its instruments, to identify possible problems being encountered in this goal due to the way the instrument was written or structured, and to identify failures of effective implementation due to the way the instrument is administered by the State.

These performance indicators are required to be analysed against the criteria as follows:

- Accidents, casualties and incidents reportable to the Organization in terms of the requirements of the applicable Conventions.
- Accidents involving personal injuries leading to absence from duty of 3 days or more on board ships flying the flag of the State concerned.
- Lives lost on its ships resulting from the operation of ships flying its flag.
- Ships lost.
- Pollution incidents according to MARPOL 73/78 and other applicable instruments' reporting standards, as appropriate, including a measure of the seriousness of the incidents.
- Information provided by other States under port State control procedures in accordance with the applicable Conventions.
- Information provided by statutory surveys, audits and inspections carried out by, on behalf of and at the request of, the flag State.
- Compliance with communication of information requirements of mandatory instruments, including the serious and very serious incidents reportable to the Organization.
- Actions taken against ships, flying the flag of the State, which have been identified as not being in compliance with the requirements of mandatory instruments, including the effects of such actions. (IMO 2002, p. 4)

These criteria and performance indicators have been effectively subsumed into the resolutions that bring VIMSAS into effect. The IMO is therefore positioning itself to be able to collate and analyse data on the performance of Member States in fulfilment of their flag, port, and coastal State obligations. As VIMSAS is voluntary, and all information gained from audits is confidential to the IMO and the Member

State audited, it is not possible at present for the performance of flag States to be made public. However, the criteria agreed by the Member States of the IMO for measurement of flag State performance, and the underlying performance indicators summarised above, are still relevant and pertinent. A database that would allow analysis of the flag State performance criteria resulting from the VIMSAS audits, were they to become mandatory, has been established.

The IMO Global Integrated Shipping Information System (GISIS) database collects mandatory reporting information from Member States. GISIS currently contains fields for Maritime Security,[18] Reporting of organisations authorised by flag States (RO),[19] Condition Assessment Scheme for tankers,[20] Maritime casualties and incidents,[21] Port reception facilities,[22] Pollution prevention equipment,[23] Greenhouse gas emissions,[24] and Contact points for Member States. Information on GISIS is supplied and maintained by national maritime Administrations, directly or by submission to the IMO Secretariat as required by various instruments. The stated aim of GISIS (http://gisis.imo.org/Public/Shared/Public/Disclaimer.aspx) is to "allow on-line access to information supplied to the IMO Secretariat by maritime Administrations, in compliance with IMO's instruments". This approach is consistent with the intention of IMO Resolution A.912(22) in 2001, that the database to be established by the Organization would *inter alia* enable the Organization to identify failures of effective implementation due to the way the instrument is administered by the State. The IMO makes it very clear that they accept no liability or responsibility for the accuracy or inaccuracy of the data on GISIS through a comprehensive disclaimer (http://gisis.imo.org/Public/Shared/Public/Disclaimer.aspx).

Acceptance by the Member States of VIMSAS, and the associated audits of those States by panels of IMO appointed auditors from other Member States, is a firm step towards increased global oversight, analysis and measurement of effective implementation of its instruments by the Organization. For the IMO to have any direct enforcement powers an amendment would be required to the IMO Convention. Agreement of two-thirds of the Assembly would be required (IMO Convention, Part XVII, Articles 69–70) to broaden the scope of the IMO's functions from those articulated in the extant Article 2 of the IMO Convention. This article states that: "IMO provides for the drafting of conventions, agreements or other suitable instruments; provides machinery for consultation among Members and exchange of

---

[18] Information communicated under the provisions of SOLAS Regulation XI-2/13 and the ISPS Code.

[19] Information submitted by Member States under MSC/Circ.1010-MEPC/Circ.382.

[20] IMO Resolution MEPC.94 (46), as amended. Electronic database for the implementation of the Condition Assessment Scheme.

[21] Data on maritime casualties and incidents as defined by circulars MSC-MEPC.3/Circ.1.

[22] Data on the available port reception facilities for the reception of ship generated waste.

[23] Pollution prevention equipment required by MARPOL 73/78.

[24] Greenhouse Gas (GHG) Module based on the Interim Guidelines for Voluntary Ship CO2 Emission Indexing for use in trials (MEPC/Circ.471).

information; facilitates technical co-operation" (IMO Convention, http://www.imo. org/Conventions/mainframe.asp?topic_id = 771). The models that have already proven effective of Member States of IMO auditing other Member States indicate that it may be neither possible nor necessary for the IMO Convention to be amended to allow the Organization enforcement powers.

The IMO comprises Member States with a supporting Secretariat and it is doubtful whether these Member States would agree to involvement of the Secretariat in their internal affairs. The most achievable mechanism for the IMO to achieve effective implementation by flag States of mandatory instruments is for the Secretariat to collect, analyse, and disseminate information on the performance of its Member States and for those States to agree, as is happening under VIMSAS, to be audited by other Member States against agreed standards. Individual Member States would have the option of bringing into effect, through their national law, sanctions that had been codified by the IMO against substandard ships through, for example, refusal of access to their internal waters and ports.

The IMO is on a steady course towards greater oversight and measurement of the effectiveness of its instruments; a role that will be necessary if the Organization is to provide leadership and coordination of global data to monitor implementation of its instruments and the performance of flag States. This matter will be brought to a head in any debate on whether the Voluntary IMO Member State Audit Scheme will be made mandatory. This debate is certain to follow the example of the ICAO and take place when confidence has been gained in the enactment and integrity of the VIMSAS process.

For the IMO audit scheme to become mandatory it would be necessary to adopt one of the resolutions associated with the VIMSAS as a mandatory instrument under the SOLAS Convention. It could be argued that the intent of SOLAS is design, construction, and equipment of ships and navigational safety. However, the mandate of the SOLAS Convention has gone well beyond these original criteria, as an examination of the 19 instruments made mandatory under SOLAS 74 demonstrates.[25] Of particular relevance to the matter of effective flag State performance in this context is the present inclusion of Resolutions A.739(18) and A.789(19) on the delegation of flag State statutory functions to ROs as mandatory instruments under SOLAS. It is logical and consistent to also mandate Resolution A.996(25), Code for the Implementation of Mandatory IMO Instruments, 2007, which sits above these two resolutions and provides required standards for effective flag, coastal and port State implementation.

11.5 Registration and Survey

The LOSC provides for a State to grant its nationality to a ship, to register ships in its territory, and to fix the conditions for the grant of its nationality (LOSC, Article 91(1)). One of the technical duties of a flag State under the LOSC is to ensure *inter*

---

[25] See Annex 5 of IMO Resolution A.973(24).

alia that each ship, before registration and thereafter at appropriate intervals, is surveyed by a qualified surveyor of ships.[26]

The clear intent of this provision is that a ship is seaworthy and in compliance with international standards before being registered and given the ability to trade under the flag of the country of registration: the flag State. This requirement is honoured more in the breach by most flag States of whatever ilk although some flag States, through Classification Societies, have requirements and procedures in place for a survey before an existing ship transfers to their register. The IMO has minimal voluntary standards in place for transfer of flag, which only require an exchange of information between States (IMO 2004, MEPC/Circ.424 MSC/Circ.1140).

As States have the sovereign right to fix conditions for the grant of their nationality under the LOSC, and there is no international standard or explicit requirement under IMO instruments for registration of ships, States have the freedom to choose not to require a survey before registration. Many flag States would see such a requirement as an unnecessary impediment, expense, and obstacle to their ability to register ships, sight unseen, on the strength of certificates that may themselves have been issued by a regulatory inefficient flag State. Thus, flag States and substandard ships have the ability to circumvent the intent of the LOSC within the extant regulatory framework.

It is concluded that there is a clear need to reflect the intent of the LOSC that a ship be surveyed before registration in IMO instruments through an amendment to the SOLAS Convention. This amendment would be to require a survey before registration and for there to be a mandatory process for transfer of ships between States that would ensure their seaworthiness and compliance with mandatory IMO and ILO instruments.

11.6 Issues of Sanctions Against Substandard Ships

If mandatory IMO Member State audits eventuate, they must provide for sanctions against those flag States that do not effectively implement and enforce the standards required by the instruments they have ratified, and/or do not accept the Organization's offers of technical assistance to improve their administration. The most obvious sanction would appear to be removal of the ability of a recalcitrant State to grant its nationality to ships but, as this sovereign right is provided to States by the LOSC (LOSC, Article 90), along with the right to fix conditions for the grant of nationality (LOSC, Article 91(1)), it is doubtful whether such sanction would withstand scrutiny or challenge in international law.

The IMO Convention could not codify sanctions that would bring into question the very cornerstone of international maritime law for jurisdiction and control of ships. Such a move would also be at variance with the LOSC and with the *pacta*

---

[26] LOSC, Article 94(4)(a).

sunt servanda principle of the Vienna Convention[27] that "every treaty in force is binding upon the parties to it and must be performed by them in good faith". The exclusivity of the right of States to grant nationality, as provided for by the LOSC, is understood by both the IMO and the ILO, and other United Nations agencies, to mean that the conditions attached to that grant of nationality are beyond the purview of the mandates of international organisations.[28]

A more practical and achievable sanction within existing international law would be for States to deny access to their ports for ships flying the flag of States that do not meet the standards required by IMO mandatory instruments.[29]

These substandard flag States could be identified through publication by the IMO of a global Black/Grey/White List of flag States. These lists could be consolidated from such lists presently published by port State control regimes and augmented by other data resulting from mandatory reports required by the IMO resolutions on casualties and oil spills, and from mandatory IMO audits of flag States.

11.7   Issues of Coastal State Control of Substandard Ships

One of the potentially fatal weaknesses of port State control is that it cannot effectively be exercised, in the sense of inspection, until the ship has voluntarily entered the internal waters, or offshore terminals, of a country.[30] By this time, the ship may have traversed many hundreds or thousands of miles of coastline in a substandard condition with the associated potential for pollution of coastal State's' exclusive economic zones or territorial waters, before it is physically possible for a port State to inspect the ship.[31] This leads to consideration of the measures a State can take in international law to prevent a ship that is known to be substandard from entering the waters over which it has jurisdiction.

There is recognition in international law of the right of a State to regulate entry by ships to its ports through reference in the LOSC to the sovereignty of a coastal State over its land territory, internal waters, archipelagic waters, and territorial sea

---

[27] Convention on the Law of Treaties, Vienna, 23 May 1969. Article 26. 1980 *UKTS* 58 6.

[28] Draft report of the ad hoc consultative meeting of senior representatives of international organizations on the "genuine link". The session in London on 7/8 July 2006 was attended by representatives from the Division for Ocean Affairs and the Law of the Sea, United Nations (DOALOS), the Food and Agriculture Organization of the United Nations (FAO), the International Labour Organization (ILO), the United Nations Conference on Trade and Development (UNCTAD) and the International Maritime Organization (IMO).

[29] As detailed in IMO resolution A.974(24) Code for the Implementation of mandatory IMO Instruments.

[30] LOSC Articles 218, 219 and 226, and IMO Resolution A.787(19), Procedures for Port State Control.

[31] This issue was the catalyst for creation of the first port State control regime in European waters, the Paris MOU on Port State Control. See Chapter Seven for a summary of the development of port State control.

(LOSC, Article 2). The LOSC does not comment upon the right of a ship to enter a port or a State's internal waters in cases of distress or *force majeure*; a right well established in customary law of the sea in order to preserve life. However, guidance has been provided by the IMO to ships and coastal States for ships seeking a place of refuge (IMO Resolution A.949(23)). The LOSC does refer to the right of a ship to stop and anchor when navigating in territorial seas (LOSC, Article 18(2)), straits used for international navigation (LOSC Article 39.1(c)), and in archipelagic waters (LOSC, Article 54). The right of a coastal State to take whatever action is necessary to protect its waters from marine pollution from ships is well established in international law.[32]

The LOSC allows a State to make laws for ships in its territorial waters[33] but the rights of innocent passage in territorial waters,[34] navigation in the EEZ,[35] transit passage through international straits,[36] and right of innocent passage through archipelagic waters[37] are jealously guarded by States. The enforcement provisions of the LOSC for port States[38] and coastal States[39] only apply when a ship is "voluntarily within a port or at an off-shore terminal of a State"; that is, in the State's internal waters.

Many of the enforcement powers of a coastal State under the LOSC are retrospective, in that they derive from "violations by ships of applicable international rules and standards for the prevention, reduction and control of pollution" in the State's territorial sea (LOSC, Article 220(2)) or exclusive economic zone (LOSC, Article 220(3)) before arrival at a port in that State. The physical inspection provided by the LOSC for the port State cannot then be effectively exercised until the offending ship has entered the State's internal waters. However, there are at least three examples of multilateral and unilateral coastal State initiatives to exclude certain ships from the waters under their jurisdiction; one of which has subsequently been translated into international law.

Refusal of access to substandard ships to ports or anchorages is attaining the status of customary law through its use, for a number of years, by all Member States of the European Union (EU).[40] The focus of the European Commission's

---

[32] LOSC, Articles 194, 195, 198, 199, 211, 221, 225, Salvage Convention, Article 9 and Facilitation Convention, Article V(2). See http://www.imo.org/Safety/mainframe.asp?topic_id = 746 "Places of refuge" – addressing the problem of providing places of refuge to vessels in distress, p. 2.

[33] LOSC, Article 21, Laws and regulations of the coastal State relating to innocent passage.

[34] LOSC, Article 17, Right of innocent passage.

[35] LOSC, Article 58, Rights and duties of other States in the exclusive economic zone.

[36] LOSC, Article 38, Right of transit passage.

[37] LOSC, Article 52, Right of innocent passage, and Article 53, Right of archipelagic sea lanes passage.

[38] LOSC, Article 218, Enforcement by port States, Article 219, Measures relating to seaworthiness of vessels to avoid pollution, and Article 226, Investigation of foreign vessels.

[39] LOSC Article 220, Enforcement by coastal States.

[40] http://ec.europa.eu/transport/maritime/safety/2000_erika_en.htm: The *Erika I* and *Erika II* Packages of Measures.

(EC) banning of ships is upon ships that have had multiple detentions, that have sailed whilst under detention, or have failed to proceed to an agreed repair port (http://eur-lex.europa.eu/LexUriServer/LexUriServer.do?uri = C E L EX:5200PCO588: EN:NOT). The majority of these ships fly the flag of States on the Paris MOU Black List.[41] This sanction provides clear warning to these flag States, that ships flying their flag may be denied entry to all ports of EU Member States. As the refusal of access presently affects a relatively small number of individual ships it does not address the systemic issue of ineffective administration by that flag State across all of the ships flying its flag, nor does it address the reality that the owners of substandard and high risk ships are attracted to such flag States precisely because of the lack of effective regulatory oversight.

The EC has recently reviewed its refusal of access criteria and proposed a strengthening of provisions by also taking into account performance of the RO and the company operating the ship. The proposed EC Directive,[42] which applies only to gas and chemical tankers, bulk carriers, oil tankers, and passenger ships, stipulates that the refusal of access will be applied if the ship:

Either

- flies the flag of a State appearing in the black list as published in the annual report of the MOU, and
- has been detained more than twice in the course of the preceding 24 months in a port of a State signatory of the MOU,

or

- flies the flag of a State described as very high risk or high risk in the black list as published in the annual report of the MOU, and
- has been detained more than once in the course of the preceding 36 months in a port of a State signatory of the MOU. (EC Proposal COM/2005/0588, Article 10)

If a ship is subject to a second refusal of access, the period shall be for 12 months. Any subsequent detention in a port of the Community shall result in the ship being permanently refused access in any port or anchorage within the community (EC Proposal COM/2005/0588, Annex XI(B)(3)).

Refusal of access by the EC is selective in the type of ship targeted. The focus would appear to be upon prevention of pollution of European waters by ships carrying large quantities of oil as cargo or bunkers; post the *Erika* and *Prestige* disasters. General cargo ships are not targeted although many substandard ships are general

---

[41] For example, 21 of the 28 bannings in 2005 were applied to ships flying a Black Listed flag. Paris MOU Annual Report 2005, p. 24.

[42] EC Proposal for a Directive, COM/2005/0588 final, Proposal for a Directive.../.../EC of the European Parliament and of the Council of [...] on port State control, Annex II, I, Ship Risk Profile, (e)(ii), p. 36 of web version. "In determining these risk profiles greater emphasis will be given to the parameters for flag State performance, recognised organisations and company performance" http://www.eur-lex.europa.eu/LexUriServ/LexUriServe.do?uri = CELEX:52005PCO 0588:EN:NOT.

cargo ships that are, on average, twice as old as other ship types and are often registered with regulatory inefficient flag States.[43]

Ships that are refused access to European ports have the ability to continue to trade in regions where there is either ineffective or non-existent port State control, or refusal of access initiatives do not exist. Apart from these issues the EC Directive could be used as a model for consideration by all regional port State control memoranda pending its possible consideration by the IMO as a global standard for refusal of access to ports through the national law of its member States.

The second initiative is OPA 90 enacted by the United States of America after the grounding of the tanker *Exxon Valdez* in Prince William Sound, Alaska in May 1989.[44] A direct outcome of this incident was passing by the United States Congress of the Oil Pollution Act 1990 (OPA 90).[45] OPA 90 imposed *inter alia* significantly greater liability upon the owners of single-hulled tankers and required the phasing out of the tankers if their owners wished their ships to continue trading to American ports. This unilateral measure effectively barred single-hulled tankers from visiting American ports and led eventually to amendments to the MARPOL Convention.[46]

Another unilateral coastal State initiative is Japan's requirement for insurance cover for non-tankers,[47] in case of spills of bunker oils, and for expenses in activities related to the removal of shipwreck, to be with designated insurers approved by the Japanese Government. All ships greater than 100 GT bound for Japanese ports have been required since 1 March 2005 to report evidence of cover with one of the 53 insurers approved by the maritime administration of Japan prior to arrival in port or entry into a designated sea area (http://www.mlit.go.jp/english/maritime/Web/insurance_portal3eng.htm). Vessels without this insurance cover are not allowed to enter or leave port. This amendment to Japanese national law[48] addresses a problem of shipwrecks abandoned in coastal waters and presaged the Bunkers Convention 2001,[49] which entered into force in November 2008.

These three unilateral and multi-lateral initiatives deal with individual ships of a known type, or with known characteristics, and all derive from concerns over

---

[43] See Chapter Ten for detailed statistics on substandard general cargo ships and associated flag States.

[44] The *Exxon Valdez* was a single-hulled tanker that spilt an estimated total of 37,000 tons of crude oil.

[45] Oil Pollution Act, 1990, (33 U.S.C. 2701 – 2761), August 1990.

[46] On 5 April 2005, amendments to Annex I of MARPOL 73/78, adopted by IMO's Marine Environment Protection Committee (MEPC) by Resolution MEPC.111(50) in December 2003, entered into force for all Parties to the MARPOL Convention.

[47] The International Convention on Civil Liability from Oil Pollution Damage, (CLC), Brussels, 29 November 1969, in force 19 June 1975, 1975 UKTS 106; requires ships covered by it to maintain insurance or other financial security in sums equivalent to the owner's total liability for one incident. The Convention applies to all seagoing vessels actually carrying oil in bulk as cargo, but only ships carrying more than 2,000 tons of oil are required to maintain insurance in respect of oil pollution damage.

[48] Law on Liability for Oil Pollution Damage.

[49] International Convention on Civil Liability for Bunker Oil Pollution Damage, London, 23 March 2001.

potential pollution of the marine environment from substandard foreign flagged vessels in a State's coastal waters. There are currently no known coastal State initiatives dealing with the vexed question of refusal of access to the waters under the jurisdiction of a State, for either individual ships or all ships flying the flag of a proven substandard flag State.

There are no extant mechanisms in international law to forbid a ship from navigating through waters under the jurisdiction of a coastal State, provided it is upon the high seas or engaged in innocent passage. However, refusal of access of a substandard ship to the internal waters and ports of a coastal State would largely obviate the need for those particular ships to navigate in the coastal waters of that State. Multilateral refusal of access to ports in adjacent coastal States, as happens under the EC Directive, would largely remove the need for substandard ships to navigate along that common coastline thus minimising or avoiding the risk of a safety or pollution incident in those waters.

There are clear benefits to be gained, in prevention of pollution, and disincentives to register or operate substandard ships, from a multilateral approach to the matter of refusal of access to ports; benefits that can be achieved through the same regional liaisons already established under the various port State control regimes. For the sake of clarity and uniform application of the refusal of access to ports, the EU standards should be considered for codification by amendment to IMO Resolution A.787(19) with that Resolution being made mandatory under the SOLAS and MARPOL Conventions. This would ensure that coastal States could bring a globally uniform standard for refusal of access to their ports into effect in their national law.

11.8 Issues of the Status of Port State Control in International Law

Port State control has been introduced as a coastal State reaction to inadequate flag State control and has proven to be increasingly effective in identifying substandard ships and flag States. The LOSC provides for port State control (PSC) in matters of environmental protection (LOSC, Article 218) and, by implication, matters of safety (LOSC, Articles 219 and 226). The universal standards, accepted by all PSC regimes, for procedures for PSC are contained in IMO Resolution A.787(19), Port State Control Procedures. Members of these regional regimes agree to use this Resolution as the standard for PSC activities and the national law of port States invariably includes a provision enabling inspection and audit of ships.[50] PSC regimes play a vital role in providing data for the analysis of flag State performance on a regional and global basis.

Codification of the resolution for port State control procedures is necessary to ensure uniform international application of this important tool in management of

---

[50] For example, s.54 of the New Zealand Maritime Transport Act 1994.

substandard ships and measurement of flag State performance. To achieve this, Resolution A.787(19) should be codified as a mandatory standard under the SOLAS and MARPOL Conventions, and other relevant mandatory IMO instruments.

11.8.1 Harmonised Target and Coding Criteria for Port State Control

Criteria to determine which ships have the highest priority for inspection by a port State have been developed by a number of port State control regimes over the past few years. The resultant target factors have proven to be appropriate, reliable, and effective in identifying high risk ships and have enabled members of PSC regimes to utilise their resources far more effectively. However, the criteria that contribute to these target factors are not uniform across all PSC regimes and, even within individual regimes, the target criteria are not used consistently, and not by all members. There are also differences between PSC regions in the coding of deficiencies issued under port State control, although this issue is currently being addressed through a joint working group of the Paris and Tokyo MOUs, including participation by the IMO (IMO 2008, Document CWGSP 8/5).

Existing target criteria should be expanded to include flag State casualty data available from the IMO database website, along with detailed data on the performance of all Recognized Organizations.[51] This would enable the IMO to collate and analyse port State control data in a globally consistent manner and to provide port States with the ability to identify poorly performing flag States and Recognized Organizations. In particular, this information would provide port States with the information necessary to identify combinations of substandard flag States and ROs, and the associated substandard ships that could be refused access to their ports or internal waters.

11.8.2 Global Analysis of Port State Control as a Measure of Flag State Performance

The principal port State control regimes presently analyse the performance of flag States using data collected from many thousands of inspections of ships by their members. The results of this regional analysis are published annually in, amongst other things, the form of Black/Grey/White lists of flag States. Research and analysis undertaken in this study has confirmed this mechanism to be effective in identifying

---

[51] The Tokyo MOU target criteria uses "IACS or non-IACS member" as the broad criteria for Recognized Organizations, largely because there is no empirical data on the performance of all individual ROs.

ships flying the flags of those States that might be either substandard or of a very good standard. The reports are, by definition, regional and not all ships trade across all regions, but it has been demonstrated that there are commonalities amongst identification of substandard ships and flag States across regions. IMO receives copies of all PSC regime annual reports but there is little discussion amongst the Member States of the IMO at FSI of the performance of flag States as presented in the reports. Neither the Secretariat nor the FSI Sub-committee presently carry out any globally coordinated analysis of the data in these reports in order to contribute to global measurement and publication of the performance of all flag States and Recognized Organizations. The minimal global analysis of port State control data currently carried out by the IMO only measures PSC detention and compliance (deficiency) rates.[52]

These matters inevitably lead to the conclusion that the IMO must assume a leadership role in the global analysis of port State data and must integrate this with mandatory reports under IMO instruments. This analysis should include casualty data in order to be able to carry out comprehensive analysis of all factors relevant to effective flag State performance, and implementation and enforcement of mandatory instruments.[53]

11.9   Summary of Issues and Proposed Remedies

The regulatory framework for flag State responsibilities is adequate but its implementation does not meet the intent of the LOSC that flag States should effectively exercise their jurisdiction and control in administrative, technical, social, and pollution prevention matters over ships flying their flag.

---

[52] The IMO has a number of external performance indicators that measure the effectives of port State control on a global basis from staistics contained in the annual reports of regional PSC MOUs/Agreements and the United States Coastguard. These are; PSC Detention Rate and PSC Non-compliance rate. See IMO document CWGSP 8/5, pp. 28–29.

[53] The IMO Secretariat recognises the need for this global and comprehensive analysis of a range of data in their document on information submitted to the *Ad Hoc* Council Working Group on the Organization's Strategic Plan (CWGSP 8/5 of 13 August 2008) Under the heading Commentary on the importance of harmonized coding for the popoulation of data in GISIS, the Secretariat comments: "In view of the recommended development of GISIS as IMO's principal data provider, it will be necessary to ensure and develop a common coding system to allow the combination of data within GISIS for the development of the PIs (Performance Indicators) In this respect, an important development is the future harmonized PSC coding system, based on a joint working group of the Paris and Tokyo MOUs, in which IMO is participating. These codes include all areas such as: flag State administrations; signatories to IMO conventions; recognized organzations; PSC deficiency codes (linked to the relevant conventions and certificates; actions taken codes; ship type codes; certificates etc. Various modules of GISIS will feed from this coding and should therefore be harmonized (e.g. PSC deficiencies with IMO Member State audits and casualty module). This will enable proper links to be established and to maintain a single standardized coding system which can then be used for the production of statistics."

Instead of wholesale change to the existing model for governance of ships, more can be achieved to ensure effective jurisdiction and control of ships through enhancement, reinforcement, and empowerment of the existing model of flag State jurisdiction and control.

The IMO has a mandate, and a burgeoning need, to assume a role of global oversight, analysis, measurement, and dissemination of information to Member States on flag State performance. The Secretariat should be adequately resourced to carry out this task on behalf of its Member States.

There is a clear need to reflect, in IMO mandatory instruments, the intent of the LOSC that a ship be surveyed before registration to ensure its seaworthiness. This can be achieved through an amendment to the SOLAS Convention to require a survey before registration, and for there to be a mandatory process for transfer of ships between flag States that would ensure their seaworthiness and compliance with IMO and ILO instruments.

The most effective tool for measurement of the effectiveness of flag State jurisdiction and control is provided by the Voluntary IMO Member State Audit Scheme (VIMSAS). This scheme will not become fully effective unless it is mandatory, and the Member States of IMO should debate this option at the earliest opportunity. For the IMO audit scheme to become mandatory it would be necessary to adopt one of the existing resolutions associated with the VIMSAS as a mandatory instrument under the SOLAS Convention. Of particular relevance in the matter of effective flag State performance in this context is the present inclusion of Resolutions A.739(18) and A.789(19) on the delegation of flag State statutory functions to Recognized Organizations as mandatory instruments under SOLAS. It is logical and consistent to also mandate Resolution A.996(25), which sits above these two resolutions and provides required standards for Administrations, as flag, port and coastal States.

If there are to be mandatory standards for flag States there must also be appropriate and effective sanctions if a flag State chooses not to meet those standards. The most effective sanction, as demonstrated by the EC, is that of refusal of access to ports of proven substandard ships. This concept can be extended to apply to all ships of a proven substandard or recalcitrant flag State. For the sake of clarity and uniform application of the refusal of access to ports the EC Directive standards should be debated by the IMO as a model for inclusion in IMO Resolution A.787(19). The sanction of refusal of access to individual ships, or all ships of a substandard flag State, could be applied through the national law of coastal States to achieve, in some cases, regional effect.

The IMO must seek a means of measuring the performance of ROs, ensuring that ROs meet the standards of the mandatory resolutions, and that the relevant flag States verify and monitor the activities of ROs. This could be achieved through the requirement for ROs to be audited independently of the flag State with the result being reported directly to the IMO. Port States should be advised of ROs that do not meet these standards in order that they could refuse to accept the certificates issued to ships by those particular ROs on behalf of a flag State.

Codification of the IMO resolution for port State control procedures, and globally harmonised coding and targeting criteria, are necessary to provide uniform international application of this important tool in monitoring and identification of substandard ships, and analysis and measurement by the IMO of flag State performance. Resolution A.787(19) should be made mandatory under the SOLAS and MARPOL Conventions and other relevant mandatory IMO instruments in order that port States could bring a uniform standard into effect in their national law.

References

Kovats L (2006) How flag states lost the plot over shipping's governance: Does a ship need a sovereign? Maritime Policy and Management Vol 33, No 1
Sasamura Y (2003) Development of Audit Scheme in ICAO and IMO. Seminar on Model Audit Scheme. London, 27 May

Documents

European Commission. Proposal for a Directive. COM/2005/0588
IMCO (1948) Convention on the Intergovernmental Maritime Consultative Organization. Geneva, 6 March. In force 17 March 1958. 289 UNTS 3
IMO (2002) Sub-Committee on Flag State Implementation (FSI), 10th session: 8–12 April
IMO (2004) MEPC/Circ.424 MSC/Circ.1140. Transfer of ships between States. 20 December
IMO (2008) Analysis of data measured against performance indicators. Document CWGSP 8/5. 13 August
UN General Assembly, 59th session, Item 51(a) of the preliminary list, Oceans and the law of the sea, Consultative group on Flag State Implementation, Report by the Secretary-General, 5 March 2004, p. 13.

National Legislation (Chronological order)

United Kingdom

- Navigation Act, 1660 (12 Cha. 2 c.18)
- An Act for prevention of Frauds and regulating Abuses in the Plantation Trade, 1696 (7 & 8 Will. 3 c.22)
- An Act for the further Increase and Encouragement of Shipping and navigation, 1786 (26 Geo. 3 c.60)
- An Act for the Registering of vessels, 1823 (4 Geo. 4 c.41)
- An Act for the Registering of British vessels, 1825 (6 Geo. 4 c.110)
- An Act for the Encouragement of British Shipping and Navigation, 1833 (3 & 4 Will. 4 c.55)
- Mercantile Marine Act, 1850 (13 & 14 Vict. c.93)
- Steam Navigation Act, 1851 (14 & 15 Vict. c.79)
- Merchant Shipping Act, 1854 (17 & 18 Vict. c. 104)
- Passenger Act, 1855 (18 & 19 Vict. c. 119)
- Merchant Shipping Act Amendment Act, 1862 (25 & 26 Vict. c. 63)
- Passenger Amendment Act, 1863, (26 & 27 Vict. c. 51)
- Merchant Shipping Act, 1871 (34 & 35 Vict. c. 110)
- Merchant Shipping Acts Amendment Act, 1872 (35 & 36 Vict. c. 73)
- Merchant Shipping Act, 1873 (36 & 37 Vict. c.110)
- Merchant Shipping Act, 1875 (38 & 39 Vict. c.88)
- Merchant Shipping Acts Amendment Act, 1876 (39 & 40 Vict. c. 80)
- Boiler Explosions Act, 1882 (45 & 46 Vict. c. 22)
- Boiler Explosions Amendment Act, 1890 (53 & 54 Vict. c. 35)
- Merchant Shipping Act, 1890 (53 & 54 Vict. c. 9)
- Imperial Merchant Shipping Act, 1894 (57 & 58 Vict. c. 60)
- Merchant Shipping Act, 1906 (6 Edw. C. 48)
- Shipping (Registration of Ships) Regulations 1993. In force 21 March 1994.

United States of America

- An Act for the Registry and Clearing of Vessels, Regulating the Coastal Trade, and other Purposes, 1789

New Zealand

– Flags, Emblems and Names Protection Act, 1981
– Ship Registration Act, 1992
– Maritime Transport Act, 1994

Australia

– Navigation Act, 1912
– Marine Order – Part 11: Substandard Ships. Issue 2 (Order No 14 of 2002)

International Instruments (Chronological Order)

- International Convention for the Unification of Certain Rules relating to Assistance and Salvage at Sea, Brussels, 23 September 1910. In force 01 March 1913. British and Foreign State Papers, Vol 103
- The Unification of Certain Rules of Law with respect to Collisions between Vessels, Brussels, 23 September 1910
- Convention for the Safety of Life at Sea, London, 20 January 1914
- Treaty of Peace between the Allied and Associated Powers and Germany, Versailles, 28 June 1919. http://www.lib.byu.edu/~rdh/wwi/versailles.html
- Minimum Wage (Sea) Convention, 1920 (C7)
- Repatriation of Seamen Convention, 1926 (C 23)
- International Convention for the Unification of Certain Rules Relating to the immunity of State-owned vessels, 1926. 179 LNTS 199; UKTS No 15 (1980) Cmnd. 7800, and Protocol of 1934, 179 LNTS 214
- Convention for the Safety of life at Sea, London, 1929. In force 1933. Treaty Series No 34 (1932), Cmd. 4198
- International Convention Respecting Load Lines, London, 5 July 1930. Treaty series No 35 (1932), Cmd. 3668
- Agreement Concerning Maritime Signals, Lisbon, 23 October 1930, Official Document of the League of Nations (Communications & Transit), No C634 M253, 1930, VIII, 13
- Agreement Concerning Manned Lightships Not on their Stations, Lisbon, 23 October 1930
- Recommendations on Lighthouse Characteristics and Radio-Beacons, Lisbon, 23 October 1930
- Forced Labour Convention, 1930 (ILO No 29)
- Convention on the Rights and Duties of States (Inter-American), Montevideo, 26 December 1933, 49 Stat 3097 Treaty series 881
- Convention Relating to the Tonnage Measurement of Merchant Ships, Warsaw, 1934
- Minimum Age (Sea) Convention (Revised), 1936 (C 58)
- Agreement for a Uniform System of Maritime Buoyage and Rules Annexed Thereto, Geneva, 13 May 1936. League of Nations (Communications & Transit), No C261 M154, 1936, VIII, 11

- Officers' Competency Certificates Convention, 1936 (C 53)
- Shipowners' Liability (Sick and Injured Seamen) Convention, 1936 (C 56)
- Medical Examination (Seafarers) Convention, 1946 (C 73)
- Food and Catering (Ships' Crews) Convention, 1946 (C 68)
- Freedom of Association and Protection of the Right to Organize Convention, 1948 (C 87)
- Convention on the Intergovernmental Maritime Consultative Organization (IMCO), Geneva, 6 March 1948. In force 17 March 1958. 289 UNTS 3
- Accommodation of Crews Convention (Revised), 1949 (C 92)
- Right to Organise and Collective bargaining Convention, 1949 (C 98)
- International Convention for the Prevention of Pollution of the Sea by Oil, London, 12 May 1954. In force 26 July 1958. 327 UNTS 3
- Convention on the High Seas, Geneva, 29 April 1958. In force 30 September 1962. 450 UNTS 11
- Discrimination (Employment and Occupation) Convention, 1958 (C 111)
- International Convention on Load Lines, London, 5 April 1966. In force 21 July 1968. #640 UNTS 133
- United Nations Flag Code and Regulations, UN doc. ST/SGB/132 (January 1967)
- Convention on the Law of Treaties, Vienna, 22 May 1969, UNTS, 1155 331
- International Convention on Tonnage Measurement of Ships, London, 23 June 1969. In force, 18 July 1982. UKTS 50
- International Convention relating to Intervention on the High Seas in Cases of Oil Pollution Casualties, Brussels, 29 November 1969, UKTS 77 (1975)
- International Convention on Civil Liability for Oil Pollution Damage (CLC Convention) Brussels, 29 November 1969, UKTS 106 (1975) Cmnd. 6183
- Medical Care and Sickness Benefits Convention, 1969 (C 130)
- Prevention of Accidents (Seafarers) Convention, 1970 (C 134)
- International Convention on the Establishment of an International Fund for Compensation for Oil Pollution Damage (Fund Convention) Brussels, 18 December 1971. 1110 UNTS 57
- Minimum Age Convention, 1973 (C 138)
- Abolition of Forced Labour Convention, 1973 (C 138)
- International Convention for the Prevention of Pollution from Ships, London, 02 November 1973, as amended by the protocol, London 01 June 1978 (MARPOL 73/78) 1340 UNTS 61, 62 (E)
- Convention concerning Minimum Standards in Merchant Ships, (C 147), Geneva, 29 October 1976
- International Convention on Standards of Training, Certification and Watchkeeping for Seafarers, London, 01 December 1978. As amended 1995. # 1984 UKTS 50
- Convention on the Law of Treaties, Vienna, 22 May 1969. In force 27 January 1980. UKTS 58 (1980)
- United Nations Convention of the Law of the Sea, Montego Bay, 10 December 1982. In force 16 November 1994. 21 ILM 1245 (1982)

- United Nations Convention on Conditions for the Registration of Ships, Geneva, 7 February 1986. Not in force. 7 LOSB 87 (1986)
- Protocol of 1996 to the Merchant Shipping (Minimum Standards) Convention, (C147) 1975, Geneva, 22 October 1996
- The International Convention on Civil Liability from Oil Pollution Damage, (CLC), Brussels, 29 November 1969, in force 19 June 1975, UKTS 106 (1975) Cmnd. 6183
- International Convention on Civil Liability for Bunker Oil Pollution Damage, London, 23 March 2001 (Not yet in force)
- Maritime Labour Convention, 2006, adopted at Geneva, 23 February 2006 (MLC)

IMO Documents

Resolutions

- A.739(18), Guidelines for the Authorization of Organizations acting on behalf of the Administration, Adopted 4 November 1993
- A.787(19), Procedures for Port State Control, as amended by Resolution 882(21), Adopted 23 November 1995
- A.789(19), Specifications on the Survey and Certification functions of Recognized Organizations acting on behalf of the Administration. Adopted 23 November 1995
- A.849(20), Code for the investigation of marine casualties and incidents, as amended by Resolution A.884(21). Adopted 27 November 1997
- A.949(23), Guidelines on places of refuge for ships in need of assistance. Adopted 5 December 2003
- A.970(24) Strategic Plan for the Organization (for the six-year period 2006 to 2010). Adopted 23 January 2006
- A.973(24), Code for the implementation of mandatory IMO instruments, Adopted 1 December 2005
- A.974(24), Framework and procedures for the Voluntary IMO Member State audit scheme, Adopted 1 December 2005
- A.996(25), Code for the implementation of mandatory IMO instruments, 2007, Adopted 29 November 2007

Maritime Safety Committee Circulars

- MSC/Circ.1140 MEPC/Circ.424 – Transfer of ships between States. 20 December 2004
- MSC/Circ.710 – MEPC/Circ.307 – Model agreement for the authorisation of organizations acting on behalf of the Administration. 9 October 1995
- MSC/Circ.788 – MEPC/Circ.325 – Authorization of recognized organizations acting on behalf of administrations, (incorporating Resolutions A.739(18) and A.739(19))

- MSC/Circ.889-MEPC/Circ.353 – Self Assessment of Flag State Performance. 17 December 1998
- MSC/Circ.1010/MEPC/Circ.382 – Communication of information on the authorization of recognized organizations (ROs) 10 July 2001
- MSC Circular 953- MEPC/Circ. 372 – Reports on Marine Casualties. 14 December 2000
- MSC-MEPC.5/Circ.2 – SURVEY AND CERTIFCATION RELATED MATTERS, Guidelines for Administrations to ensure the adequacy of transfer of class-related matters between recognized organizations (ROs). 26 September 2005

Marine Environment Protection Committee Circulars

- MEPC/Circ.318, Formats for a mandatory reporting system under MARPOL 73/78. 26 July 1996

Maritime Safety Committee papers

- MSC 77/25/4, Comparison of general cargo ship losses and fatalities, submitted by the Royal Institution of Naval Architects (RINA) to the 77th session of the Maritime Safety Committee, 25 March 2003
- MSC 82/21/19, General Cargo Ship Safety, 29 August 2006, submitted by the Russian Federation to the 82nd session of the Maritime Safety Committee

Flag State Implementation Sub-Committee papers

- FSI 7/9/2, Implications arising when a vessel loses the right to fly the flag of a State: Transfer of the flag of a ship to another State. 5 February 1999
- FSI 9/5/1/, Implications arising when a vessel loses the right to fly the flag of a State: Transfer of ships between flag State administrations. 15 December 2000
- FSI 14/4, Analysis and evaluation of deficiency reports and mandatory reports under MARPOL 73/78 for 2004. 1 March 2006
- FSI 14/4/1, Mandatory Reports under MARPOL 73/78. 1 March 2006
- FSI.3/Circ.5, Casualty Statistics and Investigations. Very serious and serious casualties for the year 2002, Annex 2. 23 February 2005
- FSI 14/5, Report of the Correspondence Group on Casualty Analysis, 3 March 2006
- FSI.3/Circ.6, Casualty Statistics and Investigations, Very serious and serious casualties for the year 2003. 23 February 2005

Appendix A

Table A.1 Changes in distribution of tonnage between flag states: 1958–2007

FLAG World total	1958 118m. GT	1982 424.7m. GT	2007 774.9 GT	% Change 1982–2007
Panama	4.4	32.6	165.3	+407
Liberia	10.1	70.7	75.3	+7
Bahamas	–	–	41.3	+41,300
Greece	1.6	40.0	35.6	−11
Hong Kong	–	3.5	35.8	+923
Singapore	–	7.2	35.0	+386
Malta	–	–	27.5	+27,500
Marshall Is.	–	–	35.1	+35,100
Cyprus	–	2.2	18.8	+755
China	0.5	8.1	23.6	+191
Norway	9.4	21.9	14.4	−34
Japan	5.5	41.6	11.7	−72
USA	25.6	19.1	9.0	−53
United Kingdom	20.3	22.5	12.7	−44
Italy	4.9	10.4	12.7	+22
Germany	4.0	7.7	12.7	+65
Denmark	2.0	5.2	8.6	+65
South Korea	-	5.5	12.5	+127
India	–	6.2	8.4	+35
Antigua & Bar.	–	–	8.6	+8,600
Netherlands	4.6	5.4	5.4	+0
Isle of Man	–	–	8.0	+8,000
St Vin. & Gren.	–	–	5.6	+5,600
Bermuda	–	0.5	8.8	+1,660
Malaysia	–	1.2	6.4	+433
Russia	3.0	23.8	4.6	−81
Iran	–	1.3	3.4	+162
Philippines	0.1	2.8	4.9	+75
France[a]	4.4	10.8	0.9	−92
Turkey	0.6	2.1	4.9	+133
Taiwan	–	2.3	2.6	+13
Sweden	3.3	3.8	3.9	+3
Indonesia	0.1	1.9	5.1	+176
Brazil	0.9	5.7	2.0	−65
Thailand	–	–	2.7	+2700

(continued)

Table A.1 (continued)

FLAG World total	1958 118m. GT	1982 424.7m. GT	2007 774.9 GT	% Change 1982–2007
Cayman Islands	–	–	2.8	+2800
Kuwait	–	2.0	2.4	+20
Spain[b]	1.6	8.1	0.5	−94
Canada	1.5	3.2	2.2	−31
Cambodia	–	–	2.0	+2000

Source: Lloyd's Register – Fairplay, World Fleet Statistics, 1958, 1982, and 2007
[a]France has 4.9m GT under the FIS register
[b]Spain has 1.9m GT under the CSR register

Table A.2 True nationality of ownership of the world's major fleets; 1 January 2007

	Panama	Liberia	Bahamas	Malta	Cyprus	Bermuda
Greece	22,211	18,834	12,632	25,832	15,540	88
Japan	112,196	5,570	3,608	27	467	0
Norway	1,580	2,695	6,836	503	791	58
Germany	5,231	30,022	2,281	1,720	4,998	747
China	15,567	2,977	211	216	238	0
USA	2,278	3,610	10,352	68	22	381
Hong Kong, China	10,579	1,116	638	46	19	2,127
South Korea	15,904	463	0	131	76	0
Singapore	2,470	4,833	389	0	30	0
Taiwan	10,202	5,793	110	0	0	0
United Kingdom	1,010	1,132	1,906	114	1,216	339
Russia	177	7,265	37	788	1,532	0
Denmark	732	231	948	197	47	0
Italy	138	1,133	461	857	11	0
India	751	154	8	38	0	0
Saudi Arabia	289	6,660	2,788	0	0	0
Malaysia	91	0	73	0	0	0
Iran	88	0	871	273	148	0
Turkey	375	53	1,933	1,254	0	0
Switzerland	9,431	280	447	852	68	3
Netherlands	321	763	32	34	159	273
Belgium	256	0	168	72	9	0
Canada	43	32	557	64	60	0
Sweden	68	380	69	9	9	1,239
Philippines	318	0	28	0	2	0
Brazil	1,101	456	149	0	0	0
France	229	131	1,187	45	0	7
Spain	422	0	1,366	17	309	0
Indonesia	541	79	102	0	0	0
Cyprus	746	272	625	484	2,439	0
Australia	80	355	95	0	0	371
Thailand	62	0	17	0	0	0
UAR	1,719	1,097	1,147	310	525	0
Kuwait	109	42	0	0	0	0
Vietnam	165	65	0	0	0	0
TOTAL	217,480	96,492	50,517	34,823	28,715	5,809

Figures for ships >1,000 GT in '000 DWT
Source: compiled by the UNCTAD Secretariat on the basis of data supplied by Lloyd's Register
– Fairplay

Table A.3 Recognized organizations on the IMO GISIS database; 2007

American Bureau of Shipping (ABS)	Korea Maritime Dangerous Goods Inspection Centre (KMDGIC)
ASIA Classification Society – (ASIA)	Korean Register of Shipping (KRS)
Associated Consultants Bureau Ltd (ACB)	Korean Society of Ship Inspection and Technology (KSSIT)
Belgian Marine Inspection Services (BMIS)	Libyan Surveyor Mr. Abdulhamid Giahmi (LS)
Belize Maritime Bureau (BMB)	Lloyd's Register (LR)
Belize Register Corporation (BRC)	Macosnar Corporation (MC)
Black Sea Bureau of Shipping (BBS)	Marconi International Marine Company (MIMC)
British Telecom plc. (BTP)	*Maritime Inspection Corporation (MIC)*
Bulgarian Register of Shipping (BRS)	Maritime Lloyd – Georgia (MLG)
Bureau Veritas (BV)	Maritime Technical Systems and Services Ltd. (MTSS)
CTM Inspection and Classification Coy (CTMICC)	National Cargo Bureau Inc. (NCB)
Central Bureau Shipping Panama (CBSP)	National Shipping Adjuster Inc. (NSA)
China Classification Society (CCS)	Nippon Kaiji Kyokai (NKK)
China Corp. Register of Shipping (CCRS)	Overseas Marine Certification Service Inc. (OMCS)
Classification Bureau of Indonesia (CBI)	Panama Bureau of Shipping (PBS)
Compana Nacional de Registro e Inspection de Naves, S. de R>L> (CNRIN)	Panama Marine Surveying and Certification Services Inc. (PMSCS)
Croatian Register of Shipping (CRS)	Panama Maritime Documentation Services (PMDS)
Cyprus Bureau of Shipping (CBS)	Panama Maritime Surveyor Bureau Inc. (PMSB)
Det Norske Veritas (DNV)	Panama Register Corporation (PRC)
Ellinikos Niognomon (EN)	*Panama Shipping Certificate Inc. (PSC)*
Ferriby Marine (FM)	Panama Shipping Register Inc. (PSR)
Fidenavis S.A. (FID)	Polski Rejstr Statkow (PRS)
Germanischer Lloyd (GL)	PT Biro Klasifikasi Indonesia (BKI)
Global Marine Bureau Inc. (GMB)	R.J. Del Pan (RJDP)
Hellenic Register of Shipping (HRS)	Registro Cubano de Buques (RCB)
Honduras International Surveying and Inspection Bureau (HINSIB)	*Regostro Internacional Naval, S.A. (REGINAV)*
Honduras Maritime Inspection Inc. (HMI)	Registro Italiano Navale (RINA)
Horizon International of Naval Surveying and Inspection Bureau, S.A. (HORINSIB)	Rinave – Registro Internacional Naval, S.A. (RIN)
Icons Marine Services PTE Ltd (IMS)	Rinave Portuguesa (RP)
IGS (IGS)	Romanian Naval Register (RNR)
INCLAMAR (INCLAMAR)	Russian Maritime Register of Shipping (RMRS)
Indian Register of Shipping (IRS)	Sociedad Andina de Certificacion Ltda Ltd (SAC)
Inspecion y Clasificacion Maritima, S. de R.L. (ICM)	Sociedad Classificadora Regsitro Italiano Navale (Brazil) (SCRIN)
Insituto Nacional de Los Espacios Acuaticos e Insulares (INEAI)	Societe Generale de Survelliance (SGS)
Intermaritime Certification Services, S.A. (ICS)	State Committee of Fisheries of Ukraine (SCFU)
International Naval Surveys Bureua (INSB)	Turkish Lloyd (TL)
International Register of Shipping (IS)	Ukraine Shipping Register (USR)
International Ship Classification (ISC)	Union Bureau of Shipping (UBS)
Iransafineh Bureau of Shipping (IRBS)	Universal Maritime Bureau (UMB)
Isthmus Bureau of Shipping, S.A. (IBS)	Universal Shipping Bureau Inc. (USB)
Isthmus Maritime Classification Society S.A. (IMCS)	Vietnam Register of Shipping (VRS)
Joson Classification Society (JCS)	Yugoslav Register of Shipping (YRS)
Jugloslavenski Registar Brodova (JRB)	

ROs in *italics* indicate that no authorized information was found for the selected organization
Source The IMO GISIS database, 2007

Table A.4 Member states of ILO and IMO and ratifications of ILO instruments; 2006: National flag states

Flag	ILO	IMO	No	147	P147[a]
Albania	Yes	Yes	3	No	No
Algeria	Yes	Yes	12	No	No
Angola	Yes	Yes	8	No	No
Argentina	Yes	Yes	11	No	No
Australia	Yes	Yes	15	No	No
Austria	No	Yes	–	No	No
Azerbaijan	Yes	Yes	9	Yes	No
Bahrain	No	Yes	–	No	No
Bangladesh	Yes	Yes	2	No	No
Belarus	Yes	No	3	No	No
Belgium	Yes	Yes	21	Yes	Yes
Bosnia and Herzegovina	Yes	Yes	13	No	No
Brazil	Yes	Yes	18	Yes	No
Benin	No	Yes	–	No	No
Brunei	No	Yes	–	No	No
Bulgaria	Yes	Yes	28	Yes	Yes
Burma/Myanmar	Yes	Yes	2	No	No
Cameroon	Yes	Yes	4	No	No
Canada	Yes	Yes	11	Yes	No
Cape Verde	No	No	–	No	No
Chile	Yes	Yes	5	No	No
China	Yes	Yes	4	No	No
Colombia	Yes	Yes	6	No	No
(Congo)	No	Yes	–	No	No
(Costa Rica)	Yes	Yes	6	Yes	No
(Cote de I)	Yes	Yes	1	No	No
Croatia	Yes	Yes	14	Yes	No
Cuba	Yes	Yes	14	No	No
(Czech Republic)	Yes	Yes	3	No	No
(Congo)	No	Yes	–	No	No
Denmark	Yes	Yes	15	Yes	Yes
(Djibouti)	Yes	Yes	13	No	No
Dominica	Yes	Yes	5	Yes	No
Dominican Republic	Yes	Yes	1	No	No
Ecuador	No	Yes	–	No	No
Egypt	Yes	Yes	16	Yes	No
(El Salvador)	No	Yes	–	No	No
Estonia	Yes	Yes	10	Yes	Yes
Ethiopia	No	Yes	–	No	No
(Fiji)	Yes	Yes	3	No	No
Finland	Yes	Yes	23	Yes	Yes
France	Yes	Yes	35	Yes	Yes
(Gabon)	No	Yes	–	No	No
(Gambia)	No	Yes	–	No	No
Georgia	Yes	Yes	1	No	No
Germany	Yes	Yes	14	Yes	No
Ghana	Yes	Yes	10	Yes	No
Greece	Yes	Yes	18	Yes	Yes
(Grenada)	Yes	Yes	5	No	No
(Guatemala)	Yes	Yes	4	No	No

(continued)

Table A.4 (continued)

Flag	ILO	IMO	No	147	P147[a]
(Guinea)	Yes	Yes	3	No	No
(Guinea Bissau)	Yes	Yes	8	No	No
(Guyana)	Yes	Yes	3	No	No
(Haiti)	No	Yes	–	No	No
(Hungary)	Yes	Yes	10	Yes	Yes
Iceland	Yes	Yes	4	Yes	No
India	Yes	Yes	4	Yes	No
Indonesia	Yes	Yes	1	No	No
Iran	Yes	Yes	1	No	No
(Iraq)	Yes	Yes	12	Yes	No
Ireland	Yes	Yes	17	Yes	Yes
Israel	Yes	Yes	7	Yes	No
Italy	Yes	Yes	24	Yes	No
Jamaica	Yes	Yes	4	No	No
Japan	Yes	Yes	10	Yes	No
Kazakhstan	No	Yes	–	No	No
(Kenya)	Yes	Yes	4	No	No
South Korea	Yes	Yes	2	No	No
DPR of Korea	No	Yes	–	No	No
(Kyrgyzstan)	Yes	No	9	Yes	No
(Kiribati)	No	Yes	–	No	No
Kuwait	No	Yes	–	No	No
Latvia	Yes	Yes	7	Yes	Yes
Lebanon	Yes	Yes	9	Yes	No
Libya	Yes	Yes	1	No	No
Lithuania	Yes	Yes	2	No	No
Luxembourg	Yes	Yes	17	Yes	No
(Madagascar)	No	Yes	–	No	No
(Malawi)	No	Yes	–	No	No
Malaysia	Yes	Yes	3	No	No
(the Maldives)	No	Yes	–	No	No
(Mauritian)	Yes	Yes	5	No	No
(Mauritius)	Yes	Yes	6	No	No
Mexico	Yes	Yes	17	No	No
(Monaco)	No	Yes	–	No	No
(Moldova)	Yes	Yes	1	No	No
Morocco	Yes	Yes	9	No	No
(Mozambique)	No	Yes	–	No	No
Namibia	No	Yes	–	No	No
(Nepal)	No	Yes	–	No	No
Netherlands	Yes	Yes	21	Yes	Yes
New Zealand	Yes	Yes	14	No	No
(Nicaragua)	Yes	Yes	7	No	No
Nigeria	Yes	Yes	9	No	No
Norway	Yes	Yes	26	Yes	No
(Oman)	No	Yes	–	No	No
Pakistan	Yes	Yes	2	No	No
(Paraguay)	No	Yes	–	No	No
Papua New Guinea	Yes	Yes	3	No	No
(Peru)	Yes	Yes	14	Yes	No
Philippines	Yes	Yes	5	No	No

(continued)

Table A.4 (continued)

Flag	ILO	IMO	No	147	P147[a]
Poland	Yes	Yes	19	Yes	No
Portugal	Yes	Yes	15	Yes	No
Qatar	No	Yes	–	No	No
Romania	Yes	Yes	15	Yes	Yes
Russia	Yes	Yes	11	Yes	No
(St Kitts and Nevis)	No	Yes	–	No	No
(St Lucia)	Yes	Yes	4	No	No
(Serbia and Montenegro)	Yes	Yes	13	No	No
(San Marino)	No	Yes	–	No	No
(Samoa)	No	Yes	–	No	No
Saudi Arabia	No	Yes	–	No	No
(Senegal)	No	Yes	–	No	No
Seychelles	Yes	Yes	5	No	No
Sierra Leone	Yes	Yes	5	No	No
Slovakia	Yes	Yes	2	No	No
(Slovenia)	Yes	Yes	17	Yes	Yes
Solomon Islands	Yes	Yes	3	No	No
(Somalia	Yes	Yes	3	No	No
(South Africa)	No	Yes	–	No	No
Spain	Yes	Yes	28	Yes	No
Sri Lanka	Yes	Yes	5	No	No
(Sudan)	No	Yes	–	No	No
(Suriname)	No	Yes	–	No	No
Sweden	Yes	Yes	19	Yes	Yes
Switzerland	Yes	Yes	5	No	No
S.A.R.	Yes	Yes	1	No	No
Taiwan	No	No	–	No	No
(Tajikistan)	Yes	No	9	No	No
Macedonia	Yes	Yes	13	No	No
Thailand	No	Yes	–	No	No
(Timor Leste)	No	Yes	–	No	No
Togo	No	Yes	–	No	No
(Trinidad and Tobago)	Yes	Yes	2	Yes	No
Tunisia	Yes	Yes	9	No	No
Turkey	Yes	Yes	13	No	No
(Turkmenistan)	No	Yes	–	No	No
Ukraine	Yes	Yes	9	Yes	No
United Arab Emirates	No	Yes	–	No	No
United Kingdom	Yes	Yes	17	Yes	Yes
(Uruguay)	Yes	Yes	13	No	No
United States of America	Yes	Yes	7	Yes	No
Venezuela	Yes	Yes	2	No	No
Vietnam	No	Yes	–	No	No
Zimbabwe	No	Yes	–	No	No

[a]P147 indicates the 1996 Protocol to ILO 147

Inactive National flag States in parenthesis

Source Member States of the ILO and ratification of ILO maritime labour instruments, including ILO 147, from Report 1(1A), Adoption of an instrument to consolidate maritime labour standards, International Labour Conference, 94th (Maritime) Session, 2006. International Labour Office, Geneva. Data for member States of the IMO as at 2006 from file://F:\International Maritime Organization_ files\mainframe.htm

Table A.5 Paris MOU average detention rates; 1999–2005[a]

Paris MOU Average	1999	2000	2001	2002	2003	2004	2005	Average
	9.15%	9.50%	9.09%	7.98%	7.05%	5.84%	4.67%	7.61%
Sao Tome and Principe		50.00	46.15					48.08
Bolivia		50.00		60.87	26.32			45.73
Albania		54.30	45.71	60.71	42.00	31.43	23.36	42.92
Tonga			33.33	42.47	41.67			39.16
DPR of Korea				28.13	49.23	37.01	29.49	35.97
Honduras	41.13	35.30	27.71	26.87	34.78	20.00	16.67	28.92
Comoros				40.00	30.61	18.42	20.00	27.26
Lebanon	29.87	33.70	35.16	26.98	26.56	22.64	7.79	26.10
Libya		37.90	14.29					26.01
Algeria	40.00	34.20	27.69	28.81	26.25	12.24	11.63	25.83
Georgia		36.00	34.21	18.92	25.65	17.12	16.67	24.76
Syria	33.06	27.60	20.13	19.82	17.50	22.86	15.38	22.34
Cambodia	30.38	32.60	23.45	22.10	22.51	12.90	10.34	22.04
Slovakia						24.00	19.74	21.87
Romania	29.58	19.10	23.53	21.82	11.11			21.03
Mongolia						19.05		19.05
Turkey	24.51	23.80	24.59	18.78	17.49	8.63	7.54	17.91
Belize	29.79	24.80	13.39	20.35	9.79	9.41	7.56	16.44
Morocco	23.64	13.60	27.50	14.52		10.34	8.77	16.40
St Vincent and the Grenadines	17.95	16.10	17.30	17.67	15.52	13.30	10.76	15.51
Egypt	21.84	12.70	17.74	13.24	13.46	13.46	10.17	14.66
Azerbaijan	17.65		10.64					14.15
Thailand	12.50	17.10					11.25	13.62
Iran		15.00			10.94			12.97
Estonia					12.64			12.64
Ukraine	15.38	13.70	14.84	11.48	13.30	7.44	8.51	12.09
Malaysia	11.90							11.90
India	12.05	10.40	16.46		10.26	9.09		11.65
Latvia	14.63						7.32	10.98
South Korea			9.68		11.11			10.40
Dominica							10.34	10.34
Cayman Is.		9.60						9.60
Tuvalu			9.52					9.52
Portugal		9.50						9.50
Kuwait		9.50						9.50
Bulgaria			15.69	9.57		6.60	5.66	9.38
Cyprus	9.97	9.70			7.40			9.02
Lithuania	9.76						7.77	8.77
Gibraltar		10.50		8.81		6.90		8.77
Philippines				8.77				8.77
Malta	10.63	11.80	9.48			7.09	4.75	8.75
Croatia		12.70		8.93	9.09	7.81	4.88	8.68
Ireland						8.57		8.57
Average %	21.23	23.25	21.74	22.11	18.71	13.90	11.79	18.96%

[a] Flag States in italics are common with the Tokyo MOU table of detention rates: Table A.6. Only flag States involved in at least twenty port State control inspections are included.

Source *ParisMOU Annual Reports* for 1999–2005 inclusive

Paris MOU Port State Control Report 2005. p. 22. "Detention rates are expressed as a percentage of the number of inspections, rather than the number of individual ships inspected to take into account that many ships are detained more than once during any one year"

Table A.6 Tokyo MOU average detention rates; 1999–2005

Tokyo MOU average	6.98% 1999	7.11% 2000	7.28% 2001	6.67% 2002	8.49% 2003	6.51% 2004	5.21% 2005	6.89% Average
DPR of Korea	30.68	35.92	40.82	59.64	58.17	37.29	20.19	49.90
Bolivia				42.86	45.00			43.93
Mongolia					48.48	28.21	22.67	33.12
Cambodia	30.04	25.70	27.76	25.53	26.59	18.30	14.72	24.09
Indonesia	16.52	22.56	28.50	21.53	26.18	28.00	21.56	23.55
Honduras	11.71	12.30	12.98	15.95	56.00			21.79
Vietnam	21.05	18.69	23.42	13.19	21.08	15.57	18.24	21.76
Belize	24.73	24.45	24.39	19.58	19.00	15.67	10.72	19.80
Tuvalu						23.53	11.27	17.40
Egypt	9.59			15.38	25.00			16.66
Tonga				12.50	25.93	7.14		15.19
Georgia							13.04	13.04
Burma/Myanmar			8.57		18.92	10.20	10.81	12.13
Turkey	14.98	13.52	11.51	12.31		8.79	6.94	11.34
Netherland Antilles				11.11				11.11
Taiwan	7.27	8.86	9.24		15.89	9.76	12.93	10.66
St Vincent and the Grenadines	14.91	12.40	9.25	9.98	8.88	6.89	6.28	9.80
Russia	8.64	10.96	12.51	8.25		7.49		9.57
Cayman Islands	8.00	7.23		13.04				9.42
Thailand	9.81	9.84	9.92	8.09	8.54	11.22	7.96	9.34
Malaysia	8.01	10.56	10.42	9.62			7.53	9.23
Iran	8.46	7.19	7.56	9.68	11.67	6.67		8.53
South Korea	7.54	9.27	7.89					8.23
Antigua and Barbuda	8.06							8.06
India		7.28		9.48			7.06	7.94
China	7.87							7.87
Average %	13.59	14.49	15.76	17.08	27.69	15.21	11.95	16.54%

Flag States in italics are common with those in the Paris MOU table of detention rates; Table A.5
Source: Tokyo MOU *Annual Reports*, 1999–2005 inclusive

Table A.7 Detentions of ships with class related detainable deficiencies per flag State: 1999–2005

	1999	2000	2001	2002	2003	2004	2005	Average
Sao Tome and Principe		43.75	27.50					35.63
Romania	24.39	17.86	32.10	4				30.15
Albania	23.08	33.33	40.00	47.20	21.80	25.40	7.10	28.27
Bolivia		20.00	50.00		10.50	16.70		24.30
Tonga			12.50	22.50	9.50			14.83
Honduras	18.46	14.89	15.80	13.30	20.60	3.60		14.44
Comoros				14.30	14.30	11.30	12.00	12.98
Georgia		11.11	25.00	16.10	3.80	6.30	9.30	11.94
Saudi Arabia	11.76							11.76
Slovakia							10.30	10.30

(continued)

Table A.7 (continued)

	1999	2000	2001	2002	2003	2004	2005	Average
Libya	**12.50**	**7.69**						**10.10**
Qatar		**10.00**						**10.00**
DPR of Korea				**15.80**	**3.80**	**8.70**	**8.20**	**9.13**
United Arab Emirates			**9.10**					**9.10**
Belize	19.80	13.92	6.40	14.50	2.70	2.70	1.70	8.82
Thailand	15.63						2.00	8.82
South Korea					8.10			8.10
Cambodia	11.11		9.20	11.90	8.00			8.04
St Vincent and the Grenadines	10.26	9.80	11.30	8.90	4.70	5.30	4.20	7.78
(Faroe Islands)					7.70			7.70
Kuwait	7.69							7.69
Lebanon	10.42	4.08	8.50	13.50	5.70	5.30	3.20	7.24
Bulgaria		6.67	11.70	7.30		2.10		6.94
Taiwan						6.70		6.70
Dominica							6.70	6.70
(Bermuda)			6.50					6.50
India	8.70	5.88	6.30			4.40		6.32
Lithuania	6.06							6.06
Egypt	5.26	6.67						5.97
Malaysia			5.90					5.90
Estonia	7.14			4.30				5.72
Iran			9.30		2.10			5.70
Morocco	7.89	5.88					2.80	5.52
Latvia							4.80	4.80
Croatia	4.76	8.11					1.40	4.76
Azerbaijan	4.55							4.55
Italy	4.35							4.35
Poland	4.62			3.50				4.06
Turkey	5.26	6.14	4.70	5.20	1.90		1.30	4.08
Syria	3.80	6.10				2.20		4.03
Ukraine		5.81	4.50		2.30	3.30		3.98
Portugal	5.45	3.42				2.70		3.86
Belgium						3.60		3.60
Cyprus	4.24	3.41	4.30	3.10		2.30		3.47
Malta	4.42	5.88	4.30	2.80	1.40		1.30	3.35
Panama	4.67	4.56	3.70	3.10		1.80	2.20	3.34
Vanuatu		3.30						3.30
(Netherlands Antilles)						2.90		2.90
China		4.00			1.40			2.70
Ireland						2.40		2.40
Averages	9.42	10.83	13.29	11.74	7.00	5.99	4.85	9.02

Statistics in bold are the fourteen flag States with class related detainable deficiencies above the total average of 9.02% for all 51 flag States identified in Table A.7

Source Paris MOU Annual Reports, 1999–2005 inclusive

Table A.8 Detentions of ships with RO related detainable deficiencies per recognized organization

Recognized Organization	1999	2000	2001	2002	2003	2004	2005	Ave. %
GL[a]	1.61	1.51	0.86	1.23	0.85	0.60	0.39	1.01
DNV[b]	1.68	1.70	1.44	0.60	0.99	0.69	0.43	1.08
ABS[c]	2.21	1.39	3.08	1.23	0.79	0.29	0.88	1.41
CCS[d]	3.08	3.88	2.86	0.00	2.14	0.00	0.00	1.70
NKK[e]	2.28	3.06	2.50	1.88	1.15	0.54	0.93	1.76
LR[f]	2.56	2.61	2.55	2.00	0.96	1.08	1.32	1.87
BV[g]	3.17	2.89	2.42	2.16	0.94	0.99	0.93	1.93
CCRS[h]	0.00	0.00	0.00	0.00	5.26	10.53	0.00	2.26
RR[i]		1.47	7.78	1.33	1.19	0.00		2.35
KRS[j]	3.0	2.97	6.60	0.96	0.93	2.34	0.00	2.40
RINA[k]	6.68	5.84	2.96	0.93	0.78	0.23	0.22	2.52
RMRS[l]	4.14	3.98	2.52	3.28	1.36	2.16	1.48	2.70
SRU[m]					0.00	6.38	3.57	3.32
IRS[n]	7.69	5.26	0.00	0.00	0.00	15.79	0.00	4.11
RSK[o]						9.09	0.00	4.55
PRS[p]	6.40	9.38	5.42	3.25	2.60	2.26	4.14	4.78
BKR[q]	3.33	13.43	14.86	8.33	1.54	1.59	5.00	6.15
TL[r]	9.46	8.14	12.09	7.78	1.79	3.60	2.21	6.44
CRS[s]	27.27	15.63	6.58	6.53	0.00	0.00	3.08	8.44
HRS[t]	13.38	7.50	8.70	12.50	8.33	9.09	3.38	8.98
RP[u]	36.36	20.00	0.00	0.00	0.00	13.33	0.00	9.96
RNR[v]	26.83	15.79	29.41	2.70	0.00	0.00	0.00	10.67
INC[x]	27.78	11.11	21.74	33.33	18.75	0.00	13.33	18.00
INSB[y]	33.33	20.59	25.58	23.44	12.28	9.52	5.45	18.60
HINSIB[z]		28.57	50.00	14.29		11.11	0.00	20.79
BS[aa]					71.43	5.56	0.00	25.66
IS[ab]			70.00	25.00	7.35	13.51	13.51	25.87
RS[ac]			50.00	50.00	32.14	40.00	11.11	36.65
PRC[ad]	33.33		40.00					36.67
RCB[ae]		40.00						40.00
Average	11.60%	9.45%	14.22%	10.16%	4.08%	5.72%	2.64%	10.42%

Cases in which more than ten inspections are involved. IACS members indicated in bold

Source Paris MOU Annual Reports, 1999–2005

[a]Germanischer Lloyd (Germany)

[b]Det Norske Veritas (Norway)

[c]American Bureau of Shipping

[d]China Classification Society

[e]Nippon Kaiji Kyokai (Japan)

[f]Lloyd's Register of Shipping (United Kingdom)

[g]Bureau Veritas (France)

[h]China Corporation Register of Shipping (Taiwan, China)

[i]Russian River (Rechnoj) Register

[j]Korean Register of Shipping

[k]Registro Navale Italiano (Italy)

[l]Russian Maritime Register of Shipping

[m]Shipping Register of Ukraine

[n]Indian Register of Shipping

[o]Register of Shipping Korea (Korean DPR)

[p]Polski Rejestr Statkow (Poland)

[q]Bulgarski Koraben Register (Bulgaria)

[r]Turkish Lloyd

Table A.8 (continued)

^sCroation Register of Shipping
^tHellenic Register of Shipping (Greece)
^uRinave Portuguese
^vRomanian Naval Register
^xINCLAMAR (Cyprus)
^yInternational Naval Surveys Bureau (Greece)
^zHonduras International Naval Survey and Inspection Bureau
^{aa}Isthmus Bureau of Shipping (Panama)
^{ab}International Register of Shipping (USA)
^{ac}Register of Shipping (Albania)
^{ad}Panama Register Corporation
^{ae}Registro Cubano De Buques

Table A.9 General cargo ships, detentions and flag states: 2004

Flag State	Inspections General Cargo Ships	Detentions	%	Inspections all ships	% General Cargo Ships
Indonesia	*145*	*55*	*37.9*	*225*	*64.4*
DPR of Korea	*161*	*55*	*34.2*	*362*	*44.5*
Mongolia	*147*	*40*	*27.2*	*156*	*94.2*
Tuvalu	*44*	*10*	*22.7*	*51*	*86.3*
Cambodia	*942*	*170*	*18.0*	*1,33*	*91.2*
Iran	*30*	*5*	*16.7*	*75*	*40.0*
Belize	*640*	*100*	*15.6*	*753*	*85.0*
Vietnam	*179*	*28*	*15.6*	*244*	*73.4*
Thailand	*110*	*13*	*11.8*	*294*	*37.4*
Myanmar	*28*	*3*	*10.7*	*49*	*57.1*
St Vincent and the Grenadines	196	19	9.7	421	46.6
Panama	1,358	110	8.1	6,96	20.9
Malta	**87**	**7**	**8.0**	**552**	**15.8**
Malaysia	**65**	**5**	**7.7**	**357**	**18.2**
Denmark	29	2	6.9	120	24.2
Antigua and Barbuda	91	5	5.5	317	28.7
Russia	*313*	*17*	*5.4*	*521*	*60.1*
Cyprus	97	5	5.2	722	13.4
Bahamas	135	6	4.4	644	21.0
Liberia	77	3	3.9	1,17	6.3
Singapore	76	3	3.9	761	10.0
Netherlands	52	2	3.8	127	40.9
Norway	40	1	2.5	253	15.8
Philippines	64	1	1.6	279	22.9
China	370	5	1.4	899	41.2
Hong Kong	239	3	1.3	1,56	20.7
South Korea	314	0	0	852	36.9
Marshall Islands	58	0	0	317	18.3
Totals/Averages	**6.05**	**673**	**11.2**	**19.53**	**31.2**

Flag States on the Tokyo MOU Black List for 2004 are indicated in bold italics, and those high on the Grey List in italics.

Source Detailed statistics on port state control inspections for 2004 and the Tokyo MOU annual report 2004

Table A.10 Reported world total losses by ship type and age at time of loss: 1996–2004

Age	0–4	5–9	10–14	15–19	20–24	25+	Total
Year							
Tankers							
1996	–	–	–	1	7	5	13
1997	–	1	–	3	4	5	13
1998	–	–	–	–	3	2	7
1999	–	–	1	–	2	3	6
2000	–	1	1	1	4	3	10
2001	–	1	–	–	2	6	9
2002	–	1	–	–	1	8	10
2003	–	–	1	–	1	7	9
2004	2	–	1	–	3	8	14
Bulk							
1996	–	–	1	5	6	2	14
1997	–	–	–	2	4	–	6
1998	1	–	–	–	7	3	11
1999	–	–	1	1	6	3	11
2000	–	2	–	6	10	3	21
2001	–	–	–	3	5	4	12
2002	–	–	1	2	3	4	10
2003	–	3	–	2	2	1	8
2004	–	1	–	2	2	–	5
Other							
1996	1	1	8	17	8	24	59
1997	3	2	6	8	16	23	58
1998	2	6	3	10	17	24	62
1999	1	3	4	11	18	18	55
2000	2	–	1	18	13	34	68
2001	1	4	4	20	14	45	88
2002	3	1	5	13	13	42	77
2003	2	1	3	7	16	45	74
2004	1	-	3	7	10	34	55

Source Lloyd's Register – Fairplay, World Fleet Statistics 2005

Index

Lightning Source UK Ltd.
Milton Keynes UK
21 August 2009
142961UK00007B/53/P